STRATEGIES
AND TACTICS
IN SECONDARY
SCHOOL
TEACHING

LEONARD H. CLARK

Jersey City State College

STRATEGIES AND TACTICS IN SECONDARY SCHOOL TEACHING

A Book of Readings

THE MACMILLAN COMPANY
COLLIER-MACMILLAN LIMITED, LONDON

Third Printing, 1969

Library of Congress catalog card number: 68–10626

THE MACMILLAN COMPANY
COLLIER-MACMILLAN CANADA, LTD., TORONTO, ONTARIO

PRINTED IN THE UNITED STATES OF AMERICA

Do not blame me if any know . . . better than I, for every man must say what he says and do what he does according to his ability.

Alfred the Great
King of the West Saxons

PREFACE

This book is meant to serve two purposes. One is to present a group of readings that will give the reader a theoretical basis and some examples of the various techniques and methods incorporated in the teaching strategies advocated in most textbooks about methods of teaching in secondary schools. The second is to present a position. That position is this: (a) Professional teachers are persons who can solve unusual pedagogical problems because they are masters of technical skills and know-how built upon well-understood, viable pedagogical theory. (b) Good teaching consists of picking the right strategy and tactics for given situations and carrying them out. Therefore, Part I of the book is an attempt to present some of the theoretical foundations for teaching method, Part II is an attempt to describe some typical teaching strategies and the tactics that one uses to make up these strategies, and Part III tries to show what we need most of all in the professional teacher.

Consequently the selections presented were not picked because they are the most recent but because they seemed to be the ones most likely to make the points that need to be made. I think that together the selections make up a book that can be used both as a basic textbook in undergraduate courses on teaching in secondary schools and as a source of supplementary readings for such courses and other courses in secondary education or methods of teaching.

The emphases in the book are just a little unusual. As the title suggests, the book is mostly concerned with strategies and tactics. That is to say that the whole book is really concerned about planning, for, after all, a strategy or a tactic is really a plan. Part I presents the many variables that should affect one's choice of strategy; Part II presents different kinds of strategies and tactics.

These kinds of strategies and tactics are useful for different purposes and for different pupils. As they stand, however, they are merely types. The student should remember that the real strategy or tactic is the specific plan he adopts in a specific situation. It is hoped that this book will give him a repertory of types of strategies and tactics and theoretical background enough so that he will know what strategy or tactic is best for what occasion. In other words, the book will have served a major part of its purpose if the student learns how to plan lessons by which pupils learn well.

A greater purpose is to encourage teachers to teach their pupils to think. Of all the instructional techniques available, the ones that help pupils to become resourceful, independent thinkers are the most important. The central purpose of American education should be to help to develop the rational powers of American boys and girls. This book emphasizes strategies and tactics that will foster that central purpose.

Before I close this preface, I wish to thank all the people who have helped me. The editors of the publishing houses and journals have been most kind and helpful. Among them Warren Seyfert, of the *Bulletin of the National Association of Secondary School Principals*, has been extraordinarily understanding and cooperative, as has Mrs. Mildred Sandison Fenner, of the *NEA Journal*, whose special features are an excellent source of first-class articles miniaturized by top-notch authors from their larger research-oriented articles and books. The kindness and friendliness of the authors was overwhelming. I hope the work warrants the kindness and good wishes they bestowed on me. Once again I must express my appreciation to my wife, Maria Aleksandra Clark, who doubles as a typist, proofreader, researcher, and triple checker in all my literary ventures. To say that this book could not have been finished without her aid is an understatement.

Finally, I would like to commit this book, even though primarily a book of readings, to the memory of my father, Ridgley Colfax Clark, teacher, headmaster, superintendent of schools—whose lifelong interests and concerns centered upon his pupils. Since I have acknowledged my indebtedness to the authors whose works I have borrowed, I think it is only right that I acknowledge my father as the source of most of my own notions concerning education and, for that matter, almost everything else.

L. H. C.

CONTENTS

STRATEGIES
AND TACTICS
IN SECONDARY
SCHOOL
TEACHING

Part I

THE FOUNDATION OF METHOD

Teaching is becoming a profession. One of the differences between professional workers and other workers is that the professional is master of skills and knowledge that laymen do not have. Faced with a new difficult case, the professional can cope with the situation because he has specialized information and know-how that he can apply. Harry Broudy, in a speech at the 1967 convention of the American Association of Colleges of Teacher Education, made the difference between professionals and nonprofessionals clear. In his example he compared three teachers who taught equally well. Of these three, Teacher A taught as she did in various situations as a result of intuition; Teacher B taught as she did because she followed the rule: in such a situation do thus and so; but Teacher C taught as she did because of theoretical reasons. She was the only one who knew why she took the various steps that she took. In this example, Teacher C, who knew why, was a professional; Teacher B, who blindly followed the rule, was a craftsman; and Teacher A, who taught well by following her impulses, was a miracle.

The professional differs from the artisan, who is also skilled and knowledgeable, in that the professional's skill is based on scholarship and theoretical background rather than sheer empiricism. One cannot learn to be a real professional worker by apprenticeship only. Becoming a professional requires practice of course, but the practice must be based on theory—in fact it should be practice in selecting and using the right theory.

As we have seen, the professional teacher has certain skills and knowledge that are not shared by lay people. It is these skills and knowledge that distinguish him from the crowd and make him a professional. With these skills and knowledge, the teacher can carry out his peculiar functions, which are to make and carry out decisions that will result in the most effective, efficient teaching of his pupils possible. These skills and knowledge make up educational method.

1

Not all teachers are professionals. The lecturer who merely tells pupils what he knows and the teacher who just listens to pupils recite do not qualify as professional teachers. Neither is using skill or knowledge that is not available to any lay person. The professional teacher, rather, would estimate the situation and then select the most suitable strategy and tactics in accordance with his diagnosis of what the situation calls for.

Teaching is helping pupils to learn. It is not just presenting information to pupils. In the final analysis, the test of how successful one's teaching has been is how well the pupils have learned. At the professional level, teaching is indeed complex. Like other professions, teaching requires learned practitioners. When all teachers acquire really professional competency, then the practice of teaching will become much more effective, just as the practice of medicine has become more effective in the last several decades. This level will not be attained, however, until teachers master the methods of teaching and the theories undergirding them.

Educational method is made up of strategies and tactics. In this context, a strategy refers to the overall approach to teaching; a tactic is a specific operation that with other tactics makes up a strategy. In defining any strategy or tactic it is important to remember that content—i.e., the subject to be taught—is part of the strategy or tactic and, in this sense, method includes content. Therefore, critics who try to separate content and method are bound to fail. One cannot teach content without method, or vice versa. The heart of educational methodology is decision-making or selection. The teacher must decide what goals it would be best to teach for under the circumstances, and what strategy and tactics are best suited for reaching these goals under the conditions prevailing. In deciding what strategy to use, one crucial factor is deciding what subject matter to include. Thus, content is part of strategy.

Selection or decision-making is the basic problem of teaching method. The problem is to select the proper strategy and tactics under the circumstances. This problem is complicated by the many variables that enter into teaching. It is the complexity of these variables that makes it necessary for teachers to be professionals rather than craftsmen. Part I of this book deals briefly with some of these variables. Teachers should not always stop to consider all of these variables before making classroom decisions, of course. More often, teachers will have to use their knowledge and skills automatically as bases for their decisions—applying principles to make snap judgments in the midst of an intense classroom situation.

Although the specific strategies and tactics suitable for particular situations are contingent on many variables, such as those discussed in the following paragraphs, one general pattern does seem desirable in most teaching. The pattern consists of the following five steps, which are usually found in much the same order:

1. Diagnosis
2. Preparation

3. Guiding learning
4. Evaluating the results of learning
5. Follow-up or follow-through

Diagnosis is the step in which the teacher determines what should be done. Preparation refers to the teacher's getting himself ready to teach, motivating the pupils, and planning. Guiding learning includes the class proper—the presentation, discussion, or whatever is done. In the evaluating step, the teacher attempts to assess the success of his teaching by finding out how much the pupils have learned. The follow-through is the process of filling in the spots that pupils seem to have missed, reteaching if necessary, and building on what the pupils have learned. At this time, if possible, the teacher clinches the learning and prepares to move on to the next sequence. After a while, some of the steps in succeeding sequences tend to run together, but in good teaching they are always there even though somewhat truncated. The key step in this pattern is, of course, diagnosis. Without good diagnosis one does not have an adequate basis on which to make a selection of strategy or tactics. Obviously, good diagnosis depends upon an analysis of as many of the variables in the particular teaching-learning situation as possible under the circumstances.

The first of the variables that affect the teaching method are the objectives. Objectives come in two or more types. There are the overall objectives that influence the type of curriculum and overall strategy, or grand strategy, and the more specific objectives that influence the choice of content and teaching strategies and tactics. The type of goal for which one is striving makes a great difference in one's strategies. The strategy suitable for bringing about a skill may be greatly different from that most suitable for teaching a concept. Different goals in the "cognitive domain" also require quite different approaches, both in teaching techniques and also in teaching content.

The pupils themselves also make up a variable. Each is, of course, unique. He has his own interests, abilities, attitudes, potentials, background, goals, and style of learning. Consequently, if the teaching content and techniques one uses are to be successful with him, they must be selected for him. It follows, then, that teachers need professional knowledge of both pupils in general and individual pupils in particular.

But the teacher's decisions are not influenced only by his knowledge of pupils, they are also influenced by his knowledge of group dynamics, especially as they pertain to his class group. Understanding and utilizing group process can make one's teaching effective. Because all groups do not necessarily behave in the same way, an understanding of interpersonal relationships in the group one is teaching can be especially helpful.

Another variable that should determine one's teaching method is the nature of the subject matter. This includes not only the structure of the disciplines but also the organization of the subject matter for teaching, and one's philosophical base for teaching it. The role of subject matter differs considerably in the eyes of teachers of different philosophical persuasions. One's classroom teaching, wittingly or not, is predicated on his real beliefs concerning the role and structure of subject matter.

Another variable is the technology available. By technology we mean both the techniques and tools of teaching. The teacher who has a large repertory of teaching techniques, backed up with a good store of materials and equipment, has potentially a great advantage over the teacher who does not have these assets. Fortunately, it is becoming increasingly easier to acquire both the techniques and the paraphernalia of teaching. The trick is to select the right combination of techniques, equipment, and materials for specific occasions.

Still another variable is the environment surrounding the school. This includes both the community in which one lives and society at large. Indeed, the environment of the school itself is also important. A physically dingy school, housing a social milieu hostile or indifferent to learning, usually requires somewhat different techniques from those suitable for schools containing more favorable environments. In this respect the organization of the school must be considered. As far as method is concerned, junior high schools probably differ from middle schools, and six-year high schools from four-year high schools. Certainly boys' schools differ from girls' schools. Teaching in a highly departmentalized school probably requires a methodology somewhat different from that required in a self-contained classroom or core curriculum. The comprehensive high school of the United States undoubtedly requires the development of many different teaching strategies and techniques not necessary in the selective schools of Europe.

The last of the variables to be discussed here, although not the last one that could be discussed, is the teacher himself. Like everyone else, every teacher has strengths and weaknesses, likes and dislikes. One's decisions invariably are influenced by one's inclinations. These in turn are influenced by one's competence, ideals, general attitudes, and personality. Individual differences in teachers cause individual differences in teaching style. It is only natural that a teacher should follow the style of teaching he finds compatible. Within reason it is right that he does so.

Because these differences do exist, it would seem logical that not only should teachers try to pick the best techniques, content, materials, and equipment to do the specific tasks required in a particular situation, but also that particular tasks be apportioned out to the individual teachers who can best do them, and to relegate to assistants, machines, and other persons and devices the tasks that can best be done by them. In this way the energies of each teacher can be saved to do those important things he can do better than anyone or anything else. Perhaps, therefore, the ultimate objective in teaching methodology should be to develop a man-machine system that will allow each teacher to make the most of his capabilities by utilizing his talents and the capabilities of assistants and teaching devices to the utmost.

The chapters of Part I present some of the variables that teachers should consider in deciding what strategies and tactics to use. Being bases for teaching strategies and tactics, these variables are the foundations of teaching method.

Chapter I

WHAT TEACHING IS

W HAT does it mean to teach? According to Edgar Dale, "To teach is to transform by informing, to develop a zest for lifelong learning, to help pupils become students—mature independent learners, architects of an exciting, challenging future . . . a kind of communion, a meeting and merging of minds." * Less poetically, to teach is to help or guide someone's learning. It is not just telling or hearing lessons. Its forms are myriad. The selections in this chapter have been chosen to give the reader some idea of the number of kinds of strategies and tactics in the pedagogical repertory. One of the teacher's principal tasks is to pick the right strategies and tactics for the particular situations he faces.

EDUCATORS AND COMMUNICATION
RESEARCH

Wilbur Schramm †

Communication theory has a direct bearing on educational theory because the heart of teaching is communication. Good teaching is good communication. Therefore the teaching strategies and tactics should be consistent with good communication techniques.

Because learning is dependent on successful teacher-pupil intercommunication, we teachers should avail ourselves of all the techniques and knowledge developed by the communications researchers to make our

---

* Edgar Dale, "What Does It Mean to Teach", *The News Letter*, Vol. 30 (March 1965), p. 4.

† From *Educational Leadership*, Vol. 13 (May 1956), pp. 503–508. Reprinted with permission of the Association for Supervision and Curriculum Development and Wilbur Schramm. Copyright © 1956 by the Association for Supervision and Curriculum Development.

*salesmanship more effective. After all, our product is more valuable and
often less appealing than most of those touted by the merchandisers
and advertisers. Evidently, however, the classroom, from the communi-
cator's point of view, presents a difficult, complex communications
problem.*

Let us begin by saying a few words about communication itself.

By *communication* we mean the process by which information is trans-
mitted from a source to a destination. The word comes from *communis*,
common, and communication implies a degree of commonness or in-tune-
ness between the systems which are communicating. The act of communication, from the sender's point of view, is the construction and delivery of a
message which will contain the desired information and (promise to) awaken
the desired in-tune-ness in the receiver. From the receiver's point of view, the
act of communication is the selection among messages and the disposition of
those selected—the attaching of meaning to them, their storage or rejection,
and such further response to them (for example, a reply) as may be indicated.
Thus the discrete elements of the communication process are, at the least,
sender, message, and receiver. But a message always travels in a channel (such
as speech or writing, gesture, print, or film), and the whole process is necessarily interwoven into a social context. In this context the group relationships
of sender and receiver are particularly important to communication. Therefore, at least five elements enter into the description of even the simplest
act of communication.

This is the process with which communication research men are concerned,
whether the process goes on between human beings, between machines, or
between machines and humans. Educators are, of course, concerned primarily with communication between humans. Human communication is a—
perhaps *the*—fundamental social process. It is the glue that holds society
together. It is the homeostatic fluid that flows among the dynamic organs of
society, keeping them in balance. It makes it possible for men to live in
groups, and for groups to deal with each other. It makes it possible for society
to get quick reports from watchers on the horizon, to reach consensus on
what to do about these reports, and to transmit funded culture to new members of the society. It is responsible for much of our entertainment and makes
possible our commerce. Society has institutionalized its need to know under
such large organizational forms as the mass communication media and formal education. Thus, when we ask what importance communication research
has for educators, we are really dealing with intra-family relationships.

The research problems that come under the heading of communication
have traditionally been classified under such a grouping as this:

Who
says what

through what channel
to what audience
in what context
with what effect?

The problem of "who" is the problem of source, what motivates and controls the source, and how it operates in encoding the message. "What" is the problem of content, its symbols, themes, and form. "Channel" introduces problems of the differences between the media as carriers of messages. "Audience" research is concerned with the description and enumeration of receivers of messages. "Context" with the worlds of the sender and receiver at the time of sending and receiving, including especially, as we have already suggested, their group relationships. "Effect," of course, implies a study of the responses to messages.

It is fair, I think, to say that sizable bodies of communication research have begun to grow up around all these foci, with the possible exception of channels. The greatest mass of information deals with the *audiences* of the mass media, which the sociologists have studied most intensively, and the advertising men most extensively. Perhaps the oldest body of research and recorded fact deals with *source*, for example the structure and operation of the mass media, the pressures and forces on mass communication, the relation of the mass media to law and government, and the development of the mass media. This has been the province of political scientists, sociologists, and historians. Another large group of studies relate to *content analysis* —the quantitative description of messages, the analysis of propaganda, the study of symbols. This was begun by political scientists, taken up by sociologists, and lately contributed to by linguists and experimental psychologists. The greatest activity in recent years, however, has been in the areas of *effects* and contextual *group relationships*. The kinds of problem most often chosen here have had to do with the meaning derived from messages, the formation of opinions and attitudes, the process of persuasion, and the dynamics of communication in groups. This area has come to be chiefly the province of the social psychologist. . . .

COMMUNICATION PROBLEMS

But all this aside, it is likely that what we already know about communication is sufficient to be of help to the educator in a number of areas. Let us consider a handful of educational problems which are also communication problems.

1. *Administrative communications.* Few school administrators need to be told that they have communication problems. Some school executives go through their careers with a vague but pervasive sense of being misunderstood; others awaken suddenly, when they face a crisis in their school system or an angered public, to the realization that communication has broken down. Every executive must endlessly explain, persuade, strive to understand, keep

his antenna tuned to faint signals, and repair the circuits. A very large part of his work is communication. Yet when a communication researcher looks at the peculiar problems of a school administrator, he finds them quite familiar. These are the same problems that have been classified and studied in large industry—for example, the need for efficient horizontal and vertical communication within the organization, the relation of communication patterns to morale, the problem of maintaining good public relations. The school executive, in trying to pass a bond issue or meet an attack on "progressive" education, is facing the same kind of problem which has been studied in dozens of informational and social action campaigns. Indeed, any school administrator would benefit from reading such an article as Hyman and Sheatsley's "Some Reasons Why Information Campaigns Fail." [1] The school administrator's problems in persuasion are the classical problems treated in a book like that by Hovland, Janis and Kelley. His problems of combining personal influence with mass media influence are the same as those treated by Katz and Lazarsfeld. This is not to suggest that there is any single book available to the school administrator which would instantly and easily clarify all his communication problems. But on the other hand we are at the point where such a book might be written in the foreseeable future, and in the meantime there are many research bridges between the needs of the educator and the resources of communication.

2. *Communication in the classroom.* When the communication researcher looks at the classroom, he is impressed with the complexity of what looks so simple. The receivers in the classroom vary greatly one from another, hence in theory require different messages. How often, in a group teaching situation, does the teacher achieve the degree of "in-tune-ness" which really good communication requires? We know from experiments in introspective recall that students are often engaged in the most varying and widely ranging mental activities when they are supposed to be listening to and absorbing a lecture. In addition to facing the ordinary problem of communicating with a varied group of receivers, the teacher is trying to combine a dozen or more channels in the average day's work—the spoken word, the written word, the blackboard, pictures, textbooks, films, "acting it out," etc. This act of combination is not simple, and is not well understood. To make it harder, the teacher is dealing with messages which carry not only "facts" about subject matter and "demonstrations" of skills, but also "concepts" of life, roles, values. Furthermore, the teacher is dealing with a functional group or series of groups, so that all communication within the classroom must have reference not only to individual needs and interests, but also to group norms and group dynamics. How differently a group functions when its communication is differently organized is illustrated by Bavelas' experiments in comparing groups in which communication passed around a circle, and groups in which all communication passed through a leader at the center of a star pattern, or Lewin's classic experiment on authoritarian vs. democratic groups. Finally,

---

[1] *Public Opinion Quarterly*, Vol. II, 1950. pp. 412–23.

to make the situation as difficult as possible, all receivers in the class are subject to a very large amount of uncontrolled and uncoordinated communication outside the class, some of which undoubtedly conflicts seriously with the communication they receive *in* class. We shall talk of this later. Here it is sufficient to say that the communication research man makes no pretense, at the present stage of his research, of being able to unravel all the communication problems of the classroom, but he would urge the teacher to be on the lookout for certain danger signals of inefficient communication. And he sees the classroom as a good and needy laboratory for future communication research.

3. *Communication aids to teaching.* Most of our "teaching aids" are no more than auxiliary channels of communication to the student. The communication researcher has studied some of these—notably films, broadcasts, and certain printed texts—has tried to make some order out of their characteristics and to estimate which combinations of characteristics make for greater learning, and has gained at least a few useful insights into their construction and use. He has learned enough to know that many aids are poorly made, and many more misused. For an example of what has been done in one field, see the annotated bibliography by Hoban and Van Ormer, *Instructional Film Research, 1918-1950.* For an examination of another teaching aid field see the little book by Cronbach and others, *Text Materials in Modern Education.*

4. *The test as communication.* Lee Cronbach, who is president-elect of the American Psychological Association, gained a fresh and useful insight into test making by thinking of the test as a communication channel from pupil to teacher. And in truth, that is what it is. It communicates baseline information, or "feedback" after a period of instruction. It asks the student to put into the channel what he knows or can do on a given subject or problem. We are really sampling the student's knowledge or skill, just as we sample a population with a public opinion poll, and therefore it is appropriate to ask some of the same questions: have we sampled adequately? have we put the information into a clear channel, uncontaminated by interviewer (teacher) influence or other noise? have we established in-tune-ness so that we can interpret the message correctly when it comes through? Cronbach was able to work out information theory mathematics to apply to test theory, but this need concern us here less than the simple idea of the test as a communication channel, subject to all the difficulties and misfunctions which may upset other communication.

5. *The world outside and the world within.* A few paragraphs back, we pointed out that students were exposed outside the classroom to a great deal of communication over which the school has no control. This is very potent communication. It includes a large share of the primary and peer groups' messages, and two to five hours per day from the mass media. It can safely be said that a child probably derives more of his idea of environment, more of his sense of values and his knowledge of roles, from outside the classroom than from inside it. Furthermore, there are likely to be notable contrasts and

conflicts as between the classroom and the outside world—popular art as against classical art, peer group values as against older-generation values, violence in the media as against restraint in the school, etc. To the communication researcher, this seems a fact of major importance. What, he asks, does it mean in terms of curriculum-making and educational policy? For one thing, how can the school make most use of the great wealth of communication the student receives outside? Are there some parts of this outside communication which are so rich as to replace some of the classroom work and free the class for more advanced things? On the other hand, what can the school do to guard the student against possible ill effects of this outside communication, and to make sure that the student selects well from what he has available? Is it not the obligation of the school to teach students to use the mass media critically and well? The people who panicked at Orson Welles' broadcast of the fictitious invasion from Mars were the uncritical listeners. The people who fall for the unscrupulous users of news columns are the uncritical readers. Should the school not be getting its students ready for a time when attempted manipulation by mass media may be even more prevalent than now? The communication researcher can ask these questions better than he can answer them, but when the educators get into these problems they will find that communication research can help them with a great deal of material on what is in the channels of mass communication, what is selected from these channels by children of different ages, and what are the dynamics and effects of the different kinds of groups in which the school child moves.

These are only a few of the problems in which the interests of educator and communication researcher coincide. For example, we have said nothing of the problem of extending the classroom: adult education, extension service, education television and radio. This is a problem in which the communication research can surely be of some aid. But our task here has not been to make an exhaustive list of problems; rather it has been to indicate by example some of the areas in which educator and communication researcher might go forward together.

PSYCHOLOGICAL ENGINEERING

Harold W. Bernard *

In his Psychology of Learning and Teaching, *Harold Bernard has adapted an outline used by Edward Bernays in describing how to use*

* From *Psychology of Learning and Teaching*, sec. ed., by Harold W. Bernard. Copyright 1965 McGraw-Hill Book Company, New York. Used by permission of McGraw-Hill Book Company.

public relations to gain support for a cause, activity, or institution. This outline describes admirably the way strategy and tactics fit into the professional approach to a teaching problem. It is just as important for a teacher to sell his wares to his pupils as it is for a public relations man to sell his products to potential buyers. Sometimes the teacher must overcome greater sales resistance than the public relations man does. It is important that teachers pay careful attention to the engineering of consent.

The role of psychology in teaching can be described in terms of engineering concepts, as Bernays did in *The Engineering of Consent*.† Bernays has described how public relations—information, persuasion, and adjustment—can be used to gain support for a cause, activity, or institution. Instead of dealing with prescriptions of minutiae, Bernays describes the underlying processes that can be adapted to specific situations. The headings he uses can be readily transferred to the use of psychology in teaching.

Define your objectives. This is the first task of a teacher as he studies the broad purposes of education, the courses of study, and the parts of the curriculum for which he is responsible. . . .

Research your public. In part, this is accomplished in college courses in child, adolescent, and educational psychology, in which the general nature of pupils is studied. Research is continued as individuals are studied through test data, sociometric ratings, questionnaires, school records, and observation.

Modify objectives to reach goals that research shows are attainable. This is done in part by curricular allocations, studying the phenomena of readiness, and knowing the status of one's pupils. In part, it is a matter of modifying objectives as the status of the class changes from day to day.

Decide on strategy. The strategies of teaching can be derived directly from the strategies of public relations, which include timing, forbearance, teaching techniques, surprise, participation, and association (hero worship and the use of ideals).

Set up themes, symbols, and appeals. This could include appeals to the pupils' desires for health, achieving good grades, learning how to get along with peers, and vocational choice and preparation. It would seem that meeting children's needs could provide themes, symbols, and appeals appropriate to educational motivation.

Blueprint an effective organization. Two approaches are of outstanding importance in educational planning. One is to capitalize on pupil skills and interests to carry out democratic participation in student activities and

† Edward L. Bernays, *The Engineering of Consent* (Norman, Okla.: University of Oklahoma Press, 1955), ed.

academic work. The other is to chart the daily and monthly lesson plans, including library resources, audio-visual equipment, and laboratory and field activities.

Chart the plan for timing and tactics. The sequence of studies, the successive skills and knowledges to be acquired, and the techniques used to evaluate progress are included in this step. The tactics are the tools and methods used to convey thought—lecture, discussion, demonstration and testing are among the tactics of communication.

Carry out the tactics. Here the problem is one of adjusting the foregoing steps to the exigencies of the moment. One cannot expect immediate results, but in education, as in public relations, there must be trust in the cumulative effect. Education is a slow process, and faith in sound planning and sound techniques must be maintained.

Examination of the above eight points suggests that educational effort, like public relations, can become more effective when carefully engineered. . . .

TEACHING: WHAT IT IS AND WHAT TO DO ABOUT IT

B. Othanel Smith *

Teaching includes both strategies and tactics. In the words of B. O. Smith, "Strategies are the large-scale maneuvers by which the teacher frames the general direction of student behavior," and "Tactics are the means by which the subject matter of instruction is manipulated and controlled from moment to moment." The theories of instruction in the past have centered on teaching strategy. Teachers today need to place an increasing emphasis on teaching tactics. Although teachers must adopt the proper teaching strategies for the goals at which they are aiming, the success of the strategy rests on the skillful use of the appropriate teaching tactics. In choosing his tactics, the teacher must consider not only his teaching goals but also the subject matter, pupils, and other classroom variables. These choices present difficult problems for which teachers are often ill prepared.

* From *The Bulletin of the National Association of Secondary-School Principals*, Vol. 47 (April 1963), pp. 98–105. Reprinted by permission of the NASSP and the author.

There is a profession of teaching and it rests upon something other than speculation and common experience. There is an extensive and rapidly growing research literature on teaching and education in general. Much more has been written about teaching than has been written, let us say, about plumbing, glassblowing, journalism, or business administration. There is an extensive body of hard facts about the teaching of reading, spelling, arithmetic, and a number of other subjects of study; about how to deal with boys and girls; and about how to organize and operate the school. This body of professional knowledge has been accumulated through painstaking research over the last hundred years. But after all of this is said, it is still the case that the profession is as yet undecided about what the program of teacher education should be.

Part of the difficulty arises because there is no unified theory of teaching. Those who are studying teaching are like the blind men feeling the elephant. Some investigators feel one part of the anatomy of teaching and come up with a partial picture. Other investigators feel another part of the anatomy and construct a different picture. So today we have diverse views of teaching, each having its own theories.

One set of theories look at teaching as a way of working with students. These theories hold that teaching is a process of interaction, somewhat like that between players in a tennis match or dogs in a fight. The teacher does something to students; the students do something in return. As a result of these reciprocal actions, the student learns. If interpersonal relations in the classroom are good, it is assumed that learning will occur. If they are bad, it is assumed that learning is not apt to occur; or, if it does occur, it will occur in less degree and with less stability.

This view of teaching emphasizes the necessity for good classroom atmosphere; it holds that relationships between teacher and student must be friendly, cooperative, and conducive to give and take in class work.

It is assumed also that, if students become involved in unsettled situations, they will engage cooperatively in trying to work out such situations and, in so doing, they will learn. It is understood that infrequently the teacher will instruct the students; that he reserves instruction for those points where the difficulties threaten to become overwhelming.

According to this view, learning to teach consists in learning to ingratiate students, to enlist them in activities, and to cooperate in ventures jointly worked out. To learn to teach, one must also learn to be alert to situations challenging to students; he must learn to use materials to frame situations that will involve students.

To learn to identify and create situations in the classroom and how to manipulate and maneuver students so as to involve them is more important, in this view, than to know how to handle the subject matter of instruction. For the subject matter is introduced into situations by students who bring it from reference materials and are responsible for its manipulation and organization as they themselves deal with the situation. To be sure, it is expected that the teacher will introduce and control the use of subject matter at points where the situation is too difficult for students to handle. But it is assumed in the training program that the teacher needs no special work in the control and manipulation of subject matter itself. Rather the training is to emphasize the teacher's understanding of students and how to work with them.

This is a bobtailed view of teaching. It is not the whole picture, and it emphasizes factors that are not unique features of teaching. Teaching behavior may be interactive, it may be ingratiating, it may involve individuals in situations, it may be attended by wholesome social atmosphere, it may eventuate in learning, but these are not uniquely characteristic of teaching. These features are to be found in political, economic, and administrative behavior as well.

Were these factors to constitute teaching in its entirety, there would be no reason for a theory of teaching or for a program of teacher education as such. For teaching behavior would then be the same as any other social behavior. All that would be required for teacher education, in this view, is a general theory of social behavior and a program that trains the teacher in the patterns and techniques of such behavior with slight adaptations to the classroom. Basically, the training of the teacher would be the same as that of the politician, the commercial worker, or any other individual whose work requires him to engage cooperatively with others at an interactive level.

While the foregoing factors are certainly involved in teaching behavior, teaching is more than a way of working with students. It is also a way of working with the subject matter of instruction. Behavior is pedagogical to the extent that it is determined by considerations of the subject matter of instruction and what the concepts, principles, norms, and facts of that subject matter require for their explication. What distinguishes teaching from all other forms of social behavior is that teaching behavior is controlled by the requirements of a body of knowledge and by the commitment to develop cognitive structures coordinate with that knowledge. While the behavior of the teacher is influenced by his understanding of the student—by his perception and diagnosis of the student's behavior—still the determining factor in the teacher's behavior is not his understanding of the student but his comprehension of the subject matter and the demands which clear instruction in it makes upon him.

Although teaching entails the handling of subject matter, the teacher is taught practically nothing about how to use subject matter in the process of teaching. Teacher education programs have had considerable influence upon the behavior of the teacher with respect to his dealing with students, but it has had practically no effect upon the teacher's behavior in handling subject matter. It is true that the teacher is taught to divide his subject matter into so-called units and to break these units down into significant elements. But the teacher's knowledge of how to handle subject matter as he teaches is not increased by what he learns about units and their components. His ability to analyze and explicate subject matter remains at about the same level as that of the layman.

How does a teacher deal with subject matter? It is generally believed that to deal with the content of instruction is to talk about it. The teacher lectures. He asks questions and then corrects the answers when those given by students are unsatisfactory. But anyone who observes teaching as it actually goes on in the classroom knows that the manipulation of subject matter by the teacher is more diversified and involved than the simple operations of lecturing and asking questions.

From analyzing classroom discourse—the discourse of both the teacher and the student—it can be seen that the teacher engages in a number of logical operations. These operations are called logical because they have a structure and are rule-oriented in the sense that rules can be applied to decide whether or not the operations are performed in accord with strict logical requirements.

These operations are the instruments by which facts, concepts, principles, and norms comprising the content of instruction are manipulated and controlled. As the teacher teaches, he deals with concepts but he does so by defining terms, classifying objects and events, and comparing and contrasting them. He deals with principles, but he seldom deals with them as such. Instead, they are brought into play as explanations are given, conditional inferences are made, and so on. He deals with values, that is, evaluating concepts, but he does so as he decides the worth of objects or the desirability of events or what is the right and proper thing to do. The teacher thus defines, classifies, explains, and evaluates as he teaches. All of these are logical operations. And the teacher cannot carry on instruction without engaging in such operations, or involving his students in the performance of them. To teach is to manipulate content; to manipulate content is to perform logical operations upon it; and to teach well is to perform these operations at a high level of insight and understanding. This, too, is a partial picture, but it is needed to help round out a unified view of teaching.

We now know from research that the teacher employs some twelve logical operations as he teaches. We also know something about the frequency with which each of these operations is performed in the classroom as well as their logical structures and sub-types. Of the total number of logical operations performed by teachers, about four per cent consist in defining; about three per cent are classifying; and about four per cent consist in comparing and contrasting. Conditional inferring makes up about seven per cent of the operations and explaining about thirteen per cent. The operation of evaluating comprises about five per cent of the total; while describing, designating, stating, reporting, substituting, and opining make up the remainder.

At the common sense level, the tendency is to think that each of these operations is homogeneous; that all defining or all explaining is the same. But this is clearly not the case. To define a term like "progress" is different from defining a term like "chair." The word "chair" is used to refer to an object which is observable and can be pointed to. The word "progress" is used to refer to nothing that is observable and identifiable. For "progress" is not an object or event, nor even a characteristic of events, but a judgment about events—a rating of them, whereas, the term "chair" refers to an object or a class of objects.

Furthermore, to define a term like "rain" is not the same process as defining a term like "triangle." The class of things called triangles, being abstract, can be set apart from other concepts such as circles, squares, and the like. But with "rain," it is different. The term "rain" must be defined in such a way as to distinguish condensations such as dew from those which count as rain. But even after this has been accomplished, there is still the problem of deciding how much precipitation will count as rain. It is like deciding how many hairs a man must lose before he is said to be bald. How many drops make a rain? There is no answer to this question save an arbitrary one. If an insurance company writes a policy to insure against rain, it defines the term by indicating how much precipitation will count as rain. But this amount, whatever it be, is but a convention.

Additional examples will give further testimony of how diverse are these general categories of logical performance. To explain *how* a fish gets oxygen from water is quite a different process from explaining *why* President Jackson vetoed the Maysville Road Bill or why Coolidge chose not to run again. To explain *how* something occurs is to describe a physical process performed by, or occurring in, an animal or a plant or in the physical world. But to explain *why* President Jackson vetoed the Maysville Road Bill is to give his purposes and his ideas of the role of government as well as his conceptions of political expediency.

Again, to explain why one uses the word "rapidly" instead of the word "rapid" in a given sentence is to refer to a rule of grammar. This is quite a different sort of explanation from that called for in deciding why there are three branches in the Federal government. In the latter case, one would be required to give the purposes for the divisions of government; namely, to prevent the concentration of power. The first of these is a normative explanation—an explanation based upon rules; the second is a teleological explanation—one based upon purpose.

Whether one looks at the college or the high school, he will conclude that instruction goes on at a low level of logical sophistication. The teacher's logical manipulation of the content of instruction seldom shows any superiority to that of the student. They both perform at a common-sense level of logical behavior. For this reason, when instruction falls into logical and linguistic traps, as it does over and over again, the teacher does not know how to spring the jaws of the trap. If he runs into trouble with concepts, as when students begin to argue about the meanings of words, he does not know enough about the logical structure of defining to handle the situation. Then instruction breaks down at the very point at which it could become fruitful. The same observation could be made about all other logical operations performed by teachers and students in the classroom.

Logical operations are the tactics of teaching. They take place within a larger pattern of performance called strategy. Strategy is a large-scale maneuver by which the teacher frames the general direction of student behavior. While tactical elements—logical operations—are the means by which the subject matter of instruction is manipulated and controlled from moment to moment, strategies consist of ways by which the materials of instruction are deployed for the purposes of either constricting or releasing the behavior of the student. For example, a teacher may start out with the notion that the student is to understand a particular point of view. The discussion leading up to an understanding of the point of view may extend over a considerable period of time—say, 15 to 20 minutes. In the course of this development, the teacher may use a number of logical operations. He may define, or he may ask the students to define. He may give explanations, or he may ask the students to give explanations, *etc.* These tactical moves lead the student from general considerations to more specific points. Such a movement might be called a *framing* strategy. It limits the students' behavior so that their ideas and verbal expressions are progressively confined and driven toward a particular end.

Neither time nor knowledge permits me to say anything further on this subject. Suffice it to say that we are now attempting to study strategies employed by teachers and to relate these to the tactics of instruction—logical operations. When these two components of teaching behavior have been identified, analyzed, and described, we should know much more about the manipulation and control of subject matter in the process of instruction. It should then be possible to test the relative effects of different strategies and tactical moves in terms of achievement. And these operations and strategies would yield a content for education courses directly relevant to the work of the teacher in the classroom. . . .

DIRECT VS. INDIRECT TEACHERS

Edmund J. Amidon and Ned A. Flanders *

Studies of the teacher's role in the classroom yield some startling implications for classroom procedures. If the inferences drawn by the authors of the following selection are correct, most teachers use the wrong tactics more than half of the time. Evidently, teachers' efforts to be efficient and to raise their pupils to intellectual excellence often tend to defeat their purpose. If teachers can learn to be flexible and adjust their tactics

* From "Research on Teacher Behavior," *The Role of the Teacher in the Classroom,* Chapter IV (Minneapolis, Minn.: Paul S. Amidon and Associates, 1963), pp. 55–62. Reprinted by permission of the publisher.

and strategies to the teaching situations, they can be quite sure of a greater degree of success than if they do not do so.

In the study, indirect influence refers to tactics in which the teacher accepts and clarifies the feeling tones of pupils in a nonthreatening manner, praises or encourages pupil action or behavior, accepts or uses pupils' ideas, or asks questions. Direct influence includes lectures and other telling activities, giving direction, and criticizing or justifying authority.

A STUDY OF TEACHER ROLE

The remainder of this chapter presents the report of a two-year project based on several theoretical ideas about the relationship between teacher influence patterns and the achievement and attitudes of students. This relationship was tested under two conditions of student goal perception, goal clarity and goal ambiguity; in two subject areas, geometry and social studies. The hypotheses of the study were concerned with the effect of direct and indirect teacher influence and various conditions of goal perception on student achievement.

Testing of these hypotheses involved the use of two general kinds of concepts. Teacher behavior was described as direct or indirect teacher influence, and student goal perception as either ambiguous or clear. . . . Goal clarity is a condition in which the student knows his ultimate goal and the steps necessary for achieving it; goal ambiguity is defined as a state of affairs in which a student either is not sure of the steps necessary to reach the goal or has an uncertain picture of the end product.

During the first year of the study the concepts of teacher influence and goal perception were used with eighth-grade students in four experimental treatments in each of two areas, geometry and social studies. These four treatments were created in a laboratory situation: (1) direct influence with goal clarity, (2) direct influence with goal ambiguity, (3) indirect influence with goal clarity, and (4) indirect influence with goal ambiguity. In each subject area a teacher role-played both direct and indirect teacher influence. Several classroom experimental groups of 20 students each were involved in each treatment, with a total of 560 students participating in the geometry and 480 different students in the social studies experiments.

The second year of the research project involved a field study that tested the same relationships as those tested in the first-year laboratory experiment. Of the 900 students participating, half were seventh-grade social studies and half eighth-grade geometry students. The 32 teachers, 16 in each subject area, were the regular classroom teachers.

RESULTS

Results of the first and second year of the study, when compared, were found to be essentially the same wherever significant differences were found.

First, a prediction was made that the more indirect teachers would act most indirectly when goals were being clarified and when new content material was being introduced, and act most directly after goals had been clarified and work was in progress. Data from the second year of the study indicate that this prediction about the more indirect teachers was accurate.

Second, it was predicted that in general students of the more direct teachers would learn less as measured by written achievement tests than students of indirect teachers. Also the prediction was made that certain types of students would learn more working with direct teachers and other types of students would learn more working with indirect teachers. Results indicated that all types of students learned more working with the more indirect teachers than with the more direct teachers.

Third, students in mathematics were predicted to learn more working with a more direct teacher, and students in social studies to learn more working with a more indirect teacher. Although it was found that teachers of mathematics use time and methods differently than do teachers of social studies, in both content areas the students of the more indirect teachers scored higher on the achievement tests than did students of the more direct teachers.

The terms "indirect" and "direct" have been used in this section and throughout the manual to describe teacher behavior. However, as a result of the study, it became clear that the concept of teacher flexibility was more predictive of teaching success than was the concept of direct-indirect influence. It was found that the teachers of classes in which achievement was above average differed from the teachers of below-average classes in their ability to shift their behavior as it was necessary. That is, they could be just as direct as any teacher in certain situations, but they could be far more indirect in other situations. This ability, which was rarely found among teachers categorized as direct, meant that the teacher had the capability to make his own behavior appropriate to the requirements of the class situation at the moment.

IMPLICATIONS

Implications for classroom teachers: Perhaps the most interesting implication of the project is concerned with the timing of direct and indirect influence. The findings of the study are contrary to accepted practice. Nearly all teachers agree that immediate action should be taken in any situation in which the learning goals are ambiguous and students do not know what to do. Students who are unable to go on with their work are wasting time. Something should be done. All teachers agree with this.

Should the initial contacts made by a teacher in such a situation be more direct or more indirect? The results suggest an indirect approach, whereas most teachers use a direct approach. Teachers can find many reasons to justify their more direct approach. Often they think that telling the students what to do is only reminding them of something they already know. Sometimes teachers are quite sure that the students are lazy or pretending confusion.

Often they feel that the direct approach is the more efficient one. These and many other reasons are often mentioned by teachers as a justification for the following pattern: (a) the teacher decides students are confused; (b) the teacher makes his best guess as to the cause of this confusion; and (c) the teacher, acting on his own diagnosis, proceeds to give information, direction, and in some cases, criticism in order to help the group continue its work. The two most common situations in which a teacher faces this choice are when new material is being introduced (for example, a new topic, a new procedure, or a new method of problem solving) and when a group already at work runs into difficulty (for example, Johnny won't cooperate, information cannot be found, the answer doesn't check with an independent proof, materials are missing, and so forth).

Thus, there will be some situations in which a teacher should be primarily direct and others in which he should be primarily indirect. However, it was found that the teachers of students who learned less too often employed a pattern of direct influence in this situation, whereas higher achievement and less dependence were found when goals were clarified by an indirect approach.

A more indirect approach will stimulate verbal participation by students. It is a way of providing the teacher with the students' perceptions of the situation, regardless of whether these perceptions are correct or incorrect. Such an approach not only provides the teacher with more information, but it often results in the students' developing more responsibility for diagnosing their difficulties and suggesting a plan of action.

On the other hand, a more direct approach increases student compliance to teacher opinion and direction. It conditions students to seek the teacher's help and to check with the teacher more often to be sure they are on the right track.

A second implication for classroom teachers is that the major differences in the use of influence between the teachers whose students learned the most and whose students learned the least are illustrated by Categories 1, 2, and 3.* The direct teachers did not use those social skills of communication that are involved in accepting, clarifying, and making use of the ideas and feelings of students. The indirect teachers have these skills, even though they are not in use a major portion of the time. Although they are used sparingly, they are effective when needed.

Teachers using these social skills appropriately have less need for giving directions and criticism. When the most direct teachers were compared with the most indirect, it was found that the direct teachers give directions twice as frequently as the indirect teachers; for criticism, the contrast increases to 8 to 1. These figures are consistent with what has been said about dependence. Lack of clarifying and using student ideas places the teacher in a position of giving more direction; in short, he must work harder to keep his students at work. When dependence is higher, progress by students depends much more on continuous teacher supervision.

* That is, accepting, clarifying, and making use of ideas and feelings of students.—Ed.

There are interesting comparisons here between what has been found in this research and some of the more common criticisms of the public schools that have attained wide circulation during the last few years. Some critics of the public schools have advocated that teachers "get tough," tell students what to do, and demand high standards. The results of this research seem to indicate that higher standards can be achieved not by telling students what to do in some sort of "get tough" policy, but by asking questions and then using student ideas, perceptions, and reactions to build toward greater self-direction, student responsibility and understanding. If "getting tough" means helping students face the consequences of their own ideas and opinions, then indirect teachers in this study are much tougher.

The third implication for classroom teachers is that variability in teacher influence, what has been referred to here as flexibility, is associated with teachers whose students learned the most. For example, the better teachers showed a variety of patterns of behavior, while the poorer teachers showed patterns that were much alike. It suggests that creative teaching is a unique expression of a particular teacher's personality using her range of ability and skill in working with a particular group of students in a particular subject matter field.

One way to interpret the differences between the direct and indirect teachers is in terms of the different roles the teacher is able to play in the classroom. The direct teachers could not shift their style of interaction as much as the indirect teachers. In effect, the direct teachers had fewer ways of working with students; they could provide only a limited number of roles. On the other hand, the indirect teachers were capable of providing many different roles and they shifted their roles in a manner consistent with the theories that have already been stated.

WHEN THE TEACHER DIAGNOSES LEARNING

Madeline Hunter *

In order to know which strategies and tactics to choose, one must diagnose the situation. Diagnosis gives teachers the basic data they need in order to work with individuals. Without it the teacher does not know what is likely to motivate the various individuals in the class. Neither

* From *Educational Leadership*, Vol. 23 (April 1966), pp. 545–549. Reprinted with permission of the Association for Supervision and Curriculum Development and Madeline Hunter. Copyright © 1966 by the Association for Supervision and Curriculum Development.

does he know which subject matter is likely to meet their immediate educational needs, or whether a particular bit of reading is too hard or too easy.

The need for diagnosis is self-evident, but somehow many teachers seem to be unaware of it. On the whole, elementary school teachers seem to be more aware of this need than other teachers are. Although Madeline Hunter writes from an elementary school teacher's point of view, her comments should be taken to heart by secondary school teachers as well. Remember that the pattern common to good teaching consists of diagnosis, preparing the setting for learning, guiding the learning, evaluating the learning, and following through or following up. Of these five, diagnosis is the key. Without it the teacher has nothing to indicate the strategy and tactics he should use in a particular situation. In other words, he has no information as a basis for choosing the content and methods for his classes.

What kind of a boy is Johnny? What has he already learned? What "next" learning tasks are appropriate for him? How can a teacher increase the efficiency and economy of his accomplishment?

As the teacher confronts these questions for each learner under his supervision, small wonder he is tempted to murmur, "Please pass the crystal ball!" Fortunately, crystal balls and divining rods are not available on supply requisition lists, so professional rigor is beginning to replace folklore and fantasy as the basis for diagnosis of and for educational prescription for the learner.

This shift from routinized application of the currently recommended panacea (what is it this year, look-say or phonics?) to decision making based on critical evaluation of each learner has been the major factor in the change from the technology of teaching to the profession of education.

No longer is diagnosis restricted to or reserved for only the educationally "sick." Rather, such diagnosis has become an intrinsic part of the teaching act for *all* learners. Out of such diagnosis are created educational prescriptions. The repertoire of competencies of the teacher and alternatives offered by the school constitute a pharmacy from which such prescriptions are filled.

We first must identify the questions such diagnosis is designed to answer. Only then can we seek instruments whose validity, reliability and precision give us confidence in the accuracy of the assessment on which diagnosis is based.

DIAGNOSTIC QUESTIONS

Identification of the essential and relevant has as its irrefutable and logical counterpart identification of the nonessential and irrelevant. The latter, no matter how fascinating and tempting (with *that* home situation what can you expect of me?), must be discarded. We also must discard many of our most easily collected but relatively worthless "test results" on learners.

Each datum we use in our diagnostic procedure must pass the screen of contributing to the answer to one of the following questions:

1. What objective is appropriate for this learner to achieve? (Notice the change from "*I* am seeking to attain with this learner.")
2. What is his present status in relation to that objective?
3. What is the next learning step in attainment of that objective?
4. Based on data about this particular learner, what can the teacher do to help him take that step efficiently and economically?
5. Was he successful?
6. If so, what is the next appropriate step?
7. If not, what changes should be made?

Questions 1, 2, and 3 are content-based. Knowledge of the learning task (reading, math, or ball playing) must be related to the assessment of the learner's present degree of achievement.

Question 4 is learner-based. An assessment of the intellectual, physical, social, and emotional factors that contribute to or detract from the learning process provides the data for the answer.

Questions 5, 6, 7 are evaluation-based, where "at this moment in time" must become the qualifying phrase for any answer.

Let us begin with an inspection of these questions as they relate to a physical activity so we will not get trapped in the value-imbued educational platitudes ("competency in reading," "appreciation of the democratic process"), which are so emotionally charged. Suppose we are trying to determine the appropriate high jump objective for a boy of a given age. The first factor that becomes obvious is that other data may be more critical than his age. Does he have long or short legs? Is he fat or thin? How well is he muscled and coordinated? (It makes you stop to reconsider the statement that ten-year-old boys should be reading at a fifth grade level, does it not?)

Suppose we agree that this boy should be able to clear a five-foot bar. Now we turn to our second question—how high can he actually jump? We find (possibly to our horror) that he can comfortably clear only a 3′ 8″ bar, although on occasions he can jump a 4′ one. Obviously, at this point we are not going to insist he keep trying the 5′ bar, but plan to start teaching so he can consistently clear the 4′ one. (Hammering away at 5th grade work that is too difficult is as obviously unsound.)

Our fourth question is concerned with the use of data about the learner that will guide us in planning the learning opportunity and teaching strategy to help him accomplish his task. Will competition with other jumpers stimulate or retard his effort? What for him is the optimum ratio of success to failure? If he responds well to performance heavily weighted with success, we had better keep the bar at 3′ 10″. If he is motivated by the frustration of some failure, let us start at 4'. What does he need in the way of teacher support? Shall we stand by to encourage or let him work by himself? Does he respond well to his own perception of growth or does he need public recognition of his achievement? Will his parents contribute to his achievement motivation or do they think high jumping is a waste of time? (His parents may be getting a divorce or his father may be an alcoholic; however, these dramatic bits of information are not relevant unless we find evidence that they contribute to or detract from his accomplishment of the learning task.)

Now that we have defined the task, and applied a teaching strategy to help him accomplish it, did it work? If the answer is "yes," we are ready to move on to the next task, raise the height of the bar and proceed. If the answer is "no," we must look for factors that may need to be changed. Have we correctly assessed his jumping ability or should we have started with a lower bar? Could there be something wrong of which we were not aware (fatigue, low energy, movement or coordination difficulties)? Was our teaching strategy ineffective? Should we have given more encouragement? Should we have been "tougher" and insisted he "get at it" with consequences if he did not? Would making him the high-jump coach for less able jumpers do the trick? Are there other factors operating which we had not taken into consideration? By practicing, he may miss the opportunity to talk with fascinating girls or perhaps he may be attempting to insure our continued attention by his lack of success.

Our estimate of the correct answer to all of these diagnostic questions becomes the basis for an adjusted educational prescription. Again we fill the prescription from the pharmacy of teaching competency and the alternatives possible in the school and again assess its effectiveness by the performance of the jumper.

DIAGNOSIS IN READING

Let us now pose these same questions in the diagnosis of a learner we find in every classroom.

Bill is not performing well in reading. While not so remedial that he needs special help, he is dragging at the bottom of his group. We have the uncomfortable feeling that the only thing he is learning is that reading is a bore to be avoided whenever possible.

We begin our diagnosis with the first question, "What goal is appropriate for this learner?" Notice by using goal in the singular, we are being forced to give priority to "enjoyment of reading" *or* "skills in reading" *or* "appreciation of literature" *or* "more active participation in the reading program." Once we identify the primary goal we are able to deal with or eliminate the incompatibility of other goals. (Chaucer and enjoyment may not be compatible at this point.) Unidentified, their counter-directions can neutralize our teaching efforts.

If we select "enjoyment of reading" as the goal basic to the achievement of all others, this becomes our criterion for answering subsequent questions. (It also eliminates such temptations as having his dad make him read an hour each night.)

Our second question, "What is his present status in relation to that goal?" involves a valid assessment of Bill. The eyes and ears of a well prepared teacher continue to be among the best instruments of appraisal; however, we can validate or supplement these observations with objective tests. There is a relationship (but not one to one correspondence) between enjoyment of and skill in an activity, so we need carefully to assess Bill's reading skills. We look beyond the homogenized 5.3 grade placement score on the fact sheet of a reading test because the information we are seeking is inside the test and we will find it only if we inspect Bill's responses.

What kinds of items did he miss? Did he do the easy ones correctly and then quit? Were careless errors responsible for missing easy items while he passed harder ones? Could his errors indicate an attempt to respond correctly or was he simply filling in the blanks? Most important, how does his test performance compare with our daily perception of him? If he performs significantly better in either the test or classroom, what factors might be responsible? Obviously, a numerical grade placement score does not begin to answer these questions.

Let us assume our answer is: Bill *can* read 5th grade material with understanding but the vocabulary load slows him down. Fourth grade material insures a more comfortable pace; however, the content of both 4th and 5th grade material he finds uninteresting. When the reading is difficult he seems to turn off his effort and make wild guesses. When the content is uninteresting, he withdraws into daydreaming with a resultant lack of focus on the learning task.

Our assessment of Bill's performance should direct us to the answer to the question, "What is the next appropriate learning step?"

Now we have two criteria to guide us. The material must be easy enough to encourage his progress and interesting enough to hold his focus. This may involve abandoning, for a time, the state series and selecting a book with a low vocabulary load and exciting content. Remember, "enjoyment of reading" is the goal with highest priority at this point in time. (We are adjusting the high jump bar so he can get over it.) We have not abandoned word attack skills and extraction of meaning but we are concentrating on first things first.

Having selected an appropriate task, we now turn to our design to help him accomplish it. Here our diagnosis of the learner requires professional literacy in learning theory and personality theory. To what reward system will he respond? Will his accomplishment be positively reinforcing or do we need to add the social rewards of praise and recognition? Do we need to suppress any behavior (such as avoidance of reading) by negative reinforcement? Will *increasing* or *decreasing* anxiety result in better motivation? How long a reading period can he tolerate before negative feelings take over? How might we extend this period?

These are samples of the questions we must answer for a valid diagnosis. The questions determine whether we skillfully entice him into the reading task or arbitrarily assign it with a time limit and consequences. We may make him the star performer in a book review or may quietly converse with him when the rest of the group are busy. We may make reading a definite assignment or a leisure-time activity. We may "keep after him" or turn him loose.

Diagnosis must lead to action. As mere intellectual exercise it is useless. Consequently, based on our best judgment, we will do *something*. The results determine the validity of our diagnosis and prescription. If all goes well we will proceed to the next learning task. If not, we will reassess our answers to each of the questions, revise our diagnosis and prescription, and try again.

Many people are seeking an instrument that will diagnose, then will "tell us what to do." It is important that we remember this has not been accomplished in any profession that deals with the intricacies of a human being. The thermometer registers with considerable accuracy the temperature of the patient but a doctor must decide which medication to use. In spite of his best and learned judgment, some patients are allergic to the dose and some are beyond his ability to help. Still we have seen tremendous advances in the skill and precision of the medical diagnostician.

As educators, we too are increasing the skill and precision of our assessment of the learner, so we no longer need to keep interminable records and stockpile useless data to stuff cumulative folders. By identification of the critical elements of an assessment we may be sure that instruments will be devised so their objectivity and precision will augment but never replace the highly trained observation that guides educational decisions.

THE SYSTEMS APPROACH

William Clark Trow *

The teaching profession seems to be moving toward a man-machine system approach to teaching. This approach need not be as frightening to prospective teachers as it might seem. Basically a man-machine sys-

* From: *Teacher and Technology: New Designs for Learning* by William Clark Trow. Copyright © 1963 by Meredith Publishing Company. Reprinted by permission of Appleton-Century-Crofts.

tem is a teaching team in which machines, as well as people, are given a role, and each person and machine is allowed to do the type of work he or it can do best. If it works as it should, the systems approach should result in more efficient and effective learning, with teachers giving pupils much more personal attention than they have in any period since the advent of mass education.

Following the rationalization idea, one might start where the school is and plan successive steps that must be taken in order to bring about the conditions sought. The planning would involve both equipment and personnel. The terms *input* and *output* are applied either to the performance of a single person or group, or to the operation of a machine or industrial system or complex that manufactures some product, like an automobile. But the input cannot be dumped in all at once. Various processes are involved requiring careful selection, variation, and timing. Different parts have to be applied in the proper amounts when they are needed.

Over the years educators have given a great deal of attention to this matter of process, including such problems as those of curriculum, method, evaluation, and promotion, but all efforts have been circumscribed by the assumption that the teacher-class subsystem is necessary. It has been taken as axiomatic that one teacher teaches a "course" or "grade," the content of which takes a year (or term) to complete, and that all the students should begin and end it together. Some of the greatest scientific discoveries have been made when investigators have dared to question an axiom. And if one follows their example and questions the validity of the teacher-class axiom, he soon realizes that it is actually more mechanical than the innovations that might supersede it. The method of assigning marks is an escape, a rationalization in the psychological sense of the term. It projects the failures of the system on the children and young people, giving low or failing marks to those who have not been properly classified or adequately taught, and at the same time giving rewarding marks to those who do well, some of whom may not even have needed the instruction.

In contrast, a systems approach [1] implies a careful study of the kind of treatment (input) required by each child, and the time when it is needed, in order to attain the objectives sought. "Systems analysis is the comparison of alternative means of carrying out some function, where the means are complicated and comprise a number of interrelated elements." [2] Educationally,

---

[1] See Robert M. Gagné, ed., *Psychological Principles in System Development* (New York: Holt, Rinehart and Winston, Inc., 1962); also John F. Cogswell in *AID for Education and Training*, 5 (September, 1961), 43.

[2] James Mauch, "A Systems Analysis Approach to Education," *Phi Delta Kappan*, 43 (January, 1962), 158–162.

it is making the best use of available resources within the framework of values that the school administrator has established or ascertained in the community. As has been noted, the term *man-machine system* applies to the coordination of men and machines in producing a specific output. The machine simplifies or at least changes the performance of the man, although the overall task remains the same. It is no longer merely the process of fitting tools to man's use, but of discovering what machines can do that man does with his tools, and what they cannot. Education has long employed a hesitant, piecemeal approach—one little innovation here and another there—without much conviction and without adequately fitting the pieces together into a total, unified process. All agree on the function of teaching as that of organizing the environment to guide learning activities toward the educational objectives. A man-machine system implies that if the means and responsibilities are realigned, the task can be performed more effectively. It implies further that the components can be so arranged that compatibility and purposeful performance are achieved by organization and readjustment among them.

If we concentrate on the task to be performed, a careful description and analysis are of primary importance, and consequent decisions on training procedures should be based on these and on the input conditions and on the output (objectives) sought.[3]

The main point in setting up such a system or combination of subsystems, as has been suggested, is that any change in any component must be analyzed and evaluated in relation to its effects on and interactions with all other components, and in relation to its effects on the operation and output of the total system. For example, the effectiveness of self-instructional devices, no matter how excellent in themselves, is dependent on interactions of different types of instruction, the roles played by school personnel, the scheduling of students, and so on.

If we concentrate on the personnel components of the system, the school staff, we realize that each member must fit into the whole structure in such a way that his peculiar contribution is made as effective as possible. This is why it is necessary to define the objectives of the system, and analyze the task and functions to be performed by the human components (the school personnel) and by the machines. Then the nature and extent of the output desired—new knowledge and skill and the behavior capabilities of the learner—must be specified. Personnel must be selected and trained to do what will be needed to contribute to the objectives of the system. With new and sometimes more specific tasks to perform, procedures for selection and training call for some modification.

Due care needs to be exercised in following through the stages in systems development listed by Gagné, above. Trial runs will probably be necessary,

---

[3] Robert B. Miller, "Analysis and Specifications of Behavior for Training," in *Training, Research, and Education* (Pittsburgh: University of Pittsburgh, 1962); also "Task Description and Analysis," in Gagné, *op. cit.*, Ch. 6.

and these can sometimes be carried on experimentally in a simulated environment in which the several components can be tested, varied, and re-tested under fairly well-controlled conditions. Similarly, effective system performance may suggest the desirability of training personnel as a team under simulated conditions. This may be done by role-playing, an excellent simulator in social situations. Or "a school within a school" may be set up, involving, say, several different kinds of rooms and a control room, which will provide a feedback to improve the procedures and achieve an integrated performance.

But a systems approach necessarily involves some over-all design. Design in education has been defined by Robert W. Wagner [4] as "thoughtful artful organic use and creative control of necessary system." It is the reason why school "systems" should differ (though they may differ for less enviable reasons). Those who create them will order the parts in a variety of ways according to the materials they use and their feeling for human values.

Technology, as has been noted, does not consist of machines alone, nor the personnel, nor is it the system, but it is the source and substance of them all. As stated earlier, the word literally means the science of construction. More specifically, it means applied science or science in support of the practical arts. Physics is basic to the engineering arts, biology to the medical, and psychology to the educational, although related sciences are also drawn upon. So rapid has been the industrial development of the last few years that many have come to think of technology as applying only to hardware. But this is too narrow a conception. As a matter of fact, many of the earlier inventions of the industrial age depended less on science than on a kind of common sense empricism or a heuristic, problem-solving procedure. What looked like a good guess was tried out to see if it would work. More is now understood about the nature of the external world—the strength of metals and alloys, the permanence of dyes, the wearing qualities of building materials, tires, and textiles, and so on—so less guesswork is necessary. Similarly, education is becoming less dependent on folklore, tradition, and heuristic procedures, and more on the methods of science as they have been developed chiefly by psychologists in the area of learning, and social psychologists, in group processes. The points of view of the scientist and of the technologist are likely to differ in one interesting respect: the scientist is impressed with what we don't know, and the technologist with what we do. So the psychologically oriented writers are apt to point out the weaknesses and faults of television and of self-instructional programs, while the educationally oriented, if not hag-ridden by habit and tradition, are more apt to go ahead, make their programs, and try them out, or perhaps work out improvements in the process.

The true function of the technologist—whether industrial, consulting, military or educational—is to employ psychology in a particular setting, that is, to the problems of one or another of the arts, to translate general laws

---

[4] Robert W. Wagner, "Design in Education," *The News Letter*, The Bureau of Educational Research and Service, Ohio State University, 27 (October, 1961), 1–4.

and principles into specific operations of machines and people. As is well known, the contribution of science is threefold: knowledge and understanding of related natural phenomena; measurement and precision, hence more exact assessment; and method, including careful observation, repetition, record-keeping, control of variables, discovery of regularities, inference, and experimentation.

While these processes are not mutually exclusive, they roughly delineate the various activities employed by scientists in the quest for certainty. Technology is the scientifically-based activity involved in the development of the practical arts, in the making of new functional constructs, whether mechanical devices or organizations of people, or a combination of the two. In the latter, technology includes the design, organization, and operation of man-machine systems along the lines previously described.

Chapter 2

THE OBJECTIVES OF THE
AMERICAN SECONDARY SCHOOL

As Aristotle pointed out many years ago, both educators and laymen find it difficult to decide what they really want the schools to do. For a long time in the Western world, secondary schools were asked to provide classical-liberal education. Stemming at least partially from Aristotle's differentiation between liberal and vocational subjects, this bias continued to dominate secondary education until the middle of the nineteenth century. At that time Herbert Spencer upset tradition by claiming that in emphasizing the humanities the schoolmen had their priorities backward. In his scheme the priorities would be reversed: the classical-liberal subjects would be relegated to last place.

This reappraisal was indicative of a movement toward the ideal of what Spencer called education for complete living, which was finally expressed officially in the "Seven Cardinal Principles." The basic notion of this ideal, which continued to be expressed during the inter-bellum period, was that it was the responsibility of the school to meet the needs of pupils in all facets of their lives. One notable statement was that of the NEA's Educational Policies Commission in 1938.* Later, during and after World War II, the notion of education for complete living continued to be preeminent, although it was then commonly expressed as the needs of youth. The most fashionable of these statements of "Needs" was the 1944 statement of the Educational Policies Commission, "The Imperative Educational Needs of Youth," contained in their influential and controversial book *Education for All American Youth.*

Recently educators have become somewhat disenchanted by the immensity of the task called for by the ideal of education for complete living. Thus we see the Educational Policies Commission stating in 1961 that the central purpose of education is the development of the rational powers. Some educators have objected strongly to this orientation, but at the moment the bulk of the opinion seems to be in favor of the development of intellectual powers as the central purpose of American education. In this respect they seem to be following the lead of Whitehead and Dewey, whose aim was to make

---

* Educational Policies Commission of the NEA, *The Purposes of Education in American Democracy* (Washington, D.C.: National Education Association, 1938).

intellectual pursuits something more than a mere swallowing of subject matter.

In the long run, perhaps the ideal general objectives of secondary education do not change. But in detail, at least, the school must change. The democracy of today requires considerably more of its citizens than did that of the nineteenth century. The world that future graduating pupils will face will be quite different from that of the past. The role of the secondary school must change accordingly. Possibly its new role is the one that it should have assumed in the past but did not. The future, however, probably will not be as tolerant of mistakes as the past has been.

Recently a revival of scientific analysis of pedagogy has attempted to reduce the objectives of teaching to a system that can be useful as a basis for study as well as for teaching and testing. The hierarchy of goals in the taxonomy of educational objectives presented in this chapter has been one result. These useful analyses do not, of course, in any way supplant the need for studying the overall directions education in the secondary schools should take.

This discussion of educational objectives should help illustrate the complexity of the teaching process. The objectives of education should determine the strategies and tactics that teachers use in their teaching. These objectives should be based on the nature of the learner, the nature of society, and the nature of the subject matter to be considered. On the other hand, the subject matter or content in a particular instance is part of the strategy and so should be selected in view of the objectives chosen for this instance. Educational method, as one can see from this illustration, consists of an intertwining of rather complex elements. To be a teacher at a really professional level, therefore, requires a really good understanding of educational theory.

THE IMPERATIVE EDUCATIONAL NEEDS OF YOUTH

The Educational Policies Commission of the NEA *

The modern secondary school seems to have taken all knowledge for its province. Brubacher † implies that this movement is largely the result of the thinking of Herbert Spencer as expressed in his well-known essay

* From *Education for All American Youth* (Washington, D.C.: National Education Association, 1944), pp. 225–226. Reprinted by permission of the NEA. Footnotes deleted.

† John S. Brubacher, A *History of the Problems of Education* (New York: McGraw-Hill Book Company, 1947), p. 16.

"What Knowledge Is of Most Worth." In this essay Spencer turned the tables on contemporary educational objectives by listing the activities of human life in an order just the opposite to that presented by the secondary-school curricula of the times. In his opinion, it is the practical rather than the liberal studies that should have priority, and the knowledge of most worth is necessarily science.

The notion of education for complete living is implicit in the seven major objectives set up by the Commission on the Reorganization of Secondary Education of the National Education Association during World War I. These all-encompassing objectives—1. Health; 2. Command of the Fundamental Processes; 3. Worthy Home Membership; 4. Vocation; 5. Citizenship; 6. Worthy Use of Leisure Time; 7. Ethical Character—commonly known as the Seven Cardinal Principles, have dominated the literature of secondary education from that time to the present. For five decades their influence has been evident in statements of educational goals and in the attempts to build school curricula that would bring about education for complete living. Their spirit is exemplified in "The Imperative Educational Needs of Youth" drawn up by the Educational Policies Commission of the NEA as a guide to give direction to educational policy in the years following World War II. This statement, like many other statements of educational aims based on the ideal of education for complete living, is all-inclusive. It omits no phase of human activity.

1. All youth need to develop salable skills and those understandings and attitudes that make the worker an intelligent and productive participant in economic life. To this end, most youth need supervised work experience as well as education in the skills and knowledge of their occupations.

2. All youth need to develop and maintain good health and physical fitness.

3. All youth need to understand the rights and duties of the citizen of a democratic society, and to be diligent and competent in the performance of their obligations as members of the community and citizens of the state and nation.

4. All youth need to understand the significance of the family for the individual and society and the conditions conducive to successful family life.

5. All youth need to know how to purchase and use goods and services intelligently, understanding both the values received by the consumer and the economic consequences of their acts.

6. All youth need to understand the methods of science, the influence of science on human life, and the main scientific facts concerning the nature of the world and of man.

7. All youth need opportunities to develop their capacities to appreciate beauty in literature, art, music, and nature.

8. All youth need to be able to use their leisure time well and to budget it wisely, balancing activities that yield satisfactions to the individual with those that are socially useful.

9. All youth need to develop respect for other persons, to grow in their insight into ethical values and principles, and to be able to live and work cooperatively with others.

10. All youth need to grow in their ability to think rationally, to express their thoughts clearly, and to read and listen with understanding.

THE CENTRAL PURPOSE OF EDUCATION

The Educational Policies Commission of the NEA *

The mid-twentieth century brought a reaction against the attempts to educate for complete living and a return to the belief that the primary objective of education should be the cultivation of the rational powers of the pupils. The Educational Policies Commission of the National Education Association in 1961 adopted this view without discarding the earlier view entirely. Their contention is that the rational powers are the hub from which all other qualities of the human spirit emanate. Therefore, the schools must make the development of the rational powers the central purpose of education in order to make it possible for the pupil to develop his other qualities to their fullest potential.

THE CENTRAL ROLE OF THE RATIONAL POWERS

The cultivated powers of the free mind have always been basic in achieving freedom. The powers of the free mind are many. In addition to the rational powers, there are those which relate to the aesthetic, the moral, and the religious. There is a unique, central role for the rational powers of an individual, however, for upon them depends his ability to achieve his personal goals and to fulfill his obligations to society.

These powers involve the processes of recalling and imagining, classifying

* From *The Central Purpose of American Education* (Washington, D.C.: National Education Association, 1961), pp. 4–11. Reprinted by permission of the NEA.

and generalizing, comparing and evaluating, analyzing and synthesizing, and deducing and inferring. These processes enable one to apply logic and the available evidence to his ideas, attitudes, and actions, and to pursue better whatever goals he may have.

This is not to say that the rational powers are all of life or all of the mind, but they are the essence of the ability to think. A thinking person is aware that all persons, himself included, are both rational and nonrational, that each person perceives events through the screen of his own personality, and that he must take account of his personality in evaluating his perceptions. The rational processes, moreover, make intelligent choices possible. Through them a person can become aware of the bases of choice in his values and of the circumstances of choice in his environment. Thus they are broadly applicable in life, and they provide a solid basis for competence in all the areas with which the school has traditionally been concerned.

The traditionally accepted obligation of the school to teach the *fundamental processes*—an obligation stressed in the 1918 and 1938 statements of educational purposes—is obviously directed toward the development of the ability to think. Each of the school's other traditional objectives can be better achieved as pupils develop this ability and learn to apply it to all the problems that face them.

Health, for example, depends upon a reasoned awareness of the value of mental and physical fitness and of the means by which it may be developed and maintained. Fitness is not merely a function of living and acting; it requires that the individual understand the connection among health, nutrition, activity, and environment, and that he take action to improve his mental and physical condition.

Worthy home membership in the modern age demands substantial knowledge of the role that the home and community play in human development. The person who understands the bases of his own judgments recognizes the home as the source from which most individuals develop most of the standards and values they apply in their lives. He is intelligently aware of the role of emotion in his own life and in the lives of others. His knowledge of the importance of the home environment in the formation of personality enables him to make reasoned judgments about his domestic behavior.

More than ever before, and for an ever-increasing proportion of the population, *vocational competence* requires developed rational capacities. The march of technology and science in the modern society progressively eliminates the positions open to low-level talents. The man able to use only his hands is at a growing disadvantage as compared with the man who can also use his head. Today even the simplest use of hands is coming to require the simultaneous employment of the mind.

Effective citizenship is impossible without the ability to think. The good citizen, the one who contributes effectively and responsibly to the management of the public business in a free society, can fill his role only if he is aware of the values of his society. Moreover, the course of events in modern life is such that many of the factors which influence an individual's civic life are increasingly remote from him. His own firsthand experience is no longer an adequate basis for judgment. He must have in addition the intellectual means to study events, to relate his values to them, and to make wise decisions as to his own actions. He must also be skilled in the processes of communication and must understand both the potentialities and the limitations of communication among individuals and groups.

The *worthy use of leisure* is related to the individual's knowledge, understanding, and capacity to choose, from among all the activities to which his time can be devoted, those which contribute to the achievement of his purposes and to the satisfaction of his needs. On these bases, the individual can become aware of the external pressures which compete for his attention, moderate the influence of these pressures, and make wise choices for himself. His recreation, ranging from hobbies to sports to intellectual activity pursued for its own sake, can conform to his own concepts of constructive use of time.

The development of *ethical character* depends upon commitment to values; it depends also upon the ability to reason sensitively and responsibly with respect to those values in specific situations. Character is misunderstood if thought of as mere conformity to standards imposed by external authority. In a free society, ethics, morality, and character have meaning to the extent that they represent affirmative, thoughtful choices by individuals. The ability to make these choices depends on awareness of values and of their role in life. The home and the church begin to shape the child's values long before he goes to school. And a person who grows up in the American society inevitably acquires many values from his daily pattern of living. American children at the age of six, for example, usually have a firm commitment to the concept of fair play. This is a value which relates directly to such broad democratic concepts as justice and human worth and dignity. But the extension of this commitment to these broader democratic values will not occur unless the child becomes aware of its implications for his own behavior, and this awareness demands the ability to think.

A person who understands and appreciates his own values is most likely to act on them. He learns that his values are of great moment for himself, and he can look objectively and sympathetically at the values held by others. Thus, by critical thinking, he can deepen his respect for the importance of values and strengthen his sense of responsibility.

The man who seeks to understand himself understands also that other human beings have much in common with him. His understanding of the possibilities which exist within a human being strengthens his concept of the respect due every man. He recognizes the web which relates him to other men and perceives the necessity for responsible behavior. The person whose rational powers are not well developed can, at best, learn habitual responses and ways of conforming which may insure that he is not a detriment to his society. But, lacking the insight that he might have achieved, his capacity to contribute will inevitably be less than it might have become.

Development of the ability to reason can lead also to dedication to the values which inhere in rationality: commitment to honesty, accuracy, and personal reliability; respect for the intellect and for the intellectual life; devotion to the expansion of knowledge. A man who thinks can understand the importance of this ability. He is likely to value the rational potentials of mankind as essential to a worthy life.

Thus the rational powers are central to all the other qualities of the human spirit. These powers flourish in a humane and morally responsible context and contribute to the entire personality. The rational powers are to the entire human spirit as the hub is to the wheel.

These powers are indispensable to a full and worthy life. The person in whom—for whatever reason—they are not well developed is increasingly handicapped in modern society. He may be able to satisfy minimal social standards, but he will inevitably lack his full measure of dignity because his incapacity limits his stature to less than he might otherwise attain. Only to the extent that an individual can realize his potentials, especially the development of his ability to think, can he fully achieve for himself the dignity that goes with freedom.

A person with developed rational powers has the means to be aware of all facets of his existence. In this sense he can live to the fullest. He can escape captivity to his emotions and irrational states. He can enrich his emotional life and direct it toward ever higher standards of taste and enjoyment. He can enjoy the political and economic freedoms of the democratic society. He can free himself from the bondage of ignorance and unawareness. He can make of himself a free man.

THE CHANGES IN MAN'S UNDERSTANDING AND POWER

The foregoing analysis of human freedom and review of the central role of the rational powers in enabling a person to achieve his own goals demonstrate the critical importance of developing those powers. Their importance is also demonstrated by an analysis of the great changes in the world.

Many profound changes are occurring in the world today, but there is a fundamental force contributing to all of them. That force is the expanding role accorded in modern life to the rational powers of man. By using these powers to increase his knowledge, man is attempting to solve the riddles of life, space, and time which have long intrigued him. By using these powers to develop sources of new energy and means of communication, he is moving into interplanetary space. By using these powers to make a smaller world and larger weapons, he is creating new needs for international organization and understanding. By using these powers to alleviate disease and poverty, he is lowering death rates and expanding populations. By using these powers to create and use a new technology, he is achieving undreamed affluence, so that in some societies distribution has become a greater problem than production.

While man is using the powers of his mind to solve old riddles, he is creating new ones. Basic assumptions upon which mankind has long operated are being challenged or demolished. The age-old resignation to poverty and inferior status for the masses of humanity is being replaced by a drive for a life of dignity for all. Yet, just as man achieves a higher hope for all mankind, he sees also the opening of a grim age in which expansion of the power to create is matched by a perhaps greater enlargement of the power to destroy.

As man sees his power expand, he is coming to realize that the common sense which he accumulates from his own experience is not a sufficient guide to the understanding of the events in his own life or of the nature of the physical world. And, with combined uneasiness and exultation, he senses that his whole way of looking at life may be challenged in a time when men are returning from space.

Through the ages, man has accepted many kinds of propositions as truth, or at least as bases sufficient for action. Some propositions have been accepted on grounds of superstition; some on grounds of decree, dogma, or custom; some on humanistic, aesthetic, or religious grounds; some on common sense. Today, the role of knowledge derived from rational inquiry is growing. For this there are several reasons.

In the first place, knowledge so derived has proved to be man's most efficient weapon for achieving power over his environment. It prevails because it works.

More than effectiveness, however, is involved. There is high credibility in a proposition which can be arrived at or tested by persons other than those who advance it. Modesty, too, is inherent in rational inquiry, for it is an attempt to free explanations of phenomena and events from subjective preference and human authority, and to subject such explanations to validation through experience. Einstein's concept of the curvature of space cannot be demonstrated to the naked eye and may offend common sense; but persons who cannot apply the mathematics necessary to comprehend the concept can still accept it. They do this, not on Einstein's authority, but on their awareness that he used rational methods to achieve it and that those who possess the ability and facilities have tested its rational consistency and empirical validity.

In recent decades, man has greatly accelerated his systematic efforts to gain insight through rational inquiry. In the physical and biological sciences and in mathematics, where he has most successfully applied these methods, he has in a short time accumulated a vast fund of knowledge so reliable as to give him power he has never before had to understand, to predict, and to act. That is why attempts are constantly being made to apply these methods to additional areas of learning and human behavior. . . .

The purpose which runs through and strengthens all other educational purposes—the common thread of education—is the development of the ability to think. This is the central purpose to which the school must be oriented if it is to accomplish either its traditional tasks or those newly accentuated by recent changes in the world. To say that it is central is not to say that it is the sole purpose or in all circumstances the most important purpose, but that it must be a pervasive concern in the work of the school. Many agencies contribute to achieving educational objectives, but this particular objective will not be generally attained unless the school focuses on it. In this context, therefore, the development of every student's rational powers must be recognized as centrally important.

THE TAXONOMY OF EDUCATIONAL OBJECTIVES

If one is to judge the success of one's teaching, one must be able to measure educational progress in relationship to definite instructional goals. All too often the educational goals described in the literature are too vague for any practical purpose. The Taxonomy of Educational Objectives *is an attempt to classify definite kinds of specific objectives so that they will be usable for the teacher as he sets himself teaching tasks and as he evaluates the success of his and his pupils' efforts.*

Instructional objectives may be classified into three major categories: cognitive, affective, and psychomotor. To place all the various kinds of goals into hierarchies according to the three major classes is an immense task. So far a group of scholars have been able to produce only tentative classifications of two of the categories, the cognitive domain and the affective domain. In both the "domains" the investigators have created hierarchies from the lowest to highest types of behavior described by the objective.

The principal reason for building the taxonomy was to create a basis for measuring learning more successfully than had been done previously. The idea was to define the objectives and then determine what evidence would indicate whether the pupils had or had not reached that objective. Sample testing and measuring items have been devised for this purpose. The taxonomy should have as much significance for teachers planning lessons and units, for specific educational objectives a teacher seeks should be paramount in dictating his strategy and tactics, including both the content and techniques of teaching.

Note also that if we agree that the central purpose of education is to develop the rational powers, that we should use strategies aimed at developing the higher mental processes listed in the hierarchy of cognitive objectives. Unfortunately, most of the teaching at this time is aimed only at the lowest level—repetition or recall of information. In very few classes are strategies aiming at the higher cognitive processes used. In even fewer classes is there any attempt made to get at the affective objectives. Such strategies and tactics seem to be defeating our central purpose. Knowledge is important, of course, but unless it is used as a basis for higher learnings it becomes inert, dead information and therefore worthless.

THE AFFECTIVE DOMAIN

David R. Krathwohl, Benjamin S. Bloom, and Bertram B. Masia *

1.0 RECEIVING (ATTENDING)

At this level we are concerned that the learner be sensitized to the existence of certain phenomena and stimuli; that is, that he be willing to receive or to attend to them. This is clearly the first and crucial step if the learner is to be properly oriented to learn what the teacher intends that he will. To indicate that this is the bottom run of the ladder, however, is not at all to imply that the teacher is starting *de novo*. Because of previous experience (formal or informal), the student brings to each situation a point of view or set which may facilitate or hinder his recognition of the phenomena to which the teacher is trying to sensitize him.

The category of *Receiving* has been divided into three sub-categories to indicate three different levels of attending to phenomena. While the division points between the subcategories are arbitrary, the subcategories do represent a continuum. From an extremely passive position or role on the part of the learner, where the sole responsibility for the evocation of the behavior rests with the teacher—that is, the responsibility rests with him for "capturing" the student's attention—the continuum extends to a point at which the learner directs his attention, at least at a semiconscious level, toward the preferred stimuli.

1.1 Awareness

Awareness is almost a cognitive behavior. But unlike *Knowledge*, the lowest level of the cognitive domain, we are not so much concerned with a

* From *Taxonomy of Educational Objectives: Handbook II, The Affective Domain* by D. R. Krathwohl, B. S. Bloom, and B. B. Masia, 1964. Used by permission of David McKay Company, Inc.

memory of, or ability to recall, an item or fact as we are that, given appropriate opportunity, the learner will merely be conscious of something—that he take into account a situation, phenomenon, object, or stage of affairs. Like *Knowledge* it does imply an assessment of the qualities or nature of the stimulus, but unlike *Knowledge* it does not necessarily imply attention. There can be simple awareness without specific discrimination or recognition of the objective characteristics of the object, even though these characteristics must be deemed to have an effect. The individual may not be able to verbalize the aspects of the stimulus which cause the awareness.

Develops awareness of aesthetic factors in dress, furnishings, architecture, city design, good art, and the like.

Develops some consciousness of color, form, arrangement, and design in the objects and structures around him and in descriptive or symbolic representations of people, things, and situations.[1]

1.2 WILLINGNESS TO RECEIVE

In this category we have come a step up the ladder but are still dealing with what appears to be cognitive behavior. At a minimum level, we are here describing the behavior of being willing to tolerate a given stimulus, not to avoid it. Like *Awareness*, it involves a neutrality or suspended judgment toward the stimulus. At this level of the continuum the teacher is not concerned that the student seek it out, nor even, perhaps, that in an environment crowded with many other stimuli the learner will necessarily attend to the stimulus. Rather, at worst, given the opportunity to attend in a field with relatively few competing stimuli, the learner is not actively seeking to avoid it. At best, he is willing to take notice of the phenomenon and give it his attention.

Attends (carefully) when others speak—in direct conversation, on the telephone, in audiences.

Appreciation (tolerance) of cultural patterns exhibited by individuals from other groups—religious, social, political, economic, national, etc.

Increase in sensitivity to human need and pressing social problems.

1.3 CONTROLLED OR SELECTED ATTENTION

At a somewhat higher level we are concerned with a new phenomenon, the differentiation of a given stimulus into figure and ground at a conscious or perhaps semiconscious level—the differentiation of aspects of a stimulus which is perceived as clearly marked off from adjacent impressions. The per-

---

[1] Illustrative objectives selected from the literature follow the description of each sub-category.

ception is still without tension or assessment, and the student may not know the technical terms or symbols with which to describe it correctly or precisely to others. In some instances it may refer not so much to the selectivity of attention as to the control of attention, so that when certain stimuli are present they will be attended to. There is an element of the learner's controlling the attention here, so that the favored stimulus is selected and attended to despite competing and distracting stimuli.

Listens to music with some discrimination as to its mood and meaning and with some recognition of the contributions of various musical elements and instruments to the total effect.

Alertness toward human values and judgments on life as they are recorded in literature.

2.0 RESPONDING

At this level we are concerned with responses which go beyond merely attending to the phenomenon. The student is sufficiently motivated that he is not just 1.2 *Willing to attend*, but perhaps it is correct to say that he is actively attending. As a first stage in a "learning by doing" process the student is committing himself in some small measure to the phenomena involved. This is a very low level of commitment, and we would not say at this level that this was "a value of his" or that he had "such and such an attitude." These terms belong to the next higher level that we describe. But we could say that he is doing something with or about the phenomenon besides merely perceiving it, as would be true at the next level below this of 1.3 *Controlled or selected attention*.

This is the category that many teachers will find best describes their "interest" objectives. Most commonly we use the term to indicate the desire that a child become sufficiently involved in or committed to a subject, phenomenon, or activity that he will seek it out and gain satisfaction from working with it or engaging in it.

2.1 ACQUIESCENCE IN RESPONDING

We might use the word "obedience" or "compliance" to describe this behavior. As both of these terms indicate, there is a passiveness so far as the initiation of the behavior is concerned, and the stimulus calling for this behavior is not subtle. Compliance is perhaps a better term than obedience, since there is more of the element of reaction to a suggestion and less of the implication of resistance or yielding unwillingly. The student makes the response, but he has not fully accepted the necessity for doing so.

Willingness to comply with health regulations.
Obeys the playground regulations.

2.2 Willingness to Respond

The key to this level is in the term "willingness," with its implication of capacity for voluntary activity. There is the implication that the learner is sufficiently committed to exhibiting the behavior that he does so not just because of a fear of punishment, but "on his own" or voluntarily. It may help to note that the element of resistance or of yielding unwillingly, which is possibly present at the previous level, is here replaced with consent or proceeding from one's own choice.

Acquaints himself with significant current issues in international, political, social, and ecenomic affairs through voluntary reading and discussion.

Acceptance of responsibility for his own health and for the protection of the health of others.

2.3 Satisfaction in Response

The additional element in the step beyond the *Willingness to respond* level, the consent, the assent to responding, or the voluntary response, is that the behavior is accompanied by a feeling of satisfaction, an emotional response, generally of pleasure, zest, or enjoyment. The location of this category in the hierarchy has given us a great deal of difficulty. Just where in the process of internalization the attachment of an emotional response, kick, or thrill to a behavior occurs has been hard to determine. For that matter there is some uncertainty as to whether the level of internalization at which it occurs may not depend on the particular behavior. We have even questioned whether it should be a category. If our structure is to be a hierarchy, then each category should include the behavior in the next level below it. The emotional component appears gradually through the range of internalization categories. The attempt to specify a given position in the hierarchy as *the* one at which the emotional component is added is doomed to failure.

The category is arbitrarily placed at this point in the hierarchy where it seems to appear most frequently and where it is cited as or appears to be an important component of the objectives at this level on the continuum. The category's inclusion at this point serves the pragmatic purpose of reminding us of the presence of the emotional component and its value in the building of affective behaviors. But it should not be thought of as appearing and occurring at this one point in the continuum and thus destroying the hierarchy which we are attempting to build.

Enjoyment of self-expression in music and in arts and crafts as another means of personal enrichment.

Finds pleasure in reading for recreation.

Takes pleasure in conversing with many different kinds of people.

3.0 VALUING

This is the only cateagory headed by a term which is in common use in the expression of objectives by teachers. Further, it is employed in its usual sense: that a thing, phenomenon, or behavior has worth. This abstract concept of worth is in part a result of the individual's own valuing or assessment, but it is much more a social product that has been slowly internalized or accepted and has come to be used by the student as his own criterion of worth.

Behavior categorized at this level is sufficiently consistent and stable to have taken on the characteristics of a belief or an attitude. The learner displays this behavior with sufficient consistency in appropriate situations that he comes to be perceived as holding a value. At this level, we are not concerned with the relationships among values but rather with the internalization of a set of specified, ideal, values. Viewed from another standpoint, the objectives classified here are the prime stuff from which the conscience of the individual is developed into active control of behavior.

This category will be found appropriate for many objectives that use the term "attitude" (as well as, of course, "value").

An important element of behavior characterized by *Valuing* is that it is motivated, not by the desire to comply or obey, but by the individual's commitment to the underlying value guiding the behavior.

3.1 ACCEPTANCE OF A VALUE

At this level we are concerned with the ascribing of worth to a phenomenon, behavior, object, etc. The term "belief," which is defined as "the emotional acceptance of a proposition or doctrine upon what one implicitly considers adequate ground" (English and English, 1958, p. 64), describes quite well what may be thought of as the dominant characteristic here. Beliefs have varying degrees of certitude. At this lowest level of *Valuing* we are concerned with the lowest levels of certainty; that is, there is more of a readiness to re-evaluate one's position than at the higher levels. It is a position that is somewhat tentative.

One of the distinguishing characteristics of this behavior is consistency of response to the class of objects, phenomena, etc. with which the belief or attitude is identified. It is consistent enough so that the person is perceived by others as holding the belief or value. At the level we are describing here, he is both sufficiently consistent that others can identify the value, and sufficiently committed that he is willing to be so identified.

Continuing desire to develop the ability to speak and write effectively.
Grows in his sense of kinship with human beings of all nations.

3.2 Preference for a Value

The provision for this subdivision arose out of a feeling that there were objectives that expressed a level of internalization between the mere acceptance of a value and commitment or conviction in the usual connotation of deep involvement in an area. Behavior at this level implies not just the acceptance of a value to the point of being willing to be identified with it, but the individual is sufficiently committed to the value to pursue it, to seek it out, to want it.

Assumes responsibility for drawing reticent members of a group into conversation.

Deliberately examines a variety of viewpoints on controversial issues with a view to forming opinions about them.

Actively participates in arranging for the showing of contemporary artistic efforts.

3.3 Commitment

Belief at this level involves a high degree of certainty. The ideas of "conviction" and "certainty beyond a shadow of a doubt" help to convey further the level of behavior intended. In some instances this may border on faith, in the sense of it being a firm emotional acceptance of a belief upon admittedly nonrational grounds. Loyalty to a position, group, or cause would also be classified here.

The person who displays behavior at this level is clearly perceived as holding the value. He acts to further the thing valued in some way, to extend the possibility of his developing it, to deepen his involvement with it and with the things representing it. He tries to convince others and seeks converts to his cause. There is a tension here which needs to be satisfied; action is the result of an aroused need or drive. There is a real motivation to act out the behavior.

Devotion to those ideas and ideals which are the foundations of democracy.

Faith in the power of reason and in methods of experiment and discussion.

4.0 ORGANIZATION

As the learner successively internalizes values, he encounters situations for which more than one value is relevant. Thus necessity arises for (a) the organization of the values into a system, (b) the determination of the interrelationships among them, and (c) the establishment of the dominant and pervasive ones. Such a system is built gradually, subject to change as new values are incorporated. This category is intended as the proper classification for objectives which describe the beginnings of the building of a value system. It is subdivided into two levels, since a prerequisite to interrelating is the conceptualization of the value in a form which permits organization. *Conceptualization* forms the first subdivision in the organization process, *Organization of a value system* the second.

While the order of the two subcategories seems appropriate enough with reference to one another, it is not so certain that 4.1 *Conceptualization of a value* is properly placed as the next level above 3.3 *Commitment.* Conceptualization undoubtedly begins at an earlier level for some objectives. Like 2.3 *Satisfaction in response,* it is doubtful that a single completely satisfactory location for this category can be found. Positioning it before 4.2 *Organization of a value system* appropriately indicates a prerequisite of such a system. It also calls attention to a component of affective growth that occurs at least by this point on the continuum but may begin earlier.

4.1 CONCEPTUALIZATION OF A VALUE

In the previous category, 3.0 *Valuing,* we noted that consistency and stability are integral characteristics of the particular value or belief. At this level (4.1) the quality of abstraction or conceptualization is added. This permits the individual to see how the value relates to those that he already holds or to new ones that he is coming to hold.

Conceptualization will be abstract, and in this sense it will be symbolic. But the symbols need not be verbal symbols. Whether conceptualization first appears at this point on the affective continuum is a moot point, as noted above.

Attempts to identify the characteristics of an art object which he admires.

Forms judgments as to the responsibility of society for conserving human and material resources.

4.2 ORGANIZATION OF A VALUE SYSTEM

Objectives properly classified here are those which require the learner to bring together a complex of values, possibly disparate values, and to bring these into an ordered relationship with one another. Ideally, the ordered relationship will be one which is harmonious and internally consistent. This is, of course, the goal of such objectives, which seek to have the student formulate a philosophy of life. In actuality, the integration may be something less than entirely harmonious. More likely the relationship is better described as a kind of dynamic equilibrium which is, in part, dependent upon those portions of the environment which are salient at any point in time. In many instances the organization of values may result in their synthesis into a new value or value complex of a higher order.

Weighs alternative social policies and practices against the standards of the public welfare rather than the advantage of specialized and narrow interest groups.

Develops a plan for regulating his rest in accordance with the demands of his activities.

5.0 CHARACTERIZATION BY A VALUE OR VALUE COMPLEX

At this level of internalization the values already have a place in the individual's value hierarchy, are organized into some kind of internally consistent system, have controlled the behavior of the individual for a sufficient time that he has adapted to behaving this way; and an evocation of the behavior no longer arouses emotion or affect except when the individual is threatened or challenged.

The individual acts consistently in accordance with the values he has internalized at this level, and our concern is to indicate two things: (*a*) the generalization of this control to so much of the individual's behavior that he is described and characterized as a person by these pervasive controlling tendencies, and (*b*) the integration of these beliefs, ideas, and attitudes into a total philosophy or world view. These two aspects constitute the subcategories.

5.1 GENERALIZED SET

The generalized set is that which gives an internal consistency to the system of attitudes and values at any particular moment. It is selective responding at a very high level. It is sometimes spoken of as a determining tendency, an orientation toward phenomena, or a predisposition to act in a certain way. The generalized set is a response to highly generalized phenomena. It is a persistent and consistent response to a family of related situations or objects. It may often be an unconscious set which guides action without conscious forethought. The generalized set may be thought of as closely related to the idea of an attitude cluster, where the commonality is based on behavioral characteristics rather than the subject or object of the attitude. A generalized set is a basic orientation which enables the individual to reduce and order the complex world about him and to act consistently and effectively in it.

Readiness to revise judgments and to change behavior in the light of evidence.

Judges problems and issues in terms of situations, issues, purposes, and consequences involved rather than in terms of fixed, dogmatic precepts or emotionally wishful thinking.

5.2 CHARACTERIZATION

This, the peak of the internalization process, includes those objectives which are broadest with respect both to the phenomena covered and to the range of behavior which they comprise. Thus, here are found those objectives which concern one's view of the universe, one's philosophy of life, one's *Weltanschauung*—a value system having as its object the whole of what is known or knowable.

Objectives categorized here are more than generalized sets in the sense that they involve a greater inclusiveness and, within the group of attitudes, behaviors, beliefs, or ideas, an emphasis on internal consistency. Though this internal consistency may not always be exhibited behaviorally by the students toward whom the objective is directed, since we are categorizing teachers' objectives, this consistency feature will always be a component of *Characterization* objectives.

As the title of the category implies, these objectives are so encompassing that they tend to characterize the individual almost completely.

Develops for regulation of one's personal and civic life a code of behavior based on ethical principles consistent with democratic ideals.
Develops a consistent philosophy of life.

THE COGNITIVE DOMAIN

Benjamin S. Bloom *

1.00 KNOWLEDGE

Knowledge, as defined here, involves the recall of specifics and universals, the recall of methods and processes, or the recall of a pattern, structure, or setting. For measurement purposes, the recall situation involves little more than bringing to mind the appropriate material. Although some alteration of the material may be required, this is a relatively minor part of the task. The knowledge objectives emphasize most the psychological processes of remembering. The process of relating is also involved in that a knowledge test situation requires the organization and reorganization of a problem such that it will furnish the appropriate signals and cues for the information and knowledge the individual possesses. To use an analogy, if one thinks of the mind as a file, the problem in a knowledge test situation is that of finding in the problem or task the appropriate signals, cues, and clues which will most effectively bring out whatever knowledge is filed or stored.

1.10 KNOWLEDGE OF SPECIFICS

The recall of specific and isolable bits of information. The emphasis is on symbols with concrete referents. This material, which is at a very low level

* From *Taxonomy of Educational Objectives: Handbook II, The Affective Domain* by D. R. Krathwohl, B. S. Bloom, and B. B. Masia, 1964. Used by permission of David McKay Company, Inc.

of abstraction, may be thought of as the elements from which more complex and abstract forms of knowledge are built.

1.11 Knowledge of Terminology

Knowledge of the referents for specific symbols (verbal and nonverbal). This may include knowledge of the most generally accepted symbol referent, knowledge of the variety of symbols which may be used for a single referent, or knowledge of the referent most appropriate to a given use of a symbol.

To define technical terms by giving their attributes, properties, or relations.
Familiarity with a large number of words in their common range of meanings.[1]

1.12 Knowledge of Specific Facts

Knowledge of dates, events, persons, places, etc. This may include very precise and specific information such as the specific date or exact magnitude of a phenomenon. It may also include approximate or relative information such as an approximate time period or the general order of magnitude of a phenomenon.

The recall of major facts about particular cultures.
The possession of a minimum knowledge about the organisms studied in the laboratory.

1.20 KNOWLEDGE OF WAYS AND MEANS OF DEALING WITH SPECIFICS

Knowledge of the ways of organizing, studying, judging, and criticizing. This includes the methods of inquiry, the chronological sequences, and the standards of judgment within a field as well as the patterns of organization through which the areas of the fields themselves are determined and internally organized. This knowledge is at an intermediate level of abstraction between specific knowledge on the one hand and knowledge of universals on the other. It does not so much demand the activity of the student in using the materials as it does a more passive awareness of their nature.

1.21 Knowledge of Conventions

Knowledge of characteristic ways of treating and presenting ideas and phenomena. For purposes of communication and consistency, workers in a field employ usages, styles, practices, and forms which best suit their purposes and/or which appear to suit best the phenomena with which they deal. It should be recognized that although these forms and conventions are likely to be set up on arbitrary, accidental, or authoritative bases, they are retained because of the general agreement or concurrence of individuals concerned with the subject, phenomena, or problem.

Familiarity with the forms and conventions of the major types of works; e.g., verse, plays, scientific papers, etc.
To make pupils conscious of correct form and usage in speech and writing.

---

[1] Each subcategory is followed by illustrative educational objectives selected from the literature.

1.22 *Knowledge of Trends and Sequences*

Knowledge of the processes, directions, and movements of phenomena with respect to time.

Understanding of the continuity and development of American culture as exemplified in American life.
Knowledge of the basic trends underlying the development of public assistance programs.

1.23 *Knowledge of Classifications and Categories*

Knowledge of the classes, sets, divisions, and arrangements which are regarded as fundamental for a given subject field, purpose, argument, or problem.

To recognize the area encompassed by various kinds of problems or materials.
Becoming familiar with a range of types of literature.

1.24 *Knowledge of Criteria*

Knowledge of the criteria by which facts, principles, opinions, and conduct are tested or judged.

Familiarity with criteria for judgment appropriate to the type of work and the purpose for which it is read.
Knowledge of criteria for the evaluation of recreational activities.

1.25 *Knowledge of Methodology*

Knowledge of the methods of inquiry, techniques, and procedures employed in a particular subject field as well as those employed in investigating particular problems and phenomena. The emphasis here is on the individual's knowledge of the method rather than his ability to use the method.

Knowledge of scientific methods for evaluating health concepts.
The student shall know the methods of attack relevant to the kinds of problems of concern to the social sciences.

1.30 KNOWLEDGE OF THE UNIVERSALS AND ABSTRACTIONS IN A FIELD

Knowledge of the major schemes and patterns by which phenomena and ideas are organized. These are the large structures, theories, and generalizations which dominate a subject field or which are quite generally used in studying phenomena or solving problems. These are at the highest levels of abstraction and complexity.

1.31 *Knowledge of Principles and Generalizations*

Knowledge of particular abstractions which summarize observations of phenomena. These are the abstractions which are of value in explaining, describing, predicting, or in determining the most appropriate and relevant action or direction to be taken.

Knowledge of the important principles by which our experience with biological phenomena is summarized.

The recall of major generalizations about particular cultures.

1.32 Knowledge of Theories and Structures

Knowledge of the *body* of principles and generalizations together with their interrelations which present a clear, rounded, and systematic view of a complex phenomenon, problem, or field. These are the most abstract formulations, and they can be used to show the interrelation and organization of a great range of specifics.

The recall of major theories about particular cultures.

Knowledge of a relatively complete formulation of the theory of evolution.

INTELLECTUAL ABILITIES AND SKILLS

Abilities and skills refer to organized modes of operation and generalized techniques for dealing with materials and problems. The materials and problems may be of such a nature that little or no specialized and technical information is required. Such information as is required can be assumed to be part of the individual's general fund of knowledge. Other problems may require specialized and technical information at a rather high level such that specific knowledge and skill in dealing with the problem and the materials are required. The abilities and skills objectives emphasize the mental processes of organizing and reorganizing material to achieve a particular purpose. The materials may be given or remembered.

2.00 COMPREHENSION

This represents the lowest level of understanding. It refers to a type of understanding or apprehension such that the individual knows what is being communicated and can make use of the material or idea being communicated without necessarily relating it to other material or seeing its fullest implications.

2.10 TRANSLATION

Comprehension as evidenced by the care and accuracy with which the communication is paraphrased or rendered from one language or form of communication to another. Translation is judged on the basis of faithfulness and accuracy; that is, on the extent to which the material in the original communication is preserved although the form of the communication has been altered.

The ability to understand nonliteral statements (metaphor, symbolism, irony, exaggeration).

Skill in translating mathematical verbal material into symbolic statements and vice versa.

2.20 INTERPRETATION

The explanation or summarization of a communication. Whereas translation involves an objective part-for-part rendering of a communication, interpretation involves a reordering, rearrangement, or new view of the material.

The ability to grasp the thought of the work as a whole at any desired level of generality.

The ability to interpret various types of social data.

2.30 EXTRAPOLATION

The extension of trends or tendencies beyond the given data to determine implications, consequences, corollaries, effects, etc., which are in accordance with the conditions described in the original communication.

The ability to deal with the conclusions of a work in terms of the immediate inference made from the explicit statements.

Skill in predicting continuation of trends.

3.00 APPLICATION

The use of abstractions in particular and concrete situations. The abstractions may be in the form of general ideas, rules of procedures, or generalized methods. The abstractions may also be technical principles, ideas, and theories which must be remembered and applied.

Application to the phenomena discussed in one paper of the scientific terms or concepts used in other papers.

The ability to predict the probable effect of a change in a factor on a biological situation previously at equilibrium.

4.00 ANALYSIS

The breakdown of a communication into its constituent elements or parts such that the relative hierarchy of ideas is made clear and/or the relations between the ideas expressed are made explicit. Such analyses are intended to clarify the communication, to indicate how the communication is organized, and the way in which it manages to convey its effects, as well as its basis and arrangement.

4.10 ANALYSIS OF ELEMENTS

Identification of the elements included in a communication.

The ability to recognize unstated assumptions.
Skill in distinguishing facts from hypotheses.

4.20 ANALYSIS OF RELATIONSHIPS

The connections and interactions between elements and parts of a communication.

Ability to check the consistency of hypotheses with given information and assumptions.
Skill in comprehending the interrelationships among the ideas in a passage.

4.30 ANALYSIS OF ORGANIZATIONAL PRINCIPLES

The organization, systematic arrangement, and structure which hold the communication together. This includes the "explicit" as well as "implicit" structure. It includes the bases, necessary arrangement, and mechanics which make the communication a unit.

The ability to recognize form and pattern in literary or artistic works as a means of understanding their meaning.
Ability to recognize the general techniques used in persuasive materials, such as advertising, propaganda, etc.

5.00 SYNTHESIS

The putting together of elements and parts so as to form a whole. This involves the process of working with pieces, parts, elements, etc., and arranging and combining them in such a way as to constitute a pattern or structure not clearly there before.

5.10 PRODUCTION OF A UNIQUE COMMUNICATION

The development of a communication in which the writer or speaker attempts to convey ideas, feelings, and/or experiences to others.

Skill in writing, using an excellent organization of ideas and statements.
Ability to tell a personal experience effectively.

5.20 PRODUCTION OF A PLAN, OR PROPOSED SET OF OPERATIONS

The development of a plan of work or the proposal of a plan of operations. The plan should satisfy requirements of the task which may be given to the student or which he may develop for himself.

Ability to propose ways of testing hypotheses.
Ability to plan a unit of instruction for a particular teaching situation.

5.30 DERIVATION OF A SET OF ABSTRACT RELATIONS

The development of a set of abstract relations either to classify or explain particular data or phenomena, or the deduction of propositions and relations from a set of basic propositions or symbolic representations.

Ability to formulate appropriate hypotheses based upon an analysis of factors involved, and to modify such hypotheses in the light of new factors and considerations.
Ability to make mathematical discoveries and generalizations.

6.00 EVALUATION

Judgments about the value of material and methods for given purposes. Quantitative and qualitative judgments about the extent to which material and methods satisfy criteria. Use of a standard of appraisal. The criteria may be those determined by the student or those which are given to him.

6.10 JUDGMENTS IN TERMS OF INTERNAL EVIDENCE

Evaluation of the accuracy of a communication from such evidence as logical accuracy, consistency, and other internal criteria.

Judging by internal standards, the ability to assess general probability of accuracy in reporting facts from the care given to exactness of statement, documentation, proof, etc.
The ability to indicate logical fallacies in arguments.

6.20 JUDGMENTS IN TERMS OF EXTERNAL CRITERIA

Evaluation of material with reference to selected or remembered criteria.

The comparison of major theories, generalizations, and facts about particular cultures.
Judging by external standards, the ability to compare a work with the highest known standards in its field—especially with other works of recognized excellence.

Chapter 3

THE NATURE OF SUBJECT MATTER

IN order to teach, one must teach something to someone. The someone is the learner or pupil; the something is the content or subject matter. Just what subject matter or content is, is the cause of much confusion. In general, by subject matter we refer to a body of knowledge, and by content we mean the specific body of knowledge to be learned in a course, unit, or lesson. It may consist of information, concepts, processes, skills, or even perhaps appreciations and ideals.

It has been sometimes stated that scholars have neglected the study of subject matter. This accusation is probably unjust, for subject matter has been the concern of numerous philosophers and educators. J. Paul Leonard, for instance, has found that one's idea of the value of subject matter varies according to his philosophical position.* An examination of these positions makes it obvious that educators holding these positions will necessarily also hold quite different approaches to curriculum and method.

In any case, not all subject matter and subjects are the same. Consequently, the nature of the subject matter to be taught is an important consideration in curriculum development and an essential element in determining the proper teaching strategy and tactics for any learning situation. Different kinds of subject matter require different kinds of teaching strategies and tactics.

Recently, curriculum theorists have been greatly concerned about the structure of the disciplines. Just what the structure of a discipline is, is not clear to many educators. This lack of understanding may be partly caused by, and partly the cause of, the growing tendency of scholars to embroider and complicate the concept. Basically, however, structure refers to the principles, organization, and methods of discovery of the subject matter that makes up the discipline. In other words, structure is how a discipline is put together. The importance of making structure rather than information the center of course content is magnified by the impermanence of knowledge today. Because of the constant, rapid changes in subject matter, pupils need to know not so much old fact as how to interpret and evaluate new knowledge. To

---

* J. Paul Leonard, *Developing the Secondary School Curriculum*, rev. ed. (New York: Holt, Rinehart and Winston, 1955), Chapter 9.

learn only facts and information will not suffice because today's facts are tomorrow's old wives' tales. It is hoped that by understanding the structure, or structures, of knowledge, the pupils will be able to make use of the information they learn and to properly assimilate and adapt to new information and changes in the disciplines.

Strangely enough, there is considerable difference of opinion about what the structure of any particular discipline really is. Possibly the structure of no discipline is constant, and undoubtedly the structure of different parts of a discipline differs greatly from its other parts. Perhaps one does not learn the structure of a discipline at all, but rather each person builds his own structure for each discipline as he learns more about the relationships of the various elements that make up its subject matter.

Perhaps the disciplines are really delusions. It may be that all knowledge is really a unity and that to attempt to divide it into subject compartments is self-deluding. Certainly the subject matter of the various disciplines intertwines so that their divisions are, at best, hazy. Therefore, it may be better to tone down the differences between disciplines and instead emphasize the continuity and unity of subject matter.

So at least many curriculum builders of the 1930's thought. To prevent the curriculum from becoming artificially compartmentalized, they developed integrated curricula or core curriculum programs. Today the re-emphasis on disciplines has awakened fears of fractionated curricula, and with cause. The everyday problems we face do not fit into any particular discipline, but rather are made up of elements from a variety of disciplines. Evidently, what is needed is a curriculum or strategy that will help pupils to understand both the workings or structure of the individual disciplines and will also make clear to them the interrelationships of the content as they apply to real problems.

Subject matter and teaching method cannot be well separated. They are so interrelated and interdependent that it is hardly possible to see where one leaves off and the other begins. What the pupils learn about anything is fully as dependent on the method used in teaching it as on the content. Also the tactics in any lesson are, in part at least, dictated by the content to be taught, but the content to be taught is also to some extent dictated by methods being used. Moreover the selection of the appropriate subject matter is a particularly essential part of method *for the content of one's lessons or units should be chosen in accordance with the objectives one wishes to teach.* For example, the question of whether to use an integrated approach or the single-discipline in a particular course might well be determined by the goals the teacher is attempting to reach rather than any intrinsic advantage of either organization. One of the great faults of the teaching of the past was that too frequently the content was not the sort that could bring out the learning desired. It is imperative that in planning teachers first determine their objectives and then select the subject matter that will lead the pupils to those goals.

THREE VIEWS OF SUBJECT MATTER

Leonard H. Clark, Raymond L. Klein, and
John B. Burks *

One's view of the value of subject matter should make considerable difference in how one teaches. The following short selection has been drawn largely from an analysis of curriculum positions originally made by J. Paul. Leonard. The point is that the teacher's objectives are in part determined by his notions about the value of subject matter. His strategies and tactics in turn are based on his objectives. Consequently, the teacher's viewpoint indirectly determines his strategies and tactics. Recently the trend seems to be for teachers and educationists to favor an emphasis on method and process. Persons who make much of the structure of the discipline are likely to favor this position, as are advocates of integrated subject matter, core curricula, cooperative planning, and other similar curriculum and methodological schemes.

In line with the above are three viewpoints concerning the worth of subject matter. They are: (1) Subject matter should be taught for its own sake; (2) subject matter should be taught for use; (3) subject matter is merely a medium for the teaching of intellectual processes, skills, attitudes, ideals, and appreciations.[1]

The first of these positions derives from the belief that everything has intrinsic value. Holders of this position believe that each subject has value in and of itself. Naturally then, some subjects are more valuable than others, not because they are more useful than others but because they have greater intrinsic value. According to this position, whether or not the pupil will ever make use of Latin, algebra, or physical education, does not matter. The important thing is that he study the subjects that have the greatest intrinsic value.

---

* From Leonard H. Clark, Raymond L. Klein, and John B. Burks, *The American Secondary-School Curriculum* (New York: The Macmillan Company, 1965), pp. 30–31. Reprinted by permission of the publisher.

[1] See J. Paul Leonard, *Developing the Secondary School Curriculum*, rev. ed. (New York: Holt, Rinehart and Winston, Inc., 1955), Ch. 9, for an extended explanation of the position from which this statement is partially derived.

The second position holds that the value of a subject depends upon the use that is made of it. This position derives from the philosophical belief that value is operational. Basically this is an essentialist position. According to it, in planning curricula, priority should be given to those studies that the boys and girls most likely will need to know. In this sense these subjects are essential. The doctrine of contingent value . . . comes from this belief.

The third position is that favored by the progressives. In this changing world of changing values, no subject matter is essential for its intrinsic value, and it is very difficult to tell which subject matter is really likely to be most functional. Therefore the progressives say it is not the subject matter but the process of education that matters. In their view subject matter is only a medium by which to teach pupils the skills they need to become independent individuals. Consequently they favor flexible curricula, teacher-pupil planning, and courses in which plans evolve as the class goes along.

PHILOSOPHICAL CONSIDERATIONS

Education for Immediate or Deferred Use. Traditionally, secondary-school curricula have been based on the second of the theoretical positions concerning subject matter described above. Its purpose has been to prepare pupils for adult life. Nowadays the skills and knowledges taught in traditional schools are largely the ones that presumably the students will need when they grow up. Moral virtues are taught authoritatively now so that the pupils will know how to discipline themselves as adults. The progressivists, on the contrary, are inclined to believe that if the youth learns how to cope with his adolescent life, his adulthood will take care of itself. Therefore progressivists concentrate on subject matter that is important to the problems of youthful living and tend to slough over much of the knowledge that traditionalists feel youths should store up for possible use in adult life. After all, they imply, what is subject matter anyway but a vehicle for teaching pupils how to meet whatever situation comes along.

A MODEST PROPOSAL

Arthur W. Foshay *

Arthur W. Foshay's presidential address given at the 1961 convention of the Association for Supervision and Curriculum Development is

* From *Educational Leadership*, Vol. 18 (May 1961), pp. 506–16; 528. Reprinted with permission of the Association for Supervision and Curriculum Development and Arthur W. Foshay. Copyright © 1961 by the Association for Supervision and Curriculum Development.

something of a landmark in educational literature. In this speech a spokesman for an influential educational organization first stated clearly the need for re-examining the role of subject matter in the curriculum. His proposal is a sane mixture of the old and the new. He does not recommend deserting pupil-centered classes in favor of subject-centered ones. Rather he recommends measures he hopes will combine the merits of one with the benefits of the other. If teachers can carry out Foshay's formula, pupils of the future should find school more fruitful than they have in the past.

The reader will recognize the source of the title of this article: "A Modest Proposal." Swift's modest proposal was, to say the least, basic. His genius as a satirist lay in the simplicity of his statement of the moral consequences of the English policy of his day. I chose his title because I wanted to remind myself of two things: that it might be possible to state the problems before us as educators simply, and that I should not attempt to be a latter-day Swift, for to do so would leave me helplessly assuming that counter-invective is debate.

What I require of myself is that I get my temper back under control. Swift helps me to remember what a really great rage would be like—but he had a great rage over a great wrong. For me—for us—to respond in towering anger to those who abuse us would be to lose the perspective our responsibilities require: it would be to indulge in mere pettiness. If there are any "self-appointed experts" in education, we are they. We have actively sought educational leadership; it was not thrust upon us. No great wrong has been done us. We are merely taking the consequences of the positions we occupy and our beliefs as we have expressed them. If there is irrationality in some of what passes for "educational interpretation," we should not be surprised. We are not always completely rational, either—since we, too, are human beings.

As practicing educators, we know some things about the great national demand for excellence in our schools that we must declare candidly, for we are the national organization most directly responsible for excellence in the curriculum, both excellence in being and excellence that is to come. No other nation has asked excellence save for the few. We must have excellence for the many.

In a sense, we must make bricks without straw: a large group we are, of altogether too human human beings—often tired, often defensive when criticized, limited by less-than-glorious educations ourselves, subject to the usual way that things go in a world in which one's best ideas often go awry or unnoticed. Yet we are the people who are charged with making something better than the world has ever seen—a nation full of schools that are excellent. The nation says we must do it. We respond, "We can, but you have to learn to listen to us, just as we have to learn to understand what you are saying."

Learning to listen to someone else was never easy; for two large groups to learn to listen to each other, as groups, is even more difficult. What is required of us is that we learn to listen to the doubt behind the questions that are showered upon us, and that we learn to speak in a way that makes our values, as well as our practical proposals, clear.

What we have to get used to is that our best efforts in the past are taken for granted, now that the nation demands of us an average public school as good as our present best. In a word, we have to get used to the era we live in. The battles of the 'Thirties were not won, nor were the issues clearly resolved; but it would be a grotesque anachronism for us to man those battlements as if the times had not changed. The times have changed as profoundly as they could have. We grew up with an 18th century nursery rhyme about the cow jumping over the moon, into a time when she just might do it, with the help of a little rocketry.

We have, I repeat, to respond to the doubt behind the question. To respond to an anxious public with, "You never had it so good, educationally," is no response at all. The question is not, "Did we ever have it so good?" The question is not, really, "Are the schools any good?" In fact, there is scarcely any question at all. What exists is a demand—that we make the schools "excellent," and a doubt—that we in education take intellectual excellence seriously. You say, "How can people have such a doubt? What do they think we've been doing?" The point is, the doubt exists. Acting offended—even though this is justified—won't make the doubt go away. Let's look at what we *have* been doing.

We, in the schools, have caused the entire population to live at a higher level culturally than is true of any similar population in the world. If you doubt this, look at the level and distribution of our mass publications. With all their faults, and they are many and grievous, our daily newspapers, taken as a whole, are the least sensational and the most informative in the world, and more people read them. As Jacques Barzun said in 1954 (sometimes I wish he would remember that he had said it), "Well, we asked for this: we in the West wanted to emancipate mankind and we have nearly done it. Nobody should be surprised if it does not speak, write, and act like Lord Chesterfield. Let us rather stay calm and keep on working."

CHILD AND SOCIETY

We have paid close attention to the field of child development, and in the last two generations, have developed nothing less than a humane school, to replace the school that used to lose a good half of its students before the eighth grade. We revised the teaching of reading in the primary grades over the country as a whole during the 'Twenties. We successfully experimented with the development of social responsibility in school, and the development of the school as a socially responsible institution, in the 'Thirties. That is part of what we have done, and we have a right to feel proud of it. However, we have no right to rest on our oars, or to go on living off the fat of the ideas developed by educational leaders of a generation ago.

When I first began to study curriculum development, I was taught to believe that the curriculum arose from two fields; the nature of the growing child, and the nature of society. These two fields, I learned, had been essentially ignored during an earlier era. Ignoring the nature of the child had led to centuries of Gradgrinds and Ichabod Cranes, who thought that all you had to know to be a teacher was a little subject matter and a lot of discipline. We say to the public: the Gradgrinds are always with us. Attack the schools indiscriminately, and they will turn on you. They will show you what "tough" really means. To be like them is to be narrow-minded, like Sir Thomas Overbury's Pedant: "He treads in a rule, and one hand scans and the other holds his scepter. He does not think a thought, that the nominative case governs not the verb; and he never had meaning in his life, for he traveled only for words. His ambition is criticism, and his example Tully. He values phrases, and elects them by the sound, and the eight parts of speech are his servants. To be brief, he is a heteroclite, for he wants the plural number, having only the single quality of words."

My task as a teacher was, of course, to teach the subjects to which I was assigned. However, my more basic task was to help the child before me to grow up in such a way as to be culturally knowledgeable, socially effective and responsible. Later, as a curriculum developer, my task was to help teachers to understand the fact that emotional and social inadequacies often fatally detract from the possibility of learning academic subject matter. With respect to the latter, especially in the field of teacher education, I learned that we relied on the academic departments of a college or a university to educate future teachers in these fields; our task was to equip them with knowledge of the child and of society, and with ways of teaching that would take advantage of these two fields of knowledge, so that the learning effectiveness of students would be increased.

These things are profoundly true. A teacher who does not understand how a child grows into adolescence, and how an adolescent grows into adult life, is seriously handicapped. A teacher who does not understand the obvious fact that education is a moral affair, and that a skill has to be learned in a way that makes it likely that a person will use it for moral ends in a good and democratic society, is not discharging his responsibility. To overlook this latter point would be to act as if the cataclysmic events of the past 30 years had not happened. To overlook it would be to betray—I do not exaggerate— the men who defended us during World War II and Korea. Surely, it means something that during the 'Forties we were at war with two of the most literate nations in the world—nations in which the institution of the public schools had been perverted to social purposes at war with our own; nations in which (if one is to believe what their nationals will tell you now, and I believe it) the subject matter of the schools was thought to be intended solely for private purposes, to carry no public obligation beyond simply obeying the law, and to have no public meaning.

Armed with some knowledge of child development, and some knowledge of society, I entered upon a career in education convinced that I was different from my pedagogical forebears, that my era was one full of freshness and vigor. And I, along with you, did my bit to bring about the ideal of a mass education dedicated to self-fulfillment within a framework of social awareness and responsibility.

FLAWED THEORY

I have to say that the theory on which I was behaving now seems to me to have been true, but inadequate. Hindsight says that it was flawed from the beginning by a failure to acknowledge a third element necessary for the making of intelligent curriculum decisions.

I learned that curriculum decisions should be based on a knowledge of the child and of society. Included in the term, "society," was the culture society represents. What was left out of this theory was the nature of organized knowledge. As professional educators, we have taken organized knowledge— the disciplines out of which man's knowledge is made—for granted. In teacher education, we left formal knowledge to the "academic departments," and did little further about it ourselves. What we did, instead, was to try to make a curriculum out of two fields neither of which takes formal knowledge into account. When you come right to it, what is it that people in child development had to say to us about the curriculum? What they had to say can be summed up as a serious warning: "Do not violate the necessities for a child's development, for if you do you will mar him in ways you wot not of, and interfere with the possibility that he will learn academic subject matter well." These warnings are real, and they must be attended to. But I call to your attention the fact that they do not tell us what to do—only what not to do. The same thing is *not* true of the knowledge about society that has been gathered.

During the 'Thirties, when much of what we know now about the curriculum was first put into practical form, social needs were on everybody's mind. That was a decade of social upheaval; the need for better housing, better health, a more humane economy, a more civilized attitude toward crime— these and other similar problems were on everybody's mind and in the daily press. If one were to build a curriculum out of child development and society, what would the curriculum consist of? It would be a curriculum about society, in which children's needs were not violated. And that is precisely the curriculum we tried to put into effect. Naturally, social utility became the major criterion we applied—social utility, that is to say, in a fairly narrow sense: the kind of social utility that would help us to solve the problems that were upon us at that time. These problems are still upon us. We are still not housed as well as we should be—if you don't believe me, let me take you on a tour of New York City. Juvenile crime, especially, appears to have increased greatly during these recent years of affluence. To these we have added yet another societal problem of great magnitude—the need for a feeling of national military security.

However, there are realities in the fields of knowledge that historically we have overlooked, in taking knowledge for granted. Chemistry, as a discipline, exists apart from our attempts to understand it. It knows no national boundaries; it has a long history. As a field of knowledge, it will survive us, no matter what the future holds, short of universal disaster. The same thing can be said for the other major fields of man's knowledge: mathematics, philosophy, literature, history, economics, etc.

So I come to my modest proposal. It is simply this: that we educators take directly into account the nature of the organized bodies of knowledge, in addition to the nature of the growing child and the nature of our society, as we try to make curriculum decisions.

Curriculum theorizing in the future will have to take the nature of the various fields of knowledge, and the nature of knowledge generally, directly into account. Future graduate programs in education will have to deal with these matters with at least as much correspondence with the scholars and the scholarship involved as we have known with the scholars and the scholarship in the behavioral sciences. I do not propose that we become "subject-centered," either in a new or an old sense. What I propose is that we examine the subject matter we teach with the same rigor, and with the same kinds of help, that we have used in examining the child and society.

This will be difficult to do, but there is room for optimism about it. My optimism is based on the fact that the nature—the basic nature—of the conception of academic subject matter is being reconceived. The Physical Sciences Study Commission has approached physics in a basically new way. Professor Karplus of the University of California, with the help of some members of ASCD, has extended this basically new way into the elementary grades, thus creating for us a portion of a new vision of elementary school science. Somewhat similar efforts have been made in mathematics at Illinois and Yale, in England, and in France—I refer to the Dienes and the Cousinière approaches. Arno Bellack, former Executive Secretary of the Association for Supervision and Curriculum Development, is working with a national committee in ecenomics, again in the same direction. Every one of these projects is imperfect. The MIT physics program has had difficulty consistently with the fact that some otherwise able students cannot handle it for reasons so far not well understood. The mathematics programs too often amount to a mere refurbishing of the subject—a mere updating of it—without sufficient attention to its reconception. The economics program is in a very early stage, though it looks promising.

THE METHOD OF DISCOVERY

The generalization that fits all of these programs and others has been attempted by Professor Jerome Bruner in his book of last fall, *The Process of*

Education. He speaks, for example, of the arithmetic project at the University of Illinois which has:

> . . . emphasized the importance of discovery as an aid to teaching. They have been active in devising methods which permit a student to discover for himself the generalization that lies behind a particular mathematical operation, and they contrast this approach with the "method of assertion and proof" in which the generalization is first stated by the teacher and the class asked to proceed to the proof. It has also been pointed out by the Illinois group that the method of discovery would be too time-consuming for presenting all of what a student must cover in mathematics. The proper balance between the two is anything but plain. . . .[1]

Why do I set such high store by these efforts? It is not because they have been brought to fruition, for they have not. It is not because they have been so heavily publicized, for those who publicize them are looking for panaceas. It is because they are consistent with what has been discovered about the way children learn to think; it is because they are consistent with what teachers have discovered and rediscovered: learning "comes alive" for children when they discover their own generalizations. It is consistent with the New Education, as the movement is called in France, where for nearly 10 years the "method of rediscovery" has been under development in fields like history and physics. It is basically consistent with the theory that has governed education since 1930.

What can be discovered through the method of discovery? Two things: one can discover the discipline one is studying; one can discover one's self as a learner. This itself was the discovery of the project method as described in part by Ellsworth Collings and William Heard Kilpatrick, 40 years ago. Applied to the discovery of the disciplines through which man's knowledge is made, this brings to a new fruition the promise that Dewey held out to us 50 years ago when he began talking to us about the method of intelligence.

What can be discovered, I say, is the discipline itself. I should like to expand on this point, for it is the direct study of the disciplines that offers us a new approach to the development of subject matter.

A discipline is a way of making knowledge. A discipline may be characterized by the phenomena it purports to deal with, its domain; by the rules it uses for asserting generalizations as truth; and by its history. Chemistry deals with chemical phenomena, according to the rules of science applicable to chemistry; both the rules and the domain of the field are in some degree a product of the history of the field. Literature deals with literary phenomena, and literary analysis has its own set of rules and its own history. The same may be said for biology, mathematics, geography, any organized discipline at all. But the physicists, especially, have been telling us that it is possible for

[1] Jerome Bruner, *The Process of Education.* Cambridge, Mass.: Harvard University Press, 1960, p. 21.

children and youth to come to an understanding of physics directly. This approach to a discipline directly, not indirectly, is, I say, the chief meaning of the subject matter projects now being developed with such vigor.

This idea—that the disciplines may be approached directly—has very great power. It contrasts sharply with the subject-centered approach that we have known. It is not a new subject-centeredness; to call it subject-centered is to misname it. It is centered upon an attempt to teach children to grasp the intellectual means through which knowledge is discovered, in the hope that they may thus become active, not passive, learners. The disciplines themselves, understood as ways of making knowledge, not merely as knowledge ready-made, offer suggestions about how they may themselves be learned. The approach to learning through discovery of the disciplines is radically different both from the subject-centered approach of the past, and from the project-centered approach of more recent times.

Let us consider an illustration of how the approach works, in the field of history. It is eleven o'clock in the morning. The date is March 13, 1961, and the teacher has proceeded in American History to the immediate post-Civil War period. I want to suggest what he would do. He would begin—if he had not already done so—by remembering what history is. History is a disciplined way of confronting the past. It deals with periods, within a chronology. It seeks consistencies within these periods, and generalizations about them. The historian constantly deals with ambiguities—with the haunting knowledge that the events he studies can never be known directly—only the records that happen to remain of these events. The historian feels his responsibility to deal with the record accurately, fully, and in a way that honestly reflects the point of view he has chosen to adopt. He knows his discipline as being in part an art, in part a science; he acknowledges that aesthetic judgment plays a significant part in his decisions as historian. History, he knows, does not exist apart from the historian's interpretation of it.

Our teacher, I say, remembers these things. Now, what does he do about the post-Civil War period? If he wishes to pursue the ideal of intellectual excellence that is represented by an attempt to study the disciplines directly, he carries the children to a confrontation of the historian's problem. He asks of the children, that is, in the Progressive tradition, that they be producers of knowledge, not mere passive consumers of it. He raises with them the question, therefore, "What kinds of events after Lincoln would be most worth knowing?" (Does this seem too advanced? You should see how children handle it!) "Now," he goes on, "how can we discover what these events were?" (We can read, ask, search, tell one another.) "What do historians say they were?" (Not one historian—several, for not all historians choose to deal with the same events, and the sooner we understand this, the more liberated we are from a naive view of our past and of the historian's place in understanding it.) "What are the principal ways the period has been interpreted by the historians?" "Do you, as a student, think of other ways?" "What information do you think the historians might include that they appear to have omitted?" "Why do you suppose they omitted this information? Because they couldn't find it? Because it didn't fit with their interpretation?"

This is how a teacher might conceive of his work in teaching history, if he meant to pursue the idea that the discipline of history might be confronted directly.

THE OUTLINE APPROACH

Contrast this with another approach—the dominant one. I refer to the outline approach. This requires that the teacher have in mind a specific number of facts and interpretations he wants to put over. To do this, he may well use a class discussion—but it will be intended to elicit the correct interpretation, and can only follow a presentation of some kind—or a series of presentations: the assigned reading of a well organized text, or a lecture, perhaps on TV. In any case, the outline approach is a flat betrayal of the discipline of history, as the historians see that discipline. The fact that this is the way it is usually done, and that the materials and tests we now use depend upon it, contributes nothing whatever to its validity.

Ah, you state, we are already doing what you say. Well, maybe. Let us agree that you have to look a long way to find it. Let us agree, further, that we are not testing for it, either in our standardized tests or in our college entrance examinations. The fact is that a student has a better chance of getting into college now on the basis of sheer rote memory than he has of getting in on the basis of an understanding of how an historian makes history, the way a physicist makes physics, the way a poet makes poetry. We have never successfully won the battle of facts versus understanding, primarily because we never really confronted the question of what we mean by understanding in a field like history, or mathematics, or chemistry, or literature. The facts are winning, because you can still win the academic game through memorizing, and it is a lot easier than thinking. In spite of all the work that Ralph Tyler and the others did during the late 'Thirties in the Progressive Education Association, the idea that thinking can be taught and learned has never really taken root until, perhaps, now.

I think that the chances that it will take root now are greatly increased because, with help, we have managed to think of a place for the roots to go down. The place is into the disciplines of the major fields of knowledge themselves.

I think I am not laboring the obvious in stating these things. Nor do I think it will be easy for us to win the battle for understanding, even though it will be fought on these new grounds. Our whole pedagogical history is against this kind of thing. We seem heavily committed to the externals—to formalism. We pedagogues have brought up a whole population that does not know the difference between grammar and composition, because we taught the one in the name of the other. Similarly, we have taught prosody in the name of poetry, thus killing poetry in our culture. We have taught places in the name of geography, thus almost losing this vitally important and interesting field to our schools. We have taught facts and canned interpretations in the name of history, thus betraying a basic discipline. We have taught computation in the name of mathematics, and facts and principles in the name of laboratory sciences. It will not do. It would not do in 1900, when Dewey and the others rebelled against it. It was not good enough in the 'Thirties, when I joined many of the persons who read this article in rebelling against the "subject-centered" curriculum. It certainly will not do now.

Our history is against it. Yet there is more than our history against it. There is our tendency in education to want to classify people into sheep and goats —to want to grade them, like eggs, or peas, or lumber. This is not limited to teachers, unfortunately. There are whole groups of people in our society who, for reasons that are essentially ugly, wish to see people classified and their potentialities limited. The fact that this kind of thing is urged in the name of the early identification of talent does not make it legitimate. The fact that studies of school organization are confused with curriculum improvement merely aggravates matters. The early identification of talent, which certainly is necessary, is not a matter of finding out who are the sheep and who are the goats in our society. This tendency to sort people out, instead of helping them toward individual fulfillment, is the ugly underside of the present drive toward excellence-through-college-entrance. It accounts for the sad truth that John Gardner mentions in his new book, *Excellence*, ". . . that for many of us the learning process comes to an end very early indeed. And others learn the wrong things." [2] What we require is a version of education, and a view of our society, that foster perpetual self-discovery and self-fulfillment. Our tendency to use the schools as a giant screening device is precisely contradictory to this idea.

In order that we do this, it seems clear that we must give renewed attention to three things:

1. A contemporary view of the subject matter of the curriculum

2. A view of our proper roles as educators vis-à-vis knowledge, the child, and society

3. A view of the goals of education that is consistent both with what is possible in the schools, and what is possible for growing children, and with what is required by our society.

I have, so far, been talking about the importance of teaching the disciplines directly—a contemporary view of subject matter. I have asserted that a view of the disciplines through which men make knowledge that is consonant with the view held by the producing scholars in these disciplines is suggestive to us of how the disciplines may themselves be learned. My illustrations, so far, have all had to do with the academic disciplines. There is more.

It seems to me that we would do well to consider that behind every subject matter we teach in school a discipline lies, or should lie. It is the discipline behind the subject matter that contains whatever life is there. I think that we should look toward the development of a whole series of new subjects, with old names: history, geography, mathematics, the sciences. But let me consider some other fields which we also teach. What, one might say, is to be said of the crafts we teach, like those in the shops and business courses? I should like to see the proposition examined carefully that behind each of these crafts, occupying the same place with respect to it that a discipline occupies with respect to an academic subject, there is a technology, and that we should cause the students learning the craft to study the technology directly. Behind automobile repairing is the technology of the automobile itself, which could be studied. Behind the typewriter is the technology of typing and of other communication devices. Behind the woodshop is the technology and the art of woodwork. There is a very considerable lore and literature in each of these fields, and the industrial arts concept goes in this direction.

In the degree that we take the fundamentals of woodwork to be the care of the tools and the performance of a few simple operations, we have over-looked the technology, the rich old technology, and the art, of woodwork. In the degree that we overlook the technology and the art of metal work, we contribute to the present shocking lack of pride and creativity in the metal shop that foremen consistently complain of. I do not ask that every mechanic become a master machinist. But the slovenly workmanship that is so fre-quently the object of complaint—the tendency to compare American and European craftsmen with respect to their pride of workmanship—may be at least in part a product of a too narrow version of what is "fundamental" to good workmanship as taught in our school shops and other technical classes. The idea seems to me to be at least worth examining. If plumbing is not a discipline, and philosophy is, it does not follow that the plumber should have no knowledge of the technology behind his immediate work. As John Gardner points out, a society which settles for mediocrity in both philosophy and plumbing develops neither theories nor pipes that will hold water.

It seems to me to be helpful to make a distinction between a discipline and a subject matter which suggests the proper roles as between an educationist and a scholar. I have called here for an attempt to teach the disciplines. Experience during the past few years has redemonstrated the difficulty of doing this. What is required is that the disciplines as known by producing scholars be translated into viable experiences in school. This translation we may call a school subject. If we make this distinction, certain clarifications become possible. For example, it is possible to look at the materials and curriculum guides in geography and ask whether they, as proposed school sub-jects, faithfully reflect the discipline of geography as viewed by the geogra-phers. As it happens, they do not, any more than the school textbooks in history (no matter how authoritative) faithfully reflect the discipline of his-tory as modern historians interpret their discipline.

TRANSLATING THE DISCIPLINES

When we view subject matter and disciplines in this fashion, our role as educators becomes clearer. Our task is to translate the disciplines into viable subject matter. In the course of doing this, we have precisely the task of bringing to bear on the disciplines as the scholars tell us of them, the knowledge we have of the practical necessities of child development, the nature of society and of the school's place in it, and learning theory as it continues to grow. We have neither the skill nor the responsibility, as educationists, to remake the academic disciplines or the basic technologies. Our task is to demand of the people whose business it is to make these disciplines and technologies, that they speak to us in a way that we can understand concerning their fields, so that our translations may be both effective and true to the original. It does little good to ask a mathematician, or an historian, or a designing engineer what should be taught in the first grade, what in the fifth, or what in the tenth. These people often think they know the answers to these questions, but the fact is they ordinarily do not understand what the questions themselves entail. We need to learn how to ask them to tell us what kinds of generalizations are appropriate to the disciplines they know well, and what is required if these generalizations are to be discovered by students.

When we ask questions in this fashion, the historian will say that, first, the generalization he seeks is the definition and explication of a period in history. He may go on to point out that some periods are far more complicated than others to understand, and that we should know this when we try to decide what periods in history shall be studied at what time. He, the historian, can indicate to us what he means by "complicated." It is in the terms of the demands of his discipline that we should devise school subject matter through which the discipline can be discovered. A considerable stride in this direction has been made in France, where a magnificent album, "Documents of the History of France," has been prepared by the Ministry. The album is put in the hands of the student in the lycée, who is directed to do no less than to rediscover French history from the primary sources on which it is based. These sources have been selected by historians, to be sure. But they constitute a universe of material so vast that the student must make many selections within it if he is to attempt historical generalizations. By comparison with what we do now, even in our most traditional and subject-centered classes, this is a vastly more demanding approach to history. However, if such experimentation as has been undertaken in other fields has any transfer value to this field, we can be confident that many of our students can learn to undertake it.

As educationists, too, we have another kind of responsibility. We have to see to it (and we in ASCD have a special responsibility in this regard) that the curriculum taken as a whole is consistent with the goals that the school exists to achieve. So far, in the course of the great public discussion of education, it has not yet become clear what a whole curriculum would be like if we saw it as a whole, nor—for that matter—what the education of all the people would be like if we intended to educate all of them. The fact that they are all in school is obviously considered by some individuals to be unfortunate, though, thank heaven, this is a very small number of persons, and likely to grow smaller. Of course this approach does not solve everything. Indeed, it reproposes some old curriculum questions.

Given this new and more vital approach to intellectuality in school subjects, how are we to view the need that children have when they leave school to deal with the practical problems of the world in a way that is better because they have been in school? Or are we to say that the school has no responsibility for equipping people to deal with the practical problems of life? The assumption the academics make is generally that if one knows the principal fields of knowledge in depth—and this is what I am proposing that we teach—one can use such knowledge to grasp practical problems in depth. This claim is very plausible, but largely unexamined.

The fact is that many a sophisticated scientist is a very naive citizen when he tries to deal with public matters, and the reverse is also true. Consider how dangerous it was when Winston Churchill demonstrated in his directive authorizing the development of the atomic bomb in England that he did not deeply understand how big a million is. As Bronowsky, the British scientist who reported this fact, pointed out, the only thing that saved England from Churchill's ignorance was her democratic government. There was nothing to save Germany from Hitler's similar ignorance. We have to have it both ways. We have to have people who are deeply knowledgeable, in a disciplined fashion, in the principal fields of knowledge, and who at the same time are capable both of understanding and participating intelligently in public decisions, and living adequate personal lives.

It is up to us in ASCD to rethink this problem and to conceptualize how it may be solved. As educators, we are receiving no help with it at present, though John Gardner's new book exhorts us to attend to it. It is our duty to do so, if we are satisfactorily to discharge the tasks of educational leadership that these times demand of us. A balance in the curriculum clearly must be maintained between what is rigorous and deep, and what is immediate and practical. We are called upon, both by the times we live in and by these new possibilities, to strike a new balance.

In doing so, we would be foolhardy indeed to follow that line of public argument which would cause us to act as if we knew nothing of child development and had no knowledge of how the school affects the society around it. If we follow our noses, and simply react to the pressures being put upon us, we will betray a whole generation of children by implying to them that a pedant is a whole man, or that only the intellectual aspect of man is worth official attention. In pursuing high intellectual goals, it is not necessary for a moment that we overlook the fact that man, in addition to being an intellectual creature, is also an emotional, a social, an aesthetic, a biological, a creative, and a spiritual creature.

It is necessary for us to acknowledge that many of our most illustrious and humane figures are deeply learned in their disciplines, and derive their humanity and liberalism from their knowledge. These things are not in conflict with one another—not at all. However, we are tempted by the power struggle in the world and by the uncertainty of the future to act as if we believe that they were. One of the questions we have to learn to ask of the scholars is exactly in what way each of their disciplines contributes to the wholeness of a whole man. For if we educate less than the whole man—if we mean to bring about a school which deals with less than the whole man, and implies a partial or distorted version of what it means to be a human being, we will have betrayed not only our heritage but the future of the children we teach.

Our task in ASCD, therefore, is greatly complicated by the opportunities and perils of our times. We have come to a deeper knowledge of the child we teach and the man we hope he will become than we have ever known, in order that we may properly take into account the nature of organized knowledge in the service of the society we would have. It is in the unity of these three—the child, the society, and organized knowledge—that future excellence in the schools will be found.

THE STRUCTURE OF THE DISCIPLINES

Jerome S. Bruner *

The September 1959, Woods Hole Conference to discuss how education in science might be improved in elementary and secondary schools has proved to be one of the most influential meetings about education in modern times. At this meeting of scholars representing several different academic disciplines, there was general agreement that learning should be basically a process of discovery. In his report on the conference, Jerome S. Bruner introduced many of his readers to two concepts: the discovery method and the structure of subjects. Although neither of these concepts was really new, Bruner's book first brought them to the attention of a populace looking for answers to its educational dilemmas. Very soon The Process of Education *became one of the most frequently cited books in the literature. It is principally responsible for the present interest in the structure of the disciplines.*

* Reprinted by permission of the publishers from Jerome S. Bruner, *The Process of Education*, Cambridge, Mass.: Harvard University Press, Copyright, 1960, by the President and Fellows of Harvard College.

Bruner's concept of structure is a relatively simple one. Structure, he says, is simply the way a discipline is put together. It is important because, once the pupil sees the relationships of things in a subject, he can place new things into their proper relationships. Recent attempts to explain structure have become much more complex and obscure. Some scholars doubt whether some disciplines have any structures at all. It would probably be wise for the reader to remember Bruner's simple explanation when he is discussing or reading further about the structure of the disciplines.

Structure has two implications as far as teaching strategies and tactics are concerned. One is that if structure is as important as writers like Bruner think it is, then teachers must choose strategies that will bring out the structure of the disciplines. The second is that the teacher must select strategies that suit the structure of the discipline being taught— in other words the structure of the discipline should in some measure determine the strategy.

Whether one accepts the principle or importance of the "structure" or not, one must recognize that for a long time scholars have known that the various disciplines are different from each other. Aristotle was one of the first to note the differences. He believed that there were three kinds of subjects or disciplines: the theoretical, that is, the ones in which the aim is to know; the practical, that is, the subjects concerned with doing things and making choices; and the productive, that is, those devoted to making things. Teachers must recognize these kinds of differences in their teaching. Unfortunately, one of the most unhappy characteristics of contemporary teaching is that some teachers have forgotten this fact and so are trying to use the same approach in all subjects. Such strategies must fail.

It is interesting that around the turn of the last century the conception of the learning process as depicted by psychology gradually shifted away from an emphasis upon the production of general understanding to an emphasis on the acquisition of specific skills. The study of "transfer" provides the type case—the problem of the gain in mastery of other activities that one achieves from having mastered a particular learning task. Whereas the earlier emphasis had led to research studies on the transfer of formal discipline—the value obtained from the training of such "faculties" as analysis, judgment, memory, and so forth—later work tended to explore the transfer of identical elements or specific skills. In consequence, there was relatively little work by American psychologists during the first four decades of this century on the manner in which the student could be trained to grasp the underlying structure or significance of complex knowledge. Virtually all of the evidence of the last two decades on the nature of learning and transfer has indicated that, while the original theory of formal discipline was poorly stated in terms of the training of faculties, it is indeed a fact that massive general transfer can be achieved by appropriate learning, even to the degree that learning properly under optimum conditions leads one to "learn how to learn." These studies have stimulated a renewed interest in complex learning of a kind that one finds in schools, learning designed to produce general understanding of the structure of a subject matter. Interest in curricular problems at large has, in consequence, been rekindled among psychologists concerned with the learning process.

A word is needed at this point to explain in fuller detail what is meant by the *structure* of a subject, for we shall have occasion return to this idea often in later pages. Three simple examples—from biology, from mathematics, and from the learning of language—help to make the idea clearer. Take first a set of observations on an inchworm crossing a sheet of graph paper mounted on a board. The board is horizontal; the animal moves in a straight line. We tilt the board so that the inclined plane or upward grade is 30°. We observe that the animal does not go straight up, but travels at an angle of 45° from the line of maximum climb. We now tilt the board to 60°. At what angle does the animal travel with respect to the line of maximum climb? Now, say, he travels along a line 75° off the straight-up line. From these two measures, we may infer that inchworms "prefer" to travel uphill, if uphill they must go, along an incline of 15°. We have discovered a tropism, as it is called, indeed a geotropism. It is not an isolated fact. We can go on to show that among simple organisms, such phenomena—regulation of locomotion according to a fixed or built-in standard—are the rule. There is a preferred level of illumination toward which lower organisms orient, a preferred level of salinity, of temperature, and so on. Once a student grasps this basic relation between external stimulation and locomotor action, he is well on his way toward being able to handle a good deal of seemingly new but, in fact, highly related information. The swarming of locusts where temperature determines the swarm density in which locusts are forced to travel, the species maintenance of insects at different altitudes on the side of a mountain where crossbreeding is prevented by the tendency of each species to travel in its preferred oxygen zone, and many other phenomena in biology can be understood in the light of tropisms. *Grasping the structure of a subject is understanding it in a way that permits many other things to be related to it meaningfully. To learn structure, in short, is to learn how things are related.**

Much more briefly, to take an example from mathematics, algebra is a way of arranging knowns and unknowns in equations so that the unknowns are made knowable. The three fundamentals involved in working with these equations are commutation, distribution, and association. Once a student

---

* Italics added by editor.

grasps the ideas embodied by these three fundamentals, he is in a position to recognize wherein "new" equations to be solved are not new at all, but variants on a familiar theme. Whether the student knows the formal names of these operations is less important for transfer than whether he is able to use them.

The often unconscious nature of learning structures is perhaps best illustrated in learning one's native language. Having grasped the subtle structure of a sentence, the child very rapily learns to generate many other sentences based on this model though different in content from the original sentence learned. And having mastered the rules for transforming sentences without altering their meaning—"The dog bit the man" and "The man was bitten by the dog"—the child is able to vary his sentences much more widely. Yet, while young children are able to *use* the structural rules of English, they are certainly not able to say what the rules are.

The scientists constructing curricula in physics and mathematics have been highly mindful of the problem of teaching the structure of their subjects, and it may be that their early successes have been due to this emphasis. Their emphasis upon structure has stimulated students of the learning process. The reader will find the emphasis reflected many times in the pages that follow.

Clearly there are general questions to be faced before one can look at specific problems of courses, sequences, and the like. The moment one begins to ask questions about the value of specific courses, one is asking about the objectives of education. The construction of curricula proceeds in a world where changing social, cultural, and political conditions continually alter the surroundings and the goals of schools and their students. We are concerned with curricula designed for Americans, for their ways and their needs in a complex world. Americans are a changing people; their geographical mobility makes imperative some degree of uniformity among high schools and primary schools. Yet the diversity of American communities and of American life in general makes equally imperative some degree of variety in curricula. And whatever the limits placed on education by the demands of diversity and uniformity, there are also requirements for productivity to be met: are we producing enough scholars, scientists, poets, lawmakers, to meet the demands of our times? Moreover, schools must also contribute to the social and emotional development of the child if they are to fulfill their function of education for life in a democratic community and for fruitful family life. If the emphasis in what follows is principally on the intellectual side of education, it is not that the other objectives of education are less important.

We may take as perhaps the most general objective of education that it cultivate excellence; but it should be clear in what sense this phrase is used. It here refers not only to schooling the better student but also to helping each student achieve his optimum intellectual development. Good teaching that emphasizes the structure of a subject is probably even more valuable for the less able student than for the gifted one, for it is the former rather than the latter who is most easily thrown off the track by poor teaching. This is not to say that the pace or the content of courses need be identical for all students—though, as one member of the Conference put it, "When you teach well, it always seems as if seventy-five per cent of the students are above the median." Careful investigation and research can tell us wherein differences must be introduced. One thing seems clear: if all students are helped to the full utilization of their intellectual powers, we will have a better chance of surviving as a democracy in an age of enormous technological and social complexity. . . .

To recapitulate, the main theme of this chapter has been that the curriculum of a subject should be determined by the most fundamental understanding that can be achieved of the underlying principles that give structure to that subject. Teaching specific topics or skills without making clear their context in the broader fundamental structure of a field of knowledge is uneconomical in several deep senses. In the first place, such teaching makes it exceedingly difficult for the student to generalize from what he has learned to what he will encounter later. In the second place, learning that has fallen short of a grasp of general principles has little reward in terms of intellectual excitement. The best way to create interest in a subject is to render it worth knowing, which means to make the knowledge gained usable in one's thinking beyond the situation in which the learning has occurred. Third, knowledge one has acquired without sufficient structure to tie it together is knowledge that is likely to be forgotten. An unconnected set of facts has a pitiably short half-life in memory. Organizing facts in terms of principles and ideas from which they may be inferred is the only known way of reducing the quick rate of loss of human memory.

TEACHING AND THE EXPANDING KNOWLEDGE

Albert Szent-Györgyi *

Knowledge is "a sacred cow." As knowledge becomes greater, it also becomes simpler. The barriers between the sciences have disappeared and the barriers between science and humanities are disappearing. These

* From *Science*, Vol. 146 (Washington, D.C.: American Association for the Advancement of Science, December 4, 1964), pp. 1278–1279. Reprinted by permission of *Science* and the author. Copyright 1964 by the American Association for the Advancement of Science.

comments by a famed scientist make one wonder about the place of the various disciplines in secondary education. Obviously, if Szent-Györgyi is right, the day for just learning content has passed. The implications of the explosion of knowledge have made that kind of education obsolete. Like Whitehead and others before him, Szent-Györgyi is against teaching dead subject matter to living minds. Instead he wants pupils to develop their rational powers by living things so that they can "stand erect with their eyes on the future."

One of the banes of pre-World War II educationists was the fragmentation of the curriculum. Each subject had been taught in a separate idea-tight compartment without any notice of relationships to other subjects or to the lives of the pupils. As a result of such teaching, the subjects in the subject-centered curricula tended to become mere formalities. Their meaning, and therefore their life, was gone. So teachers tried to build broad courses that combined or integrated the subject matter from two or more disciplines. These broad field or core curriculum courses, some of which were built around series of pupil-centered problems, demanded great skill of the teachers, but where they were done well they were usually extremely successful. Although the core-curriculum movement has lost its impetus, the merits of the arguments for the core curriculum have not lost their force. They are implicit in much of what Szent-Györgyi says.

Our attempt to harmonize teaching with expanding—or rather exploding—knowledge would be hopeless should growth not entail simplification. I will dwell on this sunny side. Knowledge is a sacred cow, and my problem will be how we can milk her while keeping clear of her horns.

One of my reasons for being optimistic is that the foundations of nature are simple. This was brought home to me many years ago when I joined the Institute for Advanced Studies in Princeton. I did this in the hope that by rubbing elbows with those great atomic physicists and mathematicians I would learn something about living matters. But as soon as I revealed that in any living system there are more than two electrons, the physicists would not speak to me. With all their computers they could not say what the third electron might do. The remarkable thing is that it knows exactly what to do. So that little electron knows something that all the wise men of Princeton don't, and this can only be something very simple. Nature, basically, must be much simpler than she looks to us. She looks to us like a coded letter for which we have no code. To the degree to which our methods become less clumsy and more adequate and we find out nature's code, things must become not only clearer, but very much simpler, too.

Science tends to generalize, and generalization means simplification. My own science, biology, is today not only very much richer than it was in my student days, but is simpler, too. Then it was horribly complex, being fragmented into a great number of isolated principles. Today these are all fused into one single complex with the atomic model in its center. Cosmology, quantum mechanics, DNA and genetics, are all, more or less, parts of one and the same story—a most wonderful simplification. And generalizations are also more satisfying to the mind than details. We, in our teaching, should place more emphasis on generalizations than on details. Of course, details and generalizations must be in a proper balance: generalization can be reached only from details, while it is the generalization which gives value and interest to the detail.

After this preamble I would like to make a few general remarks, first, about the main instrument of teaching: books. There is a widely spread misconception about the nature of books which contain knowledge. It is thought that such books are something the contents of which have to crammed into our heads. I think the opposite is closer to the truth. Books are there to keep the knowledge in while we use our heads for something better. Books may also be a better place for such knowledge. In my own head any book-knowledge has a half-life of a few weeks. So I leave knowledge, for safekeeping, to books and libraries and go fishing, sometimes for fish, sometimes for new knowledge.

I know that I am shockingly ignorant. I could take exams in college but could not pass any of them. Worse than that: I treasure my ignorance; I feel snug in it. It does not cloud my naiveté, my simplicity of mind, my ability to marvel childlishly at nature and recognize a miracle even if I see it every day. If, with my 71 years, I am still digging on the fringes of knowledge, I owe it to this childish attitude. "Blessed are the pure in heart, for they shall see God," says the Bible. "For they can understand Nature," say I.

I do not want to be misunderstood—I do not depreciate knowledge, and I have worked long and hard to know something of all fields of science related to biology. Without this I could do no research. But I have retained only what I need for an understanding, an intuitive grasp, and in order to know in which book to find what. This was fun, and we must have fun, or else our work is no good.

My next remark is about time relations. The time spent in school is relatively short compared to the time thereafter. I am stressing this because it is widely thought that everything we have to know to do our job well we have to learn in school. This is wrong because, during the long time which follows school, we are apt to forget, anyway, what we have learned there, while we have ample time for study. In fact, most of us have to learn all our lives, and it was with gray hair that I took up the study of quantum mechanics, myself. So what the school has to do, in the first place, is to make us learn how to learn, to whet our appetites for knowledge, to teach us the delight of doing a job well and the excitement of creativity, to teach us to love what we do, and to help us to find what we love to do.

My friend Gerard quoted Fouchet as advising us to take from the altar of knowledge the fire, not the ashes. Being of more earthly disposition, I would advise you to take the meat, not the bones. Teachers, on the whole, have a remarkable preference for bones, especially dry ones. Of course, bones are important, and now and then we all like to suck a bit on them, but only after having eaten the meat. What I mean to say is that we must not *learn* things, we must *live* things. This is true for almost everything. Shakespeare and all of literature must be *lived*, music, paintings, and sculptures have to be *made*, drama has to be *acted*. This is even true for history: we should live through it, through the spirit of the various periods, instead of storing their data. I am glad to say that this trend—to live things—is becoming evident even in the teaching of science. The most recent trend is not to *teach* the simpler laws of nature, but to make our students *discover* them for themselves in simple experiments. Of course, I know data are important. They may be even interesting, but only after we have consumed the meat, the substance. After this we may even become curious about them and retain them. But taught before this they are just dull, and they dull, if not kill, the spirit.

It is a widely spread opinion that memorizing will not hurt, that knowledge does no harm. I am afraid it may. Dead knowledge dulls the spirit, fills the stomach without nourishing the body. The mind is not a bottomless pit, and if we put in one thing we might have to leave out another. By a more live teaching we can fill the soul and reserve the mind for the really important things. We may even spare time we need for expanding subjects.

Such live teaching, which fills both the soul and the mind, may help man to meet one of his most formidable problems, what to do with himself. The most advanced societies, like ours, can already produce more than they can consume, and with advancing automation the discrepancy is increasing rapidly. We try to meet the challenge by producing useless things, like armaments. But this is no final answer. In the end we will have to work less. But then, what will we do with ourselves? Lives cannot be left empty. Man needs excitement and challenge, and in an affluent society everything is within easy reach. And boredom is dangerous, for it can easily make a society seek excitement in political adventure and in brinkmanship, following irresponsible and ignorant leaders. Our own society has recently shown alarming signs of this trend. In a world where atomic bombs can fly from one end to the other in seconds, this is tantamount to suicide. By teaching live arts and science, the schools could open up the endless horizons and challenges of intellectual and artistic life and make whole life an exciting adventure. I believe that in our teaching not only must details and generalizations be in balance, but our whole teaching must be balanced with general human values.

I want to conclude with a few remarks on single subjects, first, science. Science has two aspects: it has to be part of any education, of humanistic culture. But we also have to teach science as preparation for jobs. If we distinguish sharply between these two aspects then the talk about the "two cultures" will lose its meaning.

A last remark I want to make is about the teaching of history, not only because it is the most important subject, but also because I still have in my nostrils the acid smell of my own sweat which I produced when learning its data. History has two chapters: National History and World History. National history is a kind of family affair and I will not speak about it. But what is world history? In its essence it is the story of man, how he rose from his animal status to his present elevation. This is a fascinating story and is linked to a limited number of creative men, its heroes, who created new knowledge, new moral or ethical values, or new beauty. Opposing this positive side of history there is a negative, destructive side linked to the names of kings, barons, generals, and dictators who, with their greed and lust for power, made wars, fought battles, and mostly created misery, destroying what other men had built. These are the heroes of the history we teach at present as world history. Not only is this history negative and lopsided, it is false, too, for it omits the lice, rats, malnutrition, and epidemics which had more to do with the course of things than generals and kings, as Zinsser ably pointed out. The world history we teach should also be more truthful and include the stench, dirt, callousness, and misery of past ages, to teach us to appreciate progress and what we have. We need not falsify history; history has a tendency to falsify itself, because only the living return from the battlefield to tell stories. If the dead could return but once and tell about their ignominious end, history and politics would be different today. A truer history would also be simpler.

As the barriers between the various sciences have disappeared, so the barriers between science and humanities may gradually melt away. Dating through physical methods has become a method of research in history, while x-ray spectra and microanalysis have become tools in the study of painting. I hope that the achievements of human psychology may help us, also, to rewrite human history in a more unified and translucent form.

The story of man's progress is not linked to any period, nation, creed, or color, and could teach to our youngsters a wider human solidarity. This they will badly need when rebuilding political and human relations, making them compatible with survival.

In spite of its many chapters, our teaching has, essentially, but one object, the production of men who can fill their shoes and stand erect with their eyes on the wider horizons. This makes the school, on any level, into the most important public institution and the teacher into the most important public figure. As we teach today, so the morrow will be.

Chapter 4

THE PUPIL

T HE importance of understanding pupils can hardly be exaggerated. Although it is true that teachers must teach subject matter, it is also true that they must teach it to boys and girls. If teachers do not have a reasonably good understanding of their pupils, they are not in a position to know which strategies and tactics are likely to be most effective for those pupils. When a teacher fails, it is more likely to be because he does not understand his pupils than because he does not understand his subject matter.

It is easy to oversimplify what pupils are like. Of course there are similarities, but on the whole the most interesting fact about pupils is that each one is himself—an individual with his own personality. It is therefore common for teachers to endow individual pupils with supposedly typical characteristics that the pupils do not, in fact, possess. Because preconceptions can cause us to misjudge our pupils—particularly the creative, the slow, the hard to reach, and the disadvantaged—it is necessary that we teachers try to get to know our pupils as individual persons as well as possible. In this process we can be aided by school records, tests, observations, and the other techniques of diagnosis. Perhaps the best way of all is friendly informal conversation. In any case if we wish to motivate pupils and provide for their individual differences, we must learn what their different interests, ambitions, problems, potentials, and other characteristics are. Otherwise we have very little data to use in choosing the strategies and tactics that will arouse our pupils and meet their needs.

KIDS A.D. 1967

John M. Culkin, S.J.[*]

Whether we like it or not, the pupil must be the central figure in any school. Schools exist for pupils. Unless pupils learn in them, they have

* From John M. Culkin, "A Schoolman's Guide to Marshall McLuhan," *Saturday Review*, Vol. 11 (March 18, 1967), pp. 71–72. Reprinted by permission of the *Saturday Review* and the author.

no reason for existing. Instruction that does not result in pupil learning is virtually useless. Therefore, we teachers must learn how to communicate with young people as they are today—products of the twentieth century.

Whether or not one accepts McLuhan's theses concerning education, there is little doubt that he is right that instructional media have not kept up with the times. The chances are good that "drill and grill" teaching never was very effective, but nowadays it is even less so. The following excerpt from an essay on Marshall McLuhan by John M. Culkin, S.J., director of the Center for Communications at Fordham University, places youth and the problem of educating him into contemporary perspective. For the modern youth described here total reliance on mind filling, information-giving teaching strategies is surely obsolete.

Kids are what the game is all about. Given an honest game with enough equipment to go around, it is the mental, emotional, and volitional capacity of the student which most determines the outcome. The whole complicated system of formal education is in business to get through to kids, to motivate kids, to help kids learn stuff. Schools are not in business to label kids, to grade them for the job market or to babysit. They are there to communicate with them.

Communication is a funny business. There isn't as much of it going on as most people think. Many feel that it consists in saying things in the presence of others. Not so. It consists not in saying things but in having things heard. Beautiful English speeches delivered to monolingual Arabs are not beautiful speeches. You have to speak the language of the audience—of the *whom* in the "who-says-what-to-whom" communications diagram. Sometimes the language is lexical (Chinese, Japanese, Portuguese), sometimes it is regional or personal (125th Street-ese, Holden Caulfield-ese, anybody-ese). It has little to do with words and much to do with understanding the audience. The word for good communication is "Whom-ese"—the language of the audience, of the "whom."

All good communicators use Whom-ese. The best writers, film-makers, advertising men, lovers, preachers, and teachers all have the knack for thinking about the hopes, fears, and capacity of the other person and of being able to translate their communication into terms which are *relevant* for that person. Whitehead called "inert ideas" the bane of education. Relevance, however, is one of those subjective words. It doesn't pertain to the object in itself but to the object as perceived by someone. The school may decide that history is *important for* the student, but the role of teachers is to make history *relevant to* the student.

If *what* has to be tailored to the *whom*, the teacher has to be constantly engaged in audience research. It's not a question of keeping up with the latest slang or of selling out to the current mores of the kids. Neither of these tactics helps either learning or kids. But it is a question of knowing what values are strong in their world, of understanding the obstacles to communication, of sensing their style of life. Communication doesn't have to end there, but it can start nowhere else. If they are tuned in to FM and you are broadcasting on AM, there's no communication. Communication forces you to pay a lot of attention to other people.

McLuhan has been paying a great deal of attention to modern kids. Of necessity they live in the present since they have no theories to diffract or reflect what is happening. They are also the first generation to be born into a world in which there was always television. McLuhan finds them a great deal different from their counterparts at the turn of the century when the electric age was just getting up steam.

A lot of things have happened since 1900 and most of them plug into walls. Today's six-year-old has already learned a lot of stuff by the time he shows up for the first day of school. Soon after his umbilical cord was cut he was planted in front of a TV set "to keep him quiet." He liked it enough there to stay for some 3,000 to 4,000 hours before he started the first grade. By the time he graduates from high school he has clocked 15,000 hours of TV time and 10,800 hours of school time. He lives in a world which bombards him from all sides with information from radios, films, telephones, magazines, recordings, and people. He learns more things from the windows of cars, trains, and even planes. Through travel and communications he has experienced the war in Vietnam, the wide world of sports, the civil rights movement, the death of a President, thousands of commercials, a walk in space, a thousand innocuous shows, and, one may hope, plenty of Captain Kangaroo.

This is all merely descriptive, an effort to lay out what *is*, not what should be. Today's student can hardly be described by any of the old educational analogies comparing him to an empty bucket or a blank page. He comes to the information machine called school and he is already brimming over with information. As he grows his standards for relevance are determined more by what he receives outside the school than what he receives inside. A recent Canadian film tells the story of a bright, articulate middle class teen-ager who leaves school because there's "no reason to stay." He daydreams about Vietnam while his teacher drones on about the four reasons for the spread of Christianity and the five points such information is worth on the exam. Only the need for a diploma was holding him in school; learning wasn't, and he left. He decided the union ticket wasn't worth the gaff. He left. Some call him a dropout. Some call him a pushout.

The kids have one foot on the dock and one foot on the ferryboat. Living in two centuries makes for that kind of tension. The gap between the classroom and the outside world and the gap between the generations is wider than it has ever been. Those tedious people who quote Socrates on the conduct of the young are trying vainly to reassure themselves that this is just the perennial problem of communication between generations. 'Tain't so. "To-day's child is growing up absurd, because he lives in two worlds, and neither of them inclines him to grow up." Says McLuhan in *The Medium is the Massage*, "Growing up—that is our new work, and it is *total*. Mere instruction will not suffice."

Learning is something that people do for themselves. People, places, and things can facilitate or impede learning; they can't make it happen without some cooperation from the learner. The learner these days comes to school with a vast reservoir of vicarious experiences and loosely related facts; he wants to use all his senses in his learning as an active agent in the process of discovery; he knows that all the answers aren't in. The new learner is the result of the new media, says McLuhan. And a new learner calls for a new kind of learning.

Leo Irrera said, "If God had anticipated the eventual structure of the school system, surely he would have shaped man differently." Kids are being tailored to fit the Procrustean forms of schedules, classrooms, memorizing, testing, etc., which are frequently relics from an obsolete approach to learning. It is the total environment which contains the philosophy of education, not the title page in the school catalogue. And it is the total environment which is invincible because it is invisible to most people. They tend to move things around within the old boxes or to build new and cleaner boxes. They should be asking whether or not there should be a box in the first place.

The new learner, who is the product of the all-at-once electronic environment, often feels out of it in a linear, one-thing-at-a-time school environment. The total environment is now the great teacher; the student has competence models against which to measure the effectiveness of his teachers. Nuclear students in linear schools make for some tense times in education. Students with well developed interests in science, the arts and humanities, or current events need assistance to suit their pace, not that of the state syllabus. The straight line theory of development and the uniformity of performance which it so frequently encourages just don't fit many needs of the new learner. Interestingly, the one thing which most of the current educational innovations share is their break with linear or print-oriented patterns: team teaching, non-graded schools, audio-lingual language training, multi-media learning situations, seminars, student research at all levels of education, individualized learning, and the whole shift of responsibility for learning from the teacher to the student. Needless to say, these are not as widespread as they should be, nor were they brought about through any conscious attention to the premises put forward by McLuhan. Like the print-oriented and linear mentality they now modify, these premises were plagiarized from the atmosphere. McLuhan's value is in the power he gives us to predict and control these changes.

There is too much stuff to learn today. McLuhan calls it an age of "information overload." And the information levels outside the classroom are now higher than those in the classroom. Schools used to have a virtual monopoly on information; now they are part-time competitors in the electronic informational surround. And all human knowledge is expanding at computer speed.

Every choice involves a rejection. If we can't do everything, what priorities will govern our educational policies? "The medium is the message" may not be bad for openers. We can no longer teach kids all about a subject; we can teach them what a subject is all about. We have to introduce them to the form, structure, gestalt, grammar, and process of the knowledge involved. What does a math man do when a math man does do math? This approach to the formal element of a discipline can provide a channel of communication between specialists. Its focus is not on content or detail but on the postulates, ground rules, frames of reference, and premises of each discipline. It stresses the modes of cognition and perception proper to each field. Most failures in communication are based on disagreement about items which are only corollaries of a larger thesis. It happens between disciplines, individuals, media, and cultures.

The arts play a new role in education because they are explorations in perception. Formerly conceived as a curricular luxury item, they now become a dynamic way of tuning up the sensorium and of providing fresh ways of looking at familiar things. When exploration and discovery become the themes, the old lines between art and science begin to fade. We have to guide students to becoming their own data processors to operate through pattern recognition. The media themselves serve as both aids to learning and as proper objects of study in this search for an all-media literacy. Current interest in film criticism will expand to include all art and communication forms.

And since the knowledge explosion has blown out the walls between subjects, there will be a continued move toward interdisciplinary swapping and understanding. Many of the categorical walls between things are artifacts left over from the packaging days of print. The specialist's life will be even lonelier as we move further from the Gutenberg era. The trends are all toward wholeness and convergence.

These things aren't true just because Marshall McLuhan says they are. They work. They explain problems in education that nobody else is laying a glove on. When presented clearly and with all the necessary examples and footnotes added, they have proven to be a liberating force for hundreds of teachers who were living through the tension of this cultural fission without realizing that the causes for the tension lay outside themselves. McLuhan's relevance for education demands the work of teams of simultaneous translators and researchers who can both shape and substantiate the insights which are scattered through his work. McLuhan didn't invent electricity or put kids in front of TV sets; he is merely trying to describe what's happening out there so that it can be dealt with intelligently. When someone warns you of an oncoming truck, it's frightfully impolite to accuse him of driving the thing. McLuhan can help kids to learn stuff better.

THE SLOW GIFTED CHILD

Frank Riessman *

As we all know, categorizing pupils is dangerous at best. Sometimes it can be disastrous. By branding slow or disadvantaged pupils as unintelligent, teachers sometimes make boys and girls believe that they really are stupid. Many an adolescent's life has been blighted, in part at least, because teachers have mislabeled them and so consigned them to a school life of uninspiring boredom leading to a curtailment of the intellect.

It is often contended that deprived children are non-verbal, that they think in a slow, inadequate manner, and cannot conceptualize. While there are elements of truth in this portrayal, we think that it is a somewhat distorted picture, particularly in the invidious interpretation given the "elements."

How do deprived children learn and think? What are the characteristics of their so-called "cognitive style?" Do they have any creative potential? These are questions to which educators must give serious attention.

POOR OR SLOW?

An interesting confusion prevails in education circles between the "poor learner" and the "slow learner." The two are assumed to be identical. But need this be so? In a pragmatic culture such as ours, oriented toward quantity, speed, and measurement, this error can be fallen into readily. In the classroom it is terribly easy to believe that the child who learns the lesson quickly is a better learner than one who takes a long period of time. And sometimes this is the correct conclusion, as in reading, where studies show that faster readers understand better what they have read. The same thing appears to be true with regard to learning subject matter, such as history or geography. But here the problem is more complicated. The child who learns history more slowly is likely to be ignored and, unwittingly, discouraged by the teacher. Even if she does not ignore him but, on the contrary, gives him

* Chapter VII, "The Slow Gifted Child" from *The Culturally Deprived Child* by Frank Riessman. Copyright © 1962 by Frank Riessman. Reprinted by permission of Harper & Row, Publishers.

special attention, she may reflect to him her implicit assumption that he is a poor student. She may demand less of him, for example. The point is that she never sees the slowness as simply another style of learning with potential strengths of its own; nor does she see potential weaknesses (not *necessary* weaknesses) in the fast learner, who may become glib or impatient with tasks requiring protracted attention. *Because of the treatment he receives in the school system, the slow learner then may become the poor learner.*

It is time to put an end to the negative description of the term "slow" in the learning process. Slowness can reflect many things. It can indicate caution, a desire to be very thorough, great interest that may constrain against rushing through a problem, or a meticulous style. Or it may indicate a desire to mull things over, an emphasis on the concrete and physical. It may also indicate intellectual inadequacy. Extreme slowness probably does connote inadequacy in the absence of counter-indications. Even here we have to be very careful to check all possible blocks, not only the obvious emotional disturbances. There may be many other types of blockage as well, such as auditory blocks, reading difficulties (not of emotional origin), antagonism to the teacher, etc.

The nature of the slowness itself also has to be carefully examined. A delayed end product does not necessarily mean a slow process of thinking. Because a child takes a long time to arrive at an answer does not mean that his thinking is retarded. It may be that his thinking is more circuitous, that he is easily distracted, that he will not venture an answer until he is certain; and there is a host of other possibilities.

While our culture emphasizes speed, there is really no reason to assume that gifted, creative people have to learn rapidly or perform rapidly. Some people take a long time to learn basic concepts, but when they finally do so, they may use these ideas in a thoughtful, penetrating fashion. Others may learn a concept rapidly and then switch to some other area without ever pursuing the concept in depth. There are many slow people who only demonstrate their intellectual power on tasks in which it takes them a long time to get interested, and which have no time requirements. We have seen a fairly large number of college students whose grades and I.Q. scores were low, but who performed quite brilliantly on particular problems or in subjects in which they were deeply immersed. Their poor averages were simply a reflection of the pace required in college that is not attuned to their own style of work. They often fail courses where they could do extremely well if given more time. Actually, an extended college program, say, of five years, would benefit these students immeasurably. Educators tend to think of shortening college to three years for students who supposedly do not require the usual four years. But is there any reason why college could not be lengthened for these students who have a different style and pace of work? Many of these youngsters do, in fact, attend college for five or more years because they have to go to summer school to make up the courses they fail when carrying a schedule that is too heavy for them.

There is little doubt that the deprived child typically works on academic problems in a slower manner. This is shown in many different ways: he requires more examples before seeing a point, arriving at a conclusion, or forming a concept. He is unwilling to jump to conclusions or to generalize quickly (exceptions to the rule bother him). He is a slower reader, slower problem solver, slower at getting down to work, slower in taking tests.

It is important to note that in many areas of life the underpriviliged individual is not at all slow; quite the contrary, he is frequently remarkably quick. By way of illustration, in athletic activities and many games he functions rapidly and seems to think quickly. He seems to be both perceptive and quick in judging expressions on people's faces. When verbalizing in his own idiom, he does not appear to be sluggish at all. In figuring out ways of "beating the system" in the factory he is often astoundingly fast. These observations suggest that part of his slowness in the academic sphere is probably due to unfamiliarity with the subjects, limitations with formal language, and insecurity in this setting. But these "defensive" reasons for cautious slowness do not tell the whole story either. It appears at first glance that in the more direct sensory and physical areas, the deprived individual can be fast and acute, while in the middle-class settings in which he is unsure, slow caution prevails. The problem gets much more complex, however, once we begin to notice that there are a great many physical activities in which the deprived are notably slow. We had the opportunity of observing over a long period of time a highly skilled mechanic who came from a deprived background. Whenever he built anything in his house such as a cellar or a table, he did so in a meticulous fashion; likewise, when he worked on his car. He seemed to like to work in this manner, mulling things over, taking his time. Most old-time skilled workers like a leisurely pace. The shoemaker does not rush through his work, as a rule, but tends to do it carefully, patiently, at a moderate clip. This is often connected with pride in the product produced. Apparently, then, in things that are taken very seriously, things of deep concern, matters of personal pride, the slow style takes over. Workmanship is not a game or a party, but something enduring. It is also likely that many of the off-the-job pursuits of people like our mechanic—who, incidentally, likes to fish as well as to build furniture—are a reaction against the fast pace of modern industry.

Another source of the slow pace, which is not a sign of inadequacy or insecurity, may lie in the physical, less world-centered approach of the deprived person. It is not as easy to get into a problem or to cope with it as quickly if one has to go through all the steps physically. A word-oriented person can deal with most academic problems facilely, albeit sometimes glibly. A physical individual, on the other hand, likes to *do* as much as he can in thinking through a problem. This is often time-consuming.

While there are various special classes for slow learners, these classes do not really aim at developing advanced conceptual skills. They assume that the slow learner's ability is basically limited, rather than recognizing that he has a different style of learning that may have positive attributes. They do not envision any potentially gifted children among the slow learners.

DO AND SEE VS. TALK AND HEAR

In Chapter IV, the physical or motoric style of deprived groups was noted. This style is evidenced in a number of familiar ways:

1. They often appear to do better on performance tests of intelligence.
2. They like to draw.
3. Role-playing is an attractive technique to them.
4. They often use their fingers when counting, and move their lips when reading.
5. They like to participate in sports.
6. They employ physical forms of discipline.
7. They appear to think in spatial terms rather than temporal terms (they often have poor time perspective).

While their more limited temporal perspective undoubtedly produces difficulties, the spatial focus has a positive side to it. Spatial conceptualization permits an entire problem to be seen at once—it does not have temporal restrictions.[1]

The physical learner is, as was noted earlier, usually a slower learner, particularly in the early stages. But it is quite likely that he achieves a different kind of understanding of a problem than the faster, symbolic learner. Unfortunately, because our school system rewards speed, physical learners are discouraged and do not develop, while the symbolic learner is encouraged and moves forward.

While the deprived child does not easily get into problems, and has a short attention span, once he does become involved he is often able to work tenaciously for long stretches at a time. This may be a characteristic of the physical learner, because in order for him to learn he needs to have more of his whole body responding, and this requires a longer "warm-up" period. We are reminded here of the warming-up required in role-playing, which is more "physical." Highly verbal people, who, incidentlly, often resist role-playing or function in it in a highly intellectual manner, seem to need much less of a warm-up period in studying. Since they use their "muscles" less in thinking, this is perhaps comprehensible.

HOW DEEP IS THE PHYSICAL APPROACH?

It is interesting to note that the deprived child's motoric style or approach may not actually be as imbedded as might appear at first glance. There is the possibility that the difference in approach is more of a *set* which is capable of manipulation and change under certain circumstances. This interpretation is suggested by a finding of Miller and Swanson.[2] On one of tests (the Carl

---

[1] This positive aspect of spatial conceptualization was suggested by Irving Taylor in a personal communication.

[2] Daniel R. Miller and Guy E. Swanson, *Inner Conflict and Defense*, (New York: Henry Holt, 1960), p. 346.

Hollow Square Test) employed to determine whether people tended to be "conceptual" or "motoric," the researchers wanted to see if their subjects could switch their orientations if the instructions were altered slightly. That is, could a physical person perform in a conceptual fashion and vice versa. Miller and Swanson used two sets of instructions. One encouraged the subjects to take a conceptual approach: ". . . it helps to work these problems if you spend some time trying to figure out what is the best way to do them. . . ." Another set of instructions encouraged the subjects to be motoric: ". . . you can solve the problem better by trying all the possible ways to fit these together that you can in the time allowed. . . ." Under these conditions both groups were able to use styles that were not characteristic of them. *Deprived children could perform conceptually about as well as the non-deprived groups.*[3] This is one more example of their hidden intelligence. It is also further evidence that the early environment of the deprived child has not produced irreversible effects.

THE CONCRETE AND THE ABSTRACT

Abstract thinking is ultimately rooted in concrete sensory phenomena. But most of us in the course of educational experience have come to appreciate abstractions for their own sake. This is true whether we are talking about scientific theories or artistic—literary productions. We do not have to see the concrete applications or origins of Shakespeare in order to appreciate him. But deprived children have a very different attitude toward abstract concepts. They need to have the abstract constantly and intimately pinned to the immediate, the sensory, the topical. This is not to say that they dislike abstract thinking. It is, rather, that they do it differently. Moreover, after they have acquired some feeling for broad generalizations from seeing their derivation and application in practice, then the deprived individual may, to some degree, begin to appreciate abstract formulations per se. This probably comes at a later stage of development, and possibly even then the abstractions will be more firmly connected to things that can be seen, felt, and acted upon.

Since the deprived child approaches abstractions from the concrete, the immediate, the teacher must do likewise. The following is a vivid illustration reported to us recently by a junior high school teacher: [4]

[3] Siller found that low-status children do more poorly than high-status children on a variety of tests of conceptual ability and that they are less adequate in handling abstract concepts. In light of Miller and Swanson's findings, there is the possibility that this is due more to a "set" than a basic ability. An interesting residual finding of Siller's is that the differences between the high and low status groups is due to a small number of especially "low scorers" in the deprived groups. "When the groups were examined with these subjects removed, there were no significant status differences." See Jerome Siller, "Socioeconomic Status and Conceptual Thinking," *Journal of Abnormal and Social Psychology,* November, 1957, p. 365–371.

[4] Personal communication from Harold Kirsch, a New York City Junior High School teacher.

"On the day before the following lesson, the teacher told the class the story of Caliban from Shakespeare's *The Tempest*. The next day, the class walked into a darkened classroom and the teacher, walking around the room and reading by a flickering flashlight, recited the poem by Louis Untermeyer called 'Caliban in the Coal Mines.' It is a plaintive, almost sacrilegious, appeal to the Lord for better conditions in the mines: 'God, if You wish for our love, Fling us a handful of stars.' The lights in the classroom were turned on near the ending of this last line of the poem. Allowing the class to come out of its trance slowly, the teacher distributed copies of the poem and requested, and received, acceptable meanings to certain words. In the discussion that followed the teacher asked why the poet had called his miner Caliban. The answer supplied by a thirteen-year-old girl was: 'They were both in the dark.'"

This same teacher states further: [5]

"Announce a lesson in 'literature'—especially one in poetry—and you will receive an assortment of groans. Announce that you will tell the class a story and you will receive respectful but reserved expectancy. State further that this is the story of two sets of parents who, because of their unwillingness to adapt to the present time, contributed to the destruction of their own children. You will have your audience in the palm of your hand. On the basis of a sympathetic, even empathic approach to the point of view of the adolescent, you have motivated the class to the study of Shakespeare's *Romeo and Juliet*. Will deprived children respond to these techniques? Having used them in my classes, I shall vouch that arguments have started because somebody said that Juliet was a fool to destroy herself for a man. Somebody else wondered if we sometimes learn the truth too late (speaking of the elder Montagues and Capulets). It is not difficult to direct such thinking into the value of having a mind stretched by studying and observing and learning."

THE OUTSIDE VS. THE INSIDE

Deprived children for the most part are not introspective or introverted; nor are they greatly concerned with the self. They respond much more to the external, to the outside. They are not given to self-blame or self-criticism, but rather are more likely to see the causes of their problems in external forces. Sometimes this can take the form of scapegoating and projection, but it may also lead to appropriate placement of censure and accompanying anger.

That they are not introspective in focus does not mean that they are incapable of inner thought, imagination, and feeling. But rather, again, as in the case of the concrete and the abstract—the external stimulation must precede the inner development. They are not given to direct enjoyment of introspection qua introspection, but instead require, at least at first, that it be stimulated by external sources.

[5] *Ibid.*

THE GAMES FORMAT

Anyone who has worked with deprived children knows that one of the surest ways to involve them in an activity is to make it into a game. Now, this is true of all children to some extent, but it is especially true of the under-privileged. Davis and Eells have capitalized on this idea by developing an intelligence test in the form of a game. Cartoon-like personality tests such as the Rosenzweig Picture Frustration Test are much more appealing to under-privileged individuals.

Teachers have told about setting up a mock court in the classroom which enabled the class to discuss discipline, justice, and government in a meaning-ful way. Originally they had found it difficult to interest the deprived children in these subjects, but the excitement of a make-believe court attracted con-siderable attention and provided a good beginning for discussion on a higher, more abstract level.

One of the reasons why the new teaching machines are likely to appeal to the deprived child is that they operate pretty much like games. In this con-nection, we are reminded of the exciting work of O. K. Moore at Yale, where, by using special mechanical devices constructed in the form of games, he has been able to teach three-year-old children to read, write, and type.[6] The use of machines of this kind on a pre-school level with deprived children holds great promise. Perhaps even more important could be their use in special classes for "retarded" children. These game-like devices might enable these children to catch up rapidly and return to the main educational "track," and thus reduce the present "two track" character of the educational system.

What is the source of the "games" orientation of the deprived? Apparently, it is related to their down-to-earth, spontaneous approach to things. Their extra-verbal communication (motoric, visual) is usually called forth in games, most of which are not word-bound. Also, most games (not all, by any means), are person-centered and generally are concerned with direct action and visible results. Games are usually sharply defined and structured, with clear-cut goals. The rules are definite and can be readily absorbed. The deprived child enjoys the challenge of the game and feels he can "do" it; this is in sharp contrast to many verbal tasks.

---

[6] The effectiveness of the teaching machines ultimately has to be evaluated in the frame-work of the long-range learning sets produced by such devices. The present hue and cry concerning their apparent effectiveness has to be weighed in relation to the attitudes toward learning and thinking which eventuate. Also, much of their observed effectiveness may be due to a "gimmick" or novelty (placebo) effect, and not to the intrinsic learning principles presumably involved. Moore's work with small children would not seem to be subject to this effect, but the long-term effects on the child's attitudes toward learning will have to be appraised carefully. See *Time Magazine*, November 7, 1960, p. 103, for a brief presen-tation of O. K. Moore's methods.

WHY DOES THE PROGRESSIVE APPROACH FAIL?

Progressive education emphasizes "learning by doing." This fits in with the physical approach of the deprived child. Progressive education emphasizes concrete, experience-centered learning, attuned to the pace of the child. This is exactly what the deprived child needs so much. Why, then, does the progressive approach appear to fail with these children—why do they find it so unappealing on the whole? This is a puzzling problem. Certainly, it must be said, there are a fair number of progressive-minded teachers who, in stressing vivid, example-centered lessons, have been successful with deprived children. But on the average, it is the old-style, strict, highly structured teacher who appears to be most popular and effective with underprivileged children. When this teacher is also lively, and builds concepts from the ground up, and makes an effort to "win the children to learning," she is the model teacher for these youngsters.

The progressive approach by itself, however, does not catch on. It has too many features that are essentially alien to the culture of the deprived: the permissiveness; the accent on self—the internal—the introspective; creativity and growth as central goals of education; the stress on play; the underestimation of discipline and authority. All these values are contradictory to the traditional attitudes and personality characteristics of the deprived.

What is needed is a perfect marriage of the traditional and the progressive. The traditionalist contributes structure, rules, discipline, authority, rote, order, organization, and strong external demands for achievement. He fights to win the child to a high level of conceptual learning. The progressivist places the emphasis on the importance of motivation; the down-to-earth learning by doing; examples drawn from the experience of the child—beginning in the present and moving toward the broad, the abstract, the cultural heritage.

This is the combination that can break through the block which separates the child and the school.

A DIFFERENT WAVELENGTH

In summary, then, it can be said that the following characteristics are fairly typical of the deprived child's style:
  1. Physical and visual rather than aural.
  2. Content-centered rather than form-centered.
  3. Externally oriented rather than introspective.
  4. Problem-centered rather than abstract-centered.
  5. Inductive rather than deductive.
  6. Spatial rather than temporal.
  7. Slow, careful, patient, persevering (in areas of importance), rather than quick, clever, facile, flexible.

It can readily be seen that many of these characteristics overlap. They seem to form a pattern that, according to Irving Taylor, is very similar to that found among one type of highly creative person.[7] Why then does the potential creativity of the underprivileged child fail to materialize? There are a number of reasons, but perhaps the most important is his verbal difficulties. . . .

THE CASE OF BRAD

John W. M. Rothney [*]

Brad is an example of a poorly motivated hard-to-reach pupil. The school has failed him. Perhaps you can think of ways that his school experiences could have been made more successful. Note the data-gathering devices and techniques used in this school that can be used to get to know the pupil and as a basis for remedial work. Taken singly, these devices are not conclusive; but used in a battery, they can yield a great deal of significant information. With such knowledge, a teacher can make his diagnosis and select his strategy with much more confidence than he can without it.[†]

Brad was one of three students who were not graduated with their high school class of 220 students. A stuttering, confused lad whose unshaven face, greasy clothes, grimy hands, and dirty fingernails made him the worst-groomed boy in school, Brad began losing contact with reality, lapsed into word-salad language, and deteriorated rapidly in the last two years of high school. Needing sympathy and encouragement, Brad received only abuse, threats, and flunks until he felt so bitter about "this educational clambake" that he wanted to leave school. When he tried to do so in order to begin an apprenticeship in his chosen work, he found that a high school diploma was needed. Forced back into the school that he hated and into the classes of teachers who, he hoped, might "approach me with something a little bit less deadly than a double-bit axe," Brad stuck out four years of misery in high school.

[7] Personal communication from Irving Taylor.

[*] From *The High School Student:* A Book of Cases by John W. M. Rothney. Copyright 1953 by Holt, Rinehart and Winston, Inc. Reprinted by permission of Holt, Rinehart and Winston, Inc.

[†] See also Madeline Hunter, "When the Teacher Diagnoses Learning," in Chapter I.

Brad expressed himself in his inimitable way in a letter written to his junior English teacher.

Miss Shannon,

You wanted to hear the story of my peculiarities so here goes:

I reside at 240 Appian Street and I live with my mother and dad and two brothers and as a result there is a lot of noise and assorted miscellanious etc. around all of the time so I have a quiet room upstairs on the top floor where I got my start in the electifying hobby, electricity. I have a background in same and I find there is one thing that is necessary in even this—money. The absence of this one thing leaves me in a financial quandary—most of the time. So I went out and found a job—oddly enough in electricity. You have probably heard of the enterprise called the sound business. Well, I work there; That is, for Sound By Johnson. I figure that I might as well get into something that I'm interestedin. I've seen a lot of various characters in Senior high that don't have the slightest idea what they want to do when they get out of this educational clambake. They get out of school and they look around for a job. They probably find one working with the city's finest in a six foot ditch excavating for a sewer. Well, That should can up that barbecued edition of philosophical soufflé. (In other words, thats the end trailer of that model of kibitizing.)

I also spend a lot of time up at the local kilocycle kitchen, amiably captioned KPOP. (Sounds like champagne, k-pop) Among the staff in the workhouse down there are a few names you might recognize. KPOP is an odd scene when a baseball game is in progress. Sam Jones is quietly dozing at the console and Curly is curled up on the couch over in behind the organ in Studio B with the speaker blaring in the corner of the control room. And all this time Harry out at the ball park hopefully ringing the control room at KPOP trying to wake Sam up to tell him that Curly has thirty seconds to get into Studio A and tell a microphone that "This is KPOP; We now return you to the baseball park for the remains of tonights ball game." Then Curly crawls back into Studio B to get some more sleep and Sam leans back in his revolving chair and daintily parks his head on the left hand turntable in the hope that no one turns it on before he wakes up again. (Just in time to sign the station off and go back to sleep or go home.)

Another paragraph-same thing. The only place I went this summer is where my work took me. We covered the fairs in two cities and a half dozen firemans picnics scattered about the area.

My aim for a job is engineer at the soda water station, KPOP. I'd better sign off cold now before this cigar of mine burns up and or goes out and warms things up a bit. Theres my essay—hope you will approach me with something a little bit less deadly than a double bit axe.

Examination of Brad's academic record shows quite clearly that his teachers did not consider him to be a satisfactory student. He gave *his* reaction to some of their courses when he said that he wished he had not taken either sophomore English ("Who cares about Ivanhoe?") or junior English ("Who wants to know about the great and mighty English men?") He said that after leaving high school he would not strongly object to taking any kind of training "except more English." He made sarcastic comments about all school subjects except biology, physics, and auto mechanics. He said that he was too busy to do any homework in any subject.

Most of his teachers believed that Brad could have done good work if he had chosen to do so, and their beliefs, except about mathematics, seemed to be validated by his test scores. The low score on language usage can be discounted since, by the time he took that test, he had developed so strong an aversion to English that he would not put forth effort on tests that attempted to measure what had been covered in English classes.

SUBJECT	GRADES							
	9		10		11		12	
English	C	B	D	F	F	–	D	F
Amer. History								
Civics								
Social Science	C	C						
Algebra	D	F	D	F	F	Dropped		
Arithmetic					C	D		
Biology			D	D				
Chemistry							D	F
General Science	B	B						
Physics					C	B		
Physical Ed.	C	C	D	D	C	F	Excused	
Manual Arts	B	C						
Drafting			D	D				
Auto Mechanics							C	B
Typing					F	Dropped		

The mechanical-test score simply elaborated the obvious in his case. Brad was one of those single-interest boys who found no time for any of the common student activities. He had wired his home for sound, with speakers in every room, and he had a "lab" in which he did his puttering. Nightly after supper Brad went to this room to experiment with machine-shop materials, chemistry, or the repairing and making of electrical equipment. He became interested in radio and tried to prepare himself for the Federal Communications Commission radio operator's examinations. The first attempt to pass the theoretical part of the test was unsuccessful, but he set out to master it on a second trial. His interest in communications was further developed when he got a part-time job with a sound-truck operator who traveled to county fairs and public events where recording and broadcasting devices were utilized. When his employer discontinued his business, Brad found some odd jobs in the repair of electrical equipment. The work he did was so satisfactory that he was paid as much as $1.50 an hour.

TESTS	PERCENTILE		
	Grade 10	Grade 11	Grade 12
Henmon–Nelson Test of Mental Ability	72		
Reading Tests			
Cooperative reading vocabulary	91	92	
Cooperative reading comprehension	95	60	
Cooperative speed of reading			
Primary Mental Abilities			
Verbal	68		
Space	70		
Reasoning	55		
Number	18		
Word fluency	15		
Differential Aptitude Tests			
Number		25	
Language usage		10	
Spelling		90	
Mechanical reasoning		99	
Space		65	
Clerical			

With his interests and his experience, it was not surprising to find that Brad had chosen a career in those areas. The first choice of engineer at a radio station remained his preference throughout his high school career, although he thought occasionally of other occupations. His father was a machinist at a machine-tool factory and, when it became apparent that Brad was not going to be successful in academic work, he proposed that his son join him in that trade. A request for an apprenticeship was filed but was rejected until he had a high school diploma. Since there seemed to be no hope of being graduated, Brad promptly gave up the apprenticeship plan. At times he thought of applying for a position as electrician in the telephone company or in the local power and light company, or of trying to start an electrical repair and equipment business of his own after a period of employment with a local construction company. Always, however, he returned to his first choice of radio engineer. He saw no reason why, with eight years of experience on electrical equipment, he could not succeed in that field, and he hoped, within five years, to be a chief engineer in a radio or television station. He said that he could "handle anything that might come along" and was sure that the future looked good because "It has electronic possibilities with the atomic business coming up, a new power source is coming and there's openings for repairmen, etc." He said that he would like to join the American Radio Relay League and then get married. After the latter statement he added, "Hah!"

When the possibility of service in the armed forces arose, Brad thought that it might present an opportunity for further training in his field. He had looked up the Navy's classification system and was impressed with the title and duties of an Interior Communications Electrician. There was some doubt about whether Brad could pass the armed forces psychiatric screening test, since his stuttering had become noticeable and his "word-salad" speech was easily recognizable as a symptom of mental disturbance, but Brad did not realize these things. He spoke about the armed forces as though they would be very fortunate to get so skilled a recruit.

Typical of Brad's condition was the fact that he seemed never to recognize his own limitations. On a self-appraisal scale filled out during his last month in high school, he placed himself not lower than the second quarter of his class. Although he knew he could not graduate with his group, he ranked himself in the second quarter of his class. Despite his knowledge that he did

In the item given below, I would be, compared to other high school seniors, in the (indicate with check)	Highest quarter	Third quarter	Second quarter	Lowest quarter
1. Achievement in my special field of interest (write it below) RADIO	✓			
2. Reading achievement		✓		
3. Intelligence test scores	✓			
4. Achievement in numbers		✓		
5. Confidence that I will succeed in my class work	✓			
6. Getting along with people	✓			
7. Rank in this senior class		✓		
8. Confidence that I have chosen the right career	✓			
9. Knowing my own strengths	✓			
10. Knowing my own weaknesses	✓			
11. Readiness for life after high school	✓			
12. Getting along in new situations	✓			

not have any close friends, he thought he was in the top quarter of his class in getting along with people. And though his weaknesses (and strengths) were apparent to all who would look, he had never given any indication that he knew what they were. He did not, for example, see any reason why he would not succeed in his post-high-school career.

At the time his class was graduated, Brad was in a dilemma. He wanted a high school diploma because he realized its importance in getting into the kind of work he wanted. Should he come back to school and endure another year of torture? Should he take a job and try to complete his work with correspondence lessons? Should he just take a full-time job and forget about the high school diploma? Or should he enlist in the armed forces? In Brad's school there was no one to counsel with him. There was no one to answer his questions, tell him where to seek the answers, or even give him a sympathetic hearing. No one regretted that Brad, the unkempt, stuttering, electrical "nut" who would not do his homework, was leaving school. There would be a new class in the fall and its members would be easier to handle if Brad's fate could be described to those among them who would not conform.

Six months after leaving school Brad reported that he was doing electrical machine repair work for a local power company. In his second year out of high school he said he hoped to be "specializing on carburetors, speedometers, and magnetos."

Chapter 5

LEARNING

O NE of the most important facets of any theory of teaching is the nature of the learning process. In spite of the protests that learning theory is in a very immature state and so is not ready to provide a basis for teaching theory, there is a considerable body of common psychological knowledge that we can trust well enough to use for a basis for teaching strategies and tactics. Usually, however, these learning theories are more useful for describing generalities in teaching technique rather than in prescribing specific tactics for particular situations. Nevertheless, they are useful for pointing out the kinds of teaching that will most likely be beneficial. Certainly, we today know enough about learning to prevent us from using tactics and strategies that work against efficient learning.

Because of this undoubted fact, we should note that the ability to retrieve and use what has been learned is the essential test of the effectiveness of teaching. This test calls for a high level of learning. We teachers must use teaching strategies and tactics most favorable to retention, transfer, the establishment of real understanding, and the development of intellectual and other abilities.

LEARNING PRINCIPLES

Wisconsin State Department of Public Instruction *

In 1961, a committee of Wisconsin educators began to develop a guide to assist Wisconsin teachers "to evaluate critically and constructively their learning clime." As part of this study, a list of learning principles that seem to be basic to the educational process was developed. In spite

* Permission to reproduce this publication: *Learning Principles* is granted by Angus B. Rothwell, State Superintendent of Wisconsin Schools, representing the State Department of Public Instruction.

*of the differences in the various schools of psychology, these principles
can be accepted with confidence. It is probably safe to assume that any
theory of instruction and all teaching strategies and tactics should be
compatible with these principles if teaching is to be truly successful.*

READINESS

Principle No. 1: *Learning is governed by the readiness of the learner.*

Readiness is a condition of the individual which makes it possible to learn.
There are varying degrees of readiness for learning a particular task. If the
learner is not ready for a given task, he learns incompletely, is frustrated,
may be blocked, or has other problems. Readiness includes physical growth
and maturation, intelligence, background of experiences, previous learning,
motivation, perception, and probably other factors which make learning
possible.

1. Individuals learn best if the tasks are closely related to their abilities,
   interests, and backgrounds.
2. Readiness for learning must be assessed, not assumed. This means, for
   example, that the teacher might administer a readiness test or observe
   carefully the behavior of students as she teaches at their presumed level
   of readiness.
3. When individuals lack readiness for a task, the task should be postponed
   until readiness can be developed or the task can be restructured to fit
   the learner.
4. Readiness for learning reflects differences in kind as well as in degree.
   For example, two individuals with the same I.Q. might have quite different patterns of mental abilities.
5. Materials, activities, and tasks must be varied according to the readiness
   factors (cognitive, psychomotor, and affective) of the various learners.

MOTIVATION

Principle No. 2: *Intent to learn is necessary for purposeful learning.*

Motivation is a state of the learner which initiates activity, governs its
direction, and fosters perseverance. Young children are naturally curious and
engage in exploratory activities in the world in which they live. This curiosity
ought to be encouraged rather than inhibited by insistence on a prescribed
formula of educational sequence taught to all learners in the same way at
the same time.

1. Not only is the individual motivated by the need to satisfy various deficiencies—biological, social or emotional—but in addition he can be
   motivated to enhance himself beyond his present standing.
2. Knowledge of progress toward a goal encourages continued effort. Ex-

periences of failure which do not mar the learner's self-image can enhance his ability to persevere in learning situations.

3. Motives governing behavior are not always clear—even to the learner. For example, the individual who seeks out particular help from a teacher may be moved more by a need for affection than a desire to achieve.

4. Motivation is influenced by personality variables, such as feelings of inferiority, hostility, or self-confidence. Over- and under-achievers may have personality problems.

5. Security and success in goal achievement tend to increase motivation to learn. Failure may produce either increased or decreased motivation, depending on other factors. Not everyone is motivated by the same thing or to do the same thing.

6. Motivation increases if the learner has reason to believe that some of his needs will be satisfied.

7. Praise and reproof from teachers, parents, and peers significantly influence motivation and behavior. The effects of praise are positive, but the effects of reproof are less predictable. Thus, reproof may motivate or discourage a behavior with which it is associated.

8. Incentives and material rewards may sometimes be of value in classroom situations. There is danger that the individual will work for the reward rather than learning per se.

9. Competition and incentive may be affective in motivating, but where chances of success are perceived as only slight, competition may discourage motivation toward the goal in question. When the learner can predict success all of the time, his degree of maturation is reduced.

10. A favorable attitude toward learning is acquired by most individuals in the course of sustained, satisfying learning experience.

11. Where learning and activity can be related to the existing interest of the learner, motivation is increased.

PERCEPTION

Principle No. 3: *A person tends to believe according to how he perceives a situation.*

Perception is the interpretation of a life situation. Each individual perceives the world differently, and these perceptions affect behaviors. A teacher may acquire a better understanding of a student's behavior if he is sensitive to how the pupil perceives a given situation.

1. Each learner senses the world differently from other learners because each learner has a different invironment. All learners do not view the same environment in the same way.

2. The learner interprets his environment according to his own goals, attitudes, motives, past experiences, health, emotional state, and abilities.

3. The ways one perceives himself are fundamental to his behavior. In a

situation, the learner tends to act according to the way he perceives himself.

4. The learner can be helped by providing opportunities for him to evaluate his own perceptions. The teacher can be a referrent of reality. Desirable behavior is dependent upon an accurate and realistic perception of a given situation. The teacher and others can help the learner evaluate his own perception.

5. Perception can be furthered by supplying to learners views of what may be perceived.

6. The accuracy of perception must be frequently checked. Group discussions of problems offer opportunities for indivduals to clarify their own perceptions.

7. Stages of growth and development of the learner will influence his view of himself.

GOALS

Principle No. 4: *Goals must be clearly in mind and accepted by the learner if adequate learning is to take place.*

A goal is the specific objective which one is attempting to obtain. This is different than purpose which may have a number of goals.

1. Goals should be commensurate with the abilities of the individual to attain them.

2. Societal demands and the individual's needs must be considered when establishing goals.

3. The learner will accept a goal if he feels that his needs will be met by the task he undertakes.

4. The purposes of the teacher and learner should be closcly related.

5. Standards set by the various social groups of which one is a member and standards set by peers and authority figures may influence goal-setting behavior by an individual. Pressures to conform to standards tend to produce rigid behavior and inhibit creativity. The over-achiever often adopts compulsive and rigid behavior.

6. The degree of active involvement of the learner influences his goal-setting behavior. The extent of the learner's commitment influences his achievement.

7. The learner's feeling about his worth and his ability affect his goal-setting behavior. If failure to attain the goal threatens the self-concept, the person may raise his sights for social prestige or lower them to avoid failure.

8. The goals to be sought in satisfying needs frequently must be shown the learner. Various goals could satisfy a given need and various needs can be satisfied by given goals. The teacher's ability to help students formulate clear and appropriate goals becomes very important.

INDIVIDUAL DIFFERENCES

Principle No. 5: *Learning varies with the individual.*

Teaching must take account of individual differences in learners if all students in a class are to achieve maximum learning. Differences become more marked as students grow older. Teaching only one level fails to be effective for all pupils. One needs to understand the backgrounds, emotions, motives, and abilities of each learner and adapt the learning materials and tasks accordingly.

1. The learner should be helped to understand his assets and limitations and to expect differences in tasks, activities, and accomplishments.
2. The learner needs to recognize his potentials and should be helped to plan and carry out his own activities.
3. The learner needs a wide variety of tasks, materials, and methods consistent with his goals, interests, and background.
4. A learner tends to select from an experience that which is consistent with his past experiences and which he feels will have meaning for him. A learner responds differently from other learners to a common experience because of his perception of that experience.
5. Opportunities for learning are enhanced when an individual is not threatened by his environment, thus feels free to engage in learning activities. When a learner has freedom to think and act as an individual, problem solving, motivation and creative efforts are increased.
6. The learner who is encouraged to develop his own strengths learns more and shows eagerness to learn. If his weaknesses are stressed, he shows dissatisfaction for learning.

TRANSFER AND RETENTION

Principle No. 6: *Learning is useful when a person can retain and apply it to new situations.*

When whatever is learned in one situation is used in a new or different situation, transfer of learning occurs. Retention is the ability to use again. Materials learned and retained can be used by the learner for application to new situations.

1. Intent to learn and remember fosters retention. Active attempts to recall or recite materials to be learned improve retention.
2. Material that is meaningful to the learner is retained best.
3. Retention is affected by the setting (psychological and physical) in which the learning was acquired. Practice should be in a realistic setting.
4. Distributed practice (drill) favors retention. However, some important learnings are acquired which may need very little drill. Learning sessions

which are distributed or broken into smaller units of time produce learning which is better retained than learning in longer sessions. The length of a learning or practice session may sometimes be determined by the internal logic or structure of the material to be learned and by the perceived need of the learner.

5. Review of factual material, skills, or concepts increases retention and transfer value. (If too much review is needed, the original material may have lacked significance to the learner.)
6. Learning tends to occur when the activities lead to satisfying consequences.
7. Personal attitudes, feeling, or emotional states of the learner lead to "selective forgetting." Thus, disagreeable material may not be as well retained as material which the learner finds pleasant.
8. Interference in learning may occur when new but similar learnings follow an initial learning. Chance of forgetting an initial learning is increased when a new but similar learning is required.
9. Knowledge of concepts, principles, and generalizations will be retained better and will transfer more effectively than by relating applications of principles learned and by illustrating similar elements.
10. Transfer of learning to new situations is facilitated (not guaranteed) when useful relationships in unique, but somewhat similar, situations are determined.
11. The final phases of learning should include efforts to draw generalizations. These, in turn, assist in retention and transfer.

COGNITIVE LEARNING

Principle No. 7: *Cognitive learning involves recognition and/or discovery.*

Cognitive learning includes rote association, concept formation, problem finding, and problem-solving skills, from which new modes of behavior are formed. Thinking, reasoning, evaluating, and imagining are mental acts related to cognitive learning. This learning occurs at levels of complexity and requires various mental activities.

1. Attention must be focused on relevant aspects of the environment before cognitive learning can take place. The learner needs to direct his attention properly if cognitive learning is to occur.
2. The outcomes of cognitive learning will vary depending upon the levels and kinds of individual differences of learners.
3. Forms of readiness—vocabulary, reading ability, mental ability, and experiences directly affect cognitive learning.
4. Learning experiences must be organized into appropriate units.
5. When presenting concepts, meaningfulness is essential. Searching behavior, application, formal definition, and evaluation are needed to make sure that concepts are meaningful.
6. In problem-solving, the learner must be aided to define and limit the

problem, to find necessary information, to interpret and analyze this problem, and be permitted divergent thinking.

7. Attention to mental processes, rather than to cognitive and affective outcomes, favors problem-solving, analysis, synthesis, and reasoning.

AFFECTIVE LEARNING

Principle No. 8: *An individual's affective learning determines how he relates himself to new experiences.*

Affective learning includes values, emotions, motives, interests, and attitudes. The learner may not be consciously aware of some affective learnings. Affective learnings include the original bases for, and the present forms of, the individual's values, emotions, motives, interests and attitudes.

1. Most life situations have an affective aspect.
2. How a learner adjusts and reacts to situations will have an impact upon and will influence his affective learnings.
3. At times, important values acquired during the childhood years remain relatively undifferentiated throughout life. Undifferentiated values, attitudes, and feelings may arrest his over-all development.
4. Attitudes and values are frequently acquired through identification with other individuals rather than by direct teaching.
5. Attitudes are modified more easily as the result of pleasing experience.
6. A learner's values are influenced by a group's standards of behavior.
7. School learning and mental health are related. Students in good mental health tend to learn more readily than those with problems.
8. Affective learnings may be developed or modified through interaction between the teacher and the class.
9. The learner may be assisted to maturity by helping him to recognize and understand his attitudes, feelings, and emotions. Respect for the learner's attitudes, feelings, and frustrations is necessary to help him gain self-understanding and maturity.

PSYCHOMOTOR LEARNING

Principle No. 9: *An individual's psychomotor learning determines how he is able to control his muscular activity.*

Psychomotor learnings have both mental and physical aspects.

1. In any given task a group will have wide variation in basic psychomotor abilities.
2. The psychomotor development of a given learner occurs unevenly.
3. An individual's skeletal-muscular structure and nervous system help determine his level of psychomotor performance.
4. Through play and informal activities the learner gains increasing control of his movements.

5. With physical and mental maturity, the learner's ability to integrate and refine movements is enhanced.
6. Environmental factors affect the type and extent of the psychomotor performance of the individual.
7. A well conceived explanation, demonstration, and active participation by the learner increase the efficiency of psychomotor learning.
8. Appropriate practice, spaced at given intervals, enhances psychomotor learning. Meaningful practice should include a complete sequence of the motor act. Spacing cannot be done purely on a timed basis.
9. Excessive practice may result in fatigue which often results in a lower level of performance.
10. Psychomotor tasks too difficult for the learner may result in frustration and early fatigue.

EVALUATION

Principle No. 10: *The kind, the extent, and the validity of evaluation affect present and subsequent learnings.*

The practice of evaluation makes it possible for an individual to assess progress toward previously identified goals. An individual's evaluation of his learning is influenced by his freedom to evaluate. Evaluation includes an awareness on the part of an individual of his level of performance, motivations for learning, and readiness to learn. The learner, interacting with other human beings in assessing his learning experiences, may improve his ability to evaluate experiences. Objective evaluation of one's own experiences is difficult. More knowledge is brought to, and insights are gained about, an experience when the learner shares with interested informed persons.

1. Evaluation gives meaning to learning and provides new direction to the learning.
2. When goals and evaluation are seen in relationship, the evaluation becomes more meaningful to the learner.
3. Teacher evaluative practices influence what the learner engages in and learns.
4. Evaluation of progress toward a goal is enhanced when the teacher and the learner exchange and accept each others thoughts, feelings, and observations.
5. Lack of, or incomplete evaluation reduces the teacher's ability to serve the learner. Conversely, comprehensive evaluations enhance the learner's ability to do self-evaluation.
6. When persistent emphasis is placed upon the teacher's evaluation of the learner's performance, patterns of dependency, withdrawal and hostility may develop.
7. The peer group can be useful in evaluation.

STYLES OF LEARNING

Frank Riessman *

Because a person's learning techniques are themselves learned, pupils do not all learn in the same way. Instead, each pupil learns in the way he has learned to learn. Teachers tend to forget this fact sometimes and therefore attempt to use the same teaching strategies for all their pupils. Such an approach is bound to break down. Just as strategies and tactics should be chosen to match the subject matter to be taught, so should they be chosen to match the way different pupils learn. To thus match method and pupil personalities is difficult, but until it is done, teaching methods will not be really effective. As Riessman points out, the strategy is to discover the individual pupil's strengths and then capitalize on them. Such a strategy must ultimately call for tactics which individualize instruction.

In any classroom, probably no two pupils learn the same things in the same way at the same pace. Some learn most easily through reading; others through listening; still others through doing things physically. Some prefer to work under the pressure of deadlines and tests; others like a more leisurely pace. Some learn by being challenged by people ahead of them; others learn best by helping people behind them.

Everyone has a distinct style of learning, as individual as his personality. These styles may be categorized principally as visual (reading), aural (listening), or physical (doing things), although any one person may use more than one. Some persons, for example, find it much easier to pace the floor while reading an assignment than to sit perfectly still at a desk. Their style may be more physical.

A common characteristic of the disadvantaged child is his physical approach to learning. He has been exposed to very little reading because his parents rarely have the time to read to him. For this reason, it may be easier for him to learn to read by acting out the words than by hearing them spoken by his

* From *NEA Journal*, Vol. 55 (Washington, D.C.: National Education Association, March 1966), pp. 15–17. Reprinted by permission of the publisher and the author.

teacher. This is borne out by the fact that children at a school in one of New York City's poorest neighborhoods are learning to read effectively by singing and dancing to the words. Since songs and physical movement have been incorporated into the teaching of reading, the percentage of retarded readers in the school has reportedly been cut in half.

For a long time now, teachers and guidance workers have tended to ignore the concept of different styles of learning. They have, instead, focused their attention on emotion, motivation, and personality as causes for learning or failure to learn. When confronted with an intellectually able student whose learning fails to measure up to his learning potential, they have tended to attribute this failure to an emotional block or personality conflict. Little attention has been given to how a pupil's learning could be improved simply by concentrating on the way he works and learns.

I believe that a careful analysis of the way a child works and learns is of greater value than speculation about his emotional state. He may indeed feel sibling rivalry or certain irrational fears, but these conditions may not affect his learning as much as the methods his teacher uses to teach him. The important consideration, in my opinion, is whether the methods of learning imposed by the teacher utilize sufficiently the strengths in a child's style of learning.

Most teachers, unforunately, have been trained to look upon learning in a general way. Their preparation, which may include no more than a few survey courses in educational psychology, neglects the idiosyncracies involved in learning.

For example, most teachers probably assume that the best way to study a reading assignment is first to survey the chapter. This is what they have been taught from the early grades through college because it is the way most people learn best. Some students, however, become so anxious and disturbed at being told to take an overall view of a chapter that they cannot function. Their style calls for reading a chapter slowly, section by section. Requiring such a person to skim the entire chapter first makes no more sense than telling a person who can't resist peeking at the last chapter of a mystery that he must read the book straight through.

The general recommendation that one must have a quiet place to study may be equally lacking in validity. Strangely enough, some people do their best studying in a noisy place, or with certain sounds such as music or even traffic in the background. The textbooks do not talk about this because, for the "average" person, peace and quiet are more conducive to learning.

Style is also very much involved in taking tests. For some individuals, the prospect of a test operates as a prod that stimulates them to absorb a great deal of material they need to master. On the other hand, being faced with a test causes many people to become disorganized, overanxious, and unable to work. After a test, some pupils are so upset over their mistakes that they develop an emotional block about remembering the correct answers to the questions on which they erred. Consequently, they repeatedly miss the same questions. For others, finding out that they gave wrong answers aids recall and challenges them to master the problems.

Each classroom is likely to include students whose styles of learning vary widely. Although the teacher cannot cater completely to each student's particular style, he can attempt to utilize the strengths and reduce or modify the weaknesses of those in his classes.

An individual's basic style of learning is probably laid down early in life and is not subject to fundamental change. For example, a pupil who likes to learn by listening and speaking (aural style) is unlikely to change completely and become an outstanding reader. I am not suggesting that such a pupil will not learn to read and write fluently but rather that his best, most permanent learning is likely to continue to come from listening and speaking.

Since the student is the person most vitally concerned, the first step is to help him discover his particular style of learning and recognize its strengths and limitations.

In identifying a style, it is extremely important to ascertain the person's work habits as precisely as possible. If a youngster is in despair because he cannot get any work done during the study time allowed in class or in the study hall, teachers should question him carefully about his routine. What does he do first when study time is announced? How does he try to make himself concentrate? What disturbs him?

Perhaps his answer will be: "At first I'm glad we have time to do the work at school so that I will be free when school is out. I open my book to the assignment, but it's noisy because kids are asking the teacher questions or flipping through their books or whispering. I go sharpen my pencils while I'm waiting for it to get quiet.

"By the time things settle down, I know I don't have too much time left and that I have to hurry or I won't get done. I try to read fast, but the words all run together and mean nothing. Some of the smart kids are already through, and I haven't even started. I usually give up and decide I may as well do it all at home like all the other dumb bunnies do."

A number of things may be involved in this boy's problem. Possibly he is a physical learner (sharpening the pencils may show some need for movement) who has difficulty with visual learning. Apparently he warms up slowly and works slowly, for when he tries to hurry, he finds he can do nothing.

The physical learner generally gets his muscles into his work, and this takes time. Such a student must realize that attempts to rush himself are of no avail, but that this does not make him a "dumb bunny." Once he gets past his warm-up point and begins to concentrate on his work, he may work very well for long periods of time.

If this student is made aware of the way he learns, he can schedule any work requiring concentration for longer periods of time, and use short periods for something less demanding, perhaps a review of the day's schoolwork. Probably his warm-up period will gradually decrease as he becomes less anxious about failing to keep pace with his fellow students.

A pupil can take advantage of the strengths inherent in his style of learning to balance his weaknesses. For example, consider the pupil who has to learn to read, although his learning style is physical rather than visual.

In order to teach reading to a youngster for whom reading is stylistically uncongenial, the teacher may want to try role playing, which is related to a physical style of learning. The pupil is more likely to be able to read about something that he just role played.

By teaching reading in this way, the teacher is not helping the pupil develop a reading style; he is helping the pupil develop a reading skill.

In a sense, the teacher is overcoming the pupil's difficulty with reading by making use of the pupil's strength, whether it be physical, aural, or whatever.

The challenge to every teacher is first how to identify the learning strengths in his pupils and then how to utilize them to overcome weaknesses. This is the central problem in the strategy of style.

Chapter 6

MOTIVATION AND DISCIPLINE

THE problem of motivation is paramount in many secondary-school classes. It seems strange that teachers should neglect the motivational aspects of teaching, but evidently they do, and as a result convince themselves that their pupils cannot learn. Some teachers seem to ignore pupil interest entirely, and others put their faith in methods that inhibit rather than encourage learning. Their classes seem to be completely irrelevant to their pupils' lives. Unmotivated pupils are liable to be bored, disinterested, and unruly. Therefore, it seems important that teachers try to create an atmosphere favorable to learning. To do this, they can emphasize the positive, appeal to pupil interests, show the value of their subject matter to the pupils, and provide clear, tempting, reasonable assignments. Although there is no royal road to learning, there is no reason why it should be completely frustrating. Let us make learning attractive. Motivation is not only the key to learning, it is also the key to good discipline.

Discipline is by far the greatest bugbear the beginning teacher must face. And truly it does present a difficult problem to both experienced and beginning teachers.

Writers do not all agree on just what discipline is or how to maintain it, but they do all agree that it is essential. If learning in schools is to be effective, classes must be orderly. The teacher must be in control at all times. This does not mean he must rule the class with a hand of iron, whether clothed in a velvet glove or not. Neither does it mean that the class must always be still as a grave. It does mean that the class should always be moving methodically toward the teacher's goals under the teacher's guidance in an atmosphere congenial to desirable learning. For this purpose the class will be most successful if it is permissive, that is, free enough from fear to allow pupils to think independently.

This is not the same as laissez-faire. Pupils should never be free to follow their every whim. Even when they are given much freedom, their freedom must be limited to activities compatible with the goals of the lesson or unit.

To establish and maintain discipline is difficult, but to tell one how to do it is even more difficult. The strategies and tactics that are effective in one situation may not be at all effective in another. Basically, however, the problem of discipline is a problem of motivation and the establishment of values and standards of behavior. Active, interesting classes are likely to elicit good behavior; enthusiastic pupils, convinced of the essential personal worth of their classes, are seldom behavior problems. Maintaining control in boring classes is likely to be more of a problem. Nevertheless, pupils should learn to be well behaved in class, no matter how much they dislike it. If one wishes to get on, one's behavior must conform fairly well to the norms set for the groups in which one lives, whether one likes it or not. Pupils must learn this simple fact; learning it is part of their discipline.

The following selections should help the reader establish and maintain classroom discipline. They do not, however, give prescriptions for dealing with particular situations. As we have said before, strategies and tactics to be used in particular situations need to be selected in view of the pupils, teachers, goals, contents, and other ingredients of each particular situation. The ability to select the proper tactic for a specific situation comes largely from experience. Nevertheless, the selections do provide valuable guidelines or principles for the beginner to follow. The key to good discipline is well-motivated, worthwhile classes that prevent disciplinary incidents from occurring.

CLUES TO POSITIVE TEACHING

Maurice E. Schmid *

In the long run, a positive, permissive atmosphere will be more effective than a negative, repressive one in motivating pupils. This excerpt from Schmid's excellent guide, prepared for use in the Saint Paul schools in Minnesota, points out ways in which the teacher can foster this positive atmosphere.

THE TEACHER AND MOTIVATION

When an experienced teacher is faced with a child at the back of the room who apparently doesn't learn and doesn't want to learn, he calls upon his knowledge of human behavior and his experience to motivate the child.

At the outset, he knows from experience only that the child does not learn or participate. He realizes, however, that such a child is not necessarily inferior. Observation of several such nonmotivated youngsters has shown him that they come from all ability groups from the lowest to the highest.

* From *Clues to Positive Teaching*, Curriculum Bulletin No. 65, revised (Saint Paul, Minn.: The Saint Paul Public Schools, 1957), pp. 4–9; 26–30. Reprinted by permission of Kenneth Koch, Supervisor Secondary Curriculum.

Wise teachers consciously select a combination of devices which may change the behavioral pattern. The devices build on a desire to learn for the "intrinsic" value of learning itself or on a desire to achieve some "extrinsic" award. Proper diagnosis of problems allows a selection of a combination of techniques, *intrinisc and extrinsic*, which can, over a period of time, change a pattern of inertness to one of successful achievement.

More and more, experienced teachers have found that success is a propellant for achievement. They know that teachers who "accent the positive" in recognizing the basic need of each child for status, security, and a feeling of accomplishment are working effectively to change the unmotivated child into a well-motivated adult.

Although other considerations are always present, the need for adequate motivation at all levels of ability still remains the central problem for teachers. The following re-examination of motivation techniques suggested by some St. Paul teachers may inspire new efforts or renewed efforts to help non-achievers of all ability levels.

Successful teachers realize that motivation must fit the individuals being motivated and at the same time be consistent with the personality of the motivator. Some pupils lack motivation. Some respond positively to methods that do not stimulate others.

The professional teacher uses methods which work, that is, methods which change or modify learning conditions so that the individual learner profits from his experiences. Not all teachers succeed with the same methods. Each one does things which work for him without pointing to a single approach as being "good" *per se* and its theoretical opposite as "bad" *per se*.

The practitioner who faces thirty or more individuals within the confines of a classroom must know the individual students if he is to do his best. He learns about them from their files in the counselor's office and from their performance in the classroom. He may have them talk about their ambitions and write autobiographies.

The important subtleties of the individual personality may not be readily or immediately noticeable. The observant teacher watches for such things as special reading problems, areas of disinterest, and the like. Since a teacher can see only the gross aspects of personality and behavior, he relies on broad principles in the initial meetings of a class,

He combines common sense with a knowledge of general behavioral patterns. He knows, for instance, that:

1. Each child needs recognition and a feeling of personal worth and competency. An educational enterprise that immediately satisfies these needs will have stronger appeal than one purported to satisfy future needs.
2. The student needs to know where he is in his work, where he can go, and what his progress is toward his goal.
3. The student needs incentives aside from the intrinsic value of the work. He expects grades, praise, and reproof in judicious combination.

4. Students expect their teacher to reveal leadership.
5. Students expect a teacher to act with an understanding of their behavior.
6. Children respond to a quiet authority based on reasonableness which they can respect without fear. Youngsters want to know what they can't do.
7. Pupils expect and want a classroom that is quiet enough for them to work without distraction when the work at hand demands it. The teacher should deal fairly with individuals who evade the accepted rules of school behavior.
8. Children respond to a teacher who gives status to their efforts and helps them see the importance of what they are doing. A teacher contributes to a feeling of value when he openly attempts to capture the imagination of a class by using devices which excite positive reactions.
9. Students appreciate quick, regular measurements of progress which show their growth. They derive immediate satisfaction from learning things that will help them fulfill their needs as humans. They benefit from comparing measurements of success with their peers. However, all students should be given opportunity to achieve in terms of their own capabilities aside from competition with their peers.

The teacher uses his knowledge of human behavior to advance his class toward an educational goal. He knows, however, that with thirty or more students in a class, he will not be able to "know" each individual immediately. Therefore, while guiding the group toward its goal, he deals with problems involving motivation for the whole group, with the reservation that he will diagnose and treat individuals as the situation permits. He realizes that it may be some time, often through the first report period, before he can evaluate each student's progress and achievement.

Even though he works with large groups, the sincere teacher plans for the class and gives his subject meaningful content by using those methods which he has found he can use most effectively.

A successful teacher finds that a social history of students can be helpful in diagnosing individual motivational problems. By making a social history similar to the one used in school records, he has a ready classroom memorandum on each student. Such a record enables a teacher to know the members of a class more quickly. The act of "telling all" seems to build a good teacher-pupil relationship and makes individuals more receptive to suggestions for improvement.

While diagnosing and identifying individual problems, he keeps in mind the following considerations:

1. Individual assignments establish responsibility. They should allow enough latitude in choice to reflect individual interest and talent.
2. Class assignments should be designed so they can be completed with-

out frustration. The wise teacher sets a high goal, but makes sufficient allowance for individual attainment.

3. Tests frequently encourages progress toward a goal. The teacher should hold out hope of improvement to those who perform unsuccessfully.

4. A syllabus or study guide provides assurance that students are on their way to a common worthwhile goal.

5. Students are motivated by units which relate vocational goals to successful work in school. Such units should be used in the ninth grade and follow through high school.

6. A problem approach excites action if care is taken to make the problem real and significant. A good problem calls upon the student's imagination and creative abilities.

7. "Talent finding" may help individuals who are otherwise unresponsive to the school situation. For example, an appearance before the class or in an assembly may provide recognition. Individuals may become increasingly responsive because they wish to fulfill the obligation of the new role among their peers.

8. A unit on effective study and reading in the early part of the year may prove that the learning process can be enjoyable. Pleasure in learning provides a vehicle for long-time motivation.

9. Students are challenged to make adult responses when they are allowed to assume adult responsibilities for planning school handbooks, TV shows, etc.

10. Individual conferences help to determine and establish the needs, wants, and attitudes of individuals. The mere definition of problems provides security which opens up areas for motivation.

11. Most students try to identify themselves with at least one teacher who is a friend and a person of status. The experienced teacher is alert to students who seek such identification.

12. Pre-tests often determine quickly what the student doesn't know. They afford a stimulant to the natural or latent curiosity of the individual. They are a challenge. A follow-up, showing the progress that an individual has made over his pre-test position, shows growth.

13. A change of plans or methods within the overall framework of a planned unit can provide stimulation to the group and overcome what may seem to be a predictable pattern of monotony.

14. The narrowing of attention and the consequent elimination of distractions through the use of devices that create a focal point of stimulation for the group set the stage for learning. The media, the means, and the learning itself provide the propulsion. Visual materials presented at the proper time bear impact.

Even though the motivation of students is one of the most complex tasks confronting teachers, a concerted and practical approach which takes into consideration school, community, student, and teacher relations, will largely overcome a multitude of individual and group problems. Basically, good motivation comes when the real needs are being met—the need for security, for status, for approval, for new ideas and new activities, for growth toward valued goals, etc.

THE TEACHER AND SCHOOL MORALE

Experienced teachers like to teach in schools which have "spirit" or high morale, because they know that students in such schools are alert to their academic responsibilities, are alive to extracurricular events, are alert to their community's responsibilities, and react positively to the challenges in their lives. Student morale is characterized by strong inner motivation.

School morale involves many factors not directly related to classroom teaching, such as community mores and educational values; an up-to-date school plant; high faculty morale and unity of educational purpose; and a feeling on the part of students, parents, and teachers for the importance of the educational program. Alert teachers assist in initiating and maintaining high morale in a school.

Such teachers know that strong, lively leadership among teachers and students is necessary to maintain good morale. They provide good leadership in their classrooms by using positive motivational procedures. They encourage a high sense of achievement from participation in curricular and extracurricular activities.

Procedures that some teachers find helpful in creating a unity of purpose are given below:

1. Giving clear, short-range goals which relate specific assignments to long-range goals is effective. Such goals serve to stimulate an interest in the scholastic purpose of a class. Some teachers relate assignments to aims by regular discussion and by an overall outline of the course which keeps the objectives constantly in mind.
2. Assigning projects which invite individual research is often helpful. Such projects encourage originality and creativity within the framework of the subject matter. Individualizing instruction is the best way to assure individual success in subject matter and pride in accomplishment.
3. Students should be allowed to participate, when it is practicable, in setting class standards of behavior and performance. Through such participation, students gain insight into the problems of leadership. Teachers know that student leaders who are academically inclined can do much to set the "tone" of a school.
4. Placing explicit value on contributions to problems under study is often effective. It emphasizes a feeling of pride in the efforts and achievements of others in the class.
5. Insisting on the observance of the amenities of courtesy and behavior, within sensible limits, is important. When done with regard for the feelings of pupils, such insistence dignifies the classroom as a place where sincere effort is put forth to achieve valuable personal and social goals.

Practical teachers know, also, that intellectually oriented extracurricular activities focus students' attention on immediate, attainable, satisfying experiences in scholastic activities. Students are proud to be identified with a school which has a good record of participation in recognized extracurricular activities.

Academic extracurricular activities extend a school's academic curriculum in the same way that organized sports extend the physical education program. Speech, drama, debate, discussion, journalism, newspaper, yearbook, creative writing and library club may give impetus to specific skills in language arts. They allow students to follow individual interests. Choir, operetta, band, and concerts may extend general music into a specific activity. Science and art clubs may allow students to put skills to meaningful use. Student councils may vitalize the executive and legislative branches of government for social studies students.

Successful teachers who serve as advisers contribute to the intellectual atmosphere of their schools by making activities alive. They encourage the alert and interested student by developing real student leadership among participants, by insuring the success of projects undertaken, and by making all students in school aware of the aims and goals of the activity.

Students can identify themselves with a "going" activity more easily than with one that is merely a school service project. Successful advisers, therefore, emphasize the personal satisfactions and benefits to be gained from participation with others in the pursuit of knowledge.

Teachers who do not participate actively in such extracurricular projects make their own jobs easier by relating classroom work to such projects whenever possible. They do this by using students who are in certain activities for special tasks and responsibilities.

1. They use speech students to prepare and deliver special reports.
2. They use drama students to dramatize stories, plays or historical events.
3. They use debate and discussion students to present "for and against" arguments on public questions.
4. They use journalism students to prepare written reports.
5. They use newspaper or journalism students to conduct interviews or give reviews of books and plays.
6. They use music students to illustrate the relationship between art forms and the history of music.
7. They use library club members as research assistants.
8. They use science and art students as resource assistants in specific problems.
9. They use student council members to establish, maintain, and improve school policy.

Successful teachers also encourage participation in extracurriculur activities in several ways because they know that students who participate are the easiest to motivate in class. They encourage this participation in many ways:

1. They seek out the persons who can profit from participation. Quite often a talented, unmotivated youngster will "find himself" in some activity.
2. They give regular support to extracurricular activities to set an example of participation.
3. They point out the exploratory aspect of extracurricular activities in relation to careers.
4. They emphasize the intellectual and cultural achievements and awards of those who participate.
5. They attend public performances of school organizations and make a point of congratulating performers.
6. They point out the leadership training possibilities of activities. Such teachers make it plain that participating in decisions is leadership even though the students do not become officers.

Professional teachers know that constructive, positive teachers' attitudes and methods play an important part in building pride in scholastic achievement. They accept, therefore, a major responsibility to work with other teachers and administrators in enlarging and vitalizing the total school program, curricular and extracurricular.

Such teachers realize that they can interpret to others on committees the psychological needs and educational motives of the children in their classrooms. School and city-wide committees rely, to a large extent, on teacher opinions and observations in making curricular and extracurricular changes meet realistic student, community, and school needs. They gladly contribute their findings because they know that a comprehensive curriculum can do much to give a school unity and seriousness of purpose.

When all school resources are brought to bear on school morale, and each person in a building accepts his responsibility toward the goal, the resulting school atmosphere is one in which each student can achieve a feeling of growth toward his own educational objective.

IN PRAISE OF PRAISE

Paul B. Diederich *

Many teachers seem to think that their principal role is to find mistakes and correct them. Yet reward is a superb motivation, and praise can be

* From *NEA Journal*, Vol. 52 (Washington, D.C.: National Education Association, September 1963), pp. 58–59. Reprinted by permission of the *NEA Journal*.

the best reward of all. Pupils need encouragement. Too often, emphasis on correcting faults causes discouragement. Whenever possible, it seems that the wise policy, even in correcting themes and papers, is to accentuate the positive.

The average English paper corrected by the average English teacher looks as though it had been trampled on with cleated boots and has about the same effect on the student. I realize that some good-hearted teachers believe that this savagery is necessary, just as "practical schoolmen" a hundred years ago knew for certain that the only way to teach a boy Latin was to whip him.

I believe that many English teachers have a false theory about how to get rid of those pesky little errors that disfigure most student writing. They seem to think that drowning them in red ink will do away with them.

The only trouble with this approach is that it doesn't seem to work. The results of a recent series of grammar and usage tests given each level of college preparatory students in one of the oldest public high schools on the Eastern seaboard indicated that errors were being eliminated at the rate of about 2 percent a year. Chances are these errors would probably have declined at about this rate if English teachers had ignored them.

I am strongly tempted to believe, although I have no way of proving it, that all this outpouring of red ink not only does no good but positive harm. Its most common effect is to make the majority of students hate and fear writing. So far as they can see, they have never done anything on paper that anybody thought was good. No matter how hard they try, every paper they hand in gets slapped down for something or other.

The art of the teacher—at its best—is the reinforcement of good things. I am reminded of an experience from my own college days. I had one of the original "theme-a-day" courses at Harvard, taught at that time by Professor Hurlbut. So far as I can remember, he practically never said anything bad about our papers. About two or three times in an average paper we did something that was worthy of praise. We usually knew it, and his comment invariably indicated that he knew it, too. The space between these high points in our papers was filled with the usual student bilge, which he never honored with a comment. Whenever he said nothing, we knew that the verdict was "undistinguished" but that he was too much of a gentleman to say so.

About all Professor Hurlbut ever did in class was to read papers that he regarded as unusually good, without telling us who had written them. We sat there gasping, wishing that we had written them ourselves. He seldom stopped to say what was good about these papers. We either knew it, or his voice told us. In rare cases he might ask, "Now what was particularly good about that?"

I cannot remember a single instance in which he ever asked what was bad about a paper. For him to express dispraise was as rare as for him to lose his temper—which was almost inconceivable.

I believe that a student knows when he has handed in something above his usual standard and that he waits hungrily for a brief comment in the margin to show him that the teacher is aware of it, too. To my mind, these are the only comments that ever do any student any good.

Up to this point, I must have given readers the impression that there is no place whatever for brutality in the treatment of student writing. Actually, there is a place for it, when it is used in the following way: Duplicate and pass out to your class one student paper on each assignment. Use an anonymous paper from a different class, so that the students who criticize it may be sure that the writer will not be present to have his feelings hurt.

Have the students study this paper as homework, grade it, and mark it up with every sort of criticism and suggestion for improvement. Next day in class, let them argue over their grades and suggestions.

During this session everything bad that can be said about a paper ought to be said, and you may count on the students to say it. You may even have to defend the paper against an unjustified attack.

Since these sessions are an exercise in criticism, I think the sample papers should be of all kinds: good, bad, and indifferent. Some teachers balk at this idea, holding that students should never see an example of admittedly poor writing lest it corrupt them. I answer them by pointing out that the way students write is the result of hearing the language used imperfectly sixteen hours a day, every day of their lives. One more instance of imperfect language, recognized as such, and followed up by devastating criticism, is not going to corrupt them more than they have been corrupted already.

I believe that student papers should be dealt with something like this:

Find in each paper at least one thing, and preferably two or three things, that the student has done well, or better than before. Then, if you must, find one thing, and preferably not more than one thing, that he should try to improve in his next paper. Whenever possible make this a suggestion, not a prescription.

Learning one new thing per paper is certainly more than most students learn at present. As for the other ninety-nine errors that disfigure the paper and disgrace the school, simply ignore them. If you mark them all, or even half of them, the student learns nothing; he only advances one step further toward a settled conviction that he can't write and there is no use trying.

If you pursue my suggested policy, a few parents may bring student themes to school, point angrily to errors they recognize, and ask why they were overlooked. You can easily work out of this jam by indicating a few of the flaws that the parent has overlooked, telling him that no student could possibly learn that much about writing from a single paper, and pointing out that you have carefully selected one weakness for the student to try to eliminate in his next paper.

If a student concentrates on one error at a time, progress is possible; if he tries to overcome all his weaknesses at once, he will only be overwhelmed. I do not know where the scientific truth lies, but I have more faith in the value of a few appreciative comments than in any amount or kind of correction.

HOW *NOT* TO MAKE AN ASSIGNMENT

William Van Til *

The assignment sets the direction and scope of the pupils' task. Good assignments clearly map out worthwhile learning activities that will lead the pupils to the instructional goals set by the teacher. Poor assignments, on the other hand, often lead to ineffectual studying and poorly done work. Sometimes by giving greater care to his assignments and assignment procedures, a teacher can avoid the frustrations of poorly done work and the disciplinary problems that result from ill prepared, unmotivated pupils.

Mrs. Jones was worried. Through press, magazine, radio, and television, the message screamed at her: Americans have low intellectual standards. Americans are soft and undisciplined. Americans don't strive for excellence. The flabby American. The materialistic American. The American who is addicted to cars and TV.

Maybe, thought Mrs. Jones, I am one of Them, the permissive, sentimental, soft teachers who are not developing trained minds. So she doubled her assignments. Not ten questions a night in the history workbook; twenty questions now. Not fifteen pages of reading a night in the textbook; thirty pages now. Nobody can blame *me* if we don't raise our intellectual level, thought Mrs. Jones.

Gregory looked at the little notebook in which day after day he carefully copied each assignment for each of his five major courses. He made a number of rapid calculations. No matter how he calculated, it looked like about five hours of homework for tonight. Last night it had been four, and the night before, five.

It's not that I mind work, Gregory told himself. I wouldn't have gotten

* From *NEA Journal*, Vol. 53 (Washington, D.C.: National Education Association, October 1964), pp. 49–51. Reprinted by permission of the *NEA Journal* and the author.

the award as leading student of the junior class if I didn't work. It's just that this work is so stupid, useless, futile. I get the central idea of a chapter the first time I read it. Why does this workbook repeat the idea over and over again in different contexts? If I could only get on to something new, instead of repeating what I already know. If I only had time to read books I want to read. Or do something important.

The phone rang. Gregory talked briefly, then decided, "It's a good idea, but I just don't have the time. Of course I like the idea of visiting patients in the mental hospital and trying to help them take an interest in things, but I just can't do it. Look, I have even given up listening to the *American Issues* panel on Thursdays at 10:00. These days I usually finish up after 11:00. Sometimes I let the movie on a late show drug me for half an hour and then I drag off to bed."

I give up, thought Tom. I know when I'm licked and this is it. It's too hard. Most of all, it's too much. If I were a brain like Gregory—but I'm not. I'm stupid. I'd better find me a way out. Better to walk out than to be kicked out. I haven't got it made and I never will.

Maybe if I took to staying away from school, Mom and Pop would get the idea. I could find a job. I wouldn't get the Navy Yard job because that calls for high school graduation. But even if I am stupid, I could do something. If they give me half a chance, I'll quit so fast it will make them dizzy.

MISS SMITH AND THE LIBRARY

"Get the name right," said Miss Smith. "Newman, James R. Newman. And get the title right. *The World of Mathematics*. Volume I. The first three chapters by Monday."

She said almost the same thing in the second period and again in the fourth period.

The public librarian, Mary Johnson, even though she knew it was no use, said again, "Can't you get it at your school library?"

"No, ma'am," said Virginia. "The school's only got one copy of the set and the kids are waist-deep waiting for that one. Any chance your copy will be returned this weekend?"

"It's out to an adult," said Mary Johnson. "If I'd known that there was going to be a run on it, I might have been able to get another set from the Midvale library."

"Do you think they'd have it?" asked Virginia hopefully. "Let me find out," said Mary Johnson. She made a brief call, then reported to Virginia, "They *do* have a copy, but there are four students over there now trying to get a chance to read it."

"Thanks," said Virginia. "I'll see if Mom will drive me over."

Mary Johnson sighed, and turned back to the growing line at the check-out counter. When she looked up a little later, she saw three worried-looking youngsters peering into the N drawer of the card catalogue. Mary Johnson sighed again and engaged in a few private thoughts about teachers and assignments.

MR. PACKARD AND CREATIVITY

"Write as many pages as you want, as long as it's about literature," said Mr. Packard. Most of the students looked blank; a few wrote down his words verbatim. "The meaning and use of literature. Any way you want to do it or say it. This gives you a lot of room for creativity and"—he paused—"independent thought." That's what we want, isn't it? Independent thought? Through the open assignment?

The bell rang, marking the end of the class. The voices rose from the student Tower of Babel.

"I don't get it. What does he mean, 'the use of literature'?"

"What'll you do?"

"I don't know how to get at it."

"Make a bluff; that's what I'm gonna do."

"Vague it up; put in some high-sounding phrases; you'd probably get away with it. . . ."

Mr. Packard read the compositions and he sighed. "Literature has a great use in that it inspires people to go to fine things and teaches them to appreciate the really good in life. Literature is really helpful to us all." They seemed so general. Whatever was happening to students' creativity? What the class seemed to lack was independent thinkers. But he hated to give them low grades; some of them were such nice youngsters. He kept on reading.

MISS AARON AND HARVARD

Miss Aaron was constructing her true-false exam in biology. Here was a good item; buried deep in a long paragraph, it might have escaped even the best masters of detail in the class.

It gets harder and harder to distinguish between the sheep and the goats, the washed and the unwashed, thought Miss Aaron. These are bright youngsters in this suburb, and nowadays an unprecedented 92 percent are going to college. A teacher really has to work to find details which they haven't memorized. Ah, I've found another good one. Here's a *really* obscure bone in a footnote!

"But you *do* want to get into Harvard, Richard, don't you?"

"I'm certainly going to try," said Richard, "My folks are set on it and I don't want to let them down."

"Then," said Miss Aaron decisively, "you will have to work harder on mastery of details. After all, you'll never be accepted by Harvard if you haven't a well-stocked mind." She liked the phrase *well-stocked mind* and often used it.

"I get the central ideas," said Richard, "and the facts that support them. It's remembering all those tiny details—like that bone mentioned in the footnote—that gives me trouble. That bone seemed to me to be a mere fact. It didn't seem to be related to the main ideas in the summary."

"There is nothing mere about a fact, Richard," said Miss Aaron. "A well-stocked mind holds many details. If you are going to study at Harvard, Richard, you must. . . ."

MEANWHILE, BACK AT HARVARD . . .

At Harvard University, William G. Perry, Jr., the director of the Bureau of Study Counsel, reported to the faculty on a twenty-year experiment in teaching Harvard students to read better. He said: "Year by year it has become more apparent that what the students lack is not mechanical skills but flexibility and purpose in the use of them. . . . What they seem to do with almost any kind of reading is to open the book and read from word to word, having in advance abandoned all responsibility in regard to the purpose of the reading to those who had made the assignment."

Mr. Perry described a study by his Bureau which had assigned 1,500 Harvard and Radcliffe freshmen a chapter from a history book, thirty pages of detailed material.

". . . The chapter in question is an admirable piece of exposition, but like many admirable chapters it makes no initial statement of its aims, and it takes a little while to get going. And as a consequence, the reader who begins at the beginning with the Battle of Hastings and reads word by word is likely to find himself at page three hopelessly bogged down. . . . What we were interested to determine was how many students in the face of this burden of detail, the purpose of which was not clear, would have the moral courage— or should we call it the immoral courage—to pull themselves out and look at the ending of the chapter."

Mr. Perry went on to report that "their capacity to answer multiple choice questions on detail was impressive."

But, he continued, "out of these 1,500 of the finest freshman readers in the country only 150 even made a claim to have taken a look ahead during twenty minutes of struggle with the chapter. And the vast majority of these seemed to have looked ahead only to determine how long the assignment was.

"We asked anyone who could do so to write a short statement about what the chapter was all about. The number who were able to tell us, in terms that had something to do with the growth of institutions, was just one in a hundred—fifteen.

"As a demonstration of obedient purposelessness in the reading of 99 percent of freshmen we found this impressive. . . .

"After twelve years of reading homework assignments in school they had all settled into the habit of leaving the point to someone else. . . ."

OUR MISGUIDED ASSIGNMENT MAKERS

Let us consider more closely our four examples of how not to make an assignment.

Mrs. Jones, who wants desperately to help the nation, should look more carefully at individuals and more deeply at what is needed for the national welfare. In addition, Mrs. Jones needs to think about the relationship between her subject (history) and her supposed goal (citizenship).

She will best help Gregory and best foster intellectual leadership in the nation if she gives assignments which challenge Gregory's thought, not merely test his endurance. She will best help Tom and best contribute to the making of a skilled worker if her individualized assignments recognize the limitations of Tom's natural ability.

The principal in Mrs. Jones' school might well become concerned about coordination of assignments, total volume of homework, and staggering of assigned work. Communication among teachers is a first step. Who is assigning what, when?

Miss Smith, who assigned the outside reading in the hard-to-find mathematics volume, could improve her working relationships with the library world. She might have taken the school librarian and the public librarian into her confidence early through long-range planning.

At the very least, she might have told the school librarian and called the public librarian concerning her assignment on the day she decided upon it. She might have thought of the inconveniences and frustrations ahead for conscientious students, as well as the built-in alibis for failure to report which she was providing for less-motivated students. Miss Smith meant well but good intentions must be accompanied by good working relationships with those who are responsible for source materials.

Mr. Packard, sponsor of the vague assignment, will never foster the creativity and independent thought he prizes until he sets clearer bounds and limits for the students and for himself. Permissiveness-run-wild too often terminates in dead ends. Possibly the students would benefit from a course in study skills. Maybe Mr. Packard would, too.

Miss Aaron, our hunter for details, is another invention of the author. But Mr. Perry is no figment of the imagination. No doubt he is busy at Harvard today attempting to undo what Miss Aaron hath wrought.

In the name of "what Harvard wants," our Miss Aaron is teaching what Harvard and the university world in general do not want. Miss Aaron stresses reading for small details and is uninterested in ideas, relationships, and concepts. Mr. Perry and his counterparts across the nation are trying to help students see details in perspective and to aim for mastery of meanings, purposes, and relationships.

If misguided Miss Aaron prevails, Richard may give up his present attempt to see the world whole and settle for details. Ironically, he may then end up in remedial work directed by Mr. Perry.

A NEW LOOK AT CLASSROOM DISCIPLINE

David P. Ausubel *

Standards of behavior must be maintained if pupils are to be taught effectively in schools. Sometimes beginning teachers forget this truism. On occasion, they seem to feel that to demand pupils to live up to certain standards will warp the psyches of their boys and girls. This belief is a distortion of the ideal of the democratic or permissive classroom. Democracy in the classroom does not condone licence in pupil behavior. In democratic classes as in other democracies, miscreants suffer from the results of their misdeeds, misbehavior results in punishment, and defiers of group standards are ostracized. Although the editor hopes that there is more to discipline than just "the imposition of external standards and controls on individual conduct" and cannot agree with the equating of permissiveness and laissez-faire, he believes that Ausubel's position of democratic discipline is well taken. What Ausubel calls democratic discipline has been called permissiveness or permissive discipline in this book. What Ausubel calls permissiveness, this book speaks of as laissez-faire or licence. The first is desirable, the second bad. In spite of the disagreement about terms, there is complete agreement concerning the principles and methods involved.

A few years ago, in one of our better New England high schools, two members of the school's counseling staff happened to be walking in the building when their attention was drawn to sounds of a disturbance in an adjoining corridor. Investigating further, they found that two boys, surrounded by a knot of curious onlookers, were engaged in an all-out switchblade fight. One counselor quickly whispered to the other, "We'd better break this up in a hurry before there's bloodshed." The latter replied heatedly, "For heaven's sake leave them alone or you'll ruin everything! Do you want the kids to think we are *disciplinarians?*" Fortunately, however, the native common sense of the first counselor prevailed over the doctrinaire permissiveness of his colleague, and a near-tragedy was averted.

* From *Phi Delta Kappan*, Vol. 43 (Bloomington, Ind.: Phi Delta Kappa, October 1961), pp. 25–30. Reprinted by permission of the publisher.

This true story is admittedly a bit extreme and unrepresentative of disciplinary attitudes in American public schools. Nevertheless, somewhat less extreme versions occur frequently enough to suggest that American teachers are more confused and disturbed about matters of discipline today than at any previous time in the history of our public school system.

It is true that superficial observation does not support this conclusion. On the surface, practically everything *appears* the same as it was ten years ago when, except in the so-called "Blackboard Jungles," these same teachers seemed supremely confident that the ideal of democratic discipline had been achieved in the American classroom. Substantially the same disciplinary philosophy is still preached in our teachers colleges; and teachers, by and large, still practice the same kind of discipline they practiced a decade ago.

To be sure, there is still an appreciable gap between the theory of discipline as taught in colleges of education and discipline as it is actually conceived and practiced in the schools. For example, in a recent survey conducted by the National Education Association, 72 per cent of the responding classroom teachers favored the judicious use of corporal punishment in the elementary school. But the gap is no greater now than it has ever been. In everyday disciplinary practice, American teachers have never gone along completely with the more extreme ideas of educational theorists. Elementary and high-school teachers, after all, have to be realistic in handling problems of discipline because they encounter them daily in doing their jobs. Unlike professors of education, who rarely if ever have to cope with disciplinary problems in the classroom, they can ill afford to be starry-eyed about these matters.

Why then should teachers be suddenly confused and disturbed about issues of discipline? Closer scrutiny reveals that everything is not *really* the same as it used to be. One important factor in the situation has undergone significant change: Although educational theory in the field of classroom discipline has remained virtually unchanged over the past two decades, the pendulum of public opinion in recent years has been swinging further and further away from the formerly fashionable cult of permissiveness. As a result, a growing estrangement has arisen between the general public, on the one hand, and educational and psychological theorists on the other—with the classroom teacher and the rank-and-file school administrator caught squarely in the middle. Teachers, of course, were also in the middle throughout the entire period of approximately 1935–1955, when American classroom discipline underwent a process of extensive democratization. But this middle position was decidedly more comfortable then than it is now, because all three groups—educational theorists, teachers, and the public at large—were moving toward the same culturally desirable goal of a less authoritarian classroom climate.

It is true that these three groups were moving toward this goal at quite different rates. Permissiveness, nondirective guidance, and the cults of extroversion, conformity, and social adjustment were much more extreme among child-centered educators, client-centered counselors, and psychoanalytically trained child study experts than among American parents and teachers generally. By 1955, however, the entirely laudable objective of more democratic pupil-teacher relationships had been reached, and perhaps overreached. Public opinion began moving away from permissiveness, but educational and psychological theorists and professors of education, with few exceptions, stood their ground tenaciously. The same relatively extreme permissive doctrines of discipline are still dominant in teachers colleges, even though educational philosophy in the post-Sputnik era has generally become less permissive in most other areas, such as curriculum.

Now, it was one thing for teachers to swim in the middle of two streams moving in the same historically necessary direction, and to enjoy the approbation of both the general public and of their own professional leaders. It is quite another for them to be caught between two opposing streams, and to be faced with the problem of having to choose between the spirit of the times, on the one hand, and the historically obsolete ideological extremism of their former professors on the other.

HISTORICAL AND CULTURAL PERSPECTIVE

Before examining how particular concepts and practices of discipline have gone astray, it might be profitable first to view the problem in historical perspective within a broader cultural context. The revolution in classroom discipline that swept American schools between 1935 and 1955 was as necessary as it was inevitable. Teacher-pupil relationships had to be brought into closer alignment with the general spirit of adult egalitarianism in American society; and a more desirable balance had to be achieved between the actual dependence of children on adult direction and their realistic capacities for exercising self-direction and self-discipline. It was inevitable, of course, that we would go too far in redressing the balance—in overdoing the permissiveness and in cutting back adult control and guidance too drastically. Much more serious, however, were the deplorable consequences of de-emphasizing certain other traditional American values in the enthusiasm of democratizing adult-child relationships.

Thus, in stressing the inherent right of children to receive the consideration to which they are entitled, we have neglected the equally valid claims of age and maturity. In debunking superficial and unilateral forms of etiquette, we have lost sight of the importance of genuine courtesy in human relationships. And in attacking despotic and abusive adult rule, we have failed to cultivate appropriate respect for just and rightful authority.

By respect for age I do not mean uncritical veneration or ancestor worship, but simply the consideration that is due all human beings at any stage in the life cycle. Yet our cultural attitude toward middle-aged and elderly persons tends to be patronizing and slightly contemptuous. Because they quite understandably lack the exuberance and venturesomeness of youth, they are often cavalierly dismissed as "has-beens" or as bumbling, ineffectual fuddy-duddies.

Courtesy is another of our most valuable cultural assets that was overlooked in the frenzy of extending democracy to home and school. It is fashionable in many quarters—not only among the younger set—to regard good manners and the more subtle amenities of interpersonal relationships as hollow formalities. But even the highly stylized bowing ceremony of the Japanese is far from being an empty gesture. It symbolizes deep and culturally ingrained respect for the dignity of the individual and genuine concern for his pride and feelings. Although bowing is obviously incongruous with our modern way of life, concern for the pride, feelings, and dignity of every human being is one of our most cherished American values. Hence, since courtesy is basically an institutionalized set of rules designed to safeguard and implement this legitimate cultural concern, those who sneer at courtesy, whether they realize it or not, sneer at nothing less than human dignity.

Finally, our culture has tended to put authority figures in an anomalous and untenable position, particularly in the school environment. We have assigned them the necessary and often distasteful task of authority figures the world over, that is, to enforce certain basic standards of conduct; but in too many instances we have failed to give them the respect, the authority, and the protection commensurate with this responsibility. When they conscientiously attempt to apply without fear or favor the community approved sanctions for violating these standards, we accuse them of being punitive, vindictive, and authoritarian. School administrators, of course, are not above criticism and reproach when they use poor judgment or exceed their authority; but society has an obligation to protect them from disrespect and abuse for simply doing their duty and exercising their just and necessary disciplinary prerogatives. In our present cultural climate, therefore, it is small wonder that many principals and superintendents of schools are more concerned with courting general popularity than with enforcing desirable norms of pupil behavior.

THE BRIGHTER SIDE OF THE COIN

In pointing out some of the failings of our recent approach to discipline, I do not mean to detract in any way from our genuine accomplishments. The latter are extremely impressive when compared with disciplinary practices in many other countries. I recently had an opportunity to study secondary schools in New Zealand, an English-speaking welfare state of British origin with a pioneering tradition not unlike our own. School discipline in New Zealand high schools connotes explicit subjection to authority and implicit habits of obedience that are enforced by a very heavy-handed set of controls and punishments. It implies a very identifiable atmosphere of classroom control which the teacher maintains with much deliberate effort—in much the same sense that he strives to have his pupils understand and assimilate the subject-matter he teaches. For example, it is not uncommon for a New Zealand high-school teacher to begin the school year by exhibiting a cane to his class and announcing that he fully intends to use it on the first pupil who steps out of line.

By contrast, the American approach to discipline seems laudably incidental. Our teachers tend to feel that the cause of discipline is adequately served if pupils exercise sufficient self-control and observe a minimum set of rules with sufficient decorum to enable classroom work to proceed in an orderly, efficient manner. They do not, in other words, strive deliberately for discipline as an explicit goal in its own right. They assume instead that good discipline is *ordinarily* a natural by-product of interesting lessons and of a wholesome teacher-pupil relationship; that the vast majority of pupils respond positively to fair and kindly treatment; that respect for the teacher is a usual accompaniment of the latter's superior knowledge, experience, and status as a leader, and does not have to be reinforced by such artificial props and status symbols as differences in clothing, mode of address, and fear of the strap. Hence they treat adolescents as maturing young adults rather than as unruly children, and implicitly expect them to respond in kind—which they usually do. And it was a very gratifying experience to discover that despite the absence of strict authoritarian controls, American high-school students, on the whole, behave more decorously than their New Zealand counterparts—particularly when not under direct supervision.

SCIENCE OR OPINION?

Discipline today is much less a science than a matter of opinion. It not only shifts in response to various social, economic, and ideological factors, but also manifests all of the cyclical properties of fads and fashions. Objective scientific evidence about the relative merits of different types of discipline is extremely sparse. Indeed it is highly questionable to what extent valid objective data are obtainable and even relevant in matters of discipline. Whether or not particular disciplinary practices are appropriate depends, in the first place, on the particular values, institutions, and kinds of personal relationships prevailing in a given culture; and, second, any definitive empirical test of appropriateness would have to be conducted over such an extended period of time that its conclusions would tend to be rendered obsolete by intervening changes in significant social conditions. For all practical purposes, therefore, the choice of disciplinary policy involves taking a rationally defensible and self-consistent position based on value preferences, on relevant considerations of child development, and on individual experience and judgment.

The fact that discipline cannot be placed on a largely scientific basis, however, does not mean that one position is as good as another or that no public policy whatsoever is warranted. Society is continually obliged to resolve issues of much greater moment with even less objective evidence on which to base a decision. Under the circumstances, all we can reasonably expect is greater humility and less dogmatism on the part of those engaged in formulating disciplinary policy. Thus, the most disturbing aspect of the entire problem is not the fact that there is precious little scientific evidence to support the disciplinary doctrines expounded in our colleges of education and educational journals and textbooks, but rather the ubiquitous tendency to represent purely personal opinions and biases as if they were the incontrovertibly established findings of scientific research.

THE DEFINITION AND FUNCTIONS OF DISCIPLINE

By discipline I mean the imposition of *external* standards and controls on individual conduct. Permissiveness, on the other hand, refers to the absence of such standards and controls. To be permissive is to "let alone," to adopt a *laissez-faire* policy. Authoritarianism is an excessive, arbitrary, and autocratic type of control which is diametrically opposite to permissiveness. Between the extremes of *laissez-faire* permissiveness and authoritarianism are many varieties and degrees of control. One of these, to be described in greater detail below, is democratic discipline.

Discipline is a universal cultural phenomenon which generally serves four important functions in the training of the young. First, it is necessary for socialization—for learning the standards of conduct that are approved and tolerated in any culture. Second, it is necessary for normal personality maturation—for acquiring such adult personality traits as dependability, self-reliance, self-control, persistence, and ability to tolerate frustration. These aspects of maturation do not occur spontaneously, but only in response to sustained social demands and expectations. Third, it is necessary for the internalization of moral standards and obligations or, in other words, for the development of conscience. Standards obviously cannot be internalized unless they also exist in external form; and even after they are effectively internalized, universal cultural experience suggests that external sanctions are still required to insure the stability of the social order. Lastly, discipline is necessary for children's emotional security. Without the guidance provided by unambiguous external controls, the young tend to feel bewildered and apprehensive. Too great a burden is placed on their own limited capacity for self-control.

DEMOCRATIC DISCIPLINE

The proponents of democratic classroom discipline believe in imposing the minimal degree of external control necessary for socialization, personality maturation, conscience development, and the emotional security of the child. Discipline and obedience are not regarded as ends in themselves but only as means to these latter ends. They are not striven for deliberately, but are expected to follow naturally in the wake of friendly and realistic teacher-pupil relationships. Explicit limits are not set routinely or as ways of showing "who is boss," but only as the need arises, i.e., when they are not implicitly understood or accepted by pupils.

Democratic discipline is as rational, nonarbitrary, and bilateral as possible. It provides explanations, permits discussion, and invites the participation of children in the setting of standards whenever they are qualified to do so. Above all, it implies respect for the dignity of the individual and avoids exaggerated emphasis on status differences and barriers between free communication. Hence it repudiates harsh, abusive, and vindictive forms of punishment, and the use of sarcasm, ridicule, and intimidation.

The aforementioned attributes of democratic classroom discipline are obviously appropriate in cultures such as ours where social relationships tend to be egalitarian. This type of discipline also becomes increasingly more feasible as children become older, more responsible, and more capable of understanding and formulating rules of conduct based on concepts of equity and reciprocal obligation. But contrary to what the extreme permissivists would have us believe, democratic school discipline does not imply freedom from all external constraints, standards, and direction, or freedom from discipline as an end in itself. And under no circumstances does it presuppose the eradication of all distinctions between pupil and teacher roles, or require that teachers abdicate responsibility for making the final decisions in the classroom.

DISTORTIONS OF DEMOCRATIC DISCIPLINE

Many educational theorists have misinterpreted and distorted the ideal of democratic discipline by equating it with an extreme form of permissiveness. These distortions have been dogmatically expressed in various psychologically unsound and unrealistic propositions that are considered sacrosanct in many teachers colleges. Fortunately, however, most classroom teachers have only accepted them for examination purposes—while still in training—and have discarded them in actual practice as thoroughly unworkable.

According to one widely held doctrine, only "positive" forms of discipline are constructive and democratic. It is asserted that children must only be guided by reward and approval; that reproof and punishment are authoritarian, repressive, and reactionary expressions of adult hostility which leave permanent emotional scars on children's personalities. What these theorists conveniently choose to ignore, however, is the fact that it is impossible for children to learn what is *not* approved and tolerated simply by generalizing in reverse from the approval they receive for behavior that *is* acceptable. Merely by rewarding honesty and good manners one cannot, for example, teach children that dishonesty and rudeness are socially unacceptable traits. Even adults are manifestly incapable of learning and respecting the limits of acceptable conduct unless the distinction between what is proscribed and approved is reinforced by punishment as well as by reward. Furthermore, there is good reason to believe that acknowledgement of wrong-doing and acceptance of punishment are part and parcel of learning moral accountability and developing a sound conscience. Few if any children are quite so fragile that they cannot take deserved reproof and punishment in stride.

A second widespread distortion of democratic discipline is reflected in the popular notion that there are no culpably misbehaving children in the classroom, but only culpably aggressive, unsympathetic, and punitive teachers. If children misbehave, according to this point of view, one can implicitly assume that they must have been provoked beyond endurance by repressive and authoritarian classroom discipline. Similarly, if they are disrespectful, then the teacher, by definition, must not have been deserving of respect. It is true, of course, that some pupil misconduct *is* instigated by harsh and abusive school discipline; but there are also innumerable reasons for out-of-bounds behavior that are completely independent of the teacher's attitudes and disciplinary practices. Pupils are also influenced by factors originating in the home, the neighborhood, the peer group, and the mass media. Some children are emotionally disturbed, others are brain-damaged, and still others are aggressive by temperament; and there are times when even the best-behaved children from the nicest homes develop an irresistible impulse—without any provocation whatsoever—to test the limits of a teacher's forebearance.

Both of the aforementioned distortions of classroom democracy are used to justify the commonly held belief among educators that pupils should not be reproved or punished for disorderly or discourteous conduct. I have, for example, observed classrooms where everybody talks at once; where pupils turn their backs on the teacher and engage in private conversation while the latter is endeavoring to instruct them; and where pupils verbally abuse teachers for exercising their rightful disciplinary prerogatives. Some educators contend that all of this is compatible with wholesome, democratic teacher-pupil relationships. Other educators deplore this type of pupil behavior but insist, nevertheless, that punishment is unwarranted under these circumstances. In the first place, they assert, reproof or punishment constitutes a "negative" and hence axiomatically undesirable approach to classroom management; and, secondly, the misbehavior would assuredly have never occurred to begin with, if the teacher's attitudes had been less autocratic or antagonistic. I have already answered the second group of educators, and to the first group I can only say that I am still sufficiently old-fashioned to believe that rudeness and unruliness are not normally desirable classroom behavior in any culture.

When such misconduct occurs, I believe pupils have to be unambiguously informed that it will not be tolerated and that any repetition of the same behavior will be punished. This action does not preclude in any way either an earnest attempt to discover why the misbehavior occurred or suitable preventive measures aimed at correcting the underlying causes. But, by the same token, the mere fact that a pupil has a valid psychological reason for misbehaving does not mean that he is thereby absolved from moral accountability or rendered no longer subject to punishment.

Still another related distortion of democratic discipline is reflected in the proposition that it is repressive and authoritarian to request pupils to apologize for discourteous behavior or offensive language. However, if we take seriously the idea that the dignity of the human being is important, we must be willing to protect it from affront; and apology is the most civilized and effective means mankind has yet evolved for accomplishing this goal. In a democratic society nobody is that important that he is above apologizing to those persons whom he wrongfully offends. Everybody's dignity is important —the teacher's as well as the pupil's. It is no less wrong for a pupil to abuse a teacher than for a teacher to abuse a pupil.

If apologies are to have any real significance in moral training, however, it is obvious that, even though they are explicitly requested, they must be made voluntarily; and they must be reflective of genuine appreciation of wrong-doing and of sincere regret and remorse. Purely formal and mechanical statements of apology made under coercion are less than worthless. Apologies are also without real ethical import unless their basis is reciprocal, i.e., unless it is fully understood that under comparable circumstances the teacher would be willing to apologize to his pupils.

A final distortion of democratic classroom discipline associated with the extreme child-centered approach to education is the notion that children are equipped in some mysterious fashion for knowing precisely what is best for them. "Scientific proof" of this proposition is adduced from the fact that nutrition is adequately maintained and existing deficiency conditions are spontaneously corrected when infants are permitted to select their own diet. If the child can successfully choose his diet, runs the argument, he must certainly know what is best for him in *all* areas, including curriculum and classroom management.

This doctrine, however, has even less face validity than the three other distorted concepts of school discipline. Because the human being is sensitive in early childhood to internal cues of physiological needs, we cannot conclude that he is similarly sensitive to complex intellectual and moral needs, or that he has sufficient experience, perspective, and judgment to make intelligent decisions in these latter areas. Even in the field of nutrition, self-selection is a reliable criterion of need only during early infancy. The current interests and opinions of immature pupils can hardly be considered reliable guideposts and adequate substitutes for seasoned judgment in designing a curriculum or in formulating rules of classroom behavior. Hence, while it is reasonable to consider the views of pupils in these matters, teachers and school administrators cannot abdicate their responsibility for making the final decisions.

WHAT NEEDS TO BE DONE

In seeking to correct these undesirable permissive distortions of classroom democracy, it would be foolhardy to return to the equally undesirable opposite extreme of authoritarianism that flourished in this country up to a quarter of a century ago, and still prevails in many Western nations. Democratic school discipline is still an appropriate and realistic goal for American education; hence there is no need to throw away the baby with the bath water. It is only necessary to discard the aforementioned permissivist doctrines masquerading under the banners of democracy and behavioral science, and to restore certain other traditional American values that have been neglected in the enthusiasm of extending democracy to home and school.

More specifically, we first have to clear up the semantic confusion. We should stop equating permissiveness with democratic discipline, and realistic adult control and guidance with authoritarianism. Permissiveness, by definition, is the absence of discipline, democratic or otherwise. We should cease instructing teachers that it is repressive and reactionary to reprove or punish pupils for misconduct, or to request them to apologize for offensive and discourteous behavior.

Second, we should stop misinterpreting what little reputable evidence we have about discipline, and refrain from misrepresenting our personal biases on the subject as the indisputably established findings of scientific research. The available evidence merely suggests that, in our type of cultural setting, authoritarian discipline has certain undesirable effects—*not* that the consequences of *laissez-faire* permissiveness are desirable. As a matter of fact, research studies show that the effects of extreme permissiveness are just as unwholesome as are those of authoritarianism. In the school situation a *laissez-faire* policy leads to confusion, insecurity, and competition for power among pupils. Assertive pupils tend to become aggressive and ruthless, whereas retiring pupils tend to withdraw further from classroom participation. The child who is handled too permissively at home tends to regard himself as a specially privileged person. He fails to learn the normative standards and expectations of society, to set realistic goals for himself, or to make reasonable demands on others. In his dealings with adults and other children he is domineering, aggressive, petulant, and capricious.

Third, we should stop making teachers feel guilty and personally responsible for all instances of misconduct and disrespect in the classroom. We do this whenever we take for granted, without any actual supporting evidence, that these behavior problems would never have arisen in the first place if the teachers involved were truly deserving of respect and had been administering genuinely wholesome and democratic discipline.

Finally, teachers colleges should terminate the prevailing conspiracy of silence they maintain about the existence of disciplinary problems in the public schools. Although discipline is the one aspect of teaching that the beginning teacher is most worried about, he receives little or no practical instruction in handling this problem. Colleges of education, as pointed out above, rationalize their inadequacies in this regard by pretending that disciplinary problems are relatively rare occurrences involving the disturbed child, or more typically the disturbed teacher. Due respect for the facts of life, however, suggests that prospective teachers today not only need to be taught more realistic propositions about the nature and purposes of democratic discipline, but also require adequately supervised, down-to-earth experience in coping with classroom discipline.

TIPS FOR THE BEGINNING TEACHER

Martha W. Hunt *

*Prevention of discipline problems is more important than remedial ac-
tion once a discipline problem has arisen. Most educational writers and
teachers in service agree. Here is a good set of tips from a classroom
teacher on how to keep your classes under control.*

May an old hand give a beginning teacher some tips about keeping classroom discipline? I have found these procedures helpful:

Learn names. Whenever possible, be familiar before your first class session
with the names of your students and with the pronunciation of each name.

Look over the permanent records. Foresight is better than hindsight. The
records will give you clues to students' hearing and vision defects or other
physical ailments, family relationships, and emotional disturbances which affect learning rates. IQ scores will give some indication of whether or not
students are working to capacity. If not, trouble will probably develop sooner
or later.

Check the classroom environment. Have the temperature and ventilation
as right as you can make them. Draw shades to cut out glare if necessary, but
be sure there are no dark corners. See that classroom furniture and accessories
are in order and that no seats are placed so that students have to face the
light.

Watch seating. Big students should not block the line of vision of smaller
students. Place students with defective vision or faulty hearing near you.

Plan the lesson. Be ready to use the first minute of class time. If you get
Johnny busy right away, he has no time to cook up interesting ideas that do
not fit into the class situation.

Learn symptoms of illness. Misconduct often has a physiological basis.
Learn the meaning of a flushed face, reddening and watering eyes, a skin rash.

Deal with individuals. Instead of having an entire class sit around marking
time while you reprimand one offender, arrange to have a private appointment with him outside class.

Practice marginal vision. You can learn to see out of the corners of your
eyes.

Mind your manners. Student behavior often reflects a teacher's good or
bad manners.

* From *NEA Journal*, Special Feature on Discipline (Washington, D.C.: National Education Association, September 1958), p. 7. Reprinted by permission of the *NEA Journal*
and the author.

Don't stay glued to your desk. Move about. Sit in the back of the room when class reports are being given—it accents student responsibility.

Use a bit of ritual. I find code signals handy. In my school, gum chewing is forbidden, so I give a person-to-person reminder by sign language. I rapidly close and open my thumb and forefinger (imitating jaw motion), and then, like a baseball umpire calling out the runner, I motion with my thumb toward the wastebasket.

The class is not distracted; I wait until I catch the eye of the offender, give my code signal, and let the business of the class go on. For talking or whispering, a finger on my closed lips may be enough. Codes are short cuts, and can save time and energy if introduced with good humor.

Relate learning to life plans. The sooner you know the career plans, interests, and even the hobbies of your students, the more successful you will be in directing all their energies into constructive channels.

Be yourself. Pick up ideas wherever you can, but be yourself and teach in the way that is right for you.

STREAMLINING ROUTINE TASKS

Carlos De Zafra, Jr.*

The teacher's job is a time-consuming one. For some it is much more time-consuming than for others. Part of the reason for these differences lies in the differences in teachers' skills in routinizing. Skilful routinizing can often help teachers become more effective in their class control. The following suggestions gathered together by Carlos De Zafra should be priceless for the beginning teacher.

These three separate facts add up to an educational problem of discouraging proportions: (1) The current shortage of qualified teachers is estimated by the National Education Association at 180,000. (2) ". . . The average rural high-school teacher, as reported by one investigator, works more than 60 hours per week. The average work week of [city] high-school teachers, as shown by a consolidation of the findings of 13 studies, was about 47 hours long. . . ."[1] (3) The AF of L-CIO has set 1960 as its target date for the 35-

* From *The Clearing House*, Vol. 33 (Teaneck, N.J.: The Clearing House, Fairleigh Dickinson University, October 1958), pp. 92–94. Reprinted by permission of the publisher.
[1] *The Clearing House*, XXX (September, 1955), p. 34.

hour work week, a goal which already has been approximated in some trades and industries.

The significance of these three isolated facts is that prospective teachers may well be dissuaded from entering the profession as much by comparatively excessive work weeks as they are by relatively low salary schedules. Certain it is that as automation increases and as leisure becomes more abundant for the mass of wage earners, this work-week aspect of the recruitment problem and of the morale of those already in the profession will inevitably grow still more menacing.

The purpose of this article is to urge a particular approach toward ameliorating this recruitment and morale problem, which thus far seems to have been neglected in our professional periodicals. It is highly possible that in the past this approach has seemed somewhat unprofessional; but the time has now come when its emphasis can contribute to the welfare of the profession; thus this approach has become professional by definition.

The theme of this approach is simply this: Our teacher-training institutions and the profession itself need to place a new emphasis upon the development by each teacher of those techniques which, without compromising conscientious and high-quality work, and in the interest of the teacher's mental and physical health and his love for teaching, will conserve the teacher's precious time and energy.

Each teacher, in other words, needs consciously to become an efficiency expert in the clerical and routine aspects of his job so his work week will be shortened and he will have more time and energy for the creative elements of teaching. Once the desirability of such efficiencies becomes apparent, there are few veteran teachers who cannot contribute to a collection of specifics. Here are a few from one teacher's experience:

Streamlining Procedures

1. Time can be saved by eliminating all superfluous motions when doing such routine chores as correcting objective tests, stapling, correcting duplicated copies, and making trips to the office. Industry has long used time-and-motion studies to increase its man-hour productivity. Surely greater efficiency will accrue to most of us teachers if we will but streamline our routine chores.

2. Expendable and often used items such as passes, paper clips, memo sheets, chalk, blotters, thumbtacks, and rubber bands should be kept in good supply and in convenient places. Good housekeeping expedites good teaching.

3. Cards or forms which need to be kept in alphabetical order (such as attendance cards, report cards, book-record cards, registration cards) can be much more quickly rearranged once they have been sequentially numbered.

4. The use for each class of a different-colored manila typing folder with its two big pockets makes a readily identified container for papers to be marked, papers to be returned, and lesson plans.

5. It is needlessly conscientious for the teachers of some subjects to correct

every word of every paper of every pupil. A valid evaluation of other than test papers can usually be obtained by concentration on a few revealing points common to all papers and by keen but rapid scanning of the remainder of each pupil's work.

6. To expedite work, every teacher who can should use typewriting and shorthand skills. The availability of duplicating services is also desirable.

7. It is convenient to have the front desk and seat of the middle row unassigned to any pupil. This desk can then serve as a table for the distribution and collection of materials, as a convenient roost for the foot-weary teacher who wants to sit while still having a commanding position among his pupils, and as a ready "hot seat" for disciplinary cases.

Saving Time

8. In view of the fact that a study by the University of Wisconsin discloses that the average person wastes three years of his life by waiting, it behooves us to *use*, not waste, those many odd moments of each day that slip by so unproductively.

9. The use of reliable pupils (sometimes strategically placed) for such chores as taking attendance, collecting monies, changing bulletin-board displays, operating audio-visual equipment, and distributing and collecting materials is not only good training in responsibility for the pupils who undertake these assignments but also a good time- and energy-saver for the teacher.

10. When well-motivated classes are working on meaningful assignments, it would seem to be legitimate for the teacher to do required clerical work at his desk, provided, of course, that pupils feel free to request necessary help and provided a work atmosphere prevails throughout the room.

11. When a quiz reveals that reteaching needs to be done, it is energy saving and good pedagogy to have the best student in the class teach the two lowest pupils, the second highest student teach the third and fourth lowest pupils, and so on until all members of the class are accounted for. The competitive spirit that can be aroused among the threesomes makes the teacher's task of motivation considerably lighter.

12. When new units of work need to be developed for a course, it is only common sense for teachers who have similar classes to exchange efforts.

13. It is important for teachers to take the time necessary to build good classroom tests, but then these tests (with desirable improvements as indicated by experience) should be capitalized upon with other classes other years. It is inefficient to build tests anew each year.

14. It is time conserving to have pupils correct one another's objective quiz answers under your supervision and explanation.

Using Forms

15. The teacher's use of a school-year "daily date book" makes it easy to keep track of committee meetings and other prearranged commitments and forthcoming chores.

16. The use of a 3″ × 5″ card for the listing of each day's special chores jogs one's memory and promotes effective working and living.

17. Dated, weekly lesson-plan sheets for the entire school year enable the teacher more readily to plan ahead for such things as showing films, taking field trips, using resource people, and giving tests.

18. When stencils are cut of an expendable item, enough copies should be run to last a considerable time. The stencil, however, should be carefully preserved for possible reruns at later dates.

19. It is efficient to make your duplicated quiz papers nonexpendable. Supply pupils with form answer sheets for your objective questions, which sheets then lend themselves to speedy correction by answer keys.

Organizing Reference Materials

20. An encyclopedia and other reference books in the classroom as the heart of a classroom library not only saves trips to the school library but also tend to result in the greater use of such reference materials.

21. When annotations on audio-visual aids are conveniently filed, they foster the ready recall of leading questions for follow-up discussions.

Using Helpful Equipment

22. A handy note-pad and desk-pen holder saves many superfluous movements.

23. A rubber stamp with the teacher's name on it can save time and writer's cramp when signatures are required on such things as schedule cards, passes, and attendance reports.

24. A long- and red-leaded automatic pencil saves sharpening those archaic and time-consuming wooden jobs. Red lead can also be erased, if need be, far more readily than can red ink.

25. A one- and adjustable-legged table whose side can rest across the arms of an occupied armchair is a great boon to the weary reader or paper-corrector.

26. Attractive posters for the classroom can be readily produced by pupils and teacher if a supply of poster card is kept on hand, together with a yardstick, a pair of shears, and a set of green, red, and black felt-point pens. Some teachers like also to keep handy a set of stencils (for more careful yet rapid lettering) and some poster paints (for greater variety of color).

27. A clever though simple punchboard device for the rapid yet manual correcting of multiple-choice answers (where the teacher wishes not to have pupils correct their own or one another's papers in class) is available from Marx-All Scoremaster, Box 4939, Portland 13, Oregon.

Clerical and routine duties are the dishwater jobs. By streamlining them, a teacher can reduce their nuisance value and thus give more attention to the artistry of teaching.

Part II

CLASSROOM STRATEGIES
AND TACTICS

Part I is devoted to considerations that are important in the developing and choosing of strategies and tactics. Part II concerns the strategies and tactics themselves and the materials necessary for carrying them out. By far the largest emphasis is placed on strategies and tactics that are supposed to help pupils learn to think and study. This emphasis is intentional. Because the editor believes that the central purpose of the schools should be the development of the rational powers, he has purposely weighted the discussions of strategies in that direction. Other types of strategies and tactics have been included because they are necessary tools for the teacher's kit and because these strategies support the development of the rational powers.

As a matter of fact, sometimes it is difficult to determine what type of goal can best be attained by any particular technique. Programed learning, lectures, television, and large group instruction are usually best suited for presenting information to pupils. Yet, still they may also be used to motivate, to summarize, and even to initiate thinking. Drill and practice are best suited for bringing about overlearning of facts that pupils must remember, and for developing skills. Questions may be used in all sorts of ways. Discussions may lead to clearer concepts and better conversation and reasoning skills. However, discussions and other group processes are perhaps more useful for changing attitudes and deep-seated ideas. In other words, capable teachers can adapt techniques for various purposes. Thus the technique itself is not the strategy or tactic. Rather the way one uses a technique for specific purposes in a specific situation is the strategy or tactic. Strategies are one's own combination of techniques and content designed to bring about a specific goal.

Pupils are different in many ways. To be really successful in teaching, teachers must devise strategies that will allow for these differences in individuals. Administrators have tried hard to find administrative strategies to solve the problems of individual differences. Among them are homogeneous grouping, ability tracking, and ungraded schools. None of these devices adequately solves the problem, however. Consequently, teachers must concoct additional strategies. Among the techniques that one could incorporate in these strategies are individualized reading, programed instruction, individualization of instruction, differentiated assignments, and committee or small group work. Some of these techniques are discussed in Chapter 11, which deals with individual differences, but others are discussed in other chapters.

Strategies for measuring and evaluating have to be devised for specific purposes just as strategies have to be devised specifically for teaching goals. Teachers sometimes forget this elementary fact and depend upon essay-type tests or objective-type tests for all their measuring. At best such tests are very undependable instruments. They cannot measure all types of learning. Consequently, teachers should make use of many other types of measuring or data-gathering devices—among them are scales, check lists, written work, performance, and so on. Also because these devices are so imprecise, it is wise for the teacher to get many measurements using several types of measuring devices. With a mixture of many measurements gained from many devices he stands a good chance of getting a really good estimate of the pupils' learning. A single test cannot give him such an estimate.

A McLuhanism having considerable vogue at the moment is, "The medium is the message"—the implication being that the medium used in a presentation influences what pupils learn from the presentation. This statement, of course, applies to the different instructional tools—television, films, textbooks, pictures, and so forth. A statement equally true, if perhaps not so catchy, is that the material is the method. On the one hand, the material one uses determines to at least some extent the method one must use; on the other hand, the method one uses determines the type of material one must use. Consequently, a chapter on materials and tools of instruction has been included in Part II. As in the other chapters that deal with strategies and tactics, it is assumed that the selection of materials and tools of teaching is contingent on the teacher's goals, his subject matter, and his pupils. It is also assumed that primacy should be given to the goals of developing the rational powers without sacrificing the other aspects of living that make life full and enjoyable.

Chapter 7

PLANNING

PLANNING is an essential element in the development of any strategy. In a sense it *is* the strategy, because a strategy is a plan. It is by far the major part of the preparation step in the common pattern of teaching.

Although each teacher is responsible for a share in the planning of the entire school curriculum, his specific personal planning responsibilities are of three types: planning the course, planning the units or topics that make up the course, and planning individual lessons. In course planning it is necessary to block out the topics or units that will be considered in the course, to determine their relative importance, to allocate the amount of time to be spent on each one, and to determine what the major assignments and approaches will be. In this connection the teacher must consider just what his major objectives for the course are. Obviously he should choose topics and emphases that will bring about these most desirable objectives. (Presumably some teachers will desire objectives different from those of other teachers and therefore select different topics and emphases.) In selecting the topics and emphases, the teacher should try to select worthwhile content relevant to the pupils' lives. He will usually find a curriculum guide or syllabus very helpful. When curriculum guides are not available, one can follow the outline of a good text. It is not necessary or desirable, however, to follow a textbook outline slavishly when making up a course plan.

Courses are usually divided into units or topics. By unit, the well informed teacher refers to a specific type of organization in which instruction in the course is centered around some unifying theme or problem for a month or so. This organization differs from a topical organization in that in the topic there is no central theme or problem. As a result, the topic is just a series of lessons about the same heading, for instance, immigration, Romeo and Juliet, or single-celled animals; but the unit, even though it may take several weeks to teach, amounts to a long lesson plan that incorporates many different learning activities, so as to allow for many individual differences, all tied around a central focus.* One of the principal sources of help in planning unit plans and plans for topics is the resource unit.

Lesson plans are plans for a single day's instruction in a course. In topically

---

* Unfortunately the word *unit* has been so loosely used that many teachers and educators use it to refer to any subdivision of a course larger than a lesson.

organized courses, they are the flesh of the course plan; in courses organized around units, they often become vestigial—the unit plan being the basic planning element. Sources of ideas for lesson plans include resource units and curriculum guides in addition to the teacher's personal resources.

PSYCHOLOGICAL AND LOGICAL ORGANIZATION

Roy O. Billett *

Subject matter can be structured in more than one way. If Robert Arnold† is right, each person who masters a discipline in effect creates his own structure for that discipline. In a similar manner, it is possible to give a subject a structure for teaching purposes that is somewhat different from the ultimate structure of the entire discipline. The first of these structures is often called the psychological organization of subject matter, and the second the logical organization of subject matter. These phrases are not really felicitous because the terms are likely to have unintended connotations to the reader. Nevertheless, the terms do seem to refer to quite different types of disciplinary structure.

The editor of this book believes that all secondary-school courses should be organized psychologically. He contends that if all courses were so organized, the attitudes reported by Mallery in "Curriculum Is Curriculum" would disappear. The following excerpt from Roy O. Billett's Fundamentals of Secondary School Teaching *is probably the clearest description of what the psychological organization of subject matter is.*

Relation of Subject Matter to Racial Experience. A few educationists have regarded subject matter as a sort of fifth wheel in secondary education. Whether they are right or wrong should be apparent from a consideration of the nature of subject matter.

A first effort at definition of subject matter is likely to stop with the state-

---

* From Roy O. Billett, *Fundamentals of Secondary School Teaching* (Boston: Houghton Mifflin Company, 1940), pp. 161–167. Reprinted by permission of the publisher.

† See Robert L. Arnold and W. Charles Lahey, *Inquiry* (New York: Selected Academic Readings, 1965), pp. i–xii.

ment that subject matter is English, social studies, mathematics, science, foreign language, practical arts, business studies, physical and health education, music, and art. This definition seems all right as far as it goes. But such a statement leaves unexpressed a number of important facts about subject matter.

In the first place, it should be recognized that the several subject-matter fields are collectively broad enough to encompass the whole of human learning. Subject matter began when some individual first represented in words or other symbols the meanings, insights, concepts, skills, and resultant ideals, attitudes, and appreciations which he had derived from interaction with his environment. Today, collectively, the subject-matter fields represent all the vital and meaningful experiences of the race.

Second, each of the subject-matter fields is elementary enough to extend down to the nursery school, and complex enough to include the farthest upward and outward reaches explored by professional workers, by university workers at the research level, and by all other creative workers.

Third, no natural boundaries separate the several subject-matter fields one from another. They are parts of a whole cloth woven on the loom of human experience.

Fourth, no subject-matter field is static. It is as dynamic as human life. It may seem at times to have been locally mummified in outmoded texts and courses of study never revised. But subject matter itself changes, now slowly, now kaleidoscopically, from year to year and from day to day as the race acquires new capacities for and tendencies toward behavior.

Fifth, because of its changing and cumulative nature, subject matter has undergone countless organizations and reorganizations. Similar reorganizations will continue to be necessary as long as civilized man endures. In the past, the organization and reorganization of subject matter has been dominated by a logical purpose, by the intent to facilitate the acquisition of new subject matter and to test out the old.

Certainly, for the specialist in a given subject-matter field the logical [1] type of organization will always be desirable and necessary, but whether logical organization suits the purposes of the elementary- or secondary-school teacher is another question. In fact, it is conceivable that the valid objection to the past use of subject matter for educative purposes at the elementary- or secondary-school level is to be found in the way subject matter has been selected and organized and not in the intrinsic nature of subject matter. To try to think of secondary education without any reference to subject matter is to conjure up teacher and pupil activities distressingly akin to the blind interplay of primitive cosmic forces. The relation of subject matter to racial experience would seem to make the former indispensable in systematic efforts to guide and direct the educative growth of individual human beings. The outcry

---

[1] The differentiae of logical and psychological organization are brought out in subsequent paragraphs.

against subject matter indicates that something is wrong somewhere, and the assertion is ventured that it is the selection and organization of subject matter and not the subject matter itself. At least, the discussion proceeds on that hypothesis. Two or three questions seem in order. What is the objection, if any, to the use of logically organized subject matter in elementary and secondary education? Is any other systematic type of organization possible? If so, how does it differ from logical organization?

Logical and Psychological Organization of Subject Matter. Answers to these questions can be suggested by stating the salient general differences between *logical* organization of subject matter and a second distinctly different type of organization, which for the time being can be referred to as *psychological*. These major differences seem to be about as follows:

First, logical organization is determined by the present level of racial development in the area represented by the subject; psychological organization is determined by the present level of development of the individual pupil in the same area.

Second, logical organization is relatively constant; psychological organization varies for different pupils at the same time and for the same pupil at different times.

Third, logical organization is comprehensive, including all the outcomes of human experience to date in the sector covered by the subject, and implies the placement of these outcomes in their proper cause and effect, or sequential, relationship from the point of view of the expert in the field;[2] psychological organization is selective, making important omissions of materials without being a mere process of omitting.

Fourth, used for educative purposes below the university level, logical organization encourages learning processes characterized by rote memory and teaching processes characterized by indoctrination; psychological organization encourages learning processes characterized by logical memory and problem-solving, and teaching characterized by guidance and direction of the pupils' experiences.

Fifth, logical organization presumes the same ratio of direct and vicarious experience for all ages and for all types of pupils; psychological organization seeks a constant proper balance between direct and vicarious experience.

In a word, subject matter can be psychologically organized only with reference to the experiential levels and rates of educative growth of the pupils for whom it is prepared. It is a practical recognition of the fact that learning is not absorption but the result of experience; that, proverbs notwithstanding, experience keeps the only school, and fools and geniuses and normal people learn in it, if they learn at all. Psychological organization in no way prevents the teacher from capitalizing on the possibilities of vicarious experience, which, after all, is one kind of experience and must play an important rôle in education. In reality, vicarious experience is the interaction of one individual

---

[2] Hence, logical organization does not proceed "from the simple to the complex," as is so often said.

with the results of the first-hand experiences of others. It is essential if the individual is to learn some things and survive. Psychological organization does not require that pupils fall off cliffs, be struck by express trains, or contract contagious or infectious disease in order to know the disastrous or unhappy results of such first-hand experiences or to know how to avoid them. On the contrary, psychological organization attempts a constantly modified and proper balance between direct and vicarious experience for each pupil. This is essential because the amount and kind of first-hand and vicarious experience which leads to optimal educative growth varies with individual

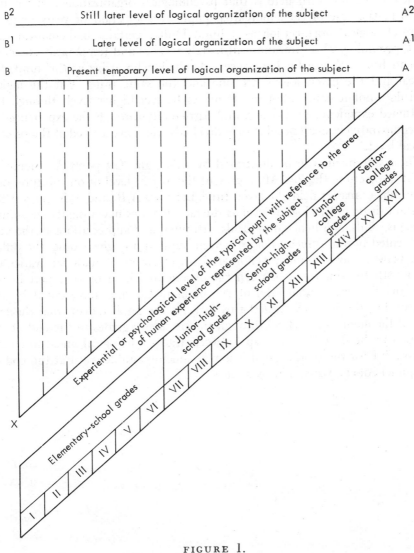

FIGURE 1.

Relating the Psychological to the Logical

pupils at a given age level, and varies with the individual pupil at different age levels. At any age level the greater the general mental ability of the pupil, the greater the possible rôle of vicarious experience; and for any given individual pupil the rôle of vicarious experience can be increased as the child grows older. Logical organization of subject matter in its very nature, not only overemphasizes vicarious experience at the elementary- and secondary-school levels, but also presents the same ratio of direct and vicarious experience to all pupils, regardless of age, aptitude, ability, interest, aim, or need.

Schematic Diagram Relating the Logical and the Psychological. The point of view being set forth here is that psychological organization is a variable which in the case of each individual pupil over a period of years tends to approach logical organization as a limit. Unlike certain mathematical variables, psychological organization ultimately reaches and temporarily coincides with its limit (Figure 1). For those individuals who arrive at this limit, the logical and the psychological are one and the same thing. But the logical level does not remain stationary. It moves to ever higher levels through the continued experience of the race, and particularly through the experiences of the comparatively small number of individuals who have arrived at the present logical level.

These statements can be illustrated by a diagram. Let point A (Figure 1) and its projection, the line AB, represent the logical level of organization of a given subject-matter field at a given time. Let lines A_1B_1 and A_2B_2 suggest the constant rising of this logical level as the race acquires new insights, meanings, concepts, skills, and hence new ideals, attitudes, and appreciations in the area represented by the subject. For any given pupil at any given time, the difference between logical and psychological organization of materials varies directly with the difference between the experiential level of an expert in the field and the experiential level of the pupil in the area represented by the subject. Let the line AX suggest this fact. As the pupil moves from the first year of the elementary school through the successive grades to the end of the secondary-school period, the gap between the psychological and the logical lessens, but for the typical pupil it is real and impassable, even at the end of the junior-college years. This is as it is.

CURRICULUM IS CURRICULUM

David Mallery *

David Mallery traveled about from school to school to ask pupils what they thought about such things as their school programs, their teachers, their teaching, and school life. Their comments were frank and refreshing. But what they thought of the curriculum was far from complimentary. Probably their judgments are more accurate than teachers like to admit. Before teachers go too far in the planning of their courses, perhaps they should ponder carefully these pupils' reactions. Perhaps if teachers were more careful to make their courses more relevant to their pupils' lives, the pupils would find the curriculum more worthwhile.

Well, curriculum is curriculum. We have it for twelve years. We haven't mentioned it to you because we wanted to tell you first about the things that really matter.

The boy who said this was announcing what turned out to be one of the major themes in this study. He was surrounded by eight other boys from the three top classes in a high school. These boys, leaders of various student councils and activities, were meeting with me after most of the students and teachers had left the building. We had been talking for more than an hour about experiences that had "really mattered" to these boys. And nothing they had talked about had anything to do with what went on inside any classroom.

This happened in one of the first schools I visited. I had not yet learned to *wait* long enough. Instead, I asked with some curiosity: "What about some things in the curriculum? What has been especially significant there? This hasn't come up at all yet. How come?"

The boy's "curriculum is curriculum" seemed to say it all. The other boys nodded, and then took the conversation back to the things that "really mattered."

This idea, that school courses were a neutral element or even irrelevant in the pattern of things that really did have significance for high school people, was repeatedly expressed in the conversations in the schools. I ran into it in advanced college preparatory sections and among vocational students—in

---

* Chapter 3 "Curriculum is Curriculum" from *High School Students Speak Out* by David Mallery. Copyright © 1962 by Educational Records Bureau. Reprinted by permission of Harper & Row, Publishers.

fast, middle, and slow groups. I heard so much on "curriculum is curriculum," and some of it was said so eloquently, that it deserves a key spot in this report. Courses that students said *did* have an impact, that did *matter*, seem all the more impressive in contrast.

Repeatedly the young people plunged into controversy or attack, or into celebration of certain courses, once the curriculum entered the picture. Did a course make any sense? Was it worth doing for any reason other than to pass or get the "A"? Was it dead or alive—and in what way? In the fragments that follow, some of the students express the urgency they feel about the chance to think and work in a course as a whole human being.

"I haven't had a chance in any course to really think. They tell us you go to school to widen your understanding and all, but where are you supposed to do it?"

The boy speaking was in a classroom group of seniors in an academic course. There was a pattern of three or four hours of work a night for these seniors and tremendous competition for marks, national test scores, and admission to college. But no chance to think?

About fifteen junior and senior girls were gathered sociably in their recreation room. Their talk shifted to "the most important things that have happened around here." One girl tried to summarize her friends' comments about certain courses in this way:

"What we study in school seems so *unreal*. I have the feeling that what's real is 'out there.' We need bridges to 'out there.'" She made a gesture in the direction of the window.

Thirty-three vocational senior boys were gathered for an English class. The teacher tipped me off in advance that this was the brightest of the seven vocational sections. The boys were impressive and had plenty to say, including this comment from a quiet-spoken fellow who appeared to carry great weight with the others: "Last year we had a new shop teacher. He was right from industry! He was pretty rough and really put it to us. We were doing new stuff and hard stuff." The others joined in to explain the work in detail, and with real eagerness. Then the same boy spoke again:

Then other teachers criticized this fellow and the things we were doing. They said this work was too advanced for us, that we were using too expensive equipment. They said the shop kids weren't responsible enough to use this equipment. Anyway the work was stopped. They told the new teacher what was usually done, and we did it. It was back to stuff we had done before, over and over again. I was even back to making doors for cabinets. It was a real letdown. But the other was great while it lasted.

I was talking during a lunch hour with an attractive girl starting her eleventh-grade year. I asked what courses she had found especially valuable last year in the tenth grade. She said, "Well, I was in the advanced section in English—I liked being in that."

I asked: "What did you read in there that struck you as particularly interesting or worthwhile?"

"Well, let's see. We read *Paradise Lost* but that was pretty cut and dried. Then . . ." (she seemed to be reaching for some memory) "there was Shakespeare . . ." (her face seemed to cloud over) "but that was pretty hard to understand a lot of the time." She thought a moment more. "We *did* read some drama." She struggled to remember names of plays. Then: "We *did* have a free reading program that we got marked on. It wasn't the *number* of books we read, it was the *kind* of books, you know what I mean?"

Asked if there were any books that meant something special to her, she thought a moment, then answered, "Well, it's hard to remember." She smiled.

In some schools there were "wonderful exceptions," some classes that really mattered, where something significant did happen. In other schools such courses did not seem to be exceptions but expected and valued experiences. And sometimes there was a sudden flash of excitement in a course. One girl described such an event as she sat in what was ordinarily an English class. The students were hard at it in an earnest discussion about the courses that struck them as most important. A girl over at the side of the room raised her hand.

You know, in physics last week, it was really great. We got into a discussion of something, and we suddenly realized that there was no answer to the question we were talking about. We went on and talked about *possibilities*, about things we couldn't know yet, on the basis of the information we had now—and about things we needed to explore this century. And it was exciting to see that the teacher didn't know the answer—that he was talking about possibilities, about unknown regions, *with* us!

A boy I was talking with remained seated at the cafeteria table after the bell, trying to explain just what was so important to him about his history course:

History is the one course where you have the feeling that we're trying to see the whole thing—not just learn about pieces. Some days it's boring as anything. But it's only boring because we don't know enough to deal with the kind of questions he's asking. And we *know* that's what is the matter. But other days it really begins to take a shape. On those days the pieces add up to something, even if it's just new questions. And the past and present seem to go together, even though the way they go together seems to change as we go along.

"Could we talk some more?"

I recognized the boy from an earlier class discussion. He joined me and soon began to talk about the school and his own outlook on life, particularly about his serious, growing interest in international affairs. "I'd like to do something in international work," he said, and without mentioning any course, he went on to explain how this feeling had come to be important to him. As I listened to him, I recognized what might have happened in certain classrooms to contribute to this feeling:

... Then one night I put my finger on a map of Russia, and I suddenly thought that my finger was running across two hundred and ten million people—across people in their homes and on the street. It was the funniest feeling—as if I suddenly was connected with them—as if even there might be a Russian boy moving his finger across a map of the U.S.A. at this same moment!

"Have you visited tenth-grade math?"

"Have you met Mr. Hunter, the math teacher?"

"Do you know about this book we're working on in tenth grade?"

"I'm no math brain, but there's something really good going on in our tenth-grade math course. . . ."

I had been inside one school less than twenty minutes before this barrage of questions about Mr. Hunter and tenth-grade mathematics began. I soon found that Mr. Hunter was indeed working on a textbook and developing it with his students. The material was on mimeographed sheets, and teacher and students were testing problems, challenging each other on precise explanations, arguing over wording, and laboring over proofs and statements of principles. The students seemed to feel a proprietary interest in developing this book. Beyond this, it looked as if they were challenged by its special approach to mathematics. They seemed to see something of the design of mathematics and were trying to describe what they saw.

These students were clearly involved in the core of mathematics, not simply in a teacher's entertaining personality. "It sure is different from just pushing numbers around the way I always did before," as one boy said. These students were encountering mathematics material before it reached the textbook editors, curriculum makers, visual-aid committees, and the rest. They were not inventing something new. They were learning what had to be learned, but with a depth that made special sense. It looked like a creative partnership of the subject, the teacher, and the students, with each important to the other.

One girl was trying to put her finger on just what this experience meant to her, and she suddenly asked this question:

You know, I wonder if this year in math is an experience that will mean something just to us. Do you think once this book gets into final shape and is published and put into the hands of eleventh-graders, say, five years from now, that it will be the basis for dead, meaningless drudgery for them just as math books used to be for me before this year?

Mr. Hunter's tenth-grade mathematics class has something to say to us about students getting into a subject beneath the answer-giving surface. This type of penetration of a subject was happening for the boy who recalled the history course where they were "trying to see the whole thing." It was happening for a few minutes in the physics class, when the students and teacher got out of the workbook and into the unknowns of physics itself. And it was happening as the boy ran his finger over the map of Russia. Surely these experiences penetrated much deeper than did the "curriculum is curriculum" feeling, into something that genuinely did "matter."

THE UNIT PROCESS

Elizabeth Berry *

For the beginning teacher who was not brought up in it, the unit plan of teaching is one of the most difficult pedagogical ideas to understand and implement. This difficulty is aggravated by the fact that educationists everywhere seem to have quite different notions of how units should be developed. Yet, the unit idea has been one of the most promising for unleashing creative spirit, for developing critical thinking, and for providing for various interests, abilities, and purposes. Although the following article presents the unit process from the point of view of a teacher of English, the methods it describes are suitable for any subject. Note that the author describes two ways to organize and teach the same unit. The second one is undoubtedly the better approach, but the first one is quite customary in unit teaching.

A few years ago I visited and observed in the classroom of an English teacher who was conducting a unit on "The Role of the Newspaper in the World Today." This teacher began the unit by announcing that the students were going to undertake a unit on the aforementioned title. The teacher spent considerable time telling the students why it was important for them to make a study of the newspaper, then she told them that the next day the class would set up objectives for the unit study.

* From *The Educational Forum*, Vol. 27 (March 1963), pp. 364–366. Used by permission of Kappa Delta Pi, An Honor Society In Education, owners of the copyright.

In the meantime, class members were to give some attention to the objectives. The next day in class, the students agreed upon a list of objectives for the unit, questions they wished to answer. It was interesting to note that their questions were primarily material that the teacher had given them in the lecture the day before. The teacher then announced a series of activities that the class would undertake in the study of the unit. These activities proceeded in a systematic way. As each activity was undertaken, the teacher brought to the class any materials needed, gave specific instructions on how each piece of work was to be done, and saw that these activities were carried out. Some of the activities undertaken included the daily reading of the local newspaper and a discussion of local news items. No attention was given to the accuracy of reporting. There seemed to be a feeling that if an article appears in the press it is valid. A local newsman spoke to the class and built up a strong argument for his paper and the press in general. He was a delightful speaker and won the support of the group. The students then wrote letters to the editor on a rather non-controversial subject. The letters were graded, returned to the students, and presumably mailed. Students were encouraged to write articles of school interest for the school newspaper. Several did. Some vocabulary words relating to the press were studied. During the month that the unit was in progress, the daily work laboriously dragged on. By the end of the unit, the students were restless and ready for a change. The teacher, realizing that the students had lost interest, decided to bring the unit to an end with a class evaluation. In the evaluation, the students agreed that they had learned how to read the newspaper, recognized the importance of reading, and expected to confirm their interest by making a daily reading of the newspaper a part of their lives. The teacher then announced that it was time to move on to another unit, which would be a study of *Macbeth*.

After I had observed the teaching of the newspaper unit, I determined to try this unit using a different approach, method, and plan. I decided to use the unit process. My own personal goals were not only to help students improve their use of specific language skills, but also to make them critical readers of newspapers. From past experiences, I knew that many of the students believed that anything in print was truth. They had probably developed such a belief because most of their educational experience had been rooted in a firm belief in the word of the press. Many had gone through school proving their points with such remarks as this, "I can prove it because I read it in . . . ." Also I had observed that many of my students equated being arrested with being guilty, considered all advertising as an honest presentation of fact, thought almost any sale a good buy, and generally felt that the highest honor that a girl could achieve would be a photograph in the society section.

Now I could have told the students the strengths and weaknesses of a newspaper, of its worth and limitations. But I knew that learning comes from within, not from without, and that students are more apt to use fruitfully knowledge gained through self-discovery. For this reason, I presented the unit in a problem solving context. I did this by making reprints of articles on the same subject but from different newspapers. I used three different newspapers for this and selected an article from each on the same topic but with varying interpretations. I passed out reprints of the first article for the class to read. Class discussion followed, but there were few comments. In general, the class members agreed with the reporter. I then gave them a second article to read. There were some comments that this article was not in complete agreement with the first, but not much excitement about it. Then I gave them the third article. But this time students were puzzled at discrepancies and differences of opinion in reporting the news. I let them wrangle over these differences in class discussion before I took action. In other words, I allowed them to come face to face with a felt difficulty and problem. Finally I halted the discussion and said, "What is the issue in this discussion? What is it that you want to know? Let's define the problem."

Now the students entered the second phase of the unit process, when they defined the problem as they saw it in view of their recent experiences. I did not define the problem for the students. Through the use of the chalkboard to examine carefully selected answers, I patiently took time for the students to agree upon a statement of the problem and a series of questions that they should answer if they were to become intelligent readers of the news. Now I asked how the class could proceed to make a study of this problem so as to gain the needed insight. The students suggested numerous ways: (1) Daily reading of different papers to see differences or similarities in reporting, (2) Reading news magazines for a similar purpose, (3) Searching for books in the library that discuss the magazine and newspaper field, (4) Calling in local reporters for class interviews, (5) Getting personal accounts of news reporting from biographies of famous newsmen, (6) Interviewing people in the community who had complained about being misrepresented in the news, (7) Practicing news reporting themselves to see what difficulties arise. I shared in the suggestions for this cooperative research, but I did not dictate them. For I did not wish to kill initiative and creativity.

Next the class co-operatively agreed upon a plan of action. They then proceeded to carry out their plans, and I acted as a catalyst and guide. As the students began the study and exploration, they found a need to go to the library for resource materials pertaining to the problem at hand. The librarian helped the students find books and materials relating to their study. Perhaps it was necessary for both librarian and students to consult the card catalogue, the *Reader's Guide*, encyclopedias, and bibliographies. In addition, students used the library to investigate current magazines and newspapers. It was through the resources of the library, for example, that they were able to compare original articles with *Reader's Digest* condensations of them. It was from the *Reader's Guide* that students discovered articles on "How to Read the Chicago Tribune" and "All the News that Fits the Pattern." (April and May issues of Harpers, 1949.) The students found especially helpful William H. Burton's *Education for Effective Thinking* and S. I. Hayakawa's *Language in*

Thought and Action. Copies of Liebling's *The Press* and Edgar Dale's *How to Read a Newspaper* were also found on the library shelves. In addition there were the autobiographies of newsmen and journalists telling their own personal experiences in the newspaper field. The unit took the students to the school library, to the public library, and into the community. It made them active researchers and problem solvers. This is quite a contrast to the self-contained English classroom where students are spoonfed from a single text or several volumes that the teacher himself has brought to them for use. The unit process makes students active seekers of knowledge, makes them creators of their own textbooks as they synthesize the source material.

As the unit proceeded, the students set up class discussion periods, small group discussion periods, panel discussions, class interviews, as well as written assignments to share their knowledge. As the unit ended they evaluated what they had learned about the original problem. Also they established guidelines for the evaluation of newspapers that would guide their future reading.

One final thought in conclusion. You have heard arguments in recent years concerning whether or not high school students should write research papers —some teachers say yes, some say no. I think such statements in themselves indicate a lack of clarification of the unit process. Students taught by the unit process write research papers from early school years on through the senior high school days. Properly done, a research paper is a write-up of a unit of study conducted by the unit process.

WRITING INSTRUCTIONAL OBJECTIVES

Thorwald Esbensen *

Good planning depends upon good objectives. Although almost any teacher would agree that this is so, evidently many are not at all sure how to use objectives in the planning of courses, units, and lessons. One of the difficulties comes from the inability to differentiate between two kinds of major goals: organizing goals and indirect or concomittant goals, which, though often very important, are not the goals one organizes one's courses for.

Another type of difficulty is that teachers lay out too many goals for there to be any focus in teaching. It is better to have fewer major goals

* From *Phi Delta Kappan*, Vol. 48 (Bloomington, Ind.: Phi Delta Kappa, January 1967), pp. 246–247. Reprinted by permission of the publisher.

that one can use for a center of one's instruction than a number of frac-tionated, unrelated little goals. That is why one major goal per lesson is usually quite enough. A third difficulty is to make objectives definite enough to be useful. In describing goals, vagueness is not much help.

For many years, educators have talked about the importance of instructional objectives. The purpose of an instructional objective is to make clear to teachers, students, and other interested persons *what it is that needs to be taught*—or what it is that *has been taught.*

A well-written instructional objective should say three things: 1) what it is that a student who has mastered the objective will be able to *do,* 2) under what *conditions* he will be able to do it, and 3) to what *extent* he will be able to do it. To put the matter in a single sentence, a well-written instructional objective should specify under what conditions and to what extent a certain kind of student performance can be expected to take place.

Performance—conditions—extent. Let us consider first the word *performance.* Performing means doing. A student who performs something does something.

Here are two statements. Which one is expressed in terms of student performance?

A. *The student will have a good understanding of the letters of the alphabet, A through Z.*

B. *The student will be able to pronounce the names of the letters of the alphabet, A through Z.*

Statement B tells what it is that the student will be able to *do.* He will be able to *pronounce* the names of the letters of the alphabet, A through Z.

Statement A tells us that the student will have a good *understanding* of the letters of the alphabet. But this is not very clear. We cannot tell what it is that the student is supposed to be able to *do* as a result of this understanding.

Let's try another pair of statements. Which one is expressed in terms of student performance?

A. *The student will have an adequate comprehension of the mechanics of punctuation.*

B. *Given a sentence containing an error in punctuation, the student will correct the mistake.*

Statement B tells what it is that the student will *do.* Statement A, which says that the student will have an adequate *comprehension* of the mechanics of punctuation, is pretty vague. We cannot tell what it is that the student is supposed to be able to *do* as a result of his comprehension.

At this point, an objection may be raised. Isn't the person who is comprehending something doing something? Isn't intellectual performance an acceptable kind of student performance?

Certainly. The difficulty is that mental activity, as such, is not directly observable. We cannot literally open up a person's head and see the thinking that is going on inside. If it is to be of use to us, a statement of performance must specify some sort of behavior that can be observed.

This does not mean that we are not concerned about intellectual performance. It does mean that since mental activity, as such, is not directly observable, some sort of behavior that is observable will have to stand for or represent the intellectual performance we have in mind.

For example, suppose that we are interested in having students know something about the writing style of Ernest Hemingway. Whatever may be intellectually involved in the attainment of this goal, it should be apparent that the language of our aim as stated leaves much to be desired.

What is the student who *knows* able to do that the student who does *not know* is not able to do? This is the important question, because we cannot measure the accomplishment of our instructional purpose until we have worked out a clear answer to it. Although there is no single answer (our objective of "knowing something" is too vague for that), here is a possible statement of desired performance: *Given 10 pairs of short prose passages— each pair having one selection by Ernest Hemingway and one by a different author—the student is able, with at least 90 percent accuracy, to choose the 10 selections written by Hemingway.*

Performance—conditions—extent. We have been talking about *performance*. Let us now consider *conditions*.

Here is one of our earlier statements concerning the alphabet: *The student will be able to pronounce the names of the letters of the alphabet, A through Z.* We have said that this statement is expressed in terms of student performance. Does this statement also set forth the *conditions* under which the performance is to take place?

It does not. For one thing, we cannot tell from our statement whether the student is to pronounce the names of the letters *at sight* or *from memory*. If the letters are to be shown, we do not know whether the student is to work with capital letters, small letters, or both. Nor do we know whether the student is to work with these letters in regular sequence or in random order. Obviously, each set of conditions is substantially different from the rest, and will make its own special demands upon the student who attempts to accomplish the objective.

Let's examine two more statements. Which one sets forth the *conditions* under which a certain kind of performance is to take place?

A. *Given the Dolch list of the 95 most common nouns, the student will be able to pronounce correctly all the words on this list.*

B. *The student will be able to pronounce correctly at least 90 percent of all words found in most beginning reading books.*

Statement A, which tells us that the Dolch list will be used, sets the conditions for the demonstration of student mastery. We are told that these particular words, and no others, are the ones at issue for this objective.

Statement B, offering us only the dubious clue of "words found in most beginning reading books," does not tell us enough. Our conditions need to be defined more precisely than this.

We come now to the matter of the *extent* and *level* of performance. A well-written instructional objective will establish an acceptable minimum standard of achievement.

Look at this objective: *Given 20 sentences containing both common and proper nouns, the student will be able to identify with very few mistakes both kinds of nouns.* Does this objective establish a minimum standard of achievement?

It does not. It leaves open the question, How many mistakes are "a very few"?

Here is the Hemingway objective we looked at earlier: *Given 10 pairs of short prose passages—each pair having one selection by Ernest Hemingway and one by a different author—the student is able, with at least 90 percent accuracy, to choose the 10 selections written by Hemingway.* Does this objective establish a minimum standard of achievement?

It does. The student is expected to be able to make at least nine correct choices out of the 10. This constitutes a minimum standard of achievement.

Let's try one more objective: *The student should be able to pronounce from memory, and in sequence, the names of the letters of the alphabet, A through Z.* Does this objective establish a minimum standard of achievement?

It does. The objective implies that we are looking for 100 percent mastery. However, we could, if we wanted to be explicit, restate our objective in this way: *The student should be able to pronounce from memory, in sequence, and with 100 percent accuracy, the names of the letters of the alphabet, A through Z.*

An instructional objective should not ordinarily be limited to specific *means* (particular materials or methods), but should be stated in terms that permit the use of various procedures. Look at this statement of an objective: *Given the California Test Bureau's E-F level programmed booklet on capitalization, the student is able to work through the exercises in this booklet with at least 90 percent accuracy.* Is this objective limited to the use of a particular instructional item or procedure?

It is. The objective is expressed exclusively in terms of performance with a specific booklet. Although the particular kind of skill development that is promoted by this booklet is presumably also fostered by other instructional materials and methods, no such options are available under the terms of our objective as it is now written.

Look at this statement of an objective: *Given 20 sentences containing a variety of mistakes in capitalization, the student is able, with at least 90 percent accuracy, to identify and rewrite correctly each word that has a mistake in capitalization.* Is this objective limited to the use of a particular instructional item or procedure?

It is. The objective as expressly stated permits us to use a number of instructional items that show promise of being able to help students attain the desired performance. Among these items are not only the California Test Bureau's E-F level material but the somewhat simpler C-D level presentation, a programmed booklet by D. C. Heath, Unit 11 of English 2200, Unit 9 of English 2600, Lessons 87 and 88 of English 3200, several filmstrips on capital letters, and so on.

Finally, a well-written instructional objective will suggest how its accomplishment can be measured. This follows from our view that a well-written objective specifies under what *conditions* and to what *extent* a certain kind of student *performance* can be expected to take place.

Look at this objective: *The student should know the alphabet.* Does this objective suggest how its accomplishment can be measured?

It does not. The reason for this judgment is that *knowing the alphabet* can mean different things to different people. Therefore, depending upon what is meant, the measuring of this knowing will take different forms.

Suppose we elaborate upon our objective so that it reads: *Shown the letters of the alphabet in random order (in both upper and lower case form), the student is able to say the name of each letter with 100 percent accuracy.* Does our objective now suggest how its accomplishment can be measured?

It does. The objective as stated makes plain how its accomplishment can be measured.

If teachers at all levels of schooling would be this explicit in writing instructional objectives, they might reasonably hope to eliminate almost immediately one major cause of learning failure among students: the traditional fuzziness of classroom assignments.

ADVERSE EFFECTS OF AD-LIB TEACHING

Roy Meadows *

Some teachers scoff at the value of lesson planning. Don't heed them, for it probably can be truly said that no one has ever been able to teach well for long without planning what he hopes the pupils will learn and how he hopes to get them to learn it. Teaching ad lib just does not come off. The best of the new "modern" methods, to say nothing of the new content, require a great deal of preparation. The teacher who does not

* From *School and Community*, Vol. 51 (May 1965), pp. 26–27. Reprinted by permission of the Missouri State Teachers Association.

take time to prepare well-conceived lesson plans will contribute to the
"mental stagnation" of his pupils. In this article, Meadows shows why.

Having taught numerous high school subjects over the years and having observed mathematics teaching in a supervisory position for the last several years, I have concluded that one of the chief weaknesses of the high school system is ad lib teaching.

By ad lib teaching I mean that there has been little or no written-out preparation to teach a particular class and subject.

The teacher knows the subject and may have taught the course before, but he has not zeroed in on the topics to be presented, the examples to be used for illustration, or the work to be assigned by specifically writing all these things out.

By way of contrast we have the carefully prepared lecture of the conscientious college teacher or the script of the TV teacher. Compared to these latter types of preparation, far too many high school teachers go into the classroom empty handed.

One might suppose that such an attack as this would of necessity be followed by a string of invectives directed at the teacher, the administrators, or someone in particular.

To the contrary, I believe that the causes are general, that this condition has evolved almost unnoticed with the growth of the high school. I find it difficult to convince some individuals that ad lib teaching is generally practiced or that there is anything wrong with it if it is.

To answer them I can only point to what I have observed and practiced, and give arguments against this type of teaching.

*   *   *

We sometimes read the charge that there is almost a total absence of scholarship among present day high school teachers. I believe there is some substantiation for this charge, and considering what the high school teacher's role has come to be, I think this condition is not surprising.

I have found that when I have been given time really to teach, or when I have made the extra time by working 10 or 11 hours a day, six days a week, that my own scholarship improves from careful, written-out preparation.

Things that would pass beneath notice in the ad lib style of teaching began to loom large, and I found it necessary to get references to clarify and extend many points.

This work stimulated my interest and that of my classes in turn, and there were numerous important by-products such as special report topics for the pupils to pursue which were not mentioned in the regular text.

Some high school teachers accept the present situation to such a degree that they argue that they do not need to use written-out preparation (some don't know how) for the lessons they teach, that they know the material and the texts practically from memory.

I have noticed as a supervisor in mathematics that a high percentage of these confirmed ad lib teachers do not want to teach the new mathematics, and if they get a new text to teach, even a conventional one, they oppose it and usually do not cover the material at first.

These ad lib teachers tend to teach the same old courses they have worked out over the years, and only slowly and gradually do they adapt to a new text.

Unlike the scholarly college lecturer, their approach does not enable them to teach a course as well the first time as they would, say, the fifth time through.

The new mathematics material, which was written for the most part by college teachers and assumes an enormous amount of daily preparation on the part of the teacher, is impossible for the ad lib teacher to teach or even to understand.

Unfortunately many administrators have the same assumptions about teaching as the ad lib teacher and are completely incredulous when told that teaching a full program of advanced modern high school mathematics may require three or four or more hours of daily preparation on the part of the teacher.

It might erroneously be assumed that although there is need for formal lesson preparation to teach modern math, such preparation is not needed in other subjects and will not be needed in math after the teacher learns the new math.

In reply to this I simply point to the charge of intellectual stagnation alleged to exist in the high school and assert that a type of teaching that does not adapt readily to new materials would cause it.

There are some minor causes of ad lib teaching which are procedural in nature. The teacher, for example, who uses hours each day marking math homework papers would do much better to put that time in on written-out lesson preparation and use some classroom checking procedure for marking homework.

Also the teacher who uses his unassigned time to give individual instruction to pupils, perhaps coddle is a better expression, is in effect robbing the class to help the individual. Private lessons for everyone in a public school system is out of the question.

I also have found that many high school and college students and also some young teachers have erroneous assumptions about a teacher's knowledge. While they would deny having such foolish notions, they nevertheless tacitly assume a teacher knows and remembers everything in his field and is ready to recite such at a moment's notice.

Students occasionally will make such outlandish demands on a teacher and the unwary teacher may go along with the student's assumption even though he can't deliver.

What this assumption amounts to is an idealization of the ad lib teacher, and the challenge created by this image is effective in promoting ad lib teaching.

The antidote is to teach the students that a teacher's primary skill is that of being able to read in his field of specialization and to prepare excellent lessons, not to know and remember all or even a small fraction of what has been written.

Given the above conditions and the undesirable consequences alleged, what can be done to improve matters?

All concerned should make a concerted effort to enable the teacher to get the bulk of his interest and attention back on the job of lesson preparation and teaching.

While most teachers make excellent and rather docile clerks, we can't afford this luxury in administration at the expense of the youngster's education.

Changes would have to be worked out gradually, but at any point where non-teaching personnel can be hired and trained to take over non-teaching duties, it should be done.

Administrators should resist the urge to call upon teachers whenever something must be done and should concentrate upon means to get the work done in some other way.

It is also quite probable that there are some non-teaching activities in any school which should simply be discontinued.

AN EFFECTIVE DAILY LESSON PLAN

Sidney L. Besvinick *

The importance of lesson planning is great; the type of format one uses is not. There are, however, some things to remember in each lesson plan. One, it is best to write down what your objective for the day is simply so you will know what it is. Another is to outline the procedure clearly and in enough detail so that you can follow it as you are teaching. A third is to write down the assignment you plan to give so that you will remember what it is and give it to the pupils. A fourth thing to remember is the materials you need for the class so that you will have them when you need them. Other things you may wish to include are notes on content, subject-matter references, or anything else you may want

* From *The Clearing House*, Vol. 34 (Teaneck, N.J.: The Clearing House, Fairleigh Dickinson University, March 1960), pp. 431–433. Reprinted by permission of the publisher.

to remember. The form advocated in the following selection is excellent.

Teachers are constantly planning. They plan the scope and sequence of courses, the content within the course, the topics or units to be covered, the activities to be used, and the tests to be given. They familiarize themselves with resource units, textbooks, and available materials. But the biggest single stumbling block to effective teaching is still a good lesson plan.

What's wrong with the lesson plans most teachers use? For one thing, the usual plan is too brief. A good lesson plan is quite lengthy and time-consuming to prepare. Second, most teachers don't use a systematic form for their plans and omit things that should be included. Third, the teacher may know from his plan what he is going to teach today but pity the poor substitute if the regular teacher is absent at the last minute!

Lesson plans should be simply stated, clearly written, and flexible, but the following rules form a better set of criteria against which to judge a lesson plan:

1. The teacher should be able to teach from it.

2. Someone else who is qualified in that subject area should be able to teach from it.

3. It should be useful as a basis for planning the lesson if it is taught again sometime in the future.

Many so-called lesson plans are really "layout sheets." They merely list what is to be covered day by day in cryptic form. For example:

Monday—Introduce *Macbeth.*

Tuesday—Biographical sketch of Shakespeare's life.

Wednesday—See film on *Macbeth.*

Thursday—Discuss major scenes.

Friday—Begin reading the play.

And so on, until the last lesson in the unit states:

Wednesday—Test on *Macbeth.*

The lesson plan form on p. 167 was designed for secondary school teachers with the criteria previously mentioned in mind. Mechanically, the form is more useful if the plans are kept in a loose-leaf notebook with page one of the plan on the left facing page two on the right.

Here are descriptions of the various sections, why they are included, and how they may be used effectively.

(1) The name blank is included so that you may have your plan returned if a supervisor or a department head checks it or another teacher wishes to borrow it.

(2) The subject is recorded in case one has to make lesson plans for more than one subject each day. A different plan sheet is obviously needed for every course.

(3) The date blank is used to provide a thread of continuity so that the plans may be linked together in a chronological order.

(4) The title of the unit or topic is listed on every plan sheet so that the planner will never forget what is under consideration. If some idea finds its way into the lesson and has no bearing on the unit, it should be stricken from the record and omitted.

(5) Forget about major and minor, specific and gross objectives. Determine the major concepts or skills learners are to acquire from this unit or topic and place them in the general unit plan. Limit yourself to six or eight and concentrate your efforts on them. List the one or two objectives which the class will examine today in the space provided.

(6) List in outline or brief form the content to be discussed and emphasized today. Don't be long winded, but don't be too brief. "Lecture on the causes of World War I" or "Demonstrate how to derive the quadratic equation" are hardly ample descriptions of content. Remember, someone else in your teaching field ought to be able to teach from this plan too.

(7) Procedures should also be listed in some detail. When this form is first used, it is surprising and embarrassing to see how many times "lecture," "discuss," and "question" are used to describe the activities to be undertaken. Gradually teachers find and utilize other teaching techniques to vary their classroom activities.

Sometimes the content is lengthy and the procedure simple. For example, the content may be a detailed development of the use of per cent in a seventh-grade arithmetic class and the procedure might be a chalkboard lecture. On the other hand, at times the content may be expressed as a single concept

DAILY LESSON PLAN FORM

Date (3) . . . . Subject (2) . . . . Teacher (1) . . . .

Unit Problem: (4)

Purposes or objectives for today: (5)

Content to be considered: (6)	Notes (11)
Procedures: (7)	
Evaluation techniques and/or questions: (8)	

Assignments: (9)
    Class
    Individuals

Pupils to see, things to do: (10)

and the procedure for developing it might be quite elaborate, such as a scientific principle and a laboratory demonstration for presenting it to the students. Since it is impossible to tell in advance which of the two sections will require the greatest description, considerable space should be allocated to both of these parts on the form.

(Because of space restrictions, items 6 and 7 have been shortened in the form shown. On the actual lesson plan at least half of a page is set aside for each of these sections.)

(8) Every plan needs to be evaluated. Each day the teacher should seek to determine, either orally or in writing, whether the learners have grown more sensitive to the concepts and skills that are being investigated. A key question, if not overused, is: "What did you learn today?" One or two objective-type test questions made up each day also provide an excellent set of items for use at the end of a unit or a reporting period as a test instrument.

Don't forget to evaluate occasionally the students' attitudes toward how they are learning; that is, the procedures being used.

(9) List the assignments, if any, for the class or for individuals.

(10) Make a note if a resource speaker needs to be contacted, a film ordered, library books obtained, or if a parent conference is due. This would be inserted in the last section on the second page.

(11) The portion of the page headed "Notes" is very important. If a certain technique goes over well or misses, or if a point of content has been omitted which should have been included, a phrase or two that will focus your attention on it in future plans should be noted in this space. Thus you can continually revise and up-date the plan, making it more interesting and worth while.

There are many teachers who will feel that this type of lesson plan asks too much of them. To do something like this would require at least an hour of preparation each day. This is true, but a perfect, complete lesson each day is not expected during the first year the form is used. In the span of two or three years, however, by building on the previous plans a teacher can develop a fairly satisfactory set of daily lessons. Naturally, some changes and variations are needed each year to tailor the plans to the needs of individual classes. Basically, though, the major concepts and procedures are still there.

Plans worked out in this fashion are thorough and complete, and give the teacher a feeling of security. Many problems of classroom disorder are averted because the students are busy with planned activities. The teacher sees direction in what he is doing; the substitute's task is simplified; the learners are more content; and the supervisor has a meaningful base for offering constructive criticism.

Helping people learn is hard work and a big responsibility. It demands a great deal of time-consuming planning, but the results are worth it.

Chapter 8

STRATEGIES AND TACTICS
INVOLVING DISCOVERY,
PROBLEM SOLVING,
AND CREATIVE THINKING

T HE first responsibility of the school is to teach boys and girls how to think and to give them the tools to think with." * This statement represents one of the assumptions underlying this book. A great number of writers and teachers of both the past and present hold this same position, although there has been considerable disagreement about how best to achieve this ideal. Evidently, many of the teaching practices teachers have been using tend to stifle thinking rather than promote it. This chapter will present some strategies and tactics designed to encourage thinking.

Thinking and creativity are much akin. Original criticism, analysis, and research, along with original writing, painting, composition, and invention are creative processes. The secret in teaching for objectives of this type seems to be to allow pupils some opportunity for free thought and expression. Just how free is moot. Some authorities make the limits of pupil freedom quite narrow so as to force pupils to come to the right conclusions, and others leave pupils almost entirely free.

At the moment the trend is toward discovery teaching utilizing inductive methods, although there is no reason not to use deductive processes. (Strangely enough, some examples of "inductive teaching" use the methods of deductive reasoning.) Discovery or inductive teaching seems to be replacing, to some extent at least, the popularity of problem solving. The difference between the two strategies seems to be that discovery teaching is more structured. In theory at least, the problem-solving strategy allows pupils to deal with real problems in rather free-wheeling ways. Discovery techniques are more likely to be designed to force pupils to rediscover what the teacher had set up for them to discover. Research papers and experiments are likely to be a form of problem solving. All of these strategies are dependent upon

---

* Leonard H. Clark, Raymond L. Klein, and John B. Burks, *The American Secondary School Curriculum*, (New York: The Macmillan Company, 1965), p. 137.

pupils' developing skills in the evaluating of their reading and other information.

Much the same thing can be said of discussion techniques. Class discussion, on the other hand, is quite useful for encouraging thinking and changing attitudes. That is why it is so often combined with large group discussion in team-teaching schemes. Unfortunately, however, class discussion is another difficult technique, for it requires the teacher to remain in the background and yet guide the discussion into fruitful paths. When effectively used, it can harness the group processes to change deep-seated beliefs and values; but when carelessly or incompetently done, it can lapse into an aimless bull session or a period of sharing ignorance and prejudiced opinion. In this respect, panel discussions and pupils' oral reports are similar to classroom discussions. Again the technique requires the teacher to guide the pupil while giving him his head enough so that he can create his own learning.

Teaching by means of discovery, problem solving and research activities is not really new. Some of these methods, the discovery method for instance, are extremely old. They are, however, rather difficult for unskilled teachers. Although many of the best teachers have advocated such approaches, mediocre, unimaginative teachers have found it easier to teach sheer information by formalized noncreative patterns. Therefore, the emphasis has been on memory rather than on thinking in most secondary school teaching. Very rarely have teachers taught for any objectives other than the very lowest of the hierarchy of cognitive objectives listed in *The Taxonomy of Educational Objectives*.†

Some teachers today seem to have become convinced that discovery teaching is the only strategy. But as the examples show, discovery teaching is only one of the techniques for teaching pupils how to think or for developing skill in the processes of thinking in a discipline. Other objectives require other strategies. There has always been and always will be need for strategies that establish skills, implant information, and change attitudes. Therefore, there will always be need for strategies that feature drill and practice, telling and showing, and persuading and convincing. The point to remember is that one should pick the strategy most likely to accomplish the desired objectives. In the past, teachers have neglected strategies that lead toward creative thought. In the future, we must stress these strategies, but not to the point of neglecting other necessary strategies.

† Benjamin S. Bloom, *op. cit.*, see Chapter 2.

THE ACT OF DISCOVERY

Jerome S. Bruner *

Many of the educational theoreticians of the past and present have emphasized the value of pupils' discovering or creating knowledge themselves. Discovery learning is basic to both the dialectical method of Socrates and the parable method of Jesus. It is implicit in the object teaching of Rousseau. A century ago, Herbert Spencer emphasized the importance of self-development through discovery in his classic Education. *Jerome Bruner and other contemporary writers are now emphasizing its importance more than ever before.*

Bruner has been the most influential of recent exponents of discovery teaching. He has several reasons for his faith in the discovery approach. One is that he believes it helps motivate youngsters; another is that it helps teach pupils how to learn; still another is that it helps pupils remember what they have learned. All in all, Bruner's arguments are most convincing. Coming, as they do, from a leading student of cognition, they have led to a considerable vogue for the use of the discovery method in the schools.

The immediate occasion for my concern with discovery is the work of the various new curriculum projects that have grown up in America during the last few years. Whether one speaks to mathematicians or physicists or historians, one encounters repeatedly an expression of faith in the powerful effects that come from permitting the student to put things together for himself, to be his own discoverer.

First, I should be clear about what the act of discovery entails. It is rarely, on the frontier of knowledge or elsewhere, that new facts are "discovered" in the sense of being encountered, as Newton suggested, in the form of islands of truth in an uncharted sea of ignorance. Or if they appear to be discovered in this way, it is almost always thanks to some happy hypothesis about where to navigate. Discovery, like surprise, favors the well-prepared mind. In playing bridge, one is surprised by a hand with no honors in it and also by one that is all in one suit. Yet all particular hands in bridge are equiprobable: to

* Reprinted by permission of the publishers from Jerome S. Bruner, *On Knowing*, Cambridge, Mass.: The Belknap Press of Harvard University Press, Copyright, 1962, by the President and Fellows of Harvard College.

be surprised one must know something about the laws of probability. So too in discovery. The history of science is studded with examples of men "finding out" something and not knowing it. I shall operate on the assumption that discovery, whether by a schoolboy going it on his own or by a scientist cultivating the growing edge of his field, is in its essence a matter of rearranging or transforming evidence in such a way that one is enabled to go beyond the evidence so reassembled to new insights. It may well be that an additional fact or shred of evidence makes this larger transformation possible. But it is often not even dependent on new information.

Very generally, and at the risk of oversimplification, it is useful to distinguish two kinds of teaching: that which takes place in the *expository mode* and that in the *hypothetical mode*. In the former, the decisions concerning the mode and pace and style of exposition are principally determined by the teacher as expositor; the student is the listener. The speaker has a quite different set of decisions to make: he has a wide choice of alternatives; he is anticipating paragraph content while the listener is still intent on the words; he is manipulating the content of the material by various transformations while the listener is quite unaware of these internal options. But in the hypothetical mode the teacher and the student are in a more cooperative position with respect to what in linguistics would be called "speaker's decisions." The student is not a bench-bound listener, but is taking a part in the formulation and at times may play the principal role in it. He will be aware of alternatives and may even have an "as if" attitude toward these, and he may evaluate information as it comes. One cannot describe the process in either mode with great precision of detail, but I think it is largely the hypothetical mode which characterizes the teaching that encourages discovery.

Consider now what benefits might be derived from the experience of learning through discoveries that one makes oneself. I shall discuss these under four headings: (1) the increase in intellectual potency, (2) the shift from extrinsic to intrinsic rewards, (3) the learning of the heuristics of discovering, and (4) the aid to conserving memory.

Intellectual potency. I should like to consider the differences among students in a highly constrained psychological experiment involving a two-choice machine.[1] In order to win chips, they must depress a key either on the right or the left side of the apparatus. A pattern of payoff is designed so that, say, they will be paid off on the right side 70 percent of the time, on the left 30 percent, but this detail is not important. What is important is that the payoff sequence is arranged at random, that there is no pattern. There is a marked contrast in the behavior of subjects who think that there is some pattern to be found in the sequence—who think that regularities are discoverable—and the performance of subjects who think that things are happening quite by chance. The first group adopts what is called an "event-matching" strategy

[1] J. S. Bruner, J. J. Goodnow, and G. A. Austin, *A Study of Thinking* (New York: John Wiley, 1956).

in which the number of responses given to each side is roughly commensurate
to the proportion of times that it pays off: in the present case, 70 on the right
to 30 on the left. The group that believes there is no pattern very soon settles
for a much more primitive strategy allocating *all* responses to the side that
has the greater payoff. A little arithmetic will show that the lazy all-and-none
strategy pays off more if the environment is truly random: they win 70 percent of the time. The event-matching subjects win about 70 percent on the
70-percent payoff side (or 49 percent of the time there) and 30 percent of
the time on the side that pays off 30 percent of the time (another 9 percent
for a total take-home wage of 58 percent in return for their labors of decision).

But the world is not always or not even frequently random, and if one
analyzes carefully what the event matchers are doing, one sees that they are
trying out hypotheses one after the other, all of them containing a term that
leads to a distribution of bets on the two sides with a frequency to match the
actual occurrence of events. If it should turn out that there is a pattern to be
discovered, their payoff could become 100 percent. The other group would
go on at the middling rate of 70 percent.

What has this to do with the subject at hand? For the person to search out
and find regularities and relationships in his environment, he must either
come armed with an expectancy that there will be something to find or be
aroused to such an expectancy so that he may devise ways of searching and
finding. One of the chief enemies of search is the assumption that there is
nothing one can find in the environment by way of regularity or relationship.
In the experiment just cited, subjects often fall into one of two habitual
attitudes: either that there is nothing to be found or that a pattern can be
discovered by looking. There is an important sequel in behavior to the two
attitudes.

We have conducted a series of experimental studies on a group of some
seventy schoolchildren over a four-year period.[2] The studies have led us to
distinguish an interesting dimension of cognitive activity that can be described as ranging from *episodic empiricism* at one end to *cumulative constructionism* at the other. The two attitudes in the above experiments on
choice illustrate the extremes of the dimension. One of the experiments employs the game of Twenty Questions. A child—in this case he is between ten
and twelve—is told that a car has gone off the road and hit a tree. He is to
ask questions that can be answered by "yes" or "no" to discover the cause of
the accident. After completing the problem, the same task is given him,
though this time he is told that the accident has a different cause. In all, the
procedure is repeated four times. Children enjoy playing the game. They
also differ quite markedly in the approach or strategy they bring to the task.
In the first place, we can distinguish clearly between two types of questions

2 J. S. Bruner and others, *The Processes of Cognitive Development*, in preparation.

asked: one is intended to locate constraints in the problem, constraints that will eventually give shape to an hypothesis; the other is the hypothesis as question. It is the difference between, "Was there anything wrong with the driver?" and "Was the driver rushing to the doctor's office for an appointment and the car got out of control?" There are children who precede hypotheses with efforts to locate constraint and there are those who are "potshotters," who string out hypotheses noncumulatively one after the other. A second element of strategy lies in the connectivity of information gathering: the extent to which questions asked utilize or ignore or violate information previously obtained. The questions asked by children tend to be organized in cycles, each cycle usually given over to the pursuit of some particular notion. Both within cycles and between cycles one can discern marked differences in the connectivity of the children's performances. Needless to say, children who employ constraint location as a technique preliminary to the formulation of hypotheses tend to be far more organized in their harvesting of information. Persistence is another feature of strategy, a characteristic compounded of what appear to be two factors: sheer doggedness and a persistence that stems from the sequential organization that a child brings to the task. Doggedness is probably just animal spirits or the need to achieve. Organized persistence is a maneuver for protecting the fragile cognitive apparatus from overload. The child who has flooded himself with disorganized information from unconnected hypotheses will become discouraged and confused sooner than the child who has shown a certain cunning in his strategy of getting information —a child who senses that the value of information is not simply in getting it but in being able to carry it. The persistence of the organized child stems from his knowledge of how to organize questions in cycles and how to summarize things to himself.

Episodic empiricism is illustrated by information gathering that is unbound by prior constraints, that is deficient in organizational persistence. The opposite extreme, what we have called cumulative constructionism, is characterized by sensitivity to constraint, by connective maneuvers, and by organized persistence. Brute persistence seems to be one of those gifts from the gods that make people more exaggeratedly what they are.

Before returning to the issue of discovery and its role in the development of thinking, there is a word more to say about the ways in which the problem solver may transform information he has dealt with actively. The point arises from the pragmatic question: what does it take to get information processed into a form best designed to fit some future use? An experiment by R. B. Zajonc in 1957 suggests an answer.[3] He gave groups of students information of a controlled kind, some groups being told that they were to transmit the information later on, others that they were merely to keep it in mind. In general, he found more differentiation of the information intended for transmittal than of information received passively. An active attitude leads to a

[3] R. B. Zajonc, personal communication (1957).

transformation related to a task to be performed. There is a risk, to be sure, in the possible overspecialization of information processing. It can lead to such a high degree of specific organization that information is lost for general use, although this can be guarded against.

Let me convert the foregoing into an hypothesis. Emphasis on discovery in learning has precisely the effect on the learner of leading him to be a constructionist, to organize what he is encountering in a manner not only designed to discover regularity and relatedness, but also to avoid the kind of information drift that fails to keep account of the uses to which information might have to be put. Emphasis on discovery, indeed, helps the child to learn the varieties of problem solving, of transforming information for better use, helps him to learn how to go about the very task of learning. So goes the hypothesis; it is still in need of testing. But it is an hypothesis of such important human implications that we cannot afford not to test it—and the testing will have to be in the schools.

Intrinsic and extrinsic motives. Much of the problem in leading a child to effective cognitive activity is to free him from the immediate control of environmental rewards and punishments. Learning that starts in response to the rewards of parental or teacher approval or to the avoidance of failure can too readily develop a pattern in which the child is seeking cues as to how to conform to what is expected of him. We know from studies of children who tend to be early overachievers in school that they are likely to be seekers after the "right way to do it" and that their capacity for transforming learning into viable thought structures tends to be lower than that of children achieving at levels predicted by intelligence tests.[4] Our tests on such children show them to be lower in analytic ability than those who are not conspicuous in overachievement. As we shall see later, they develop rote abilities and depend on being able to "give back" what is expected rather than to make it into something that relates to the rest of their cognitive life. As Maimonides would say, their learning is not their own.

The hypothesis I would propose here is that to the degree that one is able to approach learning as a task of discovering something rather than "learning about" it, to that degree there will be a tendency for the child to work with the autonomy of self-reward or, more properly, be rewarded by discovery itself.

To readers familiar with the battles of the last half-century in the field of motivation, this hypothesis will be recognized as controversial. For the traditional view of motivation in learning has been, until very recently, couched in terms of a theory of drives and reinforcements: learning occurs because a response produced by a stimulus is followed by the reduction in a primary drive. The doctrine is greatly but thinly extended by the idea of secondary reinforcement: anything that has been "associated" with such a reduction in drive or need can also serve to reinforce the connection between a stimulus

---

[4] See Note 2 above.

and the response that it evokes. Finding a steak will do for getting a food-search act connected with a certain stimulus, but so will the sight of a nice restaurant.

In 1959 there appeared a most searching and important criticism of this ancient hedonistic position, written by Robert White, reviewing the evidence of recently published animal studies, of work in the field of psychoanalysis, and of research on the development of cognitive processes in children. Professor White comes to the conclusion, quite rightly I think, that the drive-reduction model of learning runs counter to too many important phenomena of learning and development to be either regarded as general in its applicability or even correct in its general approach. Let me quote some of his principal conclusions and explore their applicability to the hypothesis stated above.

I now propose that we gather the various kinds of behavior just mentioned, all of which have to do with effective interaction with the environment, under the general heading of competence. According to Webster, competence means fitness of ability, and the suggested synonyms include capability, capacity, efficiency, proficiency, and skill. It is therefore a suitable word to describe such things as grasping and exploring, crawling and walking, attention and perception, language and thinking, manipulating and changing the surroundings, all of which promote an effective—a competent—interaction with the environment. It is true, of course, that maturation plays a part in all these developments, but this part is heavily overshadowed by learning in all the more complex accomplishments like speech or skilled manipulation. I shall argue that it is necessary to make competence a motivational concept; there is *competence motivation* as well as competence in its more familiar sense of achieved capacity. The behavior that leads to the building up of effective grasping, handling, and letting go of objects, to take one example, is not random behavior that is produced by an overflow of energy. It is directed, selective, and persistent, and it continues not because it serves primary drives, which indeed it cannot serve until it is almost perfected, but because it satisfies an intrinsic need to deal with the environment.[5]

I am suggesting that there are forms of activity that serve to enlist and develop the competence motive, that serve to make it the driving force behind behavior. I should like to add to White's general premise that the *exercise* of competence motives has the effect of strengthening the degree to which they gain control over behavior and thereby reduce the effects of extrinsic rewards or drive gratification.

In 1934 the brilliant Russian psychologist Vygotsky characterized the growth of thought processes as starting with a dialogue of speech and gesture between child and parent.[6] Autonomous thinking, he said, begins at the stage when the child is first able to internalize these conversations and "run them off" himself. This is a typical sequence in the development of competence.

[5] R. W. White, "Motivation Reconsidered: The Concept of Competence," *Psychological Review*, no. 66 (1959), pp. 317–318.

[6] L. S. Vygotsky, *Thinking and Speech* (Moscow, 1934).

So too in instruction. The narrative of teaching is of the order of Vygotsky's conversation. The next move in the development of competence is the internalization of the narrative and its "rules of generation" so that the child is now capable of running off the narrative on his own. The hypothetical mode in teaching, by encouraging the child to participate in "speaker's decisions," speeds this process along. Once internalization has occurred, the child is in a vastly improved position from several obvious points of view—notably that he is able to go beyond the information he has been given to generate additional ideas that either can be checked immediately from experience or can, at least, be used as a basis for formulating reasonable hypotheses. But over and beyond that, the child is now in a position to experience success and failure not as reward and punishment but as information. For when the task is his own rather than a prescribed matching of environmental demands, he becomes his own paymaster in a certain measure. Seeking to gain control over his environment, he can now treat success as indicating that he is on the right track, failure as indicating that he is on the wrong one.

In the end, this development has the effect of freeing learning from immediate stimulus control. When learning leads only to pellets of this or that in the short run rather than to mastery in the long run, then behavior can be readily "shaped" by extrinsic rewards. But when behavior becomes more extended and competence-oriented, it comes under the control of more complex cognitive structures and operates more from the inside out.

The position of Pavlov is interesting. His early account of the learning process was based entirely on a notion of stimulus control of behavior through the conditioning mechanism in which, through contiguity, a new conditioned stimulus was substituted for an old unconditioned stimulus. But even he recognized that his account was insufficient to deal with higher forms of learning. To supplement it, he introduced the idea of the "second signalling system," with central importance placed on symbolic systems, such as language, in mediating and giving shape to mental life. Or as Luria put it in 1959, the first signal system is "concerned with directly perceived stimuli, the second with systems of verbal elaboration." Luria, commenting on the importance of the transition from first to second signal system, says:

It would be mistaken to suppose that verbal intercourse with adults merely changes the contents of the child's conscious activity without changing its form. . . . The word has a basic function not only because it indicates a corresponding object in the external world, but also because it abstracts, isolates the necessary signal, generalizes perceived signals and relates them to certain categories; it is this systematization of direct experience that makes the role of the word in the formation of mental processes so exceptionally important.[7]

It is interesting too that the final rejection of the universality of the doctrine of reinforcement in direct conditioning came from some of Pavlov's

[7] A. L. Luria, "The Directive Function of Speech in Development and Dissolution," *Word*, no. 15 (1959), p. 12.

own students. Ivanov-Smolensky and Krasnogorsky published papers showing the manner in which symbolized linguistic messages could take over the place of the unconditioned stimulus and of the unconditioned response (gratification of hunger) in children.[8] In all instances, they speak of these as *replacements* of lower first-system mental or neural processes by higher second-system controls. A strange irony, then, that Russian psychology, which gave us the notion of the conditioned response and the assumption that higher-order activities are built up out of colligations of such primitive units, has rejected this notion while much of the American psychology of learning until quite recently has stayed within the early Pavlovian fold—as, for example, a 1959 article by Spence in the *Harvard Educational Review*, reiterating the primacy of conditioning and the derivative nature of complex learning.[9] It is even more noteworthy that Russian pedagogic theory has become deeply influenced by this new trend and is now placing much stress upon the importance of building up a more active symbolical approach to problem solving among children.

In this matter of the control of learning, then, my conclusion is that the degree to which the desire for competence comes to control behavior, to that degree the role of reinforcement or "outside rewards" wanes in shaping behavior. The child comes to manipulate his environment more actively and achieves his gratification from coping with problems. As he finds symbolic modes of representing and transforming the environment, there is an accompanying decline in the importance of stimulus-response-reward sequences. To use the metaphor that David Riesman developed in a quite different context, mental life moves from a state of outer-directedness, in which the fortuity of stimuli and reinforcement are crucial, to a state of inner-directedness in which the growth and maintenance of mastery become central and dominant.

The heuristics of discovery. Lincoln Steffens, reflecting in his *Autobiography* on his undergraduate education at Berkeley, comments that his schooling paid too much attention to learning what was known and too little to finding out about what was not known.[10] But how does one train a student in the techniques of discovery? Again there are some hypotheses to offer. There are many ways of coming to the arts of inquiry. One of them is by careful study of its formalization in logic, statistics, mathematics, and the like. If one is going to pursue inquiry as a way of life, particularly in the sciences, certainly such study is essential. Yet whoever has taught kindergarten

---

[8] A. G. Ivanov-Smolensky, "The Interaction of the First and Second Signal Systems in Certain Normal and Pathological Conditions," *Physiological Journal of the USSR*, XXXV, no. 5 (1949); Ivanov-Smolensky, "Concerning the Study of the Joint Activity of the First and Second Signal Systems," *Journal of Higher Nervous Activity*, I, no. 1 (1951); N. I. Krasnogorsky, *Studies of Higher Nervous Activity in Animals and in Man*, I (Moscow, 1954).

[9] K. W. Spence, "The Relation of Learning Theory to the Technique of Education," *Harvard Educational Review*, no. 29 (1959), pp. 84–95.

[10] *Autobiography of Lincoln Steffens* (New York: Harcourt, Brace, 1931).

and the early primary grades or has had graduate students working with him on their theses—I choose the two extremes for they are both periods of intense inquiry—knows that an understanding of the formal aspect of inquiry is not sufficient. Rather, several activities and attitudes, some directly related to a particular subject and some fairly generalized, appear to go with inquiry and research. These have to do with the *process* of trying to find out something and, though their presence is no guarantee that the *product* will be a great discovery, their absence is likely to lead to awkwardness or aridity or confusion. How difficult it is to describe these matters—the heuristics of inquiry. There is one set of attitudes or methods that has to do with sensing the relevance of variables—avoiding immersion in edge effects and getting instead to the big sources of variance. This gift partly comes from intuitive familiarity with a range of phenomena, sheer "knowing the stuff." But it also comes out of a sense of what things among many "smell right," what things are of the right order of magnitude or scope or severity.

Weldon, the English philosopher, describes problem solving in an interesting and picturesque way. He distinguishes among difficulties, puzzles, and problems. We solve a problem or make a discovery when we impose a puzzle form on a difficulty to convert it into a problem that can be solved in such a way that it gets us where we want to be. That is to say, we recast the difficulty into a form that we know how to work with—then we work it. Much of what we speak of as discovery consists of knowing how to impose a workable kind of form on various kinds of difficulties. A small but crucial part of discovery of the highest order is to invent and develop effective models or "puzzle forms." It is in this area that the truly powerful mind shines. But it is surprising to what degree perfectly ordinary people can, given the benefit of instruction, construct quite interesting and what, a century ago, would have been considered greatly original models.

Now to the hypothesis. It is my hunch that it is only through the exercise of problem solving and the effort of discovery that one learns the working heuristics of discovery; the more one has practice, the more likely one is to generalize what one has learned into a style of problem solving or inquiry that serves for any kind of task encountered—or almost any kind of task. I think the matter is self-evident, but what is unclear is the kinds of training and teaching that produce the best effects. How, for instance, do we teach a child to cut his losses but at the same time be persistent in trying out an idea; to risk forming an early hunch without at the same time formulating one so early and with so little evidence that he is stuck with it while he waits for appropriate evidence to materialize; to pose good testable guesses that are neither too brittle nor too sinuously incorrigible? And so on and on. Practice in inquiry, in trying to figure out things for oneself is indeed what is needed —but in what form? Of only one thing am I convinced: I have never seen anybody improve in the art and technique of inquiry by any means other than engaging in inquiry.

Conservation of memory. I have come to take what some psychologists might consider a rather drastic view of the memory process. It is a view that in large measure derives from the work of my colleague, George Miller.[11] Its first premise is that the principal problem of human memory is not storage but retrieval. In spite of the biological unlikeliness of it, we seem to be able to store a huge quantity of information—perhaps not a full tape recording, though at times it seems we even do that, but a great sufficiency of impressions. We may infer this from the fact that recognition, the ability to recall with maximum promptings, is so extraordinarily good in human beings and that spontaneous recall, with no promptings, is so extraordinarily bad. The key to retrieval is organization or, in even simpler terms, knowing where to find information that has been put into memory.

Let me illustrate with a simple experiment. We present pairs of words to twelve-year-olds. The children of one group are told only to remember the pairs and that they will be asked to repeat them later. Others are told to remember the pairs by producing a word or idea that will tie them together in a way that will make sense. The word pairs include such juxtapositions as "chair-forest," "sidewalk-square," and the like. One can distinguish three styles of mediators, and children can be scaled in terms of their relative preference for each: generic mediation, in which a pair is tied together by a superordinate idea: "chair and forest are both made of wood"; thematic mediation, in which the two terms are imbedded in a theme or a little story: "the lost child sat on a chair in the middle of the forest"; and part-whole mediation, in which "chairs are made from trees in the forest" is typical. Now the chief result, as you would predict, is that children who provide their own mediators do best—indeed, one time through a set of thirty pairs, they recover up to 95 percent of the second words when presented with the first ones of the pairs, whereas the uninstructed children reach a maximum of less than 50 percent recovered. Also, children do best in recovering materials tied together by the form of mediator they most often use.

One can cite a myriad of findings to indicate that any organization of information that reduces the aggregate complexity of material by imbedding it into a cognitive process a person has constructed for himself will make that material more accessible for retrieval. We may say that the process of memory, looked at from the retrieval side, is also a process of problem solving: how can material be "placed" in memory so that it can be obtained on demand?

We can take as a point of departure the example of the children who developed their own technique for relating each word pair. The children with the self-made mediators did better than the children who were given ready-made ones. Another group of children were given the mediators developed by this group to aid them in memorizing—a set of "ready-made" memory aids. In general, material that is organized in terms of a person's own interests and cognitive structures is material that has the best chance of being acces-

[11] G. A. Miller, "The Magical Number Seven, Plus or Minus Two," *Psychological Review*, no. 63 (1956), pp. 81–97.

sible in memory. It is more likely to be placed along routes that are connected to one's own ways of intellectual travel. Thus, the very attitudes and activities that characterize figuring out or discovering things for oneself also seem to have the effect of conserving memory.

SOCRATES AND THE SLAVE BOY

Plato *

Socrates, who lived in the 4th century B.C., *is famous for his teaching skill and the teaching method that still bears his name. As the following selection shows, his method is largely a series of leading questions. Although sometimes forced, the questions are open-ended. The technique is not to fill the pupil's brain, but to lead the pupil to draw his own conclusions. Even though, it must be admitted, Plato's Socrates usually saw to it that the pupil's conclusions were the same as the conclusions Socrates had in mind; to be fair to Socrates, one must also admit that he sometimes appears not to have decided what the conclusion should be and that he was always ready to accept the decision of the evidence.*

In general, the Socratic strategy was divided into two parts. First was the irony in which Socrates tried to eliminate any misconceptions or preconceptions that might cloud the student's thinking. The second was the midwivery in which Socrates tried to help the pupil give birth to a new correct concept.

The selection that follows is from Plato's Meno. Socrates, Meno, and their friends have been arguing about virtue. In this discussion, Socrates' position has been that all knowledge is innate. When we meet the players, Socrates is about to try to prove his point by teaching geometry to a slave boy who has had no previous schooling. Our selection consists of the slave's lesson. Note how Socrates develops the lesson and carries it through. The portion of the lesson up to the beginning of Socrates' words to Meno is the irony; the part following, the midwivery.

In reading this selection, the reader should note the skilful use of leading questions, the natural motivation, the logical development through questioning, and the emphasis on pupil activity, in this case pupil think-

* From *Plato: Protagoras and Meno*, translated by W. K. C. Guthrie (London: Penguin Books, 1956), pp. 133–137. Reprinted by permission of the publisher.

ing. Teachers who attempt to use this technique should not be surprised if their classes do not develop as logically as this one in Meno. Socrates himself had difficulty keeping the dialogue on the track as some of the other writings of Plato and Xenephon show. The Socratic technique is not a machine technique; it is the interaction of a teacher and pupil with the teacher guiding and helping, but not dictating, by means of questions. The technique is excellent, although rather difficult to use in large classes.

SOCRATES. Now boy, you know that a square is a figure like this?
 (*Socrates begins to draw figures in the sand at his feet. He points to the square* A B C D.)

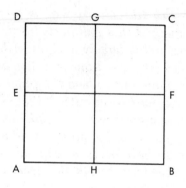

BOY. Yes.
SOCRATES. It has all these four sides equal?
BOY. Yes.
SOCRATES. And these lines which go through the middle of it are also equal? (The lines E F, G H.)
BOY. Yes.
SOCRATES. Such a figure could be either larger or smaller, could it not?
BOY. Yes.
SOCRATES. Now if this side is two feet long, and this side the same, how many feet will the whole be? Put it this way. If it were two feet in this direction and only one in that, must not the area be two feet taken once?
BOY. Yes.
SOCRATES. But since it is two feet this way also, does it not become twice two feet?
BOY. Yes.
SOCRATES. And how many feet is twice two? Work it out and tell me.
BOY. Four.
SOCRATES. Now could one draw another figure double the size of this, but similar, that is, with all its sides equal like this one?

BOY. Yes.

SOCRATES. How many feet will its area be?

BOY. Eight.

SOCRATES. Now then, try to tell me how long each of its sides will be. The present figure has a side of two feet. What will be the side of the double-sized one?

BOY. It will be double, Socrates, obviously.

SOCRATES. You see, Meno, that I am not teaching him anything, only asking. Now he thinks he knows the length of the side of the eight-feet-square.

MENO. Yes.

SOCRATES. But does he?

MENO. Certainly not.

SOCRATES. He thinks it is twice the length of the other.

MENO. Yes.

SOCRATES. Now watch how he recollects things in order—the proper way to recollect.

You say that the side of double length produces the double-sized figure? Like this I mean, not long this way and short that. It must be equal on all sides like the first figures, only twice its size, that is eight feet. Think a moment whether you still expect to get it from doubling the side.

BOY. Yes, I do.

SOCRATES. Well now, shall we have a line double the length of this (A B) if we add another the same length as this end (B J)?

BOY. Yes.

SOCRATES. It is on this line then, according to you, that we shall make the eight-feet square, by taking four of the same length?

BOY. Yes.

SOCRATES. Let us draw in four equal lines (*i.e., counting* A J, *and adding* J K, K L, *and* L A *made complete by drawing in its second half* L D), using the first as a base. Does this not give us what you call the eight-feet figure?

BOY. Certainly.

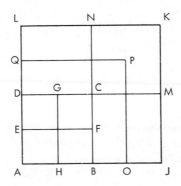

SOCRATES. But does it contain these four squares, each equal to the original four-feet one?

(Socrates has drawn in the lines C M, C N *to complete the squares that he wishes to point out.)*

BOY. Yes.

SOCRATES. How big is it then? Won't it be four times as big?

BOY. Of course.

SOCRATES. And is four times the same as twice?

BOY. Of course not.

SOCRATES. So doubling the side has given us not a double but a fourfold figure?

BOY. True.

SOCRATES. And four times four are sixteen, are they not?

BOY. Yes.

SOCRATES. Then how big is the side of the eight-feet figure? This one has given us four times the original area, hasn't it?

BOY. Yes.

SOCRATES. And a side half the length gave us a square of four feet?

BOY. Yes.

SOCRATES. Good. And isn't a square of eight feet double this one and half that?

BOY. Yes.

SOCRATES. Will it not have a side greater than this one but less than that?

BOY. I think it will.

SOCRATES. Right. Always answer what you think. Now tell me: was not this side two feet long, and this one four?

BOY. Yes.

SOCRATES. Then the side of the eight-feet figure must be longer than two feet but shorter than four?

BOY. It must.

SOCRATES. Try to say how long you think it is.

BOY. Three feet.

SOCRATES. If so, shall we add half of this bit (B O, *half of* B J) and make it three feet? Here are two, and this is one, and on this side similarly we have two plus one; and here is the figure you want.

(Socrates completes the square A O P Q.)

BOY. Yes.

SOCRATES. If it is three feet this way and three that, will the whole area be three times three feet?

BOY. It looks like it.

SOCRATES. And that is how many?

BOY. Nine.

SOCRATES. Whereas the square double our first square had to be how many?

BOY. Eight.

SOCRATES. But we haven't yet got the square of eight feet even from a three-feet side?

BOY. No.

SOCRATES. Then what length will give it? Try to tell us exactly. If you don't want to count it up, just show us on the diagram.

BOY. It's no use, Socrates, I just don't know.

SOCRATES. Observe, Meno, the stage he has reached on the path of recollection. At the beginning he did not know the side of the square of eight feet. Nor indeed does he know it now, but then he thought he knew it and answered boldly, as was appropriate—he felt no perplexity. Now however he does feel perplexed. Not only does he not know the answer; he doesn't even think he knows.

MENO. Quite true.

SOCRATES. Isn't he in a better position now in relation to what he didn't know?

MENO. I admit that too.

SOCRATES. So in perplexing him and numbing him like the sting-ray, have we done him any harm?

MENO. I think not.

SOCRATES. In fact we have helped him to some extent towards finding out the right answer, for now not only is he ignorant of it but he will be quite glad to look for it. Up to now, he thought he could speak well and fluently, on many occasions and before large audiences, on the subject of a square double the size of a given square, maintaining that it must have a side of double the length.

MENO. No doubt.

SOCRATES. Do you suppose then that he would have attempted to look for, or learn, what he thought he knew (though he did not), before he was thrown into perplexity, became aware of his ignorance, and felt a desire to know?

MENO. No.

SOCRATES. Then the numbing process was good for him?

MENO. I agree.

SOCRATES. Now notice what, starting from this state of perplexity, he will discover by seeking the truth in company with me, though I simply ask him questions without teaching him. Be ready to catch me if I give him any instruction or explanation instead of simply interrogating him on his own opinions.

(Socrates here rubs out the previous figures and starts again.)

Tell me, boy, is not this our square of four feet? (A B C D.) You understand?

BOY. Yes.

SOCRATES. Now we can add another equal to it like this? (B C E F.)

BOY. Yes.

SOCRATES. And a third here, equal to each of the others? (C E G H.)

BOY. Yes.

SOCRATES. And then we can fill in this one in the corner? (D C H J.)

BOY. Yes.

SOCRATES. Then here we have four equal squares?

BOY. Yes.

SOCRATES. And how many times the size of the first square is the whole?

BOY. Four times.

SOCRATES. And we want one double the size. You remember?

BOY. Yes.

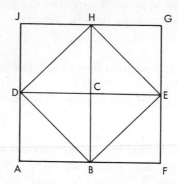

SOCRATES. Now does this line going from corner to corner cut each of these squares in half?

BOY. Yes.

SOCRATES. And these are four equal lines enclosing this area? (B E H D.)

BOY. They are.

SOCRATES. Now think. How big is this area?

BOY. I don't understand.

SOCRATES. Here are four squares. Has not each line cut off the inner half of each of them?

BOY. Yes.

SOCRATES. And how many such halves are there in this figure? (B E H D.)

BOY. Four.

SOCRATES. And how many in this one? (A B C D.)

BOY. Two.

SOCRATES. And what is the relation of four to two?

BOY. Double.

SOCRATES. How big is this figure then?

BOY. Eight feet.

SOCRATES. On what base?

BOY. This one.

SOCRATES. The line which goes from corner to corner of the square of four feet?

BOY. Yes.

SOCRATES. The technical name for it is 'diagonal'; so if we use that name, it is your personal opinion that the square on the diagonal of the original square is double its area.

BOY. That is so, Socrates.

THE GOOD SAMARITAN

Luke 10:25–37 *

Jesus of Nazareth was a master teacher. Because of his pre-eminence in other things, one sometimes forgets that his ministry was a teaching ministry. In some respects, Jesus' teaching methods were like those of Socrates. By means of questions, Jesus led his pupils to draw their own conclusions and to convince themselves. Although authoritative, his teaching was what Flanders calls "indirect." One of Jesus' favorite devices was the parable. He used this strategy often to clear up concepts his hearers found hard to understand. Briefly, what he liked to do when his pupils found the going difficult was to relate some homely anecdote well within their experience and then to ask them to draw their own inferences from the story. One of the most famous of these parables is that of the Good Samaritan. It is perhaps the best-known example of the discovery technique used as a teaching tactic.

25 And behold a certain lawyer stood up, and tempted him, saying, Master, what shall I do to inherit eternal life?

26 He said unto him, What is written in the law? how readest thou?

27 And he answering said, Thou shalt love the Lord thy God with all thy heart, and with all thy soul, and with all thy strength, and with all thy mind; and thy neighbour as thyself.

28 And he said unto him, Thou hast answered right: this do, and thou shalt live.

29 But he, willing to justify himself, said unto Jesus, And who is my neighbour?

30 And Jesus answering said, A certain *man* went down from Jerusalem to Jericho, and fell among thieves, which stripped him of his raiment, and wounded *him*, and departed, leaving *him* half dead.

31 And by chance there came down a certain priest that way; and when he saw him, he passed by on the other side.

32 And likewise a Levite, when he was at the place, came and looked *on him*, and passed by on the other side.

33 But a certain Samaritan, as he journeyed, came where he was: and when he saw him, he had compassion *on him*,

* From Luke 10:25–37, King James Version.

34 And went to *him*, and bound up his wounds, pouring in oil and wine, and set him on his own beast, and brought him to an inn, and took care of him.

35 And on the morrow when he departed, he took out two pence and gave *them* to the host, and said unto him, Take care of him; and whatsoever thou spendest more, when I come again, I will repay thee.

36 Which now of these three, thinkest thou, was neighbour unto him that fell among the thieves?

37 And he said, He that shewed mercy on him. Then said Jesus unto him, Go, and do thou likewise.

EMILE OR EDUCATION

Jean Jacques Rousseau *

J. J. Rousseau advocated a system of education in which children learned naturally. By learning naturally, Rousseau meant learning by discovery. Book learning, he thought, led only to parroting meaningless words. By the use of discovery techniques by which he induced the child to learn by himself, he hoped to make his pupil's understanding clear and whole.

Rousseau's notions have had much impact on modern educational technology. They were largely responsible for the emphasis on problem solving by the progressives and for the current stress on discovery learning by the progressives' successors and inheritors today.

In reading the excerpt from Emile, *note the emphasis on motivation, the use of questions to draw out learning, the individualized approach in the tutorial situation, and the stress on observation. Rousseau said he hated books. What he meant was that he hated accepting secondhand opinions. He preferred that his pupils know about fewer things but that their knowledge of the things they know be deep, self-discovered, and therefore real—not just empty verbalism.*

* From the book *Emile; or, Education* by Jean Jacques Rousseau. Translated by Barbara Foxley. Everyman's Library Edition. Reprinted by permission of E. P. Dutton & Co., Inc., and J. M. Dent & Sons Ltd., London.

I do not like verbal explanations. Young people pay little heed to them, nor do they remember them. Things! Things! I cannot repeat it too often. We lay too much stress upon words; we teachers babble, and our scholars follow our example.

Suppose we are studying the course of the sun and the way to find our bearings, when all at once Emile interrupts me with the question, "What is the use of that?" what a fine lecture I might give, how many things I might take occasion to teach him in reply to his question, especially if there is any one there. I might speak of the advantages of travel, the value of commerce, the special products of different lands and the peculiar customs of different nations, the use of the calendar, the way to reckon the seasons for agriculture, the art of navigation, how to steer our course at sea, how to find our way without knowing exactly where we are. Politics, natural history, astronomy, even morals and international law are involved in my explanation, so as to give my pupil some idea of all these sciences and a great wish to learn them. When I have finished I shall have shown myself a regular pedant, I shall have made a great display of learning, and not one single idea has he understood. He is longing to ask me again, "What is the use of taking one's bearings?" but he dare not for fear of vexing me. He finds it pays best to pretend to listen to what he is forced to hear. This is the practical result of our fine systems of education.

But Emile is educated in a simpler fashion. We take so much pains to teach him a difficult idea that he will have heard nothing of all this. At the first word he does not understand, he will run away, he will prance about the room, and leave me to speechify by myself. Let us seek a more commonplace explanation; my scientific learning is of no use to him.

We were observing the position of the forest to the north of Montmorency when he interrupted me with the usual question, "What is the use of that?" "You are right," I said. "Let us take time to think it over, and if we find it is no use we will drop it, for we only want useful games." We find something else to do and geography is put aside for the day.

Next morning I suggest a walk before breakfast; there is nothing he would like better; children are always ready to run about, and he is a good walker. We climb up to the forest, we wander through its clearings and lose ourselves; we have no idea where we are, and when we want to retrace our steps we cannot find the way. Time passes, we are hot and hungry; hurrying vainly this way and that we find nothing but woods, quarries, plains, not a landmark to guide us. Very hot, very tired, very hungry, we only get further astray. At last we sit down to rest and to consider our position. I assume that Emile has been educated like an ordinary child. He does not think, he begins to cry; he has no idea we are close to Montmorency, which is hidden from our view by a mere thicket; but this thicket is a forest to him, a man of his size is buried among bushes. After a few minutes' silence I begin anxiously—

Jean Jacques. My dear Emile, what shall we do to get out?

Emile. I am sure I do not know. I am tired, I am hungry, I am thirsty. I cannot go any further.

Jean Jacques. Do you suppose I am any better off? I would cry too if I could make my breakfast off tears. Crying is no use, we must look about us. Let us see your watch; what time is it?

Emile. It is noon and I am so hungry!

Jean Jacques. Just so; it is noon and I am so hungry too.

Emile. You must be very hungry indeed.

Jean Jacques. Unluckily my dinner won't come to find me. It is twelve o'clock. This time yesterday we were observing the position of the forest from Montmorency. If only we could see the position of Montmorency from the forest——

Emile. But yesterday we could see the forest, and here we cannot see the town.

Jean Jacques. That is just it. If we could only find it without seeing it.

Emile. Oh! my dear friend!

Jean Jacques. Did not we say the forest was——

Emile. North of Montmorency.

Jean Jacques. Then Montmorency must lie——

Emile. South of the forest.

Jean Jacques. We know how to find the north at midday.

Emile. Yes, by the direction of the shadows.

Jean Jacques. But the south?

Emile. What shall we do?

Jean Jacques. The south is opposite the north.

Emile. That is true; we need only find the opposite of the shadows. That is the south! That is the south! Montmorency must be over there! Let us look for it there!

Jean Jacques. Perhaps you are right; let us follow this path through the wood.

Emile. (Clapping his hands.) Oh, I can see Montmorency! there it is, quite plain, just in front of us! Come to luncheon, come to dinner, make haste! Astronomy is some use after all.

Be sure that he thinks this if he does not say it; no matter which, provided I do not say it myself. He will certainly never forget this day's lesson as long as he lives, while if I had only led him to think of all this at home, my lecture would have been forgotten the next day. Teach by doing whenever you can, and only fall back upon words when doing is out of the question.

APPROACHES TO DISCOVERY LEARNING IN MATHEMATICS

William C. Lowry *

Discovery learning requires boys and girls to learn through some sort of logical analysis. It may be by induction or deduction. It does not matter which as long as the pupils learn from deriving (or discovering) their own conclusions. Theoretically, pupils who learn in this way should learn more thoroughly and remember longer than pupils who learn in other ways. However, whether this theory always holds is moot. Undoubtedly, learning of this kind sometimes leads to half-baked ideas, false conclusions, and unnecessary confusion. Teachers should bear in mind that there are many ways to build concepts. The man who uses only one method is severely limiting his potential effectiveness; the man that claims that all concepts must be built up only by inductive learning is a charlatan. Further, for pupils to rediscover all the generalizations of a discipline would be extremely inefficient. Discovery teaching is an important technique, but like all other techniques, it should be incorporated into teaching strategies only when it seems to be the technique most likely to bring about the learning desired. The following selection presents contemporary uses of the discovery method in teaching mathematics. It should indicate to teachers of the sciences, humanities, and other subjects ways in which discovery techniques can be used.

The discovery method is not new, but it is being highlighted today largely through the efforts of very able people who seek better ways to incorporate discovery techniques into teaching. The word *the* in "the discovery method" implies *one* discovery method. The truth of the matter is that what is called "the discovery method" varies over a wide range of student and teacher activities.

Let us classify as *a* discovery method any activity through which the learner creates, invents, finds, or gains understanding of some mathematical prin-

* From William C. Lowry, "Approaches to Discovery Learning in Mathematics," *The High School Journal* (Chapel Hill, N.C.: The University of North Carolina Press, February 1967), pp. 254–260. Reprinted by permission of the publisher.

ciple, concept or procedure through his own efforts—efforts which may, however, be directed or aided by the teacher and/or the text materials. The essence is that the thing learned is not received solely by communication *from* teacher or text *to* student.

Most advocates list the following advantages of learning by discovery: (1) The student understands what he learns and is thus better able to remember it and to use it in other situations. (2) He learns a way of going about learning on his own; in mathematics he learns some techniques, or strategies, for discovering other new things. (3) He develops an interest in what he is learning.

SOME METHODS TO AID IN DISCOVERY

The inductive method. Gertrude Hendrix points out that many people incorrectly speak of the inductive method as being the discovery method.[1] By the inductive method we commonly think of procedures by which the study and analysis of the relationships in several but not all specific instances in some class leads to a generalization about those relationships for all instances in the class. For example, after several instances such as $3 + 4 = 4 + 3$, $7 + 2 = 2 + 7$, $11 + 18 = 18 + 11$, the child generalizes that in adding two whole numbers the order of adding them does not matter. He may state this in words, or he may operate successfully on the basis of his discovery without verbalizing it. Professor Hendrix says that the "fallacy of the inductive method (as practiced) lies in its confusion of verbalization of discovery with the advent of discovery itself," and she traces this emphasis on verbalization of a discovery to the psychology of Judd in his conscious generalization theory of transfer of learning, in which generalizing is synonymous with "composing a sentence which states the generalization involved." [2]

The inductive method is one method which can be used to arrive at discoveries. It is, perhaps, the major kind of thinking expected in activities in which the teacher is hoping to have the students reach a generalization by seeing a pattern existing in a collection of data. We are aware of the dangers in inductive thinking. As Henderson points out, we are dealing with the logic of probable inference when we reason inductively.[3]

The deductive method. Some teachers feel it is not possible to discover by thinking deductively. Perhaps this is because their own school experience with deduction has been almost entirely from textbooks in which the generalization is stated first, and the student's job is to apply it or to prove it a generalization (theorem) in some mathematical structure. But a student may, for example, reason that since the sum of the measures of the interior

[1] Gertrude Hendrix, "Learning by Discovery," *The Mathematics Teacher*, LIV (May, 1961), p. 290.

[2] *Ibid.*

[3] Kenneth B. Henderson, "Anent the Discovery Method," *The Mathematics Teacher*, L (April, 1957), p. 288.

angles of a triangle is 180° and since a quadrilateral can be divided into two triangles, then it is clear, without testing several instances, that the sum of the measures of the interior angles of a quadrilateral is 360°. That is, he discovers a property of quadrilaterals by deducing that it must follow from his knowledge about triangles.

For a second example, if the student accepts the properties he is familiar with from the numbers of arithmetic and the property that $a + (-a) = 0$ when negative numbers are encountered, he is forced deductively to accept that (5) $(-3) = -15$, since $5 (3 + (-3)) = 5 (0) = 0 = 15 + 5 (-3)$.

Discovery by analogy. Students can make considerable use of reasoning by analogy in mathematics. For example, the locus of all points in a plane equidistant from a given point is a circle. By analogy, the locus of all points in space equidistant from a given point is a sphere. Polya writes, "Analogy is a sort of similarity. Similar objects agree with each other in some respect, analogous objects *agree in certain relations* of their respective parts." [4] He repeatedly suggests that the person confronted with a new problem should first search his repertoire of knowledge for problems he has solved previously and which are analogous to, or have many similar elements with, or are related to the new problem.

Reasoning by analogy has its pitfalls, too, and probably has to be used with even greater care than reasoning by induction. We use analogy so much in our everyday conversations and reasoning, the young person accustomed to its rather loose use in such situations can be particularly vulnerable in his use of it in mathematics. You have seen your students do such things as the following.

(1) $\dfrac{a \not b}{\not b} = a$, for $b = 0$. By analogy, or is it? $\dfrac{a + \not b}{\not b} = a$, for $b \neq 0$.

(2) A student finds that the sum of the measures of the interior angles of a convex polyon increases as the number of sides increases. By analogy, he jumps to the guess that the same is true for the sum of the measures of the exterior angles.

(3) If $(x - 2)(x + 3) = 0$, then $x - 2 = 0$ or $x + 3 = 0$. By analogy? If $(x - 2)(x + 3) = 5$, then $x - 2 = 5$ or $x + 3 = 5$.

CAUTIONS

Consider a little experiment we might design to help students make a discovery. How many lines are determined by n points in a plane, no three of which are collinear? The students as a class gather the appropriate information for the table up to 6 points. Then we ask them to work individually

---

[4] G. Polya, *How to Solve It*, Second Edition (Garden City, New York: Doubleday and Company, Inc., 1956), p. 37.

and to continue the table for a few more entries. We watch carefully to see if we can detect those who discover the pattern.

Number of points	2	3	4	5	6
Number of lines	1	3	6	10	15

Johnny evidently has made the discovery, so we ask him how he figured out the pattern. "Well," he says, "the difference between 1 and 3 is 2, the difference between 3 and 6 is 3, between 6 and 10 is 4, and between 10 and 15 is 5. The next difference will be 6; I add it to 15 and get 21."

Jane's reasoning is as follows: "I noticed that if I add the number in the 'points' row to the number just below it in the 'lines' row, I get the next number in the 'lines' row. So $6 + 15 = 21$ gives me the number of lines for 7 points."

Jimmy appears to have discovered something. However, his entries in the "lines" row are 1, 3, 6, 10, 15, 23, 45, and his explanation is, "I had to add 2 to $(1 + 3)$ to get 6, but only 1 to $(3 + 6)$ to get 10. I had to subtract 1 from $(6 + 10)$ to get 15. So I subtracted 2 from $(10 + 15)$ and got 23; and I subtracted 3 from $(15 + 23)$ and got 45."

Jack tells us how he discovered the pattern. "For 6 points there are 15 lines. A seventh point can be combined in a pair with each of the 6 points already there. This gives 6 more lines, which added to the 15 lines already determined by 6 points gives me a total of 21 for 7 points. Moreover, I found that these points do not have to lie in the same plane."

When you turn your students loose to discover, are you prepared for the fact that there might be more than one "discovery" made, some even wrong, and that your students will make the discovery sought for in various ways? Some teachers would not know offhand whether Jack's generalization from plane to space is correct. Many more might not recognize that Jack, in his analysis of the situation, was using the thinking, and even a bit of the language, involved in a combination of m things taken n at a time.

The authors of the Cambridge *Report* comment as follows on this point. "It (teaching for insight and creativity) also requires a much deeper mastery, in a purely mathematical sense, of the subject matter. It requires that the teacher recognize, as quickly as possible, the validity of unexpected responses. It requires also that the teacher be able to tell when a response which is not correct as stated nevertheless includes a valid idea, so that the discussion can be guided in the direction of the valid idea. Such work requires far deeper understanding than lecturing does. Without deep understanding, the only responses whose validity the teacher can recognize are the expected responses given in the book. Often the result is that at moments when the students are most entitled to feel proud of themselves they get called down and marked wrong." [5]

[5] *Goals For School Mathematics*, The Report of the Cambridge Conference on School Mathematics. (Boston: Houghton Mifflin Company, 1963), pp. 26–27.

It is not a mortal sin, however, for the teacher not to be able immediately to make judgments on all student discoveries. In fact, the degree of excellence in using discovery methods might be directly proportional to the number of times a teacher comes up against such situations. This could mean he is doing such a good job that his students are off exploring several areas he is not familiar with. In a very interesting article, Stephen Willoughby writes ". . . some of the potential good in the discovery method may be missed if the teacher knows precisely what he is looking for and so does not encourage the pupils to continue to think along lines that are unfamiliar to both pupils and teacher." [6]

A second caution the teacher must be mindful of relates to the fact that not all students make a sought-for discovery, even when a generous amount of time is allowed. The teacher must help. What kind of help should be given? Kersh [7] argues from his research that there are "subtle, but highly important, differences in the way teachers guide the learning process" when students are attempting to discover mathematical principles. One of these approaches he calls that of providing "answer-giving" instructions and withholding "answer-seeking" instructions. For our points-lines problem, the teacher might give such instructions as the following to the student who has not made the discovery. "Look at this sequence of numbers; look at the differences between successive entries. Do you see a pattern?" Kersh argues that these answer-giving instructions at worst are like dangling a carrot before a donkey in order to get him to move. At best, the learner will complete the task with a meaningful knowledge of the principle involved.[8]

One benefit claimed for discovery methods is that the learner develops a power to discover principles. As Kersh puts it, the student learns a strategy for identifying new principles.[9] Answer-giving instructions on the part of the teacher do not aid in this objective. Such instructions apply to the specific problem the student is working with; they do not have the generality to help him learn a strategy for discovering.

The second approach of Kersh's is that of giving "answer-seeking" instructions and withholding "answer-giving" instructions.[10] For our points-lines example the teacher might ask the student to "think out loud," so that he can determine the student's approach. If the student has persisted in one approach and it is not "paying off," the teacher might suggest an alternate attack. Thus, he helps develop an important aspect in the process of discovering, flexibility.

We refer again to our points-line problem to discuss a third caution for the teacher. Notice that the situation in this problem is very similar to what the scientist does in using the inductive approach. If the student makes the

[6] Stephen S. Willoughby, "Discovery," *The Mathematics Teacher*, LVI (January, 1963), p. 22.

[7] Bert Y. Kersh, "Learning by Discovery: Instructional Strategies," *The Arithmetic Teacher*, XII (October, 1965), p. 414.

[8] *Ibid.*, p. 415.

[9] *Ibid.*, p. 416.

[10] *Ibid.*, p. 415.

conjecture that the number of lines for 7 points is 21, he can check this. He locates 7 points according to the restrictions on those points, draws all the lines he can, and counts them. We are not dealing with a mathematical problem only here; we are dealing with a physical situation to which we are trying to fit a mathematical model to help us generalize the situation.

Let me present you with a problem, and let us use a discovery approach. On your honor, give an answer to the following question before you read further. What is the next term in the sequence 2, 4, 6, . . . and what is the general (n^{th}) term? Is your answer 8 and 2n? If so, you are wrong. The next term is 10 and the nth term is given by the expression $\frac{1}{3}n^3 - 2n^2 + \frac{17}{3}$ n — 2. If you don't believe this, do the arithmetic in the following check.

$$\frac{1}{3}(1)^3 - 2(1)^2 + \frac{17}{3}(1) - 2 = 2$$

$$\frac{1}{3}(2)^3 - 2(2)^2 + \frac{17}{3}(2) - 2 = 4$$

$$\frac{1}{3}(3)^3 - 2(3)^2 + \frac{17}{3}(3) - 2 = 6$$

$$\frac{1}{3}(4)^3 - 2(4)^2 + \frac{17}{3}(4) - 2 = 10$$

Your generalization was wrong. Why shouldn't it be? There was nothing in this situation to help you discover what I was thinking, and that was the problem you were up against. To be sure, there is a sequence, a very obvious one, which starts 2, 4, 6, and which has 8 as the next term and 2n as the general term. But the truth of the matter is that there are an infinite number of sequences starting with 2, 4, 6. The Lagrange interpolation formula was used to produce the expression used here, one of an infinite number which will manufacture a sequence starting 2, 4, 6, 10.

The point here is that our points-lines problem and this one, the sequence starting 2, 4, 6, even though they both deal with sequences of numbers, are quite different in the way they arose. The points-lines problem is one of fitting a mathematical model to a physical situation. There is a test to determine if our conjecture continues to fit the physical situation. In the second problem there is no such test. There is an infinite number of possibilities, one very obvious one to be sure, but the discoverer has the almost impossible task of guessing which sequence the designer has in mind. Do you point out to your students the differences in the ways problems arise?

SUMMARY

Seldom do people use one type of thinking (induction, deduction, analogy) exclusively in making a discovery, but the teacher should provide pure examples of each and point out the pitfalls of each. The teacher who uses discovery methods needs a strong preparation in mathematics; but, if he is successful with these methods, he should expect some student discoveries for which he does not have the background to determine on the spot their validity. He should be willing to learn along with his students, to do some research and discovering himself. He should know the differences in ways problems arise, and he should keep in mind as he helps his students with their discoveries that a major objective is to make those students increasingly independent of his help.

ASKING QUESTIONS TO TRIGGER THINKING

M. J. McCue Aschner *

The Socratic method and many other types of discovery teaching depend largely on the skillful use of questions. The type of questions one should ask depends on the goals one is trying to achieve. Sometimes a teacher may need to answer a question that calls for a one-word factual answer. More often he should ask questions that "trigger thinking." The following article shows how to use questions for four different purposes. James Gallagher and Mary Jane Aschner in another article have categorized similar kinds of questions, as cognitive memory, convergent, divergent, and evaluative questions.† Careful study of the Taxonomy of Educational Objectives explained in Chapter 2 and the selections by Smith, and Amidon and Flanders in Chapter 1 should give the student many clues to ways of using questions to develop all sorts of cognitive and affective goals.

The classroom teacher probably devotes more time and thought to asking questions than anybody since Socrates. One might even say the teacher is a professional question maker.

* From *NEA Journal*, Vol. 50 (Washington, D.C.: National Education Association, September 1961), pp. 44–46. Reprinted by permission of the *NEA Journal* and the author.

† James J. Gallagher and Mary Jane Aschner, "A Preliminary Report of Analyses of Classroom Interaction," *The Merrill-Palmer Quarterly of Behavior and Development*, Vol. 9 (July 1963), pp. 183–194.

Asking questions—in class discussion or on assignments and tests—is one of the basic ways by which the teacher stimulates student thinking and learning. And it is by asking questions and studying the answers that the teacher measures and evaluates the thinking and learning progress of his students.

Teachers regularly stimulate four main types of thinking activities by asking questions. These types are: remembering, reasoning, evaluating or judging, and creative thinking.

MEMORY QUESTIONS

Remembering is the most common thinking activity that goes on in a classroom. It is easy to ask questions that call for remembering. "Who was the sixteenth President of the United States?" is a typical memory question. So is "What is a noun?" and "What is a prime number?"

Some questions *appear* to call for another kind of thinking—until they are given a closer look. Consider, for example, the question, "Will you please describe the nitrogen cycle?" or "What is the difference between a mammal and a marsupial?" Just because these questions require more than a single word or a short phrase for an answer does not mean that the answer will be more than a recitation of what the student has remembered. Often when the teacher believes he is triggering a more complex type of thinking, he is merely asking a slightly more complicated memory question.

Such a teacher needs to develop skill in designing better questions. He needs to ask himself, "What kind of thinking task must my students do to answer this question? Of course, they must remember something to be able to answer any kind of question. But isn't there some way I can phrase this question to call for more than remembering?" Thus the first step in designing thought-provoking questions is to analyze and plan the task which a question can set for thinking.

QUESTIONS THAT PROMPT REASONING

Reasoning is called forth in such familiar questions as these: "If two men can lay floor tile for a five-room house in three days, how many men would it take to do the job in one day?" "Why did the metal strip bend when I held it over the flame?" or, consider the following social studies discussion:

Teacher—So why would you say the Jamestown settlers were unprepared?
Bill—Well, one book said that most of them were city people. And then they had never learned to do things for themselves.
Anne—Also, since it was a new land and nobody knew much about it, they didn't know what to expect.

Reasoning goes on when there is explaining to do, when computation is called for, when someone puts two and two together and comes up with four. Reasoning takes the "given" and works its way to the necessary conclusion. Bill and Anne used the facts they had learned about Jamestown as evidence that the settlers were unprepared.

But suppose we hear the following exchange:

Teacher—All right, now, why did Jackson veto the Maysville Road Bill?
Bob—Because he was against spending government money to benefit just one community instead of the whole country.

Was Bob reasoning or remembering? How can we tell? If we know—from what has gone on before—that Bob had a limited set of facts and *derived* from them the reason he gave for Jackson's veto, then we can be fairly sure he was reasoning. But if this is a review session, or if we know the class has already dealt with the full history of Jackson's decision, then we should assume that Bob is remembering, not reasoning.

To trigger reasoning, a question must call for an answer that is not retrieved but reached. It must be reachable on the basis of the "given," but not be itself part of the "given."

QUESTIONS CALLING FOR JUDGMENT

Evaluating or judging is an important thinking and learning activity. Students need experience in weighing alternatives, in judging and making decisions. They need to learn the ways of deciding whether or not a statement is true, a plan sound, or an action wisely taken.

This time our social studies teacher asks for evaluating:

Teacher—What do *you* think of Captain John Smith's "work or starve" policy for Jamestown? Was that a good idea?
Anne—Well, I think he just about had to lay down the law. If he hadn't forced them to build houses and gather food, they wouldn't have lived through the winter.
Dick—Yes, but that just means he was doing their thinking for them. I think he should have let them learn their lesson—even if some of 'em starved or froze to death!
Teacher—Let's get some more opinions here. How about you, Lee? What do you think?

Here the teacher asked his pupils to do their own judging. He did not frame their opinions in advance by giving his own or citing others' views. In the way he phrased his question, he provided for and welcomed differences of opinion.

But suppose a teacher asks, "What was the main reason why the Pilgrims came to the New World?" Is he asking for judging or remembering? If the teacher can be sure—before he asks the question—that the children have not yet encountered *any* evaluations (in textbook or class discussion) of reasons why the Pilgrims settled in the New World, then and only then can he also be sure he is asking them to judge.

Questions *can* be designed to elicit evaluation, however, even when other opinions and authorities have been studied. Consider this way of designing the same question:

Teacher—We have seen that some historians think freedom of religion was the main reason the Pilgrims came here. Others think it was the desire for land or to set up their own government, and so forth. Now I want to hear your views on the matter. Tell me, what do *you* think? Give me *your own* opinion of what the main reason was the Pilgrims came over here.

This question signals clearly to students that they are being asked to evaluate; whether they do so or not is another question. Some students will always fall back on someone else's judgment. But at least when the teacher designs the question in this way, the students have a chance to do some judging; furthermore, they have the experience of being expected to do some judging.

QUESTIONS THAT LAUNCH CREATIVE THINKING

Creative thinking is thinking which produces ideas, proposes solutions to problems, invents ways of doing things. Creative thinking is something anyone can do, given the chance or the need to do so. In a classroom where a student is invited or required to act or think upon his own initiative, to seek instead of to receive knowledge, and to rely upon his own resources, creative thinking flourishes.

Here are some questions designed to stimulate creative thinking: "What would our world be like today if the Spanish had conquered England in 1588 instead of losing out with the Armada?" "What would happen if our nation's coal and oil reserve suddenly were to run out and go dry?" "How many ways can you get 12?"

Questions like these trigger brainstorming sessions. They are extremely useful when they are built into an over-all teaching strategy. Consider, for example, the English teacher who plans to develop his students' understanding of the structure of language. He says: "Let's invent a language for Martians. We'll give them a spoken language. Now, what will go into this language? What kinds of things must a language do so people can use it to communicate?"

In setting this problem, the teacher has accomplished much. First, with this off-beat approach, he has probably captured interest. Second, he has focused his students' thinking on the structure of language. Finally, he has put them on their own—he has launched creative thinking.

HELPING MINDS TO GROW

Remembering, reasoning, evaluating, and creative thinking can—and should—go on in any classroom, at any grade or ability level, for thinking is the catalyst of learning.

To design a good classroom question, the teacher needs to begin by analyzing and planning the kind of thinking task to be set. Then he should fit the form and phrasing of the question or problem to this task. Precision and clarity in the wording of the question will focus thinking squarely on its task.

The teacher who is a skilled designer of classroom questions and problems is the teacher who helps young minds to grow.

ON QUESTIONING

Richard L. Loughlin *

Although it is essential that teachers ask questions that bring out the educational goals they are seeking, there is more to good questioning technique than simply asking the proper questions. Richard L. Loughlin has suggested ten principles that make an excellent set of guidelines for the new teacher who wishes to develop good techniques in the use of questions.

PRINCIPLES OF QUESTIONING

I. Distribute questions so that all, including the nonvolunteers, are involved.

II. Balance factual and thought-provoking questions.

III. Ask both simple and exacting questions, so that the poorer students may participate and the brighter students may be extended.

IV. Encourage lengthy responses and sustained answers. (Avoid yes-no questions, questions overlaid with afterthoughts, fragmentary questions, and those that tug or encourage guessing. N.B. If you catch yourself asking a yes-no question, add "Explain.")

V. Stimulate critical thinking by asking: "To what extent?" "How?" "Under what circumstances?" "Why?" "Compare (*or* contrast). . . ."

   1. Avoid: "Does anyone know . . . ?" and "Who can tell us?"

   2. Allow time for thought. Wait until five or six want to speak.

   3. Be a model of exact phrasing and coherent thinking.

      a. Phrase questions clearly, within the vocabulary limits of the class, so that rephrasing and/or repeating will not be necessary.

* From *The Educational Forum*, Vol. 25 (May 1961), pp. 481–482. Used by permission of Kappa Delta Pi, An Honor Society in Education, owners of the copyright.

   b. Make each question specific, short, and provocative.

   c. Keep transitions smooth.

4. Encourage students to comment on the answers of classmates.

   a. Start the crossfire by asking, "What's your opinion of that answer, ...?"

   b. Follow up promising leads, building on contributions.

   c. Tactfully curb aggressive students. (No student or teacher domination should prevail.)

   d. Don't drop too quickly a student who seems unable to answer. If a student is nonplussed, inquire "How can we help . . . . out?"

5. Never interrupt a student who is attempting to answer nor tolerate ridicule of an honest effort.

VI. Use the *overhead* technique: (1) question, (2) pause, (3) name.

VII. Insure audibility, then refuse to repeat questions or answers.

VIII. If a student asks a question, don't answer it until you've asked the class, "How would you answer that question, ...?"

IX. Personalize questions ("Pretend you are . . . . What would *you* do?").

X. Suggest partnership by inquiring, "How can *we* . . . .?"

DISCUSSION

Don Robinson *

Teachers talk too much. Classroom discussions can do much to alter that fault. A good discussion is not teacher dominated, but is, rather, a conversation in which the pupils air their ideas and the reasoning behind them freely and openly. It is not a series of teacher questions and pupil answers. During the interplay among the pupils, the teacher leads and guides by an occasional remark or a redirecting question, as this description of a high-school discussion illustrates.

"Is the Gospel according to St. Matthew a statement of faith written by a firm believer, or should it be read as a historical document? Is St. Matthew

* From "Scraps from a Teacher's Notebook," *Phi Delta Kappan*, Vol. 48 (Bloomington, Ind.: Phi Delta Kappa, October 1966), p. 91. Reprinted by permission of the publisher.

writing what he interprets to be true or what he recognizes as a testament of faith?"

With these questions a teacher began a discussion meeting of a Great Books class, operated in a public high school on a voluntary, noncredit basis for all interested students. After these opening questions the teacher had very little to say, leaving the students free to express themselves candidly, unhampered by constant intervention.

"This writing cannot be historical," one boy asserts. "It is a statement of faith of someone who strongly believes. The style of writing shows that there is more than history here. If all this is true about the miracles. . . ."

Another lad broke in with, "I am sure he is writing what he believes to be true, but I just can't believe anyone rose out of the grave."

"Of course it's historical," added another. "It's just a recording of what he knows. It's almost like a diary."

"Well, if it's history, it's not good history. It includes too much hearsay. He is trying to write history, since he includes no personal interpretations or value judgments. Perhaps some of these miracles occurred, but St. Matthew probably exaggerates them. If two people were standing in the middle of nowhere and saw something happen, and if both wrote down exactly what they saw, they would have two entirely different accounts. And in addition to this subjectivity that attaches to every writer, here we also have the emotional faith of the writer in his Savior."

After the five boys and girls in this group had talked for a few minutes about superstition and the need for a messiah, the leader made one of his infrequent comments to direct the discussion towards the conditions in Rome at the time of the writing of the scripture, as revealed in the Gospel according to St. Matthew and without reference to other sources of information. The students decided that the rich were very rich and the poor were very poor, and that sickness and famine went with poverty everywhere.

"And his servant was healed within the selfsame hour," read one of the girls, adding her queries, "How did he know it was in the same hour, since he was in a different town? More important, how was the sick man healed?"

"Maybe it was psychosomatic," came a quick response. "Faith can do a lot, and Jesus made people have a lot of faith. It's largely a question of mind over matter, and very often mind can prevail over matter. I know this happens to people today at revivals."

A few minutes later attention focused on the phrase, "let the dead bury the dead." After the students had proposed a variety of possible meanings, one boy suggested, "Throughout the whole book Jesus gets bolder and bolder, less humble, more egotistical, more insistent that people believe in him. You begin to find him making statements like these: 'All power is given to me in heaven and earth' and 'One day I shall sit on my father's throne.' Maybe he changed as he grew older. Maybe he came to want to found a new religion."

"Rulers were all-powerful and the government was totalitarian in those days. So it was natural for Jesus to express more self-centered concern for allegiance and obedience to him if he was concerned with establishing a new religion."

One student said, "Everytime anyone asked a real important question, Jesus just asked the question back again. That's what's wrong with the whole deal. Anyone can just say 'What do you think?' and never commit himself. That way anyone can believe anything and it becomes like the Delphic oracle. It's like the blind leading the blind."

The leader now encouraged the students to seek an understanding of the meaning of the book as intended by the author, saying, "We have been refuting Jesus without trying to understand what he meant. What is Jesus trying to change? Why did he make such an impact?"

"He was trying to bring religion closer to the people. He was trying to help the people avoid the form and ritual that took the life out of religion. He wanted to reduce the reliance of the rabbis on formality and authority. He wanted reasons to be given for everything."

The students continued to talk about the relation of Jesus' words to the shortcomings of the religious life and leaders of that day, and were still discussing this matter when the bell rang to end the period.

The outstanding feature of this class was not the sharpness of the dialogue or the boldness displayed in analyzing a sacred document. These traits are conspicuous in many schools.

The unique quality of this class sprang from the ability of the leader to remain quiet and allow the students to conduct the discussion, yet without abdicating his role as leader. He was always there, ready with a cue or a question, but never imposing his interpretations on students. This is the special style of the Great Books discussion leader, a style that could improve the effectiveness of many teachers. Every teacher admits that other teachers talk too much. Few can concede that they themselves do.

Such a class discussion of the nature of the scriptures and the relation of Jesus to the life of his times obviously suggests a number of delicate questions. Some authorities question the propriety of discussing in a nonreligious setting matters about which some students have deep emotional commitments. Others will reply that schools should encourage free and frank discussion of religion in general and of the Bible as literature.

Although the discussion reported above may not exemplify the ideal student discussion, it may nevertheless represent a significant approach to learning, namely, a willingness to approach any serious topic thoughtfully, including those topics that are invested with emotional content. After all, the application of critical thinking to a subject is not a negative approach. Just as a critical analysis of American foreign policy is not unpatriotic, a critical inspection of religion need not be deemed anti-religious.

FOUR DANGERS IN CLASS DISCUSSIONS

Robert C. McKean *

Discussions should give pupils an opportunity to share and examine their thinking. It follows that teachers must conduct discussions so that pupils can talk and think freely. Thus the teacher is faced with a nice problem of how to give pupils enough freedom to allow them to think freely while at the same time structuring the discussion enough to provide impetus and direction toward the learning desired.

Teachers who think that discussion classes must be easy to teach are wrong. Conducting discussions successfully requires considerable skill and a good deal of planning. Otherwise the discussions can degenerate into aimless bull sessions in which the participants share their ignorance and re-enforce their prejudices. Skilfully conducted group discussions, however, can be an effective means of influencing pupils' attitudes, clarifying their concepts, and planting ideas.

Class discussion techniques are key tools in the successful teacher's equipment. These techniques, while most often aiming at subject matter mastery, have important values in promoting equally vital, concomitant outcomes such as the development of skill in critical thinking. However, too often class discussions tend to smother independent student thinking rather than to produce situations wherein this skill may be practiced and improved.

Inexperienced teachers find it especially difficult to plan and guide intelligent and rewarding discussion activities. Experience with student teachers and first-year teachers has pointed up four problems which seem to be most prevalent. High-school principals, as they work with these people through supervision and inservice training, might find it profitable to use these four dangers as a starting point.

1. The beginning teacher, fresh from college classes, may *phrase the questions in adult terms.* It may be very logical and possibly quite clear to adults, but often is simply not communicated or only partially communicated to the students because of the wording. The question or topic is not fully understood by the students and good discussion is impeded at the outset. Sympto-

* From *The Bulletin of the National Association of Secondary School Principals*, Vol. 42 (October 1958), pp. 82–83. Reprinted by permission of the NASSP and the author.

matic of this situation is the sight of students stumbling and fumbling verbally around the general area of the discussion subject in general terms until, through chance or trial and error, the question is clarified. There follows a surge of effort when the students finally gain understanding of what the teacher wants them to discuss.

2. The teacher may *structure the discussion in terms of the logic of the subject matter* as she sees it. Thus, it may be very abstract and there may be few if any ties with the lives of the pupils. The discussion becomes an exercise in the manipulation of verbal symbols. If the students, themselves, are encouraged to formulate the discussion topics and questions in their own words, the very statement of the problem is likely to bring the whole discussion in line with student problems, interests, and backgrounds of experience. In this way discussions are more likely to be vital and stimulating to the class.

3. *Over-emotionality* in the classroom is another condition inimical to critical, independent thinking. Often the beginning teacher is tense, striving for control and her self-concept of teacher role may impel her to pit herself against the class. Teachers should strive to promote relatively minimal conditions of emotionality in the interests of objective, logical thought. The classroom activity should be discussion rather than argument. Emotion may be desirable when you have a bear chasing you. The effects of the emotional state—amounts of sugar are released into the blood for quick energy, the heart steps up its beat making more blood available, the circulation is said to be changed sending more blood to the heavy muscles, the digestive process is stopped or reduced, *etc.*—tend to contribute to physical retreat from a dangerous or threatening situation. However, the individual's ability to reason, to think clearly, in other than habitual patterns is reduced. Thus overemotionality is not desirable as an accompaniment to mental problem solving in the classroom.

4. The teacher may actually and directly inhibit creative thinking by *over-planning*, by pre-thinking through the anticipated discussion topics or questions and carefully formulating "logical" answers or solutions. This pre-thinking should be done in general terms, of course, but, if these answers or conclusions are too rigidly adhered to, the teacher may find herself saying, "No, that is not it. That is not quite what I had in mind."

Students quickly sense what is happening (they have experienced it before), and it becomes a guessing game rather than real problem-solving activity. They watch very carefully for facial expressions, gestures, attend to subliminal cues, *etc.* for the game is to try to read the teacher's mind for *the answer* hidden there. The effect is more likely to produce students gifted in mental telepathy than in creative problem-solving skills.

As a process, classroom discussion should begin with questions which have some relevance to the lives of students and proceed to conclusions based on logic and the prizing of the authority of evidence. If inexperienced teachers are assisted in avoiding the above four dangers, they will be well on their way toward developing a vital method of teaching which fosters critical, independent thinking in our students.

ROLE-PLAYING, ANYONE?

J. Robert Jackson *

Role-playing is a dramatic technique in which people attempt to portray a situation by putting themselves in the role of the participants. The purpose of role-playing is full understanding—of one's self, of one's associates, of a group, or of a circumstance.

J. Robert Jackson has been using role-playing as a therapeutic and teaching technique for years. He has found it a powerful device—so powerful that sometimes it has led to strange results. From his experience, he points out some of the dangers as well as the advantages of this amazing technique.

Role-playing requires only three things. You need courage, love and skill. Why?

Role-playing is impromptu drama done with your students. It is a kind of super-audio-visual aid. Of all teaching methods, it is probably the most creative.

With the miracle of this teaching method, you may move anywhere in space. You may move anywhere in time—the near or distant past, or the present. You may move out of reality into the fantasy of dreams or make-believe.

This kind of movement in time and space requires courage. You may scare yourself with it, or scare your students. Powerful emotions are bound up with the past. They are triggered by events to come. Deep feelings may lie just below the surface in events of the moment.

Why should any teacher expose himself to these hazards? The answer must lie in love of one's fellowman. You take the risks of this extraordinary

* From *Language Arts Clearing House*, Vol. 2 (Jersey City, N.J.: Jersey City State College, March 1966), pp. 2–3. Reprinted by permission of the publisher and the author.

method because you love students and education enough to do so. The rewards, when they come, are immense. Almost incredible miracles of communication, insight and growth will result.

The hazards of failure are also considerable. Resistance, anger, criticism and contempt may follow a fiasco in your role-playing. You are working with the greatest goodwill and all the intelligence you can muster. And yet, in spite of this, the role-playing may fail. The negative feelings now engendered will test all your courage and all your love.

Wouldn't sufficient skill prevent the failure? Apparently not. The writer has been studying and using role-playing for fifteen years. He still fails frequently. And so does every other experienced worker in the field of group dynamics.

If the experienced often fail, are inexperienced teachers doomed to failure? No. Some of the mechanisms of role-playing are almost foolproof. Failure usually comes in more ambitious uses of the method. When resistances are high in the protagonist or group, resistances to role-playing may also run high. These resistances are likely to become great when the problem is highly personal.

The inexperienced director of role-playing may avoid difficult resistance, then, by avoiding the highly personal problem. The problems common to all of us in our past, our future, or our present will usually not evoke deep emotional involvement. How do you know that the problem for your role-playing is a common one?

A democratic selection method may be useful here. Let the group select the problem from a number which they have volunteered as important to them. If the consensus is that a problem is interesting, it is likely to be a common one.

Another danger for the inexperienced is in moving the role-playing into the far past or far future. A role-player may be taken back to the moment of his birth, be taken forward to the moment of his death. Extreme scenes of this kind may evoke powerful emotions from the Unconscious.

But to role-play the commonplace events of yesterday or tomorrow . . . you will have little difficulty here. And if, in spite of everything, the role-player gets too involved in the part, you can easily break the spell. Reverse the role. Change the scene. Freeze the action for discussion. Do a "magic shop," which means to do the scene in the perfect way all the players would like it.

In short, a teacher who can work well with students in a group has sufficient skill to do some role-playing. The teacher may wish to start with the simpler forms of role-playing to build confidence, then move on to the complex.

Should all teachers use role-playing? Will it be useful for all subjects and all age levels of students? The answers to these questions seem to lie in the answer to still another question.

Do teachers have sufficient courage, love and skill to do role-playing? In the writer's experience, the answer to this question is yes.

DYADIC ROLE-PLAYING OF CONTROVERSIAL ISSUES

Leslie D. Zeleny and Richard E. Gross *

Role-playing is a difficult technique to use. The role-playing may fail; it does so often. Moreover, the players are likely to become so involved in the role-playing that emotions may run high. Yet, if one is striving for important goals that involve changing or creating really deep affectively toned understandings rather than superficial verbalism, role-playing is one of the most powerful tools of the entire pedagogical repertory. In this selection, Zeleny and Gross suggest that because pair groups (dyads) "contain the germ of more complex human relations," and because pair groups are relatively simple to handle in the classroom, the use of dyadic role-playing is an excellent way to introduce pupils to role-playing.

Too often students of the social studies, to paraphrase Herbert J. Muller, are taught to go forward into the future while looking backward. In other words, the curriculum in the social studies too frequently emphasizes the past rather than the problems of the present; it often concentrates upon relatively isolated facts rather than interrelationships and meanings. Many teachers of the social studies, realizing the relative sterility of certain traditional content and approaches, have become interested in introducing their students to the insistent problems of our times, such as the problem of the population explosion, the problem of war, the problem of over-organization, the problem of moral irresponsibility, the problem of national survival, the capital-labor issue, and many others. But many of these same teachers, after trying to introduce the study of vital issues, have found them too "hot" to handle and have retreated into "safe" but relatively sterile practices. This withdrawal of social studies teachers from the realities and issues of our adventurous civilization, in the opinion of the authors, represents a pitiful shirking of responsibility. More than one survey points out the overriding concern for ease and security that now characterizes so many modern youth.

* From *Social Education*, Vol. 24 (Washington, D.C.: National Council for the Social Studies, December 1960), pp. 354–358. Reprinted by permission of the NCSS and the authors.

If the next generation is being taught (or allowed) to retreat from vital issues rather than face them with intelligent understanding, the survival of our nation may indeed be threatened. Social studies instruction should not, by omission or commission, contribute to such conditions!

DYADIC ROLE-PLAYING—A SUGGESTION

We have a serious problem in social studies education when, through tradition, insecurity, or fear, the insistent social problems and issues of our times tend to be bypassed in the classroom. Perhaps one cause of this serious neglect—that has characterized throughout history the schools of nations and civilizations who failed to help meet the challenges in their declining cultures—is the lack of a successful procedure for the study and discussion of contemporary issues. For those who retreat for this reason we would like to suggest a modification of role-playing as one method of teaching an understanding of social issues.

The dyad or pair group. Many years ago George Simmel pointed out that the dyad, or pair group, contained the "germ" of more complex human relations. In the small pair groups, Simmel pointed out, general forms of association may go on in a relatively "pure" fashion. Thus, conflict and cooperation, two "universal" social processes, often too complicated to understand, may go on in relatively simple and intelligible form in the dyad. Wolfe states that "these forms exist as much between two groups—families, states and groups of various kinds—as between two individuals." In their teaching experience the writers have noted the relative efficiency of committees of two (or three) individuals as contrasted with the more negative results of larger sub-groups of students or teachers with whom they have worked.

Role-playing in the dyad. Recognizing that two human beings in a dyad may initiate fundamental patterns of human relations and resolve them most effectively, the next problem is: How may real life situations or interactions be simulated in dyads in the classroom? Furthermore, how may these pair-groups be set up in a manner to achieve a desirable learning situation while, at the same time, making the teacher a "consultant" rather than an "indoctrinator?"

The significant thing about role-playing is that it provides an opportunity for students to *simulate* the real roles of representatives of groups between which there are issues, including the defense of the opposed positions, processes of accommodation, and insight into the deeper meanings of specific controversies. One who participates in the role-playing of vital issues will not only *know* life but he will *feel* it too. Thus, he may become a more intelligent and understanding member of a neighborhood community, state, or nation; and the expanded self who has "role-played" international issues could be much better prepared to understand the world scene. One who has sincerely "role-played" the issues of the day in school should find the transition from school life to real life and *role-taking* much easier than when the student has merely recited upon a social studies text.

PROCEDURE FOR DYADIC ROLE-PLAYING

Our suggested procedure for initiating role-playing in the social studies may be outlined somewhat as follows.

Student interest in a vital issue. Student interest is the vital, preliminary step in role-playing. This may be developed in a regular social studies lesson. Suppose, for example, the social studies teacher wishes to develop knowledge and understanding of the Berlin dispute by means of role-playing. What *not* to do is to say, "Tomorrow we shall study the West-East dispute over Berlin. Please read up on the subject so we can discuss it. There are several faults with this approach, as all good teachers know; but the point to be stressed here is that a teacher-decision with respect to a vital topic has been made and assigned in an arbitrary manner. Very likely, in connection with a review of key international problems, the Berlin issue will be identified by many in a class as one of significance. At this point the teacher may assist the class in deciding upon and planning their exploration of the problem by suggesting numerous, available references, by a short lecture on the history of the Berlin situation since 1944, by displaying a map or diagram of divided Berlin, or by helping the group identify the basic, divergent positions in the West and in the East with respect to the issue. Such action promotes pupil understanding of the nature of the stalemate and of the vital importance of a solution. If such procedures develop a deep interest in the issue, then the class may be ready to proceed in dyadic role-playing.

Teacher-class preparation. As the foregoing suggests, role-playing, except with respect to issues with which youth are informed because of their life experience or previous preparation, must be carefully prepared for by the teacher and the class. This is also why student interest is important; incidentally, an issue in which there is interest but which is too difficult to grasp at a certain grade level had better be postponed.

Since the teacher is to be a director-consultant in a sociodrama rather than an indoctrinator, he or she must thoroughly understand the subject and "lead" the students to a most complete study of the "facts" and "issues" related to the problem.

Another consideration of importance in the preparation is the climate of opinion in the community with respect to the issue. If the subject is too "hot" to handle in the community, it probably is too "hot" to handle in the classroom; "temperature" 98.6°F in the community is a better climate than 212°F for the classroom discussion of a vital issue.

Having decided to proceed toward the role-playing of the issue, the director-consultant and the class should study with great care the *history* of the issue. In the French-Algerian issue, for example, the problems mentioned by the class in the initial discussion should be reviewed and organized so that the full historical setting as seen by all sides is understood. This work may involve reading in books, newspapers, and magazines published during the last 25 years. But this reading must be *critical* reading for the purpose of distilling "truth" from "propaganda." Students need to be helped to see the "why" of certain positions, including their own, and the limited orientation of certain opinions, and that most issues, if studied carefully, prove to be just as complex as the many-sided Algerian crisis.

Dyadic role-playing. When a class has properly prepared itself for dyadic role-playing, using many of the customary ways of stimulating learnings, it may proceed with hope of success—that is, there may be set up dyads which simulate the real issue. To participate in a discussion of a controversial issue in a dyad requires thorough knowledge; and, in addition, the participation may be expected to promote further *insight* into the reasons for the position of two or more groups facing the issue and, possibly, in "inventing" some new and more promising "solutions" to be taken with respect to the issue, thus extending *wisdom* in a limited area.

Recognition of two positions or statuses. Role-playing begins with the recognition of two (or more) positions, statuses, or units of behavior expectancies related to the issue at hand. In the case of the Berlin issue one might say that the West (French, English, American) is expected by the situation to want to remain in Berlin in accordance with the protocol of September 12, 1944, while the Soviet Union is now expected to represent the position of a power which, since November 27, 1958, considers the 1944 protocol null and void. In addition to the mere recognition, of course, should come an understanding of the seriousness of the difference when force is suggested as a means of imposing the will of one group upon the other group. It would be equally important to delineate the varying positions of the metropolitan French, the Algerian French, the "loyal" Moslems, and the FLM "rebels" in the Algerian imbroglio.

Identification of actions (roles) associated with the statuses or positions. Class study and discussion should be able to reproduce the actions (in this case, written and spoken words) associated with the positions or statuses. Thus, according to *The New York Times*, in connection with Berlin the role or roles of the Soviet Union might be represented somewhat as follows:

1. The agreements with respect to Berlin now assume an inequitable character.
2. The Allied presence in Berlin is illegal.
3. The occupation is abnormal fourteen years after World War II.
4. Berlin should be made a demilitarized free city.

The role or roles of the West may be represented somewhat as follows:

1. Any change in the present status of Berlin would damage the West.
2. Occupation rights of the West must be continued without interruption.
3. There is no acceptable alternative to negotiation.

4. But, if the Soviet Union introduces another blockade, a nuclear war is a possibility.

Equally clear statements and lists would have to be developed about the dilemma in Algeria or for any other problem area. Of course, role-playing which merely repeats such foregoing "skeletal" phrases would be very dull, indeed. "Deep" study would bring out attitudes, values, and emotions accompanying the "official" positions.

Only after careful preparation on an issue of interest and after opposed positions (statuses) with their actions or roles have been identified can role-playing take place with hope of success. It is recommended that it begin with pair-group or dyadic interaction. As pointed out earlier, the pair-group is the most elemental social unit; and it is one which can be observed and understood most easily by the teacher-director-consultant. Consequently, it is recommended that role-playing in a class start with pair-groups, each of the two persons representing one of the two opposed positions with respect to the issue. Thus, in a class of 30 students there would be 15 pair-groups in which each of the two divergent positions would be represented.

For the classroom teacher there are many advantages in the dyadic interaction approach to role-playing. First, it involes *all* students *actively* in the learning process. Second, it encourages participation in and the development of confidence in oral discussion for the more timid members as it also prepares them for general class participation. Third, by putting the timid, the lazy, or the unprepared "on the spot" (something which general class discussion often passes by), the "natural" social pressures may motivate many not otherwise motivated. And, fourth, the teacher-consultant is more readily able to observe the work of individuals in a group of two than in a larger group. Finally, the active small-group participation provides many opportunities for the research-minded teachers to carry on objective experiments in social psychology while teaching. For example, students with varying degrees of leadership and self-confidence can be identified. Conversely, students with varying degrees of isolation and lack of self-confidence may be identified and by means of individual instruction made possible by the temporary release of the teacher from her customary dominant position, may be guided toward more successful role-playing and, consequently, the development of more effective personalities.

In role-playing, as outlined in this article, the authors see many possibilities for constructive guidance of individual students within a *social situation*. This should be much better in many ways than guidance in isolation in an office down the hall where the situation is unreal. As the article develops, the reader is urged to look for other opportunities for the development of personality by means of role-playing.

Before the pair-group role-playing is completed, the teacher-director should ask for a reversal of roles or positions; that is, the teacher should ask for each student to represent the opposite position. This work should be done thoroughly, for social insight comes from seeing one's position as others see it. This reverse of positions can be expected to have an important educational result—it requires more knowledge, more social insight, more patience, and more critical thinking, too.

When an important third position exists, as in the Algerian situation, it may be necessary to have three persons and rotate roles. Or two students can first thrash out the differences between French attitudes and then move to attempt to test a composite or compromise French position against the un-resilient rebel view. Here the students are helped to personally experience many-sided, emotionally-impacted issues and to grasp the great difficulties in their resolution.

The final exercise may be for the pair-group participants to "look at" the work they have just done to consider how well each position was represented, to ask the teacher for more information, to consult other sources of information, and to replay certain parts of their work for more accuracy.

Role-playing before and with the group. If the teacher-consultant believes the class is now ready for "more advanced" role-playing and analysis; and if he or she has identified a "successful" pair-group (or two other students who can make a good pair-group), the class can move ahead.

After a brief consultation, the selected pair-group may appear before the class. Then, while the class listens to determine the effectiveness of their role-playing, the pair-group presents as representative a discussion of the issue as is possible.

When the selected pair-group has finished, or even before it has finished, the teacher-director may call for comment and evaluation with respect to the authenticity of the role-playing. This may involve an extended discussion, including suggestions for better representation of roles. The whole or part of the activity may be repeated. Also, volunteers may be invited to "show" some possible better ways.

The teacher-director, by means of the process just outlined, has set up a second procedure which is dynamic rather than static; it has required the use of information and temporary identification with the attitudes, values, and feelings of the two group groups in the conflict.

In our illustration of the Soviet Union vs. the West over Berlin, it is intended, of course, that Americans will study the Soviet position to learn how to deal more intelligently with it in terms of our national interest and the realities of the situation that also involves varying British, French, West German, and East German outlooks.

The "invention" of "solutions." Classroom role-playing makes it possible to try out several alternative solutions to an issue and to have them considered by all pair-groups in the class and by a representative pair-group before the class, too. In the case of the Berlin issue such "solutions" as the following may be considered. Is the status-quo the answer? Is war the answer? Is a free city the answer? Or what other "solutions" are within the range of possibility? Where *should* the U.S.A. stand with respect to the Berlin crisis; and what are the possibilities for negotiation? All ideas should be "tried out" and the probable arguments of representatives of each position presented. Some "correlation" of ideas might be seen to be possible to "save the face" of both groups and a "solution" no one has thought of before may be shown to have some merit. This is true creative thinking in the area of the social studies.

All of this work should challenge the best brains in a high school class and stimulate *all* of the students. Often the weak students will not be very successful; but, on the other hand, one can expect that they will do no more poorly than otherwise. Some may do much better, and they may learn considerably from observing the dramatic role-playing situation.

The group decision. The studies of Kurt Lewin and others have shown that people are more likely to act in accord with a belief *they* have decided is sound than upon a belief someone (no matter how enticingly) has presented in a lecture. Though the representation of various positions and roles in itself can be expected to have influence, Sheriff's studies imply that a *group decision*, perhaps made by a secret ballot, will determine where the majority stand with respect to a possible solution and influence those who are in the minority group too.

USES OF DYADIC ROLE-PLAYING

So much for a brief outline of a procedure which may be used in dyadic role-playing. These techniques could vitalize history classes, for many of the issues of earlier days can be brought to life by these methods. In world history the possibilities of role-playing controversial issues are legion; and the issues are warm enough to be interesting, but they are not too hot. Take, for example, the land reform issue in Rome at the time of the Gracchi, or John Huss and the Reformation, King John and the Magna Carta, the nobility versus the peasants at the time of the French Revolution, the issues over the League of Nations at the time of Wilson, etc. Histo-dramas bringing these important conflict situations to life could make world history much more interesting and exciting.

The same procedures can be applied to make some of the issues in United States history more deeply understood. For example, the issues related to the Revolutionary War, or those facing Jefferson and Hamilton at a cabinet meeting, Lincoln and McClellan at Antietam, or the rise of the New Deal, and many others are most appropriate. The authors suggest that such issues with all their facets could be "role-played" in pair-groups (dyads) to involve the active thinking of as many in the class as possible followed by a general sociodramatic presentation, analysis, and consideration of the implications of "solutions."

Contemporary issues are probably the best medium for dyadic role-playing. Local, national, and international issues are appropriate in this connection. Locally, taxation problems, urban development problems, school segregation problems, management-labor problems—when submitted to dyadic interaction—can stimulate a great deal of interest and worthwhile study. These also serve to promote the development of insight with respect to community issues now too frequently slighted in social classes.

Issues are legion on the national scene. Here labor-capital relations become national issues; similarly taxation problems, civil rights problems, farm problems, conservation problems, problems of family policy, population policy, and many others can be treated by means of dyadic-interaction.

Finally, on the international scene, pertinent problems seem to mount. The crises touched upon in this article indicate the possible scope. Often these issues are extremely complex and they can prove difficult to handle. But these, too, can be treated by means of dyadic role-playing. Local, national, and international problems are now increasingly enmeshed. An issue of relatively local concern (a tariff on Fuller's earth) can produce national action and have international reverberation. On the other hand, the divisive question of the entrance of Red China to the United Nations can become a hot, community, election issue in a Congressional district in Illinois. Thus, related aspects of such contemporary affairs at different levels—local to international —provide excellent learning opportunities useful in several different phases of a unit. The writers would encourage teachers to explore the varying uses of role-playing in introducing a topic, for clarifying opposing viewpoints, as a part of group hypothesizing, in summarizing a lesson, and in evaluating the outcomes of instruction.

One of the alarming tendencies in education in our time is the timidity and even failure of many teachers of the social studies to face squarely social issues past and present. *One* reason for this failure has been the difficulty the teacher has had in separating himself or herself from one side or other of an issue. Another may be the lack of enough good techniques for the "fair" and "just" treatment of issues. The authors suggest dyadic role-playing, alone or in combination with sociodrama, as *one* answer to a very important problem in teaching for citizenship.

According to Simmel, the dyad or pair-group is the "social germ" in which fundamental or elemental social relationships take place. Since local, national, and international relationships over social issues are often too complicated or vast to be readily comprehended, especially by the young student, the "compression" of the essentials into a dyadic relationship may be expected to be comprehensible. Simulated interaction in the dyad with respect to an issue, frequently in conjunction with the sociodrama, is outlined here as a means that helps make social issues both real and, at the same time, "approachable" in the classroom.

BIBLIOGRAPHY

Role-Theory

CLAUDE C. BOWMAN. "Role-Playing and the Development of Insight." *Social Forces* 28:2; December 1949.

RALPH LINTON. *The Cultural Background of Personality.* New York: D. Appleton-Century, 1945.

GEORGE H. MEAD. *Mind, Self and Society.* (Charles W. Morris, editor) Chicago: University of Chicago Press, 1934.

J. L. MORENO. "The Concept of Sociodrama." *Sociometry.* November 1946.

———. *Sociodrama—A Method for the Analysis of Social Conflicts.* Psychodrama Monographs, No. 1. Beacon House, Inc., 1944.

—— and L. D. ZELENY. "Role Theory and Sociodrama." *Contemporary Sociology.* (Joseph Roucek, editor) Philosophical Press, 1958.

General Use of Role-Playing

JEAN E. ALEXANDER. *Let's Get Down to Cases.* Chicago: Anti-Defamation League of B'nai B'rith, n.d.

RICHARD E. GROSS and LESLIE D. ZELENY. *Educating Citizens for Democracy.* New York: Oxford University Press, 1958. Chapter 19.

ROBERT BARTLETT HAAS. "Sociodrama in Education." *Sociatry* 2:240–29; March 1948.

BERT HANSEN. "Sociodrama in a Small Community Therapy Program." *Sociatry* 1:92–96; March 1947.

—— "Sociodrama—A Methodology for Democratic Action." *Sociatry* 2:347–363; December-March 1948.

HELEN HALL JENNINGS. "Sociodrama as Educative Process." *Fostering Mental Health in Our School.* 1950 Yearbook. Washington, D.C.: Association for Supervision and Curriculum Development, a department of the National Education Association, 1950, p. 260–285.

HELEN JENNINGS, CHARLES E. HENDRY, RONALD LIPPITT, and ALVIN ZANDER. *Reality Practice as an Educational Method.* New York: Beacon House Inc., 1947.

ARTHUR KATONA. "Sociodrama." *Social Education* 19:23–26; January 1955.

J. L. MORENO. "Psychodramatic Treatment of Marriage Problems." *Sociometry* 3:20; 1940.

CLAIRE S. SCHUMAN and JAREN OSCARD. *To Clarify Our Problems: A Guide to Role-Playing.* Chicago: Anti-Defamation League of B'nai B'rith, n.d.

LESLIE D. ZELENY. How to Use Sociodrama. How To Do It Series, No. 20. Washington, D.C.: National Council for the Social Studies, a department of the National Education Association, 1960.

—— "The Sociodrama as an Aid in Teaching International Relations and World History." *International Journal of Sociometry.* September 1956.

—— "Sociodrama as a Means of Studying Controversial Issues." *Southern California Social Science Review.* October 18, 1948.

Role-Playing in the Elementary School

HELEN HALL JENNINGS, *op. cit.*

GEORGE and FANNIE SHAFTEL. *Role Playing the Problem Story.* New York: National Conference of Christians and Jews, 1952.

Role-Playing in the High School

RALPH GARRY. "Sociodrama in a High-School Adjustment Class." *The School Review,* March 1953.

JEAN D. GRAMBS and LUCIEN B. KINNEY. "Sociodrama in High School Classes."
    Social Education 12:341–343; December 1948.
RICHARD E. GROSS. "Role-Playing in Current Events Instruction." Civic Training.
    November 29-December 3, 1954.
—— How to Handle Controversial Issues. How To Do It Series, No. 14. Wash-
    ington, D.C.: National Council for the Social Studies, a department of the
    National Education Association, 1958.
RAYMOND H. MUESSIG. "Using Projective Pictures." Social Education 22:250–
    252; May 1958.

Role-Playing in the College and in Adult Education

MITCHELL GORDON. "Role-Playing." The Wall Street Journal. 149: March 15,
    1957.
LEOPOLD VON WIESE. "Role Playing as a Method of Academic Education."
    Group Psychotherapy 5:73–77; April, July, November, 1952 (Translation by
    Gerhard Schauer).

Supplementary Bibliography

KURT LEWIN. "Group Decision and Social Change" in T. M. Newcomb and Eu-
    gene L. Hartley, Readings in Social Psychology. New York: Henry Holt and
    Company, 1947. p. 330–344.
HERBERT J. MULLER. The Uses of the Past. New York: Oxford University Press,
    1952.
M. SHERIFF. "Group Influences Upon the Formation of Norms and Attitudes"
    in T. M. Newcomb and Eugene L. Hartley, Readings in Social Psychology.
    New York: Henry Holt and Company, 1947. p. 77–89.
KURT H. WOLFF. The Sociology of George Simmel. Chicago: University of Chi-
    cago Press, 1925.

LABOR VS. MANAGEMENT:
A SIMULATION GAME

John D. Gearon *

*Simulation techniques are a combination of role playing and problem
solving. They derive from the war games and command-post exercises
used by the military forces of all nations. They can range from highly*

* From Social Education, Vol. 30 (Washington, D.C.: National Council for the Social
Studies, October 1966), pp. 421–422. Reprinted by permission of the NCSS and the
author.

sophisticated scenarios dependent upon complicated programming by computers to the simplest kind of make-believe that children use when they "play house." Basically in any simulation exercise what happens is:

(1) The players are assigned parts in a fairly well defined situation.

(2) The players are confronted with a series of incidents in which they must take action or make decisions according to the characters they are playing and the information they have at hand. As a rule, whatever actions and decisions they take with the action and decisions of the other players lead to further incidents that require of everyone more action and more decisions.

It should be noted that in these simulations the player is not free to act in any way he wishes. He must act or decide only within the bounds of the supposed realities of the situation, which may be changed at any minute by the actions or decisions of the other players, the umpire, or the computer who is scripting the simulation.

This simulation activity through role playing can provide students many insights into the relations of labor and management in our society. The social studies model it leaves in the minds of the students can be used to define and to clarify important terms in labor history. It has served well as a stimulating and useful introductory experience for a unit on the American labor movement in United States history.

Before I begin my introduction to the game, cards are given to the students assigning them roles as citizens of Mount Van Buren, either as leader or member of one of four groups or as one of four television reporters. At the end of my introductory speech, the four groups are set up around the room and are in session working to find a solution to the labor problem threatening the economic security of Mount Van Buren.

I open by asking the class to lend me the full support of its imagination. Then I begin to set the scene and get the activity underway.

SETTING THE SCENE

We are all citizens of, and presently situated right in the middle of, our home city Mount Van Buren. Ours is by no means the smallest city in this part of the state. At the last census we had about 36,000 people. Things haven't changed much since then. Oh, a few of our restless young people have gone off to the big city, and some of our old folks have moved to California or Florida to keep warm in the winter. But it's still a good town. We like it.

Ours is a happy town. We generally have worked well together, and we have a fine community spirit. A few years ago our own Mount Van Buren High School basketball team won the state championship. We all gave the team our enthusiastic support. Yes sir! This is a good town. Never any real trouble. That is—until recently.

As everybody knows, our biggest local industry is the manufacture of welknots—that key item in American industry. Right here in Mount Van Buren we have the main plant and the head office of the Acme Welknot Manufacturing Company. The factory usually employs about 6,000 workers. They are all members of that strong industrial union, the United Welknot Workers of America. As we all know, the workers have always been contented and prosperous—until now, that is.

This brings me to the troubles that began for us nearly a week ago. At that time contract negotiations between the representatives of the union and the company broke down. Since then, production has stopped, striking pickets parade around the plant, and the entire economic welfare of the community is threatened.

The Mount Van Buren strike is in the news throughout the nation. The talk around town has grown wilder and wilder. There are rumors—and rumors about rumors. We seem to talk of nothing else. One thing is certain. We, all of us, every citizen of Mount Van Buren, should have clearly in mind the facts of the dispute. Let's get them down on paper so we will all know exactly what we are talking about.

There are three general areas of disagreement in this contract dispute between the union and the company:

Hourly wage rate
Present rate: $2.25 per hour.   Time and a half after 40 hours.
Union proposal: $2.60 per hour.   Double time after 40 hours.
Last company offer: $2.35 per hour.   Time and a half after 40 hours.

Paid vacations and sick leave
Present plan: Two weeks per year.   Five days paid sick leave.
Union proposal: Four weeks per year.   Ten days paid sick leave.
Last company offer: Three weeks per year. Five days paid sick leave.

Prospective layoffs in view of the coming of automation
1. It is known that the company plans technical changes using automated methods that will make it possible to reduce its labor force by about two thousand or more employees sometime within the next six months.

2. The union is asking that seniority be the basis on which employees will be retained on the job: last employed, first laid off. Also, the union asks that three months severance pay be given to each employee with more than two years service who is laid off.

3. So far, the company has not agreed to either of these proposals. This may prove to be the biggest block in the way of a compromise agreement.

There it is. That's what our strike is all about. Right now, the situation is very bad indeed. Company officials are meeting in their office over there in the north end of town. Down at Labor Hall on the South Side, the union's strike council is meeting. Neither side is at this time communicating in any way with the other. The first thing to do is to get them together negotiating again. Something must be done soon.

Two new groups have recently come into the picture. For the last few days some of our local business and professional leaders, a special committee of the Chamber of Commerce, have been meeting at Elks Hall here in the downtown section. Our mayor, facing another election soon, has begun meeting with a small committee of the City Council to see what can be done to bring the company and the union together. Let us hope that these two groups will be able to come up with something in their talking that can result in action.

As is the case with any people facing a crisis, we look first to our leaders. Some of us are beginning to think that our greatest hope is in the emergence of new leadership in the four groups that are now meeting to settle the conflict. Certainly, we realize that any leader has to win the support of the group with which he works. Meanwhile, through the medium of television, we are able to bring you a quick glimpse of those to whom we now look for leadership.

Here we see our most prominent local business executive, the President of the Acme Welknot Manufacturing Company. As you can see, he is hurrying to meet with the company executive group at the company office.

Now here is that important labor leader, President of Local 45 of the UWWA, on his way to Labor Hall to meet with the Union strike council.

Switching to Elks Hall, we show you the wealthy real estate dealer, President of the Mount Van Buren Chamber of Commerce, on his way to confer with his special committee.

Mounting the steps in front of City Hall, we see the familiar figure of our mayor on his way to meet with the special City Council Committee. Our hopes for a speedy end to our trouble lies with these leaders and the groups meeting with them today.

My special position in all of this, if you will excuse professional pride, is well known to each and every one of you. As news director and chief commentator on Station WMVB-TV, I have always tried to maintain impartiality. The strain, I confess, is beginning to tell, and I have a powerful urge to speak out editorially about the failure of our local leadership, of the four separate groups of fellow citizens who seem unable to get the situation moving toward a satisfactory solution.

As throughout this long crisis, we shall continue to do our best here at WMVB-TV to keep you fully informed about what is happening. We have a special camera crew at each of the four meeting places with our best reporters ready to bring you any new development, arrange interviews, and provide the freedom of our microphone and camera to any member of the concerned groups who wishes to make a statement to the public.

May I introduce our four reporters. First, at the company offices. Come in, please! Now, our regular staff correspondent at City Hall. Thank you! Then our reporter at Labor Hall. And lastly, the reporter who has been assigned to the special meeting at Elks Hall.

Shortly, we expect to bring you a special news roundup from these competent and well informed reporters. So keep your dial on Channel 3.

From this point on, the course of the game is entirely up to the students themselves. In my role as news commentator, I am able to keep in touch with what is going on. I can call for frequent news reports from each of the reporters in the field. If it appears that things need stirring up a bit, I can occasionally let my impartiality slip and offer an unfair editorial comment just to keep things moving.

AN EXPERIMENT IN PROBLEM SOLVING

Bertha Boya Thompson *

Students who have not experienced a true problem-solving situation in their secondary-school classes often find it difficult to see how problem-solving lessons work. This description of the use of problem solving in a high school geography course should make the technique a little clearer. As he reads about this problem, the reader may wish to follow the application of the steps of Dewey's reflective thinking.
 1. *Feeling a need*
 2. *Defining the problem*
 3. *Guessing hypothetical solutions*
 4. *Testing the hypotheses on the basis of evidence gathered*
 5. *Forming conclusions*
Note that in this problem-solving unit the problem is a real problem that the pupils want answered—not a canned one.

In the experimental high school geography course developed at Talawanda High School during the academic year, 1962–63, the problem-solving method of instruction was introduced in a unit of study on food production in the United States. As one of their assignments, students were asked to construct

* From *Selected Classroom Experiences: High School Geography Project*, Clyde F. Kohn, editor (Normal, Ill.: National Council for Geographic Education, Publication Center, 1964), pp. 1–14. Reprinted by permission of the editor and the author.

a dot map showing the distribution of wheat production in the fifteen leading wheat-producing states for 1959. While collecting data from the agricultural census for that year, the statistics for wheat production in Ohio for 1954 and 1959 were noted by the students. A question arose as to why wheat production in Ohio had decreased from 45 million to 29 million bushels during this five-year period.

One student asked if he might make two dot maps of wheat production for Ohio, one for 1954 and the other for 1959, to see whether or not the decline was general throughout the state (Figure 1). Upon completion of the two maps, the student concluded that a decrease did occur in all counties, but that in some counties the decline appeared to be significantly greater than in others. The student's failure to hold an identical or uniform dot size caused some slight inconsistencies in his observations.

The following "explainers," or hypotheses, were suggested by the class to account for the general decrease in production for the years 1954-59, and for the place-to-place differences observed on the completed maps:

1. The decrease in wheat production in Ohio from 1954 to 1959 was associated with a decline in the demand for United states wheat on the world market.
2. The decrease in wheat production in Ohio from 1954 to 1959 was associated with a change in the diet of the American people.
3. The decrease in wheat production in Ohio from 1954 to 1959 occurred because 1959 was a non-wheat year in the crop rotation pattern.
4. The decrease in wheat production in Ohio from 1954 to 1959 was associated with a decline in county wheat acreage allotments.
5. The decrease in wheat production in Ohio from 1954 to 1959 occurred because other crops were able to compete successfully for acreage previously used for wheat.
6. The decrease in wheat production in Ohio from 1954 to 1959 occurred because farm land had been taken out of crop production and used for other activities such as manufacturing, urban development, recreation, and mining.

TESTING THE HYPOTHESES: REJECTION AND ACCEPTANCE

After examining available data, a student reported that the United States had exported 567 million bushels of wheat in 1958, 623 million in 1959, and 712 million in 1960. He regretted his inability to secure data for 1954, but on the basis of the data obtained concluded that the increased sales from 1958–1960 did not indicate a decline in world demand for United States wheat. Hence, the first hypothesis was rejected. In other words, the decline in wheat production in Ohio between 1954 and 1959 was not due to any decline in the demand for United States wheat on the world market.

The instructor then placed the following production and sales data for Ohio on the chalkboard:

The Production and Sales of Wheat
In Ohio (1954 and 1959)

Production   1954—45,202,350 bushels   1959—29,499,714 bushels
Sales   1954—38,365,231 bushels   1959—26,115,667 bushels

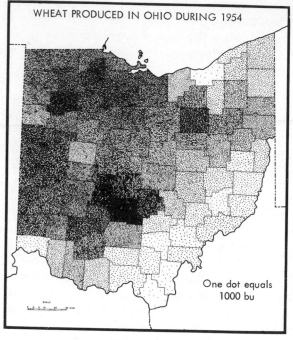

WHEAT PRODUCED IN OHIO DURING 1954

One dot equals
1000 bu

FIGURE 1A.

It was quickly noted that a larger percentage of the wheat produced in 1959 had been sold than in 1954. The class recognized that this indicated no decrease in the percentage of sales and thus rejected the second hypothesis. It was concluded that the decline in wheat production in Ohio from 1954 to 1959 did not reflect a change in the diet of the American people.

The student who proposed the third hypothesis secured wheat production data for the ten-year period, 1950 to 1959. He analyzed and graphed these data in order to determine whether or not the decrease was recurrent in any kind of recognizable pattern. He recommended that the third hypothesis be rejected, and that the class accept the conclusion that the decline in wheat production in Ohio from 1954 to 1959 was not associated with a non-wheat year in the crop rotation pattern.

To test the fourth hypothesis, which most students thought was the major reason for decreased production, data were obtained from the Agricultural Stabilization and Conservation Committee in Columbus, Ohio. Based on

their analysis of these statistics, the class decided to accept the hypothesis as
one of the important causes of decreased production. They were surprised
to find, however, that the decrease in county acreage allotments was not so
significant as they had anticipated. The following table gives some examples

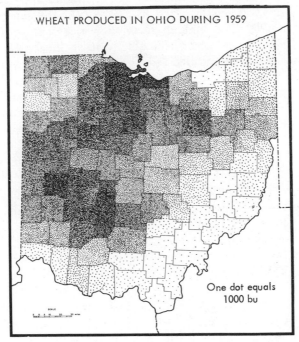

WHEAT PRODUCED IN OHIO DURING 1959

One dot equals
1000 bu

FIGURE 1B.

in which large production decreases were accompanied by relatively small
declines in acreage allotments:

	Wheat Production (in bushels)		Wheat Acreage Allotments (in bushels)		
	1954	1959	1954	1959	Difference
State Total	45,000,000	29,000,000	1,753,914	1,557,896	196,018
Paulding Co.	654,765	110,609	26,701	26,553	148
Adams Co.	308,018	71,532	13,423	12,296	1,127
Ashtabula Co.	335,821	87,280	13,109	12,769	340

It was decided that the other hypotheses had to be investigated in detail,
particularly when it was noted that the farmers of Ohio actually planted less
than the county acreage allotments permitted, as follows:

Comparison of Allotted and Planted
Acreage in Ohio (1954 and 1959)

Year	Allotted Acreage	Planted Acreage	Difference
1954	1,753,914	1,740,000	13,914
1959	1,557,896	1,264,000	293,896

One student argued that these data could be explained by increased technological knowledge, that is, farmers could get more from less acres, so less was planted to wheat. Since many thought this was the explanation, the instructor gave wheat crop yields as 27 bushels per acre in 1954 and 24.5 for 1959. The students were surprised. The instructor then asked them to multiply the 1,264,000 acres planted in 1959 by the difference in yields between 1954 and 1959. The students readily saw that more would have been produced in 1959 if farmers had been able to reach the 1954 yield. It was at this point that the students decided that unfavorable weather conditions might have accounted for the decreased yields. Hence, a seventh hypothesis was introduced: "The decrease in wheat production in Ohio from 1954 to 1959 was associated with an unfavorable growing season during the year in which the 1959 census was taken." An interview was arranged with the vocational agriculture teacher and his class to secure information relative to critical periods in the growth of winter wheat and, in addition, possible crop competitors for wheat acreage. The students then checked the acreage for other crops for 1954 and 1959. Only corn and soybeans showed an increase, with corn increases too small to be significant. It was decided that further testing of the fifth hypothesis relative to crop competition would be necessary, and that a soybean map should be made to see if areas of decreased wheat production were also areas of increased soybean production.

In order to supply relevant data for testing the sixth hypothesis, it was noted that the number of farms in Ohio declined by 37,000 from 1954 to 1959. To the unbelieving students, the instructor explained that 7,000 of these were attributed to a redefinition of the term, "farm." Some of the decline, however, was attributed to the merging of farms, for the average farm size of Ohio increased from 112.9 acres to 131.9 acres in the five-year period from 1954 to 1959. Other contributing factors suggested were increased urban sprawl, the development of new parks, and strip mining. The field consultant on the High School Project, Professor Henry J. Warman, suggested that the decline in proportion of all land in farms or the change in the number of acres of farmland cultivated might be used as indicators of competition from other activities.

Committees were selected to map the dependent variable, that is, the phenomenon whose spatial variation was to be explained. In this instance, the dependent variable was the variation in changed wheat production from 1954 to 1959 in Ohio by counties, and the tentative independent variables (the possible explainers) were: (1) county wheat acreage allotment changes, (2) monthly differences in temperature and precipitation, (3) changes in soybean acreage, and (4) changes in farm acreages. Changes in wheat acreage were mapped to depict the dependent variable and to facilitate visual correlation.

A simplified quantitative system was devised for constructing the necessary maps (Figure 2). The differences between the 1954 and 1959 data were determined for each county, for both the dependent and independent variables (with the exception of the temperature and precipitation changes). The

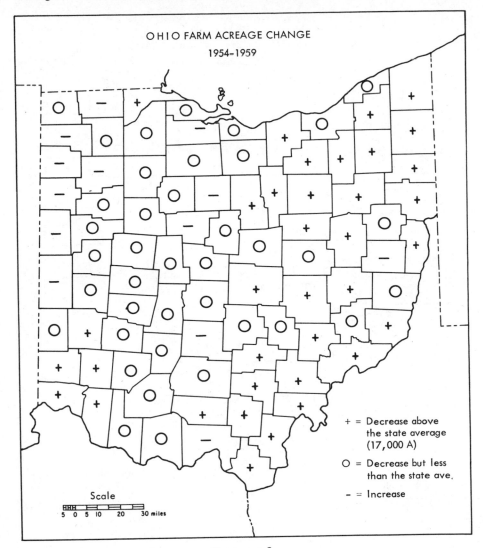

FIGURE 2.

average county change was calculated for each variable. The symbols +, —, and O were placed upon each map according to fixed criteria. For example, in the case of farm acreage changes, a "+" was placed in a county if the county decrease was equal to the state average or greater; an "O" was placed in a county if the decrease was less than the average for the state. A "—" was placed in a county if an increase occurred.

The "weather data committee" placed its information upon each of their maps using areas determined by the state climatologist. Two different colors, blue for 1954–55 and red for 1958–59, were used in recording the temperature and precipitation data on each of the climatic maps constructed. The 1954

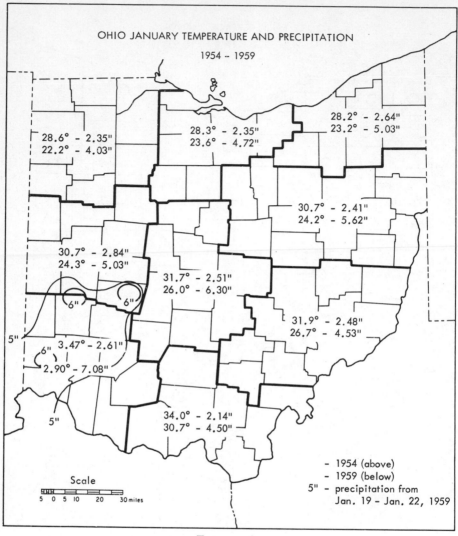

OHIO JANUARY TEMPERATURE AND PRECIPITATION

1954 - 1959

28.6° - 2.35"
22.2° - 4.03"

28.3° - 2.35"
23.6° - 4.72"

28.2° - 2.64"
23.2° - 5.03"

30.7° - 2.41"
24.2° - 5.62"

30.7° - 2.84"
24.3° - 5.03"

31.7° - 2.51"
26.0° - 6.30"

6"   6"

31.9° - 2.48"
26.7° - 4.53"

5"

6"   3.47° - 2.61"
2.90° - 7.08"

5"

34.0° - 2.14"
30.7° - 4.50"

Scale

5 0 5 10   20   30 miles

- 1954 (above)
- 1959 (below)
5" - precipitation from
   Jan. 19 – Jan. 22, 1959

FIGURE 3.

data were placed above the 1959 data as shown in Figure 3. Five-inch and six-inch isohyets for a 48-hour period were placed on the January map.

After all the maps had been constructed, they were placed upon the bulletin board. Students were urged to check the extent of spatial covariance visually. Later a class period was set aside to test hypotheses 5, 6, and 7 using this method of visual correlation. During this period students concluded that the map depicting changes in wheat production indicated that all counties had experienced a decrease in wheat production with the greatest declines in the southwestern, the central, and northwestern parts of the state (Figure 4). Similar results were noted using the map showing changes in wheat acreages.

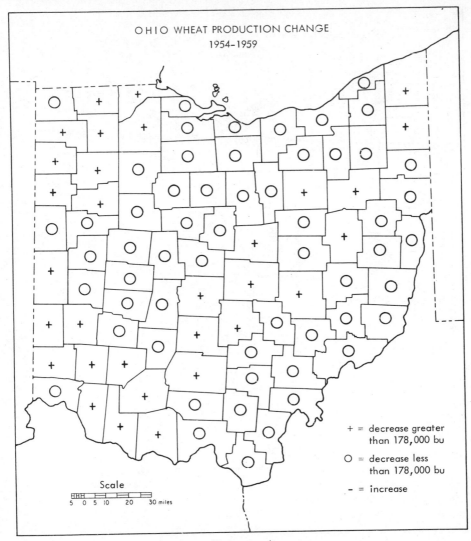

FIGURE 4.

One student noticed that the greatest decrease in wheat acreage allotment occurred in areas where the greatest changes in wheat production occurred (Figure 5). In light of this observation, the students' previous judgment relative to the wheat acreage allotment hypothesis (hypothesis 4) was reaffirmed. However, one exception was noted in the southwestern part of the state where a greater than average decrease in production occurred but where government allotment decreases were less than the average for the state. Students also observed that a less than average decrease in wheat acreage allotment change and a less than average decrease in wheat acreage change occurred in the southeast. Here, however, there was an above average decrease in total

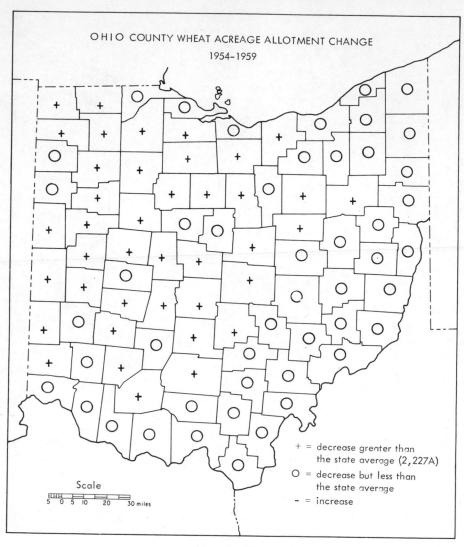

OHIO COUNTY WHEAT ACREAGE ALLOTMENT CHANGE
1954–1959

Scale
5 0 5 10 20 30 miles

+ = decrease greater than
      the state average (2,227A)

O = decrease but less than
      the state average

− = increase

FIGURE 5.

farm acreage. These observations plus their knowledge of urban sprawl, park development, strip-mining, and reforestation in Ohio led to the acceptance of the sixth hypothesis. It was concluded that the decrease in wheat production in Ohio from 1954 to 1959 was positively associated with competition for land by other activities.

In looking at both the wheat acreage and soybean acreage maps (Figure 6), the students concluded that where greater than average wheat acreage decreases occurred in western Ohio, soybeans showed an increase. Thus, on the basis of these observations they accepted the fifth hypothesis and concluded that the decrease in wheat production in Ohio from 1954 to 1959 was

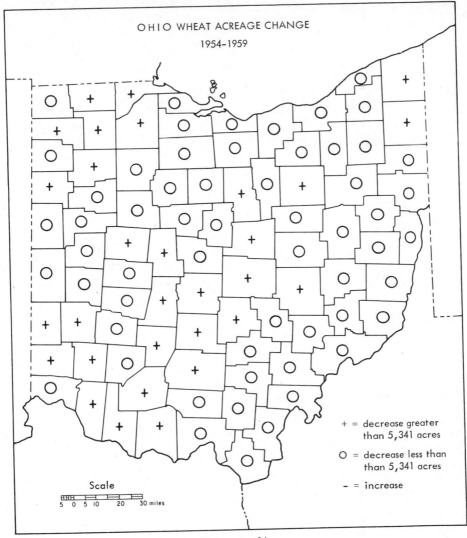

FIGURE 6A.

associated in part with the successful competition of other crops for acreage once planted in wheat. This judgment was reaffirmed when weather conditions were later investigated. The students proposed that the winter wheat crop might have been destroyed by inclement weather conditions, and that a spring planting of soybeans might have replaced the wheat crop.

Some wetness in the northwest was noted in November, 1958, for those counties where an above average decrease occurred; severe temperatures with much less precipitation and no snow cover in December of that year might have caused freezing; and flood-like conditions occurred in January of 1959 in two of the areas of greater than average decline. The isohyets of 5 and 6

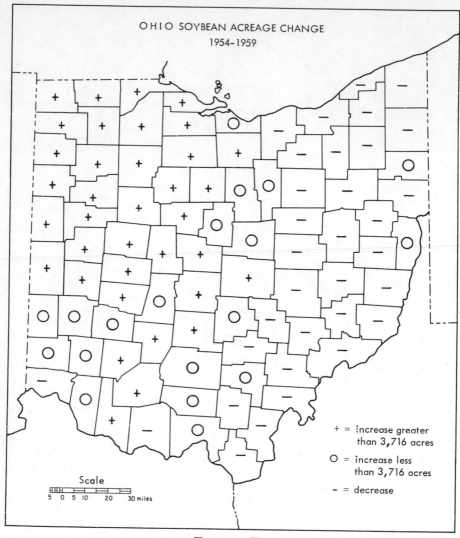

FIGURE 6B.

inches for a 48 hour period include most of these areas (Figure 3). Frozen flood waters in lowland areas possibly caused suffocation of the wheat plants. The above average precipitation of May and June, 1959, did not covary with an above average decrease. The "adverse weather condition hypothesis" was therefore accepted, and the class concluded that the decline in wheat production in Ohio from 1954 to 1959 was associated with an unfavorable growing season for the year on which the 1959 figures are based.

SUMMARY

Of the seven hypotheses proposed by the students, three were quickly rejected; but, on the basis of available data, four were accepted as possible "explainers" for changes in wheat production in Ohio between 1954 and 1959. Whereas, in the beginning, several students believed that their particular hypothesis was the *only* explanation, they all agreed that the solution was much more complex than they had anticipated originally. They were satisfied, however, that through the use of statistics and the process of visual correlation they had determined the major factors contributing to the decline in wheat production in Ohio for the years indicated.

HIGH SCHOOL STUDENT RESEARCH— FACT OR FANCY?

John R. Jablonski *

Research is another problem-solving technique that can be used in school. If it is to be profitable to the student, research should consist of a real problem whose solution would provide the researcher with some information or knowledge not available before. In this selection, Jablonski sets his standards for student research quite high. Perhaps he has made them too narrow, but however that may be, it is important that when teachers encourage pupils to do research, the research really be research and not some cookbook exercise. That real research can be done in high school classes has been demonstrated by pupils time and time again.

Among the various procedures used by teachers to guide the learning process of pupils in science are those related to the development of research techniques. The question is posed as to whether high school students can or can not participate in research activities. If so, what direction should teachers take to guide these research activities and how may these be achieved?

What is meant by research for the high school student? Perhaps one could be led to a clear understanding of what research is by describing what *is not* research.

Thus, research *is not* defined as the performance of a rigorous specific experiment copied from notes in a science journal or other source. It *is not* the

* From *The Science Teacher*, Vol. 31 (April 1964), pp. 24–26. Reprinted by permission of *The Science Teacher*.

obtaining of results by repeating these experiments and confirming or disproving the results reported by the original author. Certainly, this procedure of repetition is part of research work, but to actually repeat the same expriment done by others can not be considered *research*, as the writer hopes to define it.

Clearly, research *can not* be defined as such, when a student reports to a laboratory period, has all the materials and instructions laid out, and works to determine what happens when various trials are performed with the materials. Perhaps this might be considered only an exploratory or introductory procedure before research begins. It is a necessary procedure, but it is not *research*, as properly defined.

Some believe that research consists of giving students a standard experiment and having them discover by themselves what will happen. Assuredly, this is again only part of the exploration process to lead to real research.

To repeat, the views expressed which are not research do not limit their importance. Such activities are a necessary part of the training to conduct research and are a means to obtain the final objective. How then *can* research be explained or defined?

From my view, research is an attitude, a way, an existence, or to sum it up: *a complex of deliberations involved in the pursuit of information or knowledge.*

Embodied in the pursuit of knowledge is the direct and personal involvement of the individual in a problem. Such a problem involves an answer not already known or understood, and the unknown elements of the problem must be recognized or identified by the seeker. The seeker is the researcher or the scientist. He may be either student or teacher.

If the work is identified as research, the worker, too, must be identified. This person is an individual who has become intensely involved and interested in exploring specifically not what is already known, but what is *unknown*. To find out what is *unknown* does not in any sense limit the process to science alone. Such an individual could also be engaged in other fields, the fine arts, languages, or philosophy, for example. The important label for such an individual, however, is "one who seeks." Thus, the seeker or researcher undertakes a research activity to look for new knowledge or the unknown as related to a specific problem.

Hopefully, some clarity has been given to the researcher and research. The next important step is to have an understanding of categories or areas that identify the work procedure. Various labels are given for these as demonstration, experiments, projects, and observation.

A demonstration is a performance of a procedure by one individual to a group or to another individual to illustrate a specific reaction or chain of events which finally terminate in a statement as to what has happened.

An experiment is a series of steps usually performed to obtain answers to questions concerning a specific body of knowledge.

Projects are here defined as devices through which teachers and researchers select a variety of problems (known or unknown) to be presented for the training of a student or an assistant in research procedures. Often, the selections are not carefully chosen and do not offer the proper challenge or development necessary for a particular student of high ability. In some instances, the projects are selected by the teacher for his own use in a current course requirement. Consequently, this imposes limits on its suitability, its merits, and its rationality for the specific objective—finding unknown facts. It does not necessarily contribute to a later goal for greater depth in discovering truths. To be a legitimate project for research, it must be part of the whole, or a whole, for which answers are uncovered or investigated. Moreover, before such a springboard for pursuit is founded, certain basic elements must have been developed in the seeker or researcher. How these are provided rests in the capabilities and responsibilities of the classroom teacher. Undoubtedly, no one way exists, but the determination and the understanding of each in his own way will be a contribution. To summarize briefly, the elements of importance for the researcher (student or teacher) are:

1. Organization in problem objective
2. Dedication to seeking the truth
3. Open-mindedness
4. Accurate recording of observations
5. Control in the experiment
6. Reporting and possibly publishing the completed work
7. Advancement in knowledge in context or understanding.

LIMITATIONS

Although any writer may set up certain criteria or procedures, it is understood that certain obstacles or limits are imposed. It would be appropriate to review some of these to alert the student or teacher to their consequences. The sources of some limitations may be recognized as existing within the areas of the school systems or within the scientific communities.

Within the school, certain conditions might be affected by the teachers, the administrators, the student body, the curriculum, financial support, and the library, and other facilities available. Each of these might have a role in determining what kind of research is set up for the high school to follow.

Reviewing first the role of the library and its sources, there is no doubt as to its importance. In exploring a problem, a researcher must of necessity have available to him previous information, literature from as many sources as possible, and reports of current progress in his specific area. If such a facility is not available at the school, arrangements should be made for the students or teachers to use supplementary facilities of other institutions. Provision should also be made to give *time* for working at such facilities.

The role of the teachers, administrators, and student body are obvious and need not be elucidated here. They, together with the curriculum in force, are responsible for creating the appropriate atmosphere to engender greater fluency in the conduct of research investigations by high school students.

Support for these activities must be directed and stimulated throughout the system. A lax student body is often the result of a similar slackness among teachers and administrators. It is necessary that the positive form of cooperation and participation exists in relation to the conduct of research activities. Encouragement is needed for challenge, discussion, and a supportive attitude from administrator to teacher, to student, and finally among students themselves.

FINANCES

No matter how strong the above roles may become, unless there are added to them proper facilities and financial support, they would remain fruitless. This is *not* an argument for expensive materials and equipment, but rather a plea for rational use of funds without hindering the conduct of proper research. To be sure, many of the schools have already demonstrated their ingenuity in making things work with a limited budget and limited personnel. But with a strong supportive role from personnel, student body, and the budget, considerable contributions can be made in these areas. Certainly it takes organization and planning and the will to succeed.

SCIENTISTS

The contribution of the scientific community in this endeavor is not often explored to its fullest degree. Many students and teachers in research activities are hesitant in using the advice or help of a practicing scientist in the community. Without exception, scientists have considerable interest in this aspect of the high school program. And who, in the community, is more qualified to assist and direct the research being performed? Often the fresh approach by a student researcher even leads to the enlarged outlook or approach of the scientist in his own work. Time and again, each generation of youth has made a contribution toward the progress of new knowledge by mutually sharing in the exchange of ideas. In addition, the practitioner has gained or received a new impetus for greater effort.

To emphasize again: The working scientist in the community is available and would participate. Thus, the only possible limitation may be distance or proximity. Nevertheless, with today's advance in transportation, all that is needed is the initial action by the student or teacher to request the help of a scientist in the community.

Some teachers have reported that cooperation from a scientist in the community has failed to materialize after the teacher had written a letter of request. It is at this juncture that the writer wishes to relate the opinions of some of his fellow workers in this respect. Often, a letter is sent using the phrase ". . . tell us all you know about . . ." Such a question has resulted in preventing the establishing of the interest or cooperation of the working scientist. Of greater value would be a letter stating the specific project, the reason for the investigation, and an outright invitation to join in the completion of the problem.

In all previous experiences the writer has known of, no scientist in a community who was properly approached has failed to enter into such a cooperative effort. The responsibility to seek out this aid, however, rests with the initiative of the student or teacher. In general, most city or town governments have a bureau or organization which can render valuable aid in such a venture. Without these sources, the teacher may approach the scientist himself by letter or in person, with specific needs in mind.

As previously indicated, some of the essentials for beginning research activities lie in the availability of time, space, personnel, and budget. With these appropriately aligned, the selection of the problem for use by the students must be given thorough review.

SELECTION OF PROBLEM

Essentially, the first requirement is the framework related to attitude. Selection must not consist of a mere exercise—an exercise is *not* research. No project or problem can be identified without first reading the literature in the particular area of study. Without reading, there is no research framework with which to begin.

Along with this approach, the teacher must have an interested student who is willing to delve with him in the first approaches to any problem or project. Together, they might then consult with the practicing scientist.

For example, here is a summary of a specific case. A group of students heard a lecture by a scientist who was conducting research in the field of animal nutrition as related to tumor growth. The topic became related to the students' specific problem and one student posed the question: "Do laboratory rats eat the same amount of three different available commercial diets?"

A simple question on the surface, but the answer was not immediately available. The student had a definite interest, and it had a bearing on the experimentation of the scientist. The student read more on general nutrition, examined the use of proper controls and numbers of experimental animals to use, and—after a preliminary conference with the teacher and scientist—set out to find the answers.

What about his findings? The student reported to the interested scientist that rats *did* indeed eat different amounts of the three commercial diets. Furthermore, during his observations, a second question came to his mind: "What would happen to the rats' consumption of the diets if they were given an experimental tumor that had been previously carried in the peritoneal cavity of the donor rat?" This represented an expansion of his work toward a new goal. He prepared a procedural outline to follow and discussed it again with the teacher and scientist. After approval, he set up his experimental plan and injected the experimental rats with a subcutaneous tumor. He continued to observe the dietary habits of the animals and after about a two-week period, he observed an astounding fact.

Following the injection of the tumor and also after the tumor had an opportunity to grow, he noticed that the rats changed their preference in their choice of diet to the one which had previously been less popular. Shortly thereafter, he noticed that the tumors had disappeared.

There was considerable excitement about the finding, but the working scientist wished to have greater verification and asked that the experiment be repeated. The experiment was repeated, and similar results, but not precisely the same, were obtained.

The student reported his work in a progress report to other class members, and a second student expressed a desire to repeat the experiment. The results were not the same as those obtained in the initial experiment. She raised some questions, so that a three-school program was set up on the same project to repeat this experiment again.

Essentially, the observations of the initial observer were verified, and this led to other ramifications of the problem. One student wanted to know what the diet might contain that could have produced the effects obtained; another queried what changes were produced in the rats, and some asked specifically if something happened to the serum of the rats during the experimental conditions which existed.

The latter problem was explored by a senior college student as a tutorial investigation at the conclusion of the three-school experiment.

This was a follow-up of the high school students' efforts but was limited to an investigation in the changes in specific serum proteins.

In the preliminary planning of the work of the college student, she was able to enlist the advice of other scientists. Finally, it was shown that components in the serum did alter as a result of the diet and that specific changes in the quality and quantity of serum proteins could be produced and measured.

This verification led, concomitantly, to the cooperating scientist on the project to attempt to identify and isolate the specific serum proteins that were responsible for changes in the serum components. This work is still in progress.

This is only one example of how related research has expanded from initial attempts at the high school level to the laboratory of a working scientist. There is an inherent freedom in the "untrained" mind which ultimately leads by proper direction to worthy objectives in research.

Emphatically, then, high school research *can* be done with the proper guidance, selection, and interpretation of information, knowledge, and ideas.

The student has the same role as does the working scientist, but to start him on the way, he must receive the necessary guidance. To elaborate again: *Research* is an attitude, a way, an existence or to sum it up:

A complex of deliberations involved in the pursuit of knowledge or information.

Can a high school student do research? The answer depends on the total circumstances for each individual.

VITALIZING STUDENT
RESEARCH REPORTS

Phyllis Lieberman and Sidney B. Simon *

Reports on individual pupil research often fail because teachers neglect the important process of making assignments. The practice of giving research and report assignments without any particulars or amplification is quite futile. The pupils do not know how to select a problem or go about solving it. As a result, their reports are deathly dull and intellectually worthless when careful preparation and guidance by the teacher might have made the reports informative and stimulating.

You have been in this classroom before. You are the teacher. Your students sit before you in silent apathy. True, in one corner the three students who are "on" this morning *do* exhibit a little nervous energy. At least, as this morning's reporters, they *do* have to get up on their feet and move their mouths. But the other members of the class have little to which to look forward. They have heard reports before.

On drone the second-hand sentences until, finally, you can take little more. John declares for the whole class to hear, "The government in Brazil has alienated the people by its extreme inflationary measures." You interrupt, "John, what does that sentence mean?"

"Beats me," says John helplessly.

"How is it possible," you ask, "that you would include such a sentence in a report to our class and not know what it means?"

John stammers a moment and says, "That's what was written in the book, so I figured it must be right."

* From *Social Education*, Vol. 27 (Washington, D.C.: The National Council for the Social Studies, January 1964), pp. 24–26. Reprinted by permission of The National Council for the Social Studies and the authors.

The scene is too familiar. How many reports have you as a teacher read in your lifetime which were researched and written by *Encyclopedia Britannica* and signed by Mary Jones, grade seven? How often have you been handed a beautiful booklet that took days to complete only to find that its cutter and gluer understood little of the information it contained?

But all student reports do not have to be dull and uninspiring. Good reports, intelligently guided, can indeed foster creativity and independent study. They can widen circles of knowledge and understanding and develop the sense of accomplishment which comes from sticking to a task from beginning to end. What we need, then, is to discover ways of assuring that the reports our students prepare will be truly meaningful, reports in which "hack work" will not abound and the plagarism won't plague us unduly.

Of the three suggestions for improving the quality of reports here presented, two have often been used successfully. The third, we think offers an interesting and rewarding alternative.

1. *Reports with an emphasis upon dramatics.* Instead of standing before the class and reading, or presenting from memory, or even telling in their own words *their* encyclopedia's version of a particular incident in history or conditions in a specific country, the students are asked to present the information they have gathered concerning their topic to the class in the form of a skit. Making broad use of a narrator, the skits highlight the important points the reporters choose to make, and *all* of the information that has been collected can be printed on ditto sheets and distributed to the members of the class for further study after the presentation of the skit.

The sheer fun of dramatic play is enough to justify this approach to reports. Most children have a deep sense of the dramatic and enjoy using their creative talents to work out original presentations. In order to present an exciting, dramatic play, each student must give careful consideration to all information and ideas pertaining to the report topic, with the result that a greater familiarity with and understanding of the assigned subject matter is gained.

2. *Reports with an emphasis upon summaries.* A second way to assure that student reports will be interesting and original is to ask for written summaries of the information the children have accumulated as a result of their research. In the process of deciding what material to include and what to omit, the students will become increasingly skilled in the art of discriminating and distinguishing between the significant and the unimportant. Moreover, this summary-type report tends to eliminate the problem of students who are apt to copy directly from the book, for each student must use his own words to prepare a précis.

3. *Reports with an emphasis upon values.* This, in our opinion, is the most important way to vitalize student reports. We also believe that it does much more than bring about the creation of reports that are exciting to hear, instructive to prepare, and pleasurable for teachers to read. We feel that a very real benefit from such reports is that they re-focus for the teacher the

whole problem of what *is* worth including in a list of topics on which students may be asked to report. We see no great value in having a student list the mountains, rivers, and major cities of a country. We are not against mountains, rivers, and cities as such, but we want them to be studied for a larger purpose than that a student be able successfully to complete a crossword puzzle at some future date. Similarly, no important person will come to life in the mind of a student so long as we settle for merely listing his birth date, his five significant achievements, or the rate and date of his death. Such facts as these can be looked up at any time in the future and certainly cannot be considered worthy of student library research.

What then, you ask, is better? What do we advocate? We say we must lead our students into an inquiry, not of how a country looks or of what a person did, but rather of what that country or that person *is*, or *was*. The struggles and the joys of people seem important here. The happiness and the despair and the personal conflicts of a man take on significance. His shortcomings, the loyal support of the people close to him, or the treachery of his "best friends"—all enter into a report the emphasis of which is upon values. We seek to avoid the cardboard cut-out image of Simon Bolivar astride his horse. We are interested rather in learning his reactions when a peasant came to him for help. We want to know what he read, what made him laugh. We believe that an investigation of such matters spirals learning. Sheer memorization is not rewarded here. The inquiry becomes more complex than the mere copying of paragraphs from reference books. Moreover, the children gain a deeper understanding of the countries and peoples they are studying, and a sustained interest is stimulated that continues long after the report has been duly turned in and the appropriate letter of the alphabet entered in the teacher's grade book.

Perhaps most important of all, reports of this nature bring students to a consideration of alternative ways of life. The emphasis on the attitudes and behavior of a people provides meaningful insights for the youngster who is searching to find his own value system or philosophy of life. In a world in which it is becoming increasingly difficult to single out one right way to live and behave, an awareness of alternative values may well prove to be the most important thing we can give our students.

In order to illustrate the type of value-emphasis report we advocate, we here present the material which served as the basis for a successful seventh-grade unit on South America. The following paragraphs were mimeographed and distributed to each student:

We are starting an important unit on South America. You will be asked to work on an individual as well as a group project. During the course of this unit, I hope to bring you into contact with the people of South America. You will be dealing with those people who are living, working, and struggling today as well as with those who lived and worked and struggled in the past.

You will be getting information from books, pamphlets, and articles which will enable you to answer the questions raised below. This should prove an interesting and rewarding experience if you will make it so.

For your individual report you will choose one of the following great men who fought to free South America from foreign rule: Jose De San Martin, Bernardo O'Higgins, Antonio Jose De Sucre, Francisco De Miranda, Simon Bolivar.

Your individual reports will consider the following: What was there in the life of the man you have chosen that interested you? Are there any things in your own life which are similar to his? For what things did you admire him most? Have you known any other adults who have these qualities? What exactly did he achieve? Were his goals or aims at all like any you have dreamed up for yourself? What difficulties did he have to undergo to achieve his goals? In what ways was he weak? How did this hurt him? How would he have made out in our world? Explain. Where did his life seem less fulfilled or satisfying? Do most great men have large areas of their life which are not fulfilled? Explain. What did his friends feel about him? How important were their feelings to him? In what ways were his friends' feelings influential upon him? Where did he display his greatest courage? Where did he display his greatest wisdom? Where did he make his greatest contribution? Who benefited from this contribution? Are there any ways he lived which would be good for people to follow today?

For your group report, you must choose one of the following countries that Bolivar helped to make free: Colombia, Venezuela, Peru, Bolivia, Equador.

You will deal with the following questions as part of your group report: What does the farmer want in the country you have chosen? What stands in his way of getting it? How does he go about getting what he wants? What help does he have? What hopes do his children have? What do they know of their own country? Of ours? What do they think and know about politics or their government? What is their day like? Where do they sleep? How many in a bed? What do they fear? When do they marry? What do they do for recreation? What part does religion play in their lives? What is their idea of a good life? How does it compare with yours? (Discuss this last question with your group and come up with some ideas.)

Answer these same questions for an industrial worker and a wealthy landowner. Are your answers the same for all of these people? If not, why not? Are any answers you have the same or similar to those of another group? Which ones? (Find this out by reading and discussing work of other groups.) If your answers are similar, why do you think this is so?

Consider the impact of these questions on a group of seventh-graders. Think of your own class and imagine how they would respond to an exploration of such problems as these. We can assure you that some students will find it too unorthodox a way for them to proceed. You must be ready to help them to learn to work with this new approach. We believe you will find the rewards worth the effort.

For one thing, you will begin to see that your students can not deal with these questions in any satisfactory manner merely by copying facts from an encyclopedia. Instead they will be drawn to a wide range of source materials:

magazines, newspaper articles, materials from the various countries, as well as books which treat certain of the men or the countries in depth. The word "research" will take on real meaning and point the way to the preparation of the kind of papers which will be most apt to bring the greatest satisfaction to the authors when and if they go on to higher education.

You will find, too, that reports with an emphasis upon values force the students to analyze and interpret what they read. No longer can John merely mouth his Brazilian insights. He must now actually *have* the insight. Because the information sought after is complex and multifaceted, the students will not as readily be able to find the single right answer stated in black and white. They *must* employ their powers of reasoning and judgment to make the best use of the material they have read. We consider this an excellent way in which to open up the curriculum to a true sense of inquiry.

At this point in our discussion, many of you may be saying to yourselves, "It's all very well to handle a report in this way, but I *am* responsible for covering the rivers, mountains, etc. of Latin America, and my class must learn these facts. I can't put all of that information on ditto sheets. How will I have time to teach what my school expects me to teach?

Fundamentally, the solution to such problems as the need to cover certain material and the desire to teach specific skills in a limited amount of time leads to the all-important question of what we are trying to bring about by our teaching. Just what is important enough to spend time on in the classroom? This is a decision each teacher must make every day of the school year. If you feel it is more important for your students to know the geography and natural resources of a country, this will be reflected in your teaching. Or if you feel it more important for your students to know a country in terms of the suffering and hopes of its people, this, too, will be reflected in the type of work going on in your classroom. We strongly urge, however, that you at least choose your position from among several alternatives and that the choice you make be based upon what you firmly believe is most essential for your students. Mere expediency is not adequate grounds for such an imperative decision.

The amazing thing about the alternative we pose; namely, the possibility of building a values emphasis into your work, is that the mandatory subject matter may still be covered, perhaps with even more satisfactory results than that obtained by standard approaches. Because of the wide reading that must be done, and due in part to the heavy involvement of the student in the content, we have found that often the necessary facts "hit" the student from a variety of sources, thus making the subject matter stick in a way which seems to last longer than the learning produced by mere rote memorization. Moreover, we believe that in the preparation of reports which emphasize values, students will better understand certain facts such as natural resources and geographical characteristics and appreciate their interrelationship with the problem of people.

Furthermore, our experience has shown that such reports contribute significantly to our teaching of important research and writing skills. Our students grow in their ability to interpret and to grasp the implications of information. Stereotyped images of—and again we use Latin America as an example—sandy beaches, warm climates, and siesta-seeking gauchos in colorful costumes disappear and are replaced by a real understanding of what such often casually dropped terms as poverty, illiteracy, hunger, passivity, and hate mean to those confronted by them every day of their lives. Thus a values emphasis takes on added significance if we feel that the kind of adults we need in this baffling and sometimes frightening world are people who have compassion for others and a true desire to devote their lives to making democracy a living creed.

Chapter 9

STRATEGIES AND TACTICS
CONCERNING READING
AND STUDYING

STRATEGIES and tactics that center upon reading and studying hold a dominant position in American secondary schools. Therefore, reading deserves to be taught in the secondary schools much more effectively than it has been. Large numbers of high school pupils read so poorly that they need corrective work. In addition, most high school pupils, and for that matter adults too, do not read efficiently. Relatively few know how to vary their reading approach for different subject matter, for instance. Because of the evident need, secondary schools are now establishing developmental and remedial reading programs. To be good, these programs must be total school programs. In such programs the English teachers must accept the responsibility for teaching a large share of the basic reading skills, but they cannot carry on the special work needed for remedial cases or for reading in the content fields. These tasks must be done by the reading teachers and subject-matter specialists.

Probably all reading assignments should be individualized. Pupils have such wide differences in interests and reading ability that it seldom seems necessary for all of them to read the same text. (A possible exception may be classes of very slow readers.) Teachers inexperienced with individualized reading techniques sometimes are frightened and bewildered at the prospect of having individual pupils read different works at different levels. Teachers should not be frightened, for the techniques are really not very difficult.

Neither are the other skills needed to teach reading in a regular class very difficult. Most of the techniques recommended by the experts make very good common sense. Particular care needs to be given to comprehension skills, vocabulary study, and to showing pupils how to attack the subject matter they must read. In this connection the subject-matter textbook may well be the best reading textbook.

Closely allied to reading are study skills. One important study skill, for instance, is the ability to vary one's reading techniques according to the material being read. In spite of the recent fad of speed reading, it is more important for pupils to learn how to adapt their reading speed to the reading situation than to read fast. Sometimes one should skim, sometimes one should read, reread, and reread intensively. Another important skill is the ability to extract the important ideas from a bit of writing. Also important are the skills· of outlining and note-taking. These skills, and other skills necessary, should be taught by the subject-matter teachers as the need arises.

With the plethora of reading matter of all types and levels flooding every subject field, there seems to be no longer any excuse for teachers to complain of a dearth of material. Even the poorest classroom can be well supplied with reading materials if the teacher is alert and aggressive. In many cases the problem is that of selecting appropriate material from an overabundance rather than searching for sufficient material to read. Among the sources available in addition to the standard textbook materials are supplementary readers, paperbacks, magazines and periodicals, newspapers, monographs, government publications, advertising and library materials.

BETTER READ!

National Association of Secondary School Principals *

Boys and girls of all ability groups need continued instruction in reading during their high school years. Total-school developmental reading programs have been slow starting in the high schools. The National Association of Secondary School Principals is concerned because secondary schools have not done better in providing instruction in developmental reading. In order to encourage principals to initiate good developmental reading programs in their high schools, the Curriculum Service Center of the NASSP has issued this excellent summary of informed thinking concerning developmental reading in high schools.

Reading skills needed in high school and later years are, in their essence, the ones taught to all and learned by many elementary schoolers. However, the applications secondary school students are called upon to make of these essential skills are significantly more varied and involved than are childhood uses. True, the boy who hopes to get to the end of a ten-word sentence before

* From *Curriculum Report*, No. 7 (Washington, D.C.: National Association of Secondary School Principals, The Curriculum Service Center, November 1965), pp. 1–9. Reprinted by permission of the NASSP.

he runs out of breath is father to the man who one day will be analyzing research reports and skimming the *Congressional Record* in preparation for debating the wisdom of damming still another wild-water stream. But more is required to make a man of that boy than just the passing of time and contact with increasingly difficult subject matter.

No track coach believes a boy is ready for his mile-relay team just because he once learned to run fast enough to get to the head of the cafeteria line or to escape his mother when there were chores to be done. Acquiring mature skills in reading also necessitates knowledgeable coaching, supervised practice, and purposeful application. Specialists have been saying for years that reading is a complex and demanding act; that it is far from a simple skill that can be mastered, once and for all, somewhere in the elementary school. They have argued that *all* young people, not just those with serious reading deficiencies, ought to be given teaching assistance for the bettering of their reading competences. But while remedial reading services have been available in many schools for some time, it is only within the last half-dozen years or so that the need for comprehensive and systematic *developmental reading* programs at the high school level has been widely admitted by non-specialists.

Because of this low interest level there is no large body of either experience or "findings" to which a school can turn for advice in expanding its developmental reading activities. Nonetheless, some guides can be constructed from what is known. The reader is advised, however, that the generalizations that follow do not alone furnish a complete framework for a school's developmental reading program.

ANY SPEED LIMIT?

With all the talk going on these days about faster reading rates and about this or that procedure guaranteed to produce small miracles, it's little wonder that so many students have come to believe that "better reading rate" is the same thing as "better reading ability." Even though there is some question that rate deserves all the attention it is getting, most high school students under most circumstances do read more slowly than those circumstances either require or permit. For them, a drive for more speed does seem justified. This is a kind of adolescent acceleration everyone can applaud, but some of the facts suggest need for a brake pedal as well as an accelerator.

The fundamental generalization is this: *The accomplished reader does not have A RATE; he commands and uses a VARIETY OF RATES.* The common name for this variety is "flexible rate," which we may as well use, although to this writer the phrase does seem to play up the distance/time factor and to obscure the choice-of-procedure element in the generalization.

When the word "reading" is used to mean visual contact with most of the words on a page—close reading, that is—there is an upper speed limit set by physical conditions. Though for most people training can speed up their eye movements somewhat, muscle and nerve do take time to respond, with a minimum that no amount of training can break through. Similarly, eye or word span can be enlarged. Here, too, muscles and the facts of light set limits. A person can also learn how to be more efficient in the ways he actually combines eye movements and eye span for reading purposes, but infinite perfectibility is not possible here, either. Researchers say that *when the shortest possible times for the various physiological functions involved in close reading are summed, the upper limit for such reading is about 900 words per minute.* Furthermore, this upper limit is achievable only when the content is familiar or very easy so that the rate of reading and the rate of thinking can be about the same. This is rarely the case with school materials, so the best rate for the close reading of the compactly composed writing in textbooks or of other unfamiliar material will be less than the physiological limit.

Of course, close reading is not always called for; in fact, there are times when it is a positive handicap. Often, a reading need is best met by some form of rapid search. In contrast, getting the meaning from a technical report can require word-by-word study. And the fun and fantasy of science fiction may escape the reader entirely if he uses either of these extremes of method. To be efficient in his reading, *a student needs to become as skillful as possible in using different approaches in his reading, and he needs to have good judgment in selecting that approach or combination of approaches compatible with his purposes for reading.*

Ellen Thomas, reading consultant to the faculty of the Laboratory Schools, University of Chicago, comments on the applicability of five approaches to reading:

1. *Skimming.* The student should skim when searching through materials for a single piece of information, when seeking a general impression of the content, or when examining the selection to see if it contains what he wants. He should skim when previewing, preliminary to more careful reading.
2. *Very rapid reading.* This rate would probably be suitable when reading light, easy, fast-moving fiction for entertainment only.
3. *Rapid reading.* The student might read rapidly when the material is fairly easy and when his purpose is grasping only the more important ideas and facts. Much of the content of newspapers and magazines is intended for rapid reading, as is much recreational material.
4. *Average reading.* Average reading may be suitable for an article in *Natural History* assigned in science, for certain chapters read in social studies, and for novels in English, like *My Antonia* or *The Ox Bow Incident.*
5. *A slow and careful approach.* The student should adjust his speed downward when . . . he wants to retain details, to weigh the truth of what he is reading—with "thought time" required in addition to "reading time"—to linger over artistic wording or to compare his own experiences with a poet's sonnets.

Sometimes the accomplished reader moves through printed matter very fast in search of a date or some other reference, but to call this his rate is to tell only part of the truth. It is just as partial to define as his rate the speed with which he studies a play or reads a book review. But *all of these are his rates; his rate is flexible, and this is one reason why he is an accomplished reader.*

One purpose of a school's developmental reading program should be to help students become proficient in the use of each of various approaches to reading, such as the five described by Miss Thomas. It must be noted that many people, young and old, assume that neither skimming nor very close reading needs much teaching or learning. After all, can't everyone just run his eyes down a page or stop and go, one word at a time? The reply to this is that everyone probably can do these things, but that competent skimmers and close readers remain comparatively rare.

Further, *the program should help young people to become more self-reliant in selecting reading patterns suitable to the task at hand and to the difficulty of the material being read.* Most people do. exhibit variations in their ways of attacking reading matter, but too often these variations are random, unplanned, and academically unproductive. On the other hand, the reader who is skillful is skillful in part because he has learned how and when to make changes in his reading pattern as he proceeds through a paragraph or a chapter or a volume. The well-read man is much like the well-mannered one: each without prolonged thought or hesitation selects the act or gesture or procedure most likely to establish a cordial and productive relationship—with page or person, as the case may be.

NOT BY THE NUMBERS ALONE

Since reading rate is not a unitary personal characteristic, *scores from standardized reading tests are not the rich and dependable sources of information they are commonly thought to be.* These scores tend to be over-valued and seriously misunderstood by both test givers and test takers. Reasons for caution in using these tests ought to be clearly recognized. (The reference here is to reading rate, but the same limitations apply in the case of reading comprehension.)

An obvious reason is that a single number, a score, can carry only one or two bits of information about reading rate, and many bits are needed to give a rounded picture of a student's level of competence. Furthermore, a test score describes a youngster's performance only in terms of a comparison with the performance of other students. (What *is* meant by the observation that a student's reading rate is at the tenth grade level?) The score says almost nothing about the student's ability to carry on one or more of the processes involved in reading on the job.

A majority of the standardized reading tests used in schools were designed to obtain information on *group* performance. Many users credit them with more precision in the measurement of individual progress than their makers claim for them.

One more reason for caution. When a classroom teacher employs a standardized subject-matter test as an evaluation instrument, he has at his disposal many kinds of information about student progress. No one source need carry more than its own fair and reasonable share of the evaluation load. Moreover, from the interplay among the various sources, each gains somewhat in meaning and reliability. Unfortunately, much standardized testing in reading is not supported or supplemented by a flow of disciplined observations by teachers. This situation is improving as more teachers and schools become involved in reading activities, but mostly the score stands exposed like a frail boy expected to do a healthy man's work.

WHAT DOES IT MEAN?

Comprehension is really the only generally significant reason for reading, yet so-called comprehension scores from tests are as ambiguous as rate scores are, and for about the same reasons. But the difficulty goes beyond the shortcomings of a score: teachers have been slow to recognize that *like rate, comprehension is not a unitary quality*, at least not as it shows itself in ordinary life.

The scholarly community continues to debate the true nature of comprehension, but this need not prevent a teacher or a faculty from identifying the skills or other behaviors that common sense and professional judgment take as evidence that comprehension is taking place. It's possible that comprehension is some kind of general intellective factor, but for all practical purposes it can be considered a well-articulated assembly of entirely real parts. To the purist, a faculty's efforts to develop its own operational definition of comprehension by listing specific behaviors that can be observed, taught, learned, and measured may seem only sloppy scholarship. Perhaps so, but there is not much likelihood that developmental reading programs will have strength unless and until that venerable but vague word "comprehension" is replaced with a set of particulars.

Whatever the particulars put down, they will need to be made even more particular to fit the ability levels of actual students. They will need also to be adapted to the special characteristics of different instructional fields. A few examples, however, will indicate the nature of the first-level particulars. The good reader—that is, the comprehending reader—can for instance:

Follow a set of directions
Differentiate between fact and opinion
Draw inferences or get ideas that are implied rather than explicitly stated
Spot major points or the dominant theme
Distinguish between a generalization and the supporting details
Relate reading content to his own personal experience

Getting-the-facts is also an important comprehension skill and is not to be neglected. A great deal of teaching, however, appears to assume that it is *the* comprehension skill rather than only one member of a numerous company, each of which deserves a fair share of attention.

One final comment about reading comprehension. It is widely believed that reading rate and quality of comprehension go hand in hand. From this it is deduced that one way to understand better what is being read is to read it faster. For some classes of readers this can be true; for instance, the overly deliberate reader or the one whose reading habits generally are ill formed. It may also hold for the mythical average reader when he is dealing with comparatively easy material. But as a subject matter becomes more difficult or style and vocabulary more technical the positive relationship between speed and understanding deteriorates. It is possible, in fact, to push rate to the point where its correlation with comprehension is negative.

ALL TOGETHER, NOW

A staff member with a specialist's training in reading can be useful in assisting a faculty in designing and operating a developmental reading program, but such a specialist is by no means a minimum essential. *If such a program is to have anything like all-school coverage, there must be commitment to it and participation in it by all of the teaching staff.* That old wistful supervisory maxim—"Every teacher a reading teacher"—must be a reality. (Actually, as the discussion will show, in these days few teachers can avoid being some kind of reading teacher, no matter how much they demur or disclaim.) No reading specialist, nor even a band of specialists, can alone provide the kind of learning activities necessary for effective reading growth.

When, in times past, a teacher and his students had little more than a single textbook to read from, what that classroom teacher did about the reading practices of his students may have been of little consequence. Now, in contrast, the quality, quantity, and variety of reading materials being used in practically every subject field has expanded to the point where classroom-based reading is a major influence on the reading development of boys and girls. In present-day classrooms the teacher is a reading teacher if his teaching is at all contemporary in content and method.

In all the fuss and excitement stirred up by curriculum-making projects the increased demands new curriculum patterns and content make on students' reading competence get passed over with very little notice. Perhaps it is supposed that that competence exists in ample supply, for *unless students' reading skills are at a relatively high level substantial portions of the new curricula will have only limited effectiveness.* If for no other reason than this, reading must be a matter of all-faculty concern.

Illustrations of the relationship come easily to mind. Independent study in any significant sense is possible only if the student is a proficient reader. The use of original documents in American history or of scholarly writings in an anthropology course won't be worth the bother unless students can read and comprehend them. New mathematics texts are meant to be read and learned from; no longer are they merely hard-backed sets of exercises. Even programmed courses won't run through the machine properly unless the learner is also a reader.

There is a parallel generalization of squal importance: Modern methods and materials offer students excellent opportunities for the improvement of all of their reading skills. To recollect the nature of what goes on in, say, a new geography course or a revised freshman English course is to sense the many ways students can be helped to raise their reading competence in the entirely normal process of mastering other subject matter.

It is argued that students must improve their reading powers because they have so much reading to do. Again, the converse is true: *Students must read extensively if they are going to improve their reading skills.* Bulk is a necessity! Neither a reading teacher nor a librarian can provide a majority of students with the quantity of reading experiences they need if they are to become better readers. For most youngsters in most schools, the primary source of their reading bulk will be that which is required, recommended, and motivated by classroom teachers. Happily, modern programs provide many possibilities for supplying this bulk in beneficial amount and of suitable kind.

A reading rate of any level is real only if it can be maintained for a much longer time than just during brief practice periods or on tests. To establish a rate or to increase one requires reading at that rate for extended periods or trying for the better rate frequently and under different conditions until it becomes fixed. It follows that *extensive reading is even more necessary if students are to obtain command of a really flexible rate.* Flexing can take place within a paragraph or two, and it can be practiced on a special reading lesson. But this is not its natural habitat. Extensive reading is not the only requisite for domesticating this ability, but it is one of the requisites.

Everything that is known about the relationship of purpose or motivation to learning applies to the improvement of reading competence. It is difficult to identify any source other than his subject teachers which is likely to provide for the student the pervasive and varied stimulation which he needs if he is to increase his command of reading skills.

Two 40-minute periods a week for a school year with a reading teacher or five days a week in a special section of 8th grade English cannot meet the need for extensive and relevant reading, though such experiences can help and they do have other contributions to make to reading growth. *Purposeful, quantity-in-reading experiences will be supplied principally by the courses in which a student is enrolled and by the other reading these courses motivate him to do.*

MUTUAL SUPPORT

"But," a teacher says, "there isn't enough time for teaching as it is. Trying to teach reading is going to cut into that time even further." Could be, and it's very likely to do so initially when a teacher is becoming attentive to the reading needs of his students and aware of the potentialities of his instructional field for meeting these needs. *For the long haul, however, the teacher who aids his students to become better readers is also helping them to be-*

come better learners in his subject field. Consequently, time is going to be saved rather than lost, and both teaching and learning are going to benefit.

Two years ago, with the help of their reading consultant, the tenth grade teachers in the University of Chicago's Laboratory Schools made a year-long study of ways by which they could help their students to be better readers while still carrying on the regular business of their courses. They have reported their experiences in a manuscript to be published in the near future, but in the meantime, Miss Thomas, the consultant, has given *Curriculum Report* permission to pass on to its readers a few of the ideas in the manuscript. (The Laboratory schools are somewhat favored in resources and staffing, but there appears to be nothing this group of teachers did that teachers elsewhere could not also do, at least to some extent.)

For one thing, with the assistance of librarians, teachers searched out reading materials related to both course content and reading levels of students. Not an easy or quick job, to be sure, but a manageable one. As would be anticipated, this was beneficial in many ways, but it had *special value for relatively poor readers who began to enjoy some success with their reading and with this success in the course generally.*

From time to time during the year, many of the teachers gave student groups what amounted to guided tours through the reading required for a particular assignment so that they could really see what was involved and what choices in procedure actually were available. Doing this kind of thing in the artificial environment of a How-to-Study course or occasionally in an English course simply does not provide the variety of learning opportunities available in different courses, nor can it meet the varying needs that are generated as pupils encounter different disciplines and as they mature as learners.

The project also demonstrated once more that there is *nothing quite like a well-formulated and sensible assignment to establish purposes for reading and to improve the comprehension of what's read.* ("Read the next twenty pages" doesn't quite turn the trick.) This attention to the nature of assignments resulted in improved comprehension since both teachers and students became more aware of the specific uses to be made of what was read, more aware of the particulars of "comprehension." It seemed apparent, too, in several instances that assignments generally were better adapted to variations in student capacity as a result of the teacher's starting out merely to find reading material that was so adapted.

All the teachers, and not just the English teachers, found they had more opportunities than they had realized to promote wide reading for enjoyment by their students, thereby adding somewhat to students' knowledge as well as contributing to an enlarged interest in general reading.

When vocabulary is limited, reading rate and comprehension are seriously restricted. As a minimum, a teacher is responsible for helping his students master the technical vocabulary of his field. This involves more than making some kind of list of new words as they appear in the text or sending the student to the dictionary. Some common words will have special subject related meanings. Others will have special uses. Root study related to subject matter is worthwhile. The foreteaching of a word or a few words can make a monumental difference in what a student can or cannot do with a reading assignment—it takes only one tripped-over curb to break an ankle! Every teacher can through the subject matter of his course give youngsters at least a few hints on effective vocabulary-building techniques.

Just as there is continuity in reading skills from childhood to maturity so is there commonality among the reading requirements of the various secondary school academic fields. In the latter case as in the former, there are enough differences in emphasis to warrant attention. That is to say, a teacher should try to be sensitive to the special reading demands his field tends to make on students. For example, the vocabulary load in a Modern Problems course is quite different from that in Introduction to Probability. Probing a play to discover the leading character's motives requires abilities not much needed in tackling an article in the *Scientific American* as a supplementary reference in Advanced Biology. Even the student reader who by usual signs appears to be a competent reader will benefit from advice from a subject specialist on how most effectively to work with written material characteristic of that field.

Concludes Miss Thomas,

Many of the ways of encouraging progress in reading . . . are everyday practices of good teachers—not always recognized as methods of increasing competence in reading. Helping students read and study in a subject is not adding the teaching of reading to the teaching of the subject. It is the essence of good teaching in the subject.

BUT ARE THEY MAKING PROGRESS?

It's time now to return to the question of how to estimate the progress a student is making in increasing his reading powers, especially recalling the limitations standardized tests are likely to have for this purpose. *Here, again, the classroom teacher appears as a crucial figure.* More and more, the use of informal assessment devices is recommended. Notable among these are so-called informal reading inventories. (As used here, "informal" does not mean a casual, come-as-you-are process. Inventories—other instruments, too—must be carefully constructed and used. They will be informal mainly because they do not have the rigid monorail aspect of the usual test.)

Inventories thus far have been used more frequently in elementary than in high schools, probably just because elementary school teachers have been more interested in reading than have their high school colleagues. It's probable, too, that inventories are more difficult to devise for secondary schoolers than for younger students. It is true that a teacher of mathematics or history rarely will have either the time or the know-how to put together an instrument with enough structure to permit calling it an inventory. *He can, however, use a number of simple yet valid techniques for finding out what his students can do and what they do do when they read.*

For instance, *an open-book test* based on the textbook and requiring different reading/comprehension activities will give insight into students' ability to use the text for different purposes. (In spite of innovations, the textbook remains a basic learning tool, and one that has to be read to be useful.) A *series of precis* based on magazine articles or other short selections, roughly graded in difficulty, will give information on the points at which students begin to lose power to cope with vocabulary or concepts. *Direct observation of students at work* on an assignment which requires spotting a writer's principal thesis and his main evidence in several different instances can tell a great deal about youngsters' ability to skim and use other screening devices. Happily, informal assessment practices like these not only provide evidence of students' competence in reading but also are legitimate subject-matter-learning activities.

ANY OTHER QUESTIONS?

A few earthy questions are certain to come up in any faculty discussion of this every-teacher approach to developmental reading.

Why not have the English Department do whatever teaching of reading needs to be done? They know more about language than any other teachers. English teachers will, of course, have special contributions to make to a developmental reading program, and often they can provide needed local leadership. But they can't do everything that ought to be done. Mature reading requirements are so diverse and students' developmental needs exist in so many forms that no one department, not even the English Department, can provide all the learning opportunities and content required for full development of reading competence.

But most teachers don't know anything about teaching reading. Won't it just be a mess? It isn't entirely true that most teachers know nothing about reading. As has been said, practically all teachers, whether they realize it or not, do some teaching of reading. Not always very well, but teach they do. To the extent that the focus is on developmental rather than remedial needs of boys and girls, it will not be difficult for teachers to gain the understandings they need through in-service or independent study, particularly in view of the close relationship that has been noted between good teaching and teaching reading.

Does every teacher have to be a teacher of reading? The common-sense answer to this seems to be, "No, not really, but give it a try." If most teachers pitch in there is bound to be enough transfer of training so a few faculty exceptions will not mean the collapse of the program.

Where's the leadership to come from? What about the technical knowledge and experience the general run of teachers will want to be able to fall back on? If there is a trained reading specialist in the local school family somewhere, the answer may be apparent, although other demands on this specialist may mean little time remains to give leadership to all-teacher plans. But lacking any kind of special staffing a department or an entire faculty can still move ahead by relying on the leadership normal to curriculum-making activities in the school. A willing worker does not become a good teacher of reading skills just by being willing. But all the evidence indicates that teachers who wish to can learn to be helpful to their students in improving their reading skills, and that seemingly small but consistent contributions from many teachers produce, in total, surprisingly substantial effects.

Notwithstanding this, *experience is demonstrating the value that a reading consultant can have for a school.* An excellent analysis of the work of such a consultant is contained in the Robinson and Rauch* entry in the bibliography. Quoting from their introduction, "A reading consultant is defined as a person largely freed of classroom teaching and other school responsibilities in order that he may concentrate on assisting the staff in the coordination and facilitation of efforts to improve the reading program."

Do we have to have another program? Can't we accept what you say, that good teachers do teach reading and let it go at that? Every indication is that "letting it go at that" at the secondary school level is not good enough; some form of "program" is called for. But so far as developmental reading is concerned, a high school's "program" need not have—probably ought not to have —the evident regularity and high visibility characteristic in the elementary school years. Some "regularities" may be called for; for example, special instruction for a group of youngsters with non-English language backgrounds, who by usual measures appear to be retarded but who in actuality are only at a different developmental point. Or a course might be useful to youngsters entering a high school from elementary schools in which they had little chance to learn how to make effective use of varied reading resources.

Coordinated and purposeful faculty efforts? Yes. Elaborate and expensive professional machinery? It can wait.

READING IN SCIENCE
AND MATHEMATICS

Henry A. Bamman *

Teachers of science and mathematics seldom think of themselves as teachers of reading. Yet, reading science and mathematics presents many

* H. Allan Robinson and Sidney J. Rauch, eds., *Guiding the Reading Program* (Chicago: Science Research Associates, Inc., 1965).

* From *Perspectives in Reading* (Newark, Del.: National Reading Association, 1964), pp. 63–71. Reprinted with permission of Henry A. Bamman and the International Reading Association.

youngsters with difficulties that only science and mathematics teachers can help them solve. Teachers can save themselves considerable disappointment, and much need for reteaching, if they include the teaching of reading science and mathematics material in their courses. The techniques suggested in this article for science and mathematics teachers can be used, or adapted, equally well by teachers of history, business education, or home economics.

TEACHING READING IN THE CLASSROOM

Within this section, consideration will be given to techniques of teaching reading in the science and mathematics class. Only four aspects of reading will be considered: vocabulary, comprehension, critical reading, and rate of reading. It is assumed that any teacher, regardless of his lack of formal training in the teaching of reading, can aid students in developing increased competence in basic skills.

Vocabulary. The vocabulary of mathematics and science is often more specific, more descriptive, than vocabulary found in other content areas. Traditionally, students have been admonished to learn definitions of the words in a selection or chapter; however, the greatest difficulty in learning such specific terminology seems to lie in the inability of many students to apply a term to an exact process, a classification, or a broad concept. Many words need special attention, since they take on new meanings when they are used in science or mathematics. For instance, *product, rate, base, root, interest,* and *literal* are mathematics terms which have different connotations in other areas. Too often writers of textbooks introduce technical vocabulary under the assumption that the simpler phases of the subject have already been mastered by students. Teachers may make these same assumptions. The responsibility for introducing technical terms and relating them to processes or classifications is definitely a major task for the classroom teacher.

All scientific classifications are based on structural similarity. For example, *lepidoptera, hymenoptera, hemiptera,* and *homoptera* are terms used to describe orders of insects. Each term is descriptive of the wing (*pteron*) structure of the particular order: *lepido* (scale), *hymen* (membrane), *hemi* (half), and *homo* (same texture throughout). The student of biology, lacking the experience of examining the components of words, tends to attempt to memorize terms and examples of each. He may know that *Orthoptera* is a term which refers to the grasshopper, without realizing that *all straight-winged* insects are classified in the order *Orthoptera.* The biology teacher could help this student by taking time to explain the structural elements of biological terminology.

Considerable aid has been given to the teachers by authors of recent textbooks in both science and mathematics. It has become common practice to list new terms at the beginning or at the end of chapters or units. However, these lists of words are of little benefit to the student if they are merely assigned as word-memorization exercises. They must be related to classifications, processes, or concepts. They can be illustrated, demonstrated, and further related to similar words.

The use of prefixes, suffixes, and root forms may be one of the richest sources of word knowledge in these content areas. For instance, the Greek *mono* in biology is found in *monocotyledon;* in chemistry, we find *monomer;* physics gives us *monochromatic;* and in mathematics we use the word *monomial.* The Latin equivalent, *uni,* may be *univalve* in biology; chemistry, *univalent;* physics, *units;* and in mathematics, *union.* Hence, knowledge of a single root, prefix, or suffix may lead to understanding of the meanings of hundreds of words.

There are other approaches to teaching vocabulary. Synonyms are always useful, but there is a danger of the synonym giving no more meaning than the original word. Dictionaries and glossaries list synonyms frequently; care should be taken by the teacher to determine that the appropriate synonym is selected to fit the particular context. Most scientific and mathematical terms are monosemantic; consequently, using antonyms, or opposite meanings of words, is frequently impossible. It can be demonstrated, however, that an antonym may, by telling what a word is *not,* give more meaning to a new term than a synonym which may be as obscure as the word itself. As a simple example, *cold* is clearly the opposite of *hot* and is readily understood; synonyms for *hot* are *heated, scorching, scalding, fervid, peppery.* Consider the confusion that would result from substituting one of these synonyms in this sentence: The night was *hot.*

The major difficulty in developing vocabulary for mathematics and science in the secondary school class is that so many terms must be mastered and applied at once. An introductory chapter in a recent mathematics textbook lists as new vocabulary these terms: *closure, commutative property, associative property, distributive property, multiplicative identity, multiplicative inverses, additive identity,* and *additive inverses.* Each of these terms is listed at the beginning of the chapter and the student is cautioned to know the words. They are also listed in the glossary of the textbook. However, few students will understand these terms unless they are demonstrated, discussed at length in various contexts, and *repeated frequently* in problem solving situations.

Words are the tools of all knowledge. They must be taught as deliberately and as reservedly as they were written. If an effort were to be made by all teachers of mathematics and science to improve the teaching of vocabulary, reading skills of their students would be greatly enhanced.

Comprehension Skills. Many students who read well in literature or social sciences fail to read well in science and mathematics. They apparently lack the ability to adjust their reading to the phrase and sentence patterns that they encounter in these areas. Paragraphs are written in a terse language; they are reduced to the minimum number of words necessary for communicating ideas. To read well, to interpret literally and critically the writing of scientists and mathematicians, the student must develop habits of careful observation of details, learn to think reflectively about ideas and their relationships, and improve his skills of problem-solving.

An integral part of reading for science and mathematics is the interpretation of problems, preceded by precise, methodical reading. The student must learn that every word may be crucial to complete understanding of the problem or process. Recognizing all words, applying their specific meanings to the problems at hand, and sensing relationships among several conditions which are presented by the problem are prerequisites to actual problem-solving.

Careful questioning by the teacher may determine which students are grasping main ideas and essential details, which students are merely interpreting ideas literally and failing to think critically. Some students are incapable of seeing relationships among main ideas and need careful guidance in determining main ideas and their supporting details. Students benefit from occasional opportunities to restate main ideas in their own words and to state essential sequences of ideas. Listening and speaking become an integral part of good reading when the teacher involves the student in stating clearly and succinctly the ideas that have been encountered. Further, questions from students are important. Too often the teacher asks all of the questions and fails to recognize that many students in a class are not participating in discussions; since their questions are seldom entertained, these students feel a sense of futility that the content is beyond their grasp.

Fehr (1) has suggested six steps for improving comprehension in mathematics. The writer has adapted these steps to include both mathematics and science.

1. *Help the student adopt a problem consciousness.* A problem is not a problem simply because a teacher or a textbook suggests that it is. There must be a purpose for solving the problem, and this may be achieved by several readings and analyses. Further explorations of similar problems may be necessary. A knowledge of the contributions of scientists and mathematicians past and present may help the student develop positive attitudes towards materials and forces in the universe that will help him to live more successfully in our complex world.

2. *Develop wide experience and broad background in mathematics and science situations.* Too often at the beginning of a course we assume a level of understanding or proficiency in our students, based on normal expectancies of the curriculum of previous grades or courses. Textbooks are limited; too frequently our secondary courses are broad surveys of mathematics, physical and life sciences. For the more able students, provisions should be made for wide reading to build background for understanding the laws, principles, or processes. The young and inexperienced scientist or mathematician lacks the ability to sense and feel relationships. Here is where the teacher functions best, in pointing out essential relationships through references to previous learning and through multiple illustrations.

3. *Activate the problem.* Aid the student in the statement of the problem

in his own language. Be alert to distorted or inaccurate sequences of ideas. Use diagrams, concrete objects, blackboard illustrations to focus attention on the problem and to illustrate the practical applications of the problem to other situations.

4. *Help students ask meaningful questions.* When students have no questions, they have not read carefully. Guide them, through your own questions, to read the selection or problem again. In problem-solving there are always these questions: What are the conditions or details? What, exactly, are you asked to find? to do? What is the order in which the conditions of the problem should be used? What processes are required? What is a reasonable answer?

5. *Become sensitive to the student who is using an unsuccessful attack on the problem.* Encourage rereading, careful and critical thinking. Help the student correct his procedures.

6. *Generalize the solution to every problem* so that it may have wide application in solving new problems.

There are two particularly fine references that every teacher of mathematics and science should read for detailed suggestions for improving their teaching of reading. "Directives for Developing Reading Skills" in *The Improvement of Reading* by McCullough, Strang and Traxler (6) suggests numerous techniques for reading for the main idea, reading for details, and reading for sequence or outline. The Metropolitan School Study Council has recently revised *Five Steps to Reading Success in Science, Social Studies, and Mathematics* (2). They suggest that to read science and mathematics materials successfully, students must master certain reading skills: locating pertinent details, distinguishing between main ideas and supporting details, visualizing, following directions, and drawing inferences. Five steps of readiness, concept development, silent reading, oral or written discussion, and oral or silent rereading are outlined in detail and illustrated for the teacher.

In both areas of mathematics and science we have moved away from the format of model solutions of problems, followed by a series of similar problems or experiments to be completed by the student. Today, fewer examples are given and the student is required to supply reasons for steps, later the steps, and finally the entire proofs. This change in emphasis has handicapped the poor reader; under the traditional system of models, the poor reader could frequently work a series of similar problems in physics, chemistry, or mathematics with a minimum of reading and memorization of the model.

Nordberg, Bradfield and Odell (7) recommended open-end experiments as one means of meeting individual differences of experience and abilities. In contrast to verifying conclusions known beforehand, the student must determine the methods to employ, the apparatus to use, and the conclusions to reach. Open-endedness of the experiment is varied according to the abilities and experiences of the students. Frequently, the student who cannot read the experiment can participate successfully in the discussions of methods, apparatus, and conclusions and can complete the experiment independently.

Critical Reading. It has been stated earlier that many students are capable of literal interpretation of what they read in science in mathematics, using only the information which is explicitly stated. A question such as "What is radioactivity?" can be answered on the basis of explicitly stated facts; however, to answer the question "What uses can we make of atomic energy?" the student must go beyond the printed page and think critically, using the specific knowledge that he has about atomic energy and inferring or predicting logical future uses. He may consider the present use of isotopes in medicine and predict probable developments. He may consider the possibility of conversion of sea water into fresh water.

There are innumerable definitions of critical reading and critical thinking. What, from our knowledge of critical reading, is practical for the teacher who wishes to aid his students in developing better understanding of the concepts of science and mathematics? Maney's (5) definition of comprehension and critical reading skills, derived from her study of literal and critical reading in science, has definite implications for both science and mathematics.

1. Developing functional vocabulary, or the vocabulary which is necessary for the understanding of the subject.
2. Developing understanding of the semantic variations of vocabulary, or the use of words in other contexts.
3. Locating the central theme; separating the central topic from the subordinate topics.
4. Making inferences; drawing conclusions from facts explicitly stated.
5. Making generalizations; identifying a general conclusion or principle from information implicitly stated.
6. Solving problems; applying information to problem situations.
7. Associating ideas; relating ideas in a series.
8. Recognizing analogies; seeing relationships between two pairs of ideas.
9. Understanding antecedents.
10. Establishing and remembering sequences.
11. Recognizing extraneous ideas.
12. Following directions.
13. Visualizing; interpreting graphic representations of an idea presented verbally.

Rate of Reading. Many of our students in secondary schools have been made aware of the necessity for reading rapidly. Numerous articles in newspapers and magazines, demonstrations on television channels, and purveyors of books and programmed materials have made the student conscious of the need for accelerating his reading as he has accelerated his other activities. The amount of reading to be done in a day's assignment is increasing with each generation; the availability of a wide variety of supplementary materials for each content area has emphasized the need for selecting wisely, skimming, and reading intensively.

The student who reads science and mathematics must be prepared to make adjustments to the basic materials, both in terms of his speed of reading and his purpose for reading the material. Reading in these content areas is most frequently slow, deliberate reading. By its very nature, problem-solving is more deliberate than reading for pleasure. Skimming is seldom applicable as a skill, except to familiarize the student with new materials or to search for related ideas. Directions must be read and reread, with attention directed toward the exact use of words, the sequence of ideas, and the questions that are raised. Fortunately, many of the concepts of science and mathematics are both observable and demonstrable; many of the ideas are precise and if careful reading has been done, they may be related to known laws and principles.

The teacher of science and mathematics may occasionally advise the reader to slow down and to read deliberately and critically. If essential words, phrases, or symbols are missed in cursory reading, then rereading is necessary.

USING DIVERSIFIED MATERIALS AND ACTIVITIES

All classroom teachers are certainly aware that our textbooks are not appropriate for all of the students in a class. Problems in real life are frequently not structured like those in the text, and the necessary data for an experiment or a problem are not always obvious to the poor reader. Many textbooks present too many topics in such concentrated space that the reader cannot clearly understand the essential relationships. Frequently, summary statements at the beginning or end of chapters presuppose experiences and knowledge that students do not possess. The problem of the textbook is compounded at higher levels of education, particularly in junior and senior high schools, where the use of a *single* text is prevalent in science and mathematics classes, and where the range of reading abilities of the students may be from a third reader level to the level of a mature adult.

The unit or project plan of teaching makes possible the diversity of materials, both in terms of interests and reading abilities of the students. A textbook is less essential when a broad unit is developed and students are assigned topics in materials which are commensurate with their reading and thinking abilities. However, in mathematics we are constantly confronted by a single textbook and virtually no supplementary reading materials for the poor reader. As a result, the teacher must diversify the activities in terms of the abilities of the students. Oral reading of problems, discussions and demonstrations of problems, and numerous teaching aids are necessary to involve all students in solving the problem. Recent developments in materials for the teaching of science and mathematics have included the use of multi-sensory approaches to reading and learning: films, filmstrips, models, and a wide variety of concrete objects.

In the selection of supplementary materials for the science or mathematics program, the librarian is invaluable. Lists such as Mallinson's (4) are readily available in most libraries and offer guidance in the selection materials for slow learners and retarded readers. We should be concerned, when we select materials, that they are of a length substantial enough to constitute a valid reading situation. They should demand the same competencies of the student as are demanded in reading textbooks. The quantity of materials is not nearly so important as the quality and the usefulness.

SUMMARY

An increased emphasis upon the substance of courses in mathematics and science has not in any sense alleviated the problem of poor readers in those content areas. Mathematics and science teachers, who know the substance of their courses, are in the best position to aid their students in developing better reading and study skills for their particular courses. While their general reading skills are frequently well developed, students may lack the experiences for adapting their reading skills to science and mathematics. Teachers and students in science and mathematics courses are involved in two vital processes: the development of *knowledge* of specific content, and the development of *skills* for life-long acquisition of knowledge.

REFERENCES

1. FEHR, HOWARD F., "Teaching High School Mathematics." *What Research Says to the Teacher.* Pamphlet No. 9. Washington, D.C.: Department of Classroom Teachers, AERA of the NEA, 1955, 24–25.
2. *Five Steps to Reading Success in Science, Social Studies, and Mathematics,* Revised. Metropolitan School Study Council. New York: Teachers College, Columbia University, 1960.
3. HENDERSON, KENNETH B., "Research on Teaching Secondary School Mathematics." *Handbook of Research on Teaching.* Chicago: Rand McNally and Company, 1963, 1026–1027.
4. MALLINSON, GEORGE G., "Reading Materials for Slow Learners and Retarded Readers." *Materials for Reading,* edited by Helen G. Robinson. Chicago: University of Chicago Press, 1957, 151–154.
5. MANEY, ETHEL, "Literal and Critical Reading in Science." *Journal of Experimental Education,* XXVII (September, 1958), 57–64.
6. McCULLOUGH, CONSTANCE M., Ruth Strang and Arthur E. Traxler, *The Improvement of Reading,* Third Edition. New York: McGraw Hill Book Company, 1961, 174–175.
7. NORDBERG, H. ORVILLE, JAMES M. BRADFIELD and WILLIAM C. ODELL, *Secondary School Teaching.* New York: Macmillan Company, 1962, 291–313.
8. SMITH, NILA BANTON, *Be a Better Reader, Books I-VI.* Englewood Cliffs: Prentice-Hall, Inc., 1959.
9. WATSON, FLETCHER G., "Research on Teaching Science." *Handbook of Research on Teaching.* Chicago: Rand McNally and Company, 1963, 1034–1035.

EXTENSIVE-INTENSIVE READING
AND PAPERBACKS

Leonard H. Clark *

Individual differences in interest and ability make single-textbook teaching out of date. No single text can appeal to all pupils. It may be too hard or too easy, too childish or too mature, too elementary or too advanced for some of them. In heterogeneous classes it is quite possible to find one pupil who cannot read the book because the vocabulary and ideas are way over his head and another pupil who won't read it because he has read and understood all that years ago. Thus, by necessity, teachers are being forced to use several texts and individualized readings. Some teachers find the use of multiple readings and the individualizing of reading very difficult—some think it impossible. The techniques in the following selection should make strategies using multiple readings much less difficult than teachers fear. The techniques are useful for any kind of subject and can be adapted for all kinds of reading material with or without the help of paperback readings.

Fundamentally, there are only two basic reasons for reading anything. The first is for information; the second is for enjoyment. Which of the two is the more important does not really matter since if a selection is any good at all, we can both learn from it and enjoy it—if we read it well. Unfortunately that is where many of us fall down. We do not read things well. To do that we must read individually and analytically, intensively and extensively.

Once we thought that in order to learn to read analytically and intensively everyone in a class should read the same material at the same speed, chapter by chapter, line by line, all together. The basic reason for this was to insure that everyone had read the same material in the same way as a basis for classroom discussion. Obviously, if everyone in a class is supposed to discuss something, each person in the class should know at least a little about the matter to be discussed. To discuss intelligently a book you have not read is difficult, although lots of pupils have tried it, even as you and I.

But reading is an individual affair, even a solitary one. Groups cannot read; only individuals can read. When we speak of a group's reading together,

* From *Studies in the Mass Media*, Vol. 3 (Champaign, Ill.: NCTE, January 1963), pp. 16–18. Reprinted by permission of the National Council of Teachers of English.

what we really mean is that everyone in the group has been given the same assignment.

There seems to be no logical reason why students should always read the same assignment. Rather it seems more logical that class members should all be reading different things. No one book is equally suited to every member of the class. Pupils have different tastes, different goals, different backgrounds, different personalities, and different reading abilities. Instead of everyone's plodding along through the same book, would it not be better if each one read the things best suited to him?

Literary analysis is also an essentially individual venture. Group discussions about a work are worthwhile only if the discussants have read the book analytically before the discussion. Lectures carefully analyzing a literary work are of little value to the listener unless he too analyzes the work and assesses the lecture in the light of his own thinking. Although the lecturer can give his pupils much information and many leads, unless the pupil uses the information and leads in his own assessment, the lecturer might better have saved his breath.

So it seems that for literary analysis to be of real value one must do it oneself. This is really not so difficult to do as it seems. Reading analytically is merely reading in question marks. What the pupil must do is to ask himself and the author questions as he reads along—questions like: What is the author trying to do or say? How is he trying to say it? Is his technique effective? Does his plan seem logical? Is his style adequate and appropriate? Does he do the job skillfully? Is the job worth doing skillfully, or at all? Do his characters act like human beings? Why, or why not? Did the author have a point to make? Did he make it? And so on. The reader knows the type of questions to ask as well as the writer. Just what questions should be asked depends upon the reader and what he is reading. When the reader has discovered the answers to the right questions he has analyzed the work.

Evidently, then, pupils' reading should be both analytical and individual. But how can any teacher conduct thirty adolescents through simultaneous literary analysis of different literary works? The answer lies in the much maligned subject-centered unit approach. What the topic should be depends upon the teacher. Topics concerning literary types or even literary techniques would probably be more satisfactory than units built around themes although not necessarily so. In any case the unit must be centered around analysis.

In the beginning, the unit will probably have to be teacher centered. During this phase the teacher must present the techniques and purposes of literary analysis to the pupils. Once oriented the pupils can practice analysis with short texts if it seems desirable. At this point for several pupils or even the entire class to read and criticize the same text may be advisable. Another useful technique suitable to the early stage of development is for pupils individually, in small groups, or as a class, to develop lists of questions to use in guiding individual reading and analysis.

The heart of the unit is the individualized reading. After pupils become used to reading analytically they can start this aspect straightaway with a minimum of introduction. In order to learn to select reading matter suitable to them pupils should have many selections to choose from. However, in order to keep the teacher's task under control, pupils' choices must be somewhat limited, for teachers do not have time to read all the books in print. For optimum benefit the books should be readily available in a classroom library where each pupil can browse under supervision, sampling and rejecting until he makes his choices. Although the teacher should guide the browsing and final choices, only on rare occasions should the teacher force a particular book on a pupil.

Once he has selected his choice the pupil should read and analyze alone. To help him the teacher can provide a study guide. Sometimes the best guide sheets are made up by the pupils themselves. But no matter who makes them out the questions should not be too definite and specific. Seldom should they ask for factual information about content. Reading literature is not the same as textbook reading. In literature it is not so much the material as the handling of the material that matters. Therefore the study questions should be kept big.

At least some of the results of the reading done by the pupils independently should be shared with the group. Small group discussions, panels, and interviews are useful for this phase. However, the major report should be written analysis. This should not be a silly book report of the I-like-the-*Catcher-in-the-Rye*-because-it-was-very-interesting type. Instead it should be true criticism. For the capable student this should be a mind-stretching experience, but all pupils who can read can gain from it, if given a real chance to try.

This scheme of teaching is not new. What is new is the advent of the paperback book which can make the scheme more effective.

One purpose of the plan is to develop critical taste and the ability to select suitable reading material. Pupils cannot learn that unless they have something to choose from. Here the paperback can help. Every school and classroom should have a well-stocked library, but most of them do not. By buying paperbacks, the school library can acquire a great variety of books of all sorts to augment their more permanent collection. In the classroom, paperbacks can supplement or even replace the sets of literature anthologies and classics. Instead of sets of 30 or more copies of single classics or anthologies, each classroom can have several copies each of a multitude of paperback titles for the classroom library.

But the best thing about paperbacks is they are inexpensive enough so that pupils can buy them. Where for some reason or other the school does not provide a classroom library, the students can pool their resources and stock their own classroom library with paperbacks at no great expense. More important, pupils can build their own personal libraries and so become really intimate with their books.

When pupils own their own books, they can mark them up as they read them. Skill in marking up books is an important aid to analytical reading. The pupil should underline and label passages that seem especially significant and worthwhile. Things that strike him as good or bad, true or false, logical or not so, should be marked and commented upon. If he thinks the style is particularly suitable at this point, or that the argument limps here, let him jot it down in the margin. Of course, if he does not own the book himself, he can make similar notes to himself on cards or a notebook, but it is not quite the same. Learning to mark up books properly is so important that school districts in which pupils cannot buy their own paperback books would do well to give pupils inexpensive paperbacks to keep and mark up to their heart's content. The practice would not be so terribly expensive, and it should bring a handsome return on the investment.

Paperbacks make it possible to deal with whole books rather than with clippings. Although anthologies may be excellent for presenting snippets, the development of critical taste and analytical reading skill requires that one deal with complete works as much as possible. To ask pupils to base their interpretations from snippets is hardly fair.

The purpose of literary analysis is to increase the reader's appreciation and understanding. With the help of paperbacks and a half-century old technique perhaps teachers can foster these appreciations and attitudes more easily than ever before since the advent of mass education.

STUDY SKILLS

Walter E. Mulholland *

Not only do pupils need help in learning to read, they also need help in learning how to study. For some reason, many teachers assume that once pupils have learned the rudiments of reading, they should automatically know how to study. This assumption is false. Studying requires special skills. Pupils must be taught these skills, for they seldom pick up efficient, effective study habits on their own. This selection by Mulholland explains what some of the study skills are and suggests some ways of teaching them. Because the pupils need to learn how to study specific subject matter, every teacher should help pupils learn how to study for his classes. The assignment provides an excellent opportunity for teachers to teach pupils how to study that particular type of content. Notice

* From *The Bulletin of the National Association of Secondary-School Principals*, Vol. 45 (September 1961), pp. 119–124. Reprinted by permission of the NASSP and the author.

how the suggestions for studying in this and the following selection fit into the NASSP selection "Better Read!" Unless our teaching strategies provide for the development of reading skills, pupils will never learn to study as well as they should.

Most of the "how to study" references appear to be aimed at the college student rather than at the high-school pupil, to say nothing of the child in the elementary grades. This does not mean that effective study is not necessary at these earlier levels or that an elementary- or junior high-school pupil is incapable of studying efficiently. It does mean that here is an area of academic development which can be fostered during these earlier school years, but which has been largely overlooked by teachers. Because the principles of learning are similar for any age learner, there is no reason why we cannot begin to teach efficient study skills from the time a pupil begins to study, using such forms as out-of-class assignments, readings or reports, or class notes and examinations.

GENERAL STUDY HABITS

When to study may be the first thing to consider. It is well for pupils to know that the best time to study a subject is as soon following the class period as possible. The advantage is that the subject matter is then still "fresh" and there is not the need to recall what the topic was with which the class work was concerned. Not as good a time, but perhaps a necessary time, is to study the material at home. This study time is generally not as good as immediately after the class because there is time to forget some details of the class work. (This time, however, does have other advantages.) The least appropriate time to study, but the best time to review, is just before the class period begins.

Saying when to study almost suggests where to study—in school as the best place and at home as the second best place. There are other factors which must be considered here however. If the material is such that library resources, maps, encyclopedias, or other learning aids are necessary or helpful, it is obviously better to study where these aids are to be found—usually in school rather than in the home. On the other hand, if the material does not require such resources or if it is better to spend a longer single block of time on the assignment than is possible in school, then the home is, of course, a better place for study.

If there are several subjects to be covered in the study program, help each pupil decide in what order to do them and the appropriate time to devote to each topic; having each pupil be aware of such problems as fatigue. Some individuals require a warm-up before serious study (and an easier subject can act as the warm-up to the more difficult task) while others can plunge immediately into serious study. The further the pupils progress through school, and the more studying they are required to carry on, the more important become the habits of proper study.

READING NOTES

Before reading notes can be taken, learning how to read effectively is necessary. The topic of how to read is not included here. In taking reading notes, the first point to emphasize to pupils is that the notes are never taken until the material is understood; read at least once. This is necessary so that the note taker knows what is important in the material—otherwise, "everything" seems important, with the result that there are far too many unnecessary notes taken.

If the book is owned by the pupil, there are several methods of note taking which are possible. The first is the underlining technique. (Underlining words, phrases, sentences, or even entire paragraphs). While this is perhaps the most common technique, it has two major weaknesses: (1) it takes valuable time and (2) it adds extra parallel lines to those already on the page, making a possible visual problem.

A second technique involves jotting down key words or phrases in the margin where they are easily seen and do not interfere with the written words. This technique requires that considerable thought be given to the words or phrases used so that a minimum of words can clearly convey the thought of the paragraph. Too few words make it difficult to recall the paragraph's meaning and too many words mean the pupil is practically rewriting the book!

A third system uses a standard set of marginal notations as follows:

(a) | indicates important material. Line extends from beginning to ending line of material.

(b) || indicates summary material. Lines follow the same areas as in (a).

(c)   ⌈   indicates end of extended important passage.
     ⌊   indicates beginning of extended important passage.

(d)   *ex*   indicates an example

(e)   *il*   indicates an illustration

This technique requires a minimum of time, a minimum distraction from the written material and a standard set of symbols, easily learned. When reviewing, only the indicated passages are reread.

If the book or periodical is school or library owned, the best set of notes are those taken in outline form from the written material. The outline form offers a minimum amount of note taking while offering an easy-to-follow visual pattern when rereading the notes. Always insist that the pupils include the full bibliographical material for each book or periodical used. This is a technique which will be a required procedure in later years of study. It is also a time saving device (in the event of using the book again, later) to include, after the bibliographical data, the library call number.

Reviewing written material should be done from the reading notes only. These should contain all that is important in the original material, and no more, except for needed examples or illustrations.

LECTURE NOTES

While we do not usually think of lecturing to an elementary-school class (unless the "lecture" is in the form of a reprimand for misconduct), we do carry on lecturing at a relatively low level. Teachers "talk," "teach," and "discuss" with the class. These are actually all forms or variations of the lecture technique; the difference between this and the lecture work done at the college level is perhaps a difference of formality in the talk.

Regardless of how we define lecturing or how it is done, it is important that pupils properly prepare for the class. This preparation consists of two activities: (a) prepare for a lecture by reading before-hand as much about the topic as possible so the pupil will be able to understand and appreciate, as much as possible, the material presented in the lecture or talk; and (b) have the necessary tools—paper, pencil or pen, notebook, or whatever other tools and materials may be needed—available and ready for use before the lecture begins. In many talks or lectures, the key idea is given in the first sentence or paragraph. The pupil who is asking another person for a pencil or the one who has to stop to tear out a page of his notebook to give to a classmate may well miss hearing the most important statement given during that class period! It is essential that pupils be prepared for a lecture before it begins.

As for the notes themselves, the important thing is to learn how to keep them effectively, but yet at a minimum. We can effectively do only one thing at a time and this means, in a lecture, we are hearing the material or writing —seldom both!

The pupil should begin each set of lecture notes with the topic of the talk and the date. This is important in the event he needs to secure help later, when reviewing. Asking for help concerning a particular topic or work of a specific date can bring better results than can a request for help on an indefinite topic given on a forgotten date.

Because the important thing in a lecture is to hear what is being said (and watch for indications of what is important—visual or voice cues from lecturer), it is necessary to spend as little time as possible in writing. This means using two techniques in writing notes: (a) outline the material and (b) use abbreviations. Each of these means the pupil can get a maximum amount of information with a minimum amount of writing—minimizing the amount of time he is not concentrating on the lecture.

Assuming all teachers can, and do, teach techniques of outlining, it will be skipped here. The idea of using abbreviations is somewhat unique, however, because the thing to strive for is to have the pupils develop, for themselves, a set of "standard" abbreviations which can be used in all courses. These "standard" abbreviations may be standard only for that individual. There is no reason why everyone must use identical ones. However, some which the author has found to be valuable to many students include the following:

∴	meaning therefore
=	meaning equals, the same as
Q	meaning the question (is)
?	meaning what, why, how
→	meaning leads to
conc	meaning conclusion

Using such notes, the simple question of "what time is it" may appear in note form as: ? hr. The statement that George Washington crossed the Delaware River on December 25, 1775 may read: GW Del 12/25/75. The important thing is to have a standard set of notes which can be used as the "basic vocabulary" in all courses and which will require a minimum amount of time taken from listening to the lecture.

The next important point in taking lecture notes is the technique of asking questions. Pupils should be encouraged (and allowed) to ask questions when they arise during the talk or lecture. This is the best time because the information needed is immediate. If, for some reason, the pupil may not interrupt, encourage questions at the end of the lecture, while the material is still fresh in the pupil's mind. The third time to allow questioning—and the least effective except that it may allow for a more thorough, detailed answer—is after school.

The last step in notetaking is to rewrite the notes. This is important for several reasons: even though some notes will be "standard" symbols, others will not and when they become old, may not be understood; therefore these should be rewritten into full words, (b) information taken in class notes may not be important enough to retain as part of the permanent notebook (anecdotal material, for example) and (c) rewriting notes allows for reorganization if necessary, and also if necessary, a chance to improve on handwriting.

STUDYING FOR EXAMINATIONS

Fear of examination often develops into a major problem for pupils as they progress through school. There are basically two reasons for this: they do not know how to study for, and take, examinations, and teachers create a fear situation for them by the improper use of examinations. A few ideas here may help on both counts.

Pupils should recognize that studying for examinations is basically no different from any other kind of study or assignment. The best form of preparation for examinations is the daily preparation of lessons. If further study, or review, is necessary, it should be done in the same way, using about the same amount of time per session. If, for example, the pupil normally spends thirty to forty-five minutes in studying an assignment because this time represents the limits of his attention span in the area, it is ridiculous for him to expect to study the same object, for an examination, by two hour blocks. It is perhaps obvious to suggest that pupils review by blocks of work rather than by an arbitrary number of pages per sitting!

Cramming is of no value except for pure note learning. Since there should be a minimum of this type of material on an examination, there should be no reason for cramming. A person "learns" a thing only by thinking through the information and this can best be done over a series of learning sessions, geared, in number and time, to the material and ability of the learner.

Traditionally the time and place for studying for examinations is at home where the pupil can work and concentrate individually. However, there are subjects which contain material or ideas about which there may be varying opinions. Where there are several logical views, it is well to study, in part at least, in groups. This procedure allows for the presentation and discussion of the several viewpoints and offers each individual the opportunity to defend or change his own viewpoint if necessary or desired. While this type of review may have to be, at first, somewhat supervised to prevent the development of "bull sessions," it is a technique which is usually enjoyed by pupils and one which has very definite values.

TAKING EXAMINATIONS

The purpose of examinations should be for the pupil and teacher to see what the pupil does know and what material or information is incorrectly learned or not yet understood. It should, therefore, be seen as an opportunity to measure progress and not seen as a threat or unpleasant hurdle to be passed or avoided. In short, the attitude your class takes toward examinations is a reflection of your teaching.

There appears to be two major problems involved in writing examinations (essay type). The first is in reading the question and the second is in proof-reading. The difficulty for many pupils is not in knowing the answer on the examination, but rather in interpreting the question. What do you mean when you say "discuss" a question? How do "define," "explain," and "describe" differ? The problem is that you, as the teacher, mean one thing by the directions given, but the pupils interpret the directions differently. The answer, of course, lies in the direction of deciding what your directions mean and make this meaning clear to the class. The second problem is simply the fact that pupils fail to take a few moments to proofread their papers and, as a result, leave silly, ridiculous mistakes, such as failing to insert a "not" in a statement, and thereby making a completely wrong or foolish answer.

Beyond these major, frequent mistakes is the mistake of not answering the question completely. Too often the pupil writes several pages and assumes he has answered the question—only to find when the papers are returned to him that he has completely answered only one part of the question! Using an outline before beginning the actual writing is one of the best ways of avoiding this type of problem.

When answering short-answer type questions, the first point is for the pupil to answer, first, those questions about which he is certain of the answers, leaving the doubtful ones for later. On unit examinations, the important thing is to discover what the learner really knows and does not know, and guessing under these conditions makes this difficult. Therefore, guessing should be discouraged—and the pupils should clearly understand the reason. On a final examination, however, there is traditionally not time given following the examination to learn further what is not clearly understood. There is, therefore, no longer the need to insist on not guessing. Here the grade is the important thing and a correct guess is better than no answer, so why shouldn't a pupil guess on the final examination?

ASSIGNMENTS

Assignments are actually not different from examinations. They are, in fact, open-book, take-home examinations and the points which relate to examinations should apply to assignments: the directions should be clearly given and must be understood by the pupils. The assignment should be written and proofread just as in another examination. The use of guessing, grammar, spelling, or other essentials should be the same as any other form of examination. In fact, pupils should develop the recognition that examinations are nothing more or less than a different form of assignment, allowing the teacher and learner the opportunity to see what is known and what needs further work. This approach to assignments offers one answer to the "busy work" type of assignment. If it is only "busy work," it is useless.

HOMEWORK

Lloyd McCleary *

To improve the quality of homework is one of education's most compelling tasks, says Lloyd McCleary. In consideration of how to improve

* From *Educational Leadership*, Vol. 17 (January 1960), pp. 217–220. Reprinted with permission of the Association for Supervision and Curriculum Development and Lloyd McCleary. Copyright © 1960 by the Association for Supervision and Curriculum Development.

homework, teachers will have to pay more attention to the nature of a good assignment, to teaching how to study, and to selecting the proper strategy for the learning product desired.

Reflection upon the subject of homework seems to open a Pandora's box for the educator. Pupils, parents, teachers and administrators hold a wide range of beliefs and opinions relative to homework. Beliefs and opinions not only differ within and between each of these groups, but they also vary as attention moves along the line from the practical concerns to the deeper philosophical questions which arise whenever problems of homework require attention.

As if this were not enough, opinions are likely to be affected by "side" concerns, for administrators *are* concerned about public relations; teachers *are* concerned about how "respectable" they appear to their colleagues; and parents *are* concerned about their child's readiness for College Boards. Since standard prescriptions of policy and practice are not likely to end the intense concern over this subject, perhaps an attempt in this article to indicate some of the major problems and some of the operating principles revealed by research and by current best practice may be of value to the reader.

THE "WHAT" AND THE "WHY"

In an analysis of the topic of homework, we first face a semantic problem. To the uninitiated, perhaps it would appear that homework should mean work assigned by a teacher to be completed at home. This definition of homework is of little help in understanding what a given teacher is likely to mean by the term.

Because of the protests of some pupils, the author questioned an English teacher about the amount of homework she had assigned. The teacher in question denied vigorously that the required reading of a novel within a period of one week in addition to a strong dose of written work was unreasonable because the reading of a novel (although required) was not homework! Likewise, a Latin teacher became incensed with the author because he objected to the fact that she kept students after school each night to do the work she had assigned in class that day. She held many of her pupils until five o'clock almost daily because she didn't believe in having them do work at home! These are extreme but actual examples of the practices of teachers.

In the literature of the 1930's the term homework apparently had a very clear meaning. The assign, study, recite, test methods in common use gave rise to this parent reaction reported by Butler [1] in 1939. A parent wrote to a superintendent:

[1] Frank A. Butler. *The Improvement of Teaching in Secondary Schools.* Chicago, Illinois: The University of Chicago Press, 1939, p. 208.

I have four little girls attending your schools. I am up at five o'clock in the morning to get them off to school and to get myself off to work. It is six o'clock in the evening when I reach home again, pretty well worn out, and after we have had dinner and have tidied up the house a bit, it is eight o'clock. Then, tired as I am, I sit down and teach the little girls the lessons your teachers will hear them say over on the following day. Now, if it is all the same to you, it would be a great help and a favor to me if you will have your teachers teach the lessons during the day, and then all I would have to do at night would be to hear them say them over.

Unfortunately, as late as 1950, Burton [2] reported an investigation which showed that four-fifths of the assignment procedures in the social studies classes studied were nothing more than page assignments of a single textbook.

Curriculum workers find the need to distinguish between formal or traditional practices and modern practices relative to teaching methods and techniques including homework. Very largely the distinction is based upon the degree to which practice is related to the findings of modern research dealing with individual differences in ability, in interests, and in rates of learning. The few statistical studies which have been made show that home study of the formal sort even when accompanied by questions, study guides and the like have little effect upon achievement. As teaching methods and homework shift from the expository-memory type of activity to the problem solving-independent study type there will be many activities to be carried on outside of the scheduled class time. However, these homework activities do not resemble the "assigned textbook pages" kind of homework.

THE "HOW"

The newer approach equates study with learning. The emphasis as far as homework is concerned becomes that of teaching pupils how to learn and how to become self directing in their study. Continuity between classroom and out-of-classroom study is sought. Teachers know very well that the demands of the classroom will largely condition the approaches the pupil will use in independent study. If factual tests are a major element of the teaching method, memory will be the habit of study employed by the pupil. The habit of memorizing is likely to be employed as the means of study even in situations in which memorizing is completely inappropriate. Thus, classroom activities should require a variety of individual and group learning experiences which are completed outside the classroom. Examples of these activities are identifying and defining problems; analyzing problems through library, laboratory or action research type of activity, interviews, visits, experiments and the like.

Needless to say, this kind of homework emphasis does not reduce the range

[2] *Learning and Instruction.* The forty-ninth Yearbook of the National Society for the Study of Education, Part I. Chicago, Illinois: The University of Chicago Press, 1950, p. 227.

of opinion or the number of issues relative to homework. Rather the shifting emphasis to problem-solving and independent study type of outside of classroom learning has introduced new problems and issues. The efforts to develop independent study have largely centered upon (a) the lengthened period with time devoted to the teaching of appropriate study techniques, (b) the development of separate how-to-study courses, (c) the use of special or remedial teachers such as a reading teacher to develop certain skills, and (d) the provision of supervisory help for the teacher in teaching study habits through regular class procedures. Within any given staff one will almost certainly find advocates of these various approaches. Obviously the direction of curriculum development being taken in a given school, administrative procedures, preparation of staff and the like will determine which, if any, steps are taken to alter the quality of homework and to prepare pupils to profit fully from it.

Regardless of the teaching methods employed, teachers need to understand and to recognize good study procedures and be able to diagnose cases of inefficiency in or ignorance of study procedures. Aids to the teacher in the form of books and monographs on effective study procedures, diagnostic tests, remedial materials, guides, inventories and the like are plentiful and are of excellent quality. In addition, the teacher can detect evidence of poor study habits through observation, examination of pupils' work, conferences, and self constructed questionnaires.

Unfortunately, many schools attempt to initiate curricular changes without the proper preparation of the staff. The incidents of comic if not pathetic attempts are legend. In one school known to the author, the principal abolished all study halls and lengthened the class periods accordingly with the expectation that teachers would immediately begin teaching independent study techniques appropriate to their subject but with no preparation other than the announcement in a faculty meeting that this would be done.

During the 1940's a large number of controlled studies were conducted. The author was, however, unable to find a study which actually compared various techniques rather than various administrative schemes for facilitating study. A Project for the Improvement of Thinking, now being conducted by Professors Henderson and Smith of the College of Education of the University of Illinois, is an excellent example of a project which developed and tried out materials for improving pupil learning within the classroom. This study and others like it, however, have not directly investigated the aspect of independent study or the transfer of these learnings to use beyond the classroom. Soundly conceived experimental studies are badly needed in this area.

Although the nature of instruction and the development of sound habits of independent study are important to worthwhile out-of-class study, the assignment is a crucial element in productive homework. Regardless of the nature of the homework assignment, the pupil should clearly understand what he is to do and have definite leads to begin his work. There is ample research data to support the belief that pupil failure relative to study is as much caused by factors indicative of a poor assignment (frustration, lack of interest, failure to understand the relationship of the assignment to the class-work, etc.) than to poor study habits.

THE "WHEN" AND THE "HOW MUCH"

Definite answers to the "when" and the "how much" questions are offered from many quarters. Generally these answers are not derived from the nature of a particular unit of school work or from the needs of particular pupils. Unfortunately, the professional journals contain just as many such answers as do the newspapers and popular magazines. In a 15 minute scanning of professional journals the author found seven separate (and each surprisingly similar) statements of the amount and timing of homework. Generally these statements were policies adopted and in force in some school system and apparently their publication implied their recommendation to the profession to be used as a standard for adoption in other schools. One such statement recommends: "In kindergarten to grade four: no homework; in grades five and six: one-half hour; in grades seven and eight: one hour; (and so on). It is suggested that no homework be given over weekends or holidays." Another article with the same time requirements is headed by the words "homework may harm the child's health and the school's public relations"!

These kinds of statements are not likely to be of much help to parents or to teachers. If such policies are taken seriously they may be a source of frustration to the teacher and a cause of irritation to parents that could defeat the public relations purpose which the statement professes to serve. Louis Brumer, the father of a pupil in a New York City high school, wrote his reaction to homework policy in the June 1956 issue of *High Points:*

Do responsible members of the high school teaching corps recommend 30-50 minutes (of homework) daily in each prepared subject?

Do they believe students should be encouraged to give services to the school?

Do they believe youth should be encouraged to attend school club meetings, and/or community religious group club activities after school?

Do they believe school children at the high school level should continue with music lessons, dancing lessons, or art lessons. . . . ?

Should children develop responsibility toward the home and family by performing special duties. . . . ?

Should families be encouraged to dine together nightly for an hour to review the day's events. . . . ?

Should there be an occasional free afternoon. . . . ?

Should at least one morning a week be assigned to formal religious devotions?

Should time be set aside for shopping for a suit or dress, other wardrobe essentials, or an occasional birthday gift. . . . ?

Should any unscheduled time be left for an adolescent to read a *book of his own choice.* . . . ?

How many hours of sleep should a growing young man or lady require?

Some school-wide policies relative to homework seem to be required but it is doubtful that rather fixed time limits are either effective or meaningful. The most fruitful approach seems to lie in the direction of the study of the curriculum and the teaching procedures out of which the homework evolves. A knowledge of home conditions and the out-of-school experiences of pupils should help teachers to devise learning activities which develop into stimulating out-of-class study and which can be tailored to individual needs.

Another avenue to independent study that is important to those concerned about homework is the use of the extended school day. Shops, libraries, science and language laboratories, work space and equipment for the use of tapes, television kinescopes and the like under the care of a para-professional teacher or a laboratory assistant are already available in some schools during out-of-class study time. Such facilities with proper provision for their use create excellent study conditions and do not involve the taxation of teacher time. This kind of activity meets many of the objections to homework held by parents and teachers. These activities could be incorporated with leisure time pursuits, relieve the home of the burden of providing materials and equipment, enrich and extend classroom experiences and promote the development of independent study.

In an opinion poll of school administrators conducted by *The Nation's Schools*, 96 percent of the administrators polled favored scheduled study during the school day; 95 percent favored homework assignments for junior and senior high school pupils; 79 percent favored homework at the upper elementary school level; and 31 percent favored homework for pupils in the lower elementary grades. According to reports from the administrators involved in this poll, the average time spent doing homework was about three hours per week for elementary pupils and from four to six hours per week for high school pupils. If these reactions represent homework conditions generally, there is wide acceptance of the practice of assigning homework; and at least at the high school level, the average time spent doing assigned homework is the equivalent of one school day each week. If this time is to be employed effectively and if it can be invested to produce independent, self directing students, the effort by teachers to improve the quality of homework becomes one of education's most compelling tasks.

STRATEGIES AND TACTICS
THAT PRESENT AND FIX
INFORMATION AND SKILLS

A MONG the classroom instructional strategies that have not been discussed in this book so far are drill, programmed instruction, lecture, television teaching, and team-teaching strategies. All of these have one element in common: they are difficult to use well. Yet, each one of them has its place and should be used when the teaching objectives are appropriate.

Drill and practice are necessary in the teaching of skills and in the learning of material that must be remembered even though not very meaningful or interesting. Learning French verbs or memorizing dates are examples of the type of thing that calls for drill. So are learning to play the piano or how to type. Practice is the same as drill, except that the word *drill* connotes meaningless teacher-conducted repetition, and practice refers to more thoughtful, largely self-directed repetition. For our purpose, we can think of them as the same. They are both useful for solidifying, improving and re-enforcing; they are not good for introducing new learning. The article on drill by Ausubel applies also to practice.

Programmed learning is in some ways similar to drill, although its purpose is to bring about new learning rather than solidify and improve old learning. Just what the future of this type of teaching is, is hard to guess. At the moment, machine teaching of this type is necessarily limited to the teaching of fact and information and the cultivation of certain skills. Whether or not it will ever be really useful for teaching higher mental processes is yet to be seen, but there is no doubt that teaching machines can teach. It seems that the immediate role of teaching machines should be to teach basic information and skills so that teachers can have more time to teach the higher intellectual and affective learning so necessary if pupils are to become truly educated.

Lecture and telling techniques are also basically strategies for presenting information to pupils. This is true of almost all large group-teaching techniques, including instructional television. Sometimes these techniques can be used to start pupils thinking, or sway attitudes. Usually, though, the change in thinking or attitude must be carried out by a different strategy.

Team-teaching plans require a combination of all kinds of strategies and tactics. By grouping teachers together in teams, we hope that it will be possible to organize classes so that teachers may teach the content and strategies they find most comfortable. The plans should result in an optimal mixture of learning information and using information in thinking and developing concepts, beliefs, values and skills. Let us hope the dream comes true. That is why it is so often designed to combine large-group presentations, small-group discussions, and individual study. At present the tendency has been to emphasize the information giving elements of the plan at the expense of the information using aspects.

IS DRILL NECESSARY? THE MYTHOLOGY
OF INCIDENTAL LEARNING

David P. Ausubel *

Is drill necessary? Yes, of course, is the answer. Although some psychiatrists deplore the side effects of drill, few teachers have found it wise to completely eliminate it. In this article Ausubel shows why. He makes as good a case for drill as anyone else has done lately. Probably there never has been any real objection to drill, but to the way it has been used. Drill for drill's sake has no value, but drill for the sake of practice is something else again, and repetition is often a requisite for thorough learning. If the practice can be lively, meaningful and enjoyable, so much the better.

One of the strongest legacies of the progressive education movement and of Thorndikian educational psychology that still remains on the pedagogic scene is a confused and contradictory attitude toward structured practice or drill. On the one hand, we minimize the value of drill in educational theory, regarding it as rote, mechanical, passive, and old-fashioned, as psychologically unnecessary for the learning process, and as actually harmful for active, meaningful learning. On the other hand, as teachers, parents, coaches, and students, we still implicitly accept the old maxim that "practice makes perfect."

* From *The Bulletin of the National Association of Secondary-School Principals*, Vol. 47 (December 1963), pp. 44–50. Reprinted by permission of the NASSP and the author.

The upshot of this conflict in our beliefs is that we still place considerable reliance on drill in actual classroom practice, but do so half-heartedly, apologetically, and in ways that detract from its effectiveness.

The progressivists, of course, did not entirely deny the value of practice. As a matter of fact, both their espousal of activity programs and their battle cry of "learning by doing" carried an implied endorsement of the importance of appropriate practice. But by appropriate practice they meant direct (concrete, manipulative), nondeliberate, and autonomous learning encounters with different examples of the same concept or principle in uncontrived, "real-life" situations. Their mistake lay in assuming that all structured practice (drill) is necessarily rote; that unstructured, unguided, and unintentional (incidental) practice is maximally effective for school learning tasks; and that "doing" necessarily leads to learning simply because it involves direct experience and occurs repeatedly in natural, problem-solving situations.

Actually, for practice to result in meaningful mastery of material, the only really essential conditions are that the learning task be potentially meaningful; that the learner exhibit a meaningful learning set and possess the necessary background concepts; and that the number, distribution, sequence, and organization of practice trials conform to empirically established principles of efficient learning and retention. Not only is the uncontrived or unstructured quality of practice an unessential condition of meaningful, effective learning, but it also often leads to no meaningful mastery whatsoever.

The fetish of naturalism and incidental learning embodied in the activity program movement emphasizes these five points: (1) unstructured and uncontrived learning situations; (2) direct kinds of experience, in a concrete, manipulative sense; (3) unintentional or nondeliberate learning effort; (4) learning by autonomous, unguided discovery; and (5) exposure to diversified rather than repetitive experience.

LEARNING IN NATURAL SETTINGS

How desirable is it that factual information and intellectual skills be acquired in the real-life, functional contexts in which they are customarily encountered, rather than through the medium of artificially contrived drills and exercises? It is true, of course (providing that all other factors are equal), that learning is enhanced when the conditions of practice closely resemble the conditions under which the skill or knowledge in question will eventually be used. Wholly natural settings, however, rarely provide the practice conditions that are either necessary or optimal for efficient learning. Generally it is only during the latter stages of learning, *after* component aspects of the learning task have already been identified and mastered in structured practice sessions that naturalistic "dress rehearsals" become feasible.

This is so, in the first place, because unstructured learning settings typically fail to furnish examples that come along frequently, repetitively, and close enough together to make possible the learning of concepts and principles.

Under these circumstances there is also inadequate opportunity for differential practice of particularly difficult components. Contrary to Thorndike's generally accepted but unwarranted inferences from his well-known experiments on the "law of frequency," the weight of the research evidence clearly indicates that repetition *per se* is typically necessary both for the learning and retention of associations and meanings. Second, unstructured practice does not receive the benefit of either skilled pedagogic selection, presentation, and organization of material or of careful sequencing, pacing, and gradation of difficulty.

DIRECT EXPERIENCE

Many features of the activity program were based on the quite defensible premise that the elementary school child perceives the world in relatively specific and concrete terms, and requires considerable first-hand experience with diverse concrete instances of a given set of relationships before he can acquire genuinely meaningful concepts and propositions. Thus, an attempt was made to teach factual information and intellectual skills through the medium of direct, manipulative experience in natural settings rather than through verbal exposition and drill.

In older pupils, however, once a sufficient number of basic concepts is consolidated, new concepts are primarily abstracted from verbal rather than concrete experience, and new propositions are comprehended without any direct reference to or manipulation of concrete props. Hence, in secondary school, it may be desirable to reverse both the sequence and relative balance between abstract concepts and supportive data. There is good reason for believing that much of the time presently spent in cookbook laboratory exercises in the sciences could be more advantageously employed in formulating precise definitions, making explicit verbal distinctions between concepts, generalizing from hypothetical situations, etc.

John Dewey correctly recognized that meaningful understanding of abstract concepts and principles in childhood must be built on a foundation of direct, empirical experience, and for this reason advocated the use of activity methods in the elementary school. But he also appreciated that once a firmly grounded first-story of abstract understandings was established, it was possible to organize secondary and higher education along more abstract and verbal lines. Unfortunately, however, some of Dewey's disciples blindly generalized over the entire life span the conditions that limit abstract verbal learning during childhood.

NONDELIBERATE LEARNING

Although individuals can acquire much miscellaneous information and some skills incidentally, deliberate effort is required for the efficient learning of most types of academic material. Countless experiments show that deliberate learning in response to explicit instructions is both more effective and more precise than is unintentional or implicitly instructed learning.

Especially for long-term meaningful learning of subject matter, doing *per se* is not sufficient in the absence of the felt needs and interests that give rise to deliberate intent. Inability to see any need for a subject is the reason students mention most frequently for losing interest in high-school studies. Doing, without being interested in what one is doing, results in relatively little permanent learning. Only that material can be meaningfully incorporated into an individual's structure of knowledge, on a long-term basis, which is relevant to areas of concern in his psychological field.

Learners who have little need to know and understand, quite naturally expend little learning effort and manifest an insufficiently meaningful learning set. They fail to develop precise meanings, to reconcile new material with existing concepts, and to reformulate new propositions in their own words. Finally, they do not devote enough time and effort to practice and review. Material is therefore never sufficiently consolidated to form an adequate foundation for sequential learning. Hence it is unrealistic to expect that school subjects can be effectively learned and retained until pupils develop a felt need to acquire knowledge as an *end in itself*—since much school learning can never be rationalized as necessary for meeting the demands of daily living.

AUTONOMOUS, UNGUIDED DISCOVERY

The unquestioning faith which advocates of incidental learning have in autonomous, unguided discovery is justified neither by logic nor by research evidence. In the first place, laboratory and problem-solving exercises are not inherently or necessarily meaningful. They may lead to little or no meaningful learning if a student's learning set is simply to memorize rotely type problems or techniques of manipulating reagents and symbols, and if he has inadequate background in or appreciation of the substantive and methodological principles underlying specific problem-solving or laboratory procedures.

Second, what is typically called "the discovery method" is really a contrived type of discovery that is a far cry from the truly autonomous discovery activities of the research scholar or scientist. Pure discovery techniques could lead only to utter chaos and waste of time in the classroom, inasmuch as immature students generally lack sufficient subject-matter sophistication both to formulate workable problems and to devise appropriate and relevant research methods. Before students can "discover" concepts reasonably efficiently, problems must be structured for them in such a way as to make ultimate discovery almost inevitable.

Third, many short-term studies have demonstrated that guided discovery is more efficacious for learning, retention, and transfer than is either completely autonomous discovery or the provision of complete guidance. Guidance under these circumstances sensitizes the learner to the salient aspects of the problem, orients him to the goal, and promotes economy of learning by preventing misdirected effort. However these findings do not necessarily indicate that guided discovery is more effective for teaching subject-matter content than is simple didactic exposition. For one thing, the solving by a naive subject of a few novel problems in a laboratory setting is hardly comparable to the learning of a large body of sequentially organized material by a learner with varying degrees of subject-matter sophistication. For another, even contrived discovery techniques are incomparably more time-consuming than expository teaching.

Lastly, guidance in the form of prompting has been shown to be very helpful during the early stages of learning. At this point in the learning process, the learner has not mastered sufficient material to receive much practice benefit from unaided recitation. Furthermore, the provision of prompts can prevent the learning of errors and thus obviate the necessity for costly unlearning.

DIVERSIFIED EXPERIENCE

Proponents of activity programs tend to favor task heterogeneity in practice. That is, they seek, in part, to escape the opprobrium associated with drill by stressing diversity both in the types of learning tasks and in the examples of each type that are presented to the learner. This approach undoubtedly has merit in that, other factors being equal, the defining attributes of a new concept are learned most readily when the concept is encountered in many different contexts. Such experience obviously enhances the generality of abstract knowledge and transferable skills. It also minimizes the possibility of boredom and of a rote and rigid approach to learning.

However, if diversity of learning task content is provided at the expense of attaining mastery of the particular component tasks which comprise it, its over-all effect on learning is detrimental. Positive transfer from one learning task to another requires that particular examples of a given type of task as well as particular types of tasks first be consolidated (*i.e.*, mastered, overlearned) before new task content is introduced.

Many cases of disability in such academic skills as arithmetic, reading, spelling, and grammar can undoubtedly be attributed to overemphasis on the importance of diversified experience in unstructured learning situations. Failure to provide sufficient repetitive practice (drill) in antecedent learning tasks does not allow for the adequate mastery of these tasks that is essential if sequentially related tasks are to be successfully handled in the acquisition of concepts, generalizations, and intellectual skills.

WILL PROGRAMMED INSTRUCTION
SERVE PEOPLE?

Gerald Gleason *

Programmed instruction has been gaining acceptance in the schools slowly. Although teachers do well to be wary, they should become familiar with programming because it is one of the first attempts to use systematic analysis to improve teaching. Undoubtedly, the programs of the present will seem really amateurish in the near future, but they do provide a means for individualizing teaching and for using the teacher's time efficiently. At the moment, they seem best adapted for purposes of "drilling and grilling" information into pupils' heads so that they will not readily forget it. What the future holds for programmed instruction is still uncertain. The following selection will give some notion of how things in programmed instruction stand today and how they may go in the future.

Perhaps no innovation in recent history has caused so much furore, has captured so much interest, has been so grossly maligned and, at the same time, has resulted in such critical analysis of the teaching-learning process as has the teaching machine—or more correctly, programmed instruction. Growing from the laboratory manipulation of subhuman organisms by experimental psychologists, the teaching machine has been cited either as the answer to most of our educational problems or as the next step in the increasing pace of dehumanizing our educational system.

Few educators are unaware of the basic principles of programmed instruction. Virtually every professional convention has had sessions devoted to the topic; most professional publications have included articles describing programmed instruction; increasing attention is being given to the reports of research using programmed instruction; most major publishing companies have marketed programmed textbooks, and major corporations (IBM, Du-Pont, Xerox, U.S. Industries) have made substantial, long range investments in the development of programmed materials and devices.

This article will not attempt to describe either the basic theoretical formu-

* From *Educational Leadership*, Vol. 23 (March 1966), pp. 471–479. Reprinted with permission of the Association for Supervision and Curriculum Development and Gerald Gleason. Copyright © 1966 by the Association for Supervision and Curriculum Development.

lations or the practical applications of programmed instruction. The interested reader is referred to any one of several new books in the field (1, 2, 3). A note of caution, however. Publications more than two or three years old are badly outdated and have little more than historical value. The early pronouncements, "basic" principles, and recommendations of many self-styled authorities in the field have been reversed if not at least challenged by subsequent research and application in the past year or two.

Unfortunately, many skeptics are still basing their positions concerning programmed instruction on information which is no longer accepted by knowledgeable people or on the basis of their experience with some of the first available programs or machines. The field is in a very dynamic state. There is a real danger that premature closure on programming styles and machine design will seriously hinder the ultimate development of programmed instruction.

One of the most amazing aspects of the movement has been its rapidity of development and implementation. While Skinner's article in *Science* in 1958 (5) is regarded as the first serious proposal for utilizing teaching machines, it was not until the early 1960's that programs and machines became generally available.

In just a few short years, a promising and possibly threatening innovation has burst upon the educational scene and has influenced students, teachers, curriculum planners, textbook publishers, building designers, as well as large segments of the general public. Even more dramatic has been the widespread and enthusiastic acceptance of programmed instruction by business and industrial educators. One of the most encouraging aspects of programmed instruction has been its ability to overcome the barriers that educators so often raise when dramatic innovations are proposed.

It should also be noted that the pace of acceptance by educators has been distressingly slow from the perspective of many proponents of programmed instruction as well as publishers of programmed materials. Professional journals have had an increasing number of articles in which educators are criticized for their reluctance to embrace programmed instruction.

The point is this—programmed instruction has been accepted by educators far more rapidly than any other innovation in history.

DOES IT WORK?

Does programmed instruction work? Do students learn when using programmed textbooks or teaching machines? The most clear-cut answer has come from Schramm in his excellent summary, *Research On Programmed Instruction* (4), in which he reviews hundreds of research studies. His conclusion is very simple. Programmed instruction can be effective in helping most students achieve specified behavioral objectives, in a variety of subject areas, and using a variety of programming techniques and presentation devices. The key phrase is "specified behavior objectives." The crucial task is to specify what we want the student to learn, and the behavioral criteria he must meet to demonstrate his learning. If the behavioral objectives can be specified, there seems to be little argument that a carefully constructed program will help most students attain the objectives.

While much of the research evidence may appear to be contradictory to the casual reader, the contradictions arise from the question "Which method of programmed instruction is most effective and/or efficient?" Linear-branching? Small step-large step? Overt response-covert response? Textbook-machine? Inductive-deductive? These are the research questions that are receiving attention today. As the head of a large corporation recently declared, "We know programmed instruction works. Now we're trying to find the most effective way to use it."

Unfortunately, many educators are still demanding research which compares the results of programmed instruction with the results of "conventional instruction." Schramm cites some 36 studies which have been attempted. Such efforts are no longer necessary and are probably misguided from a research point of view. While it is essential for the programmer to specify the prerequisites, the sequence, the style and the outcome of his learning experience, it is virtually impossible to specify and control these characteristics in a conventional classroom setting to the extent which would permit valid generalization to larger populations. Our efforts should be expended in defining our instructional objectives and then searching for the most effective and efficient ways to help students attain those objectives.

Is efficiency a "dirty word" in education? Many persons would say it is and object strenuously to the demonstrated capability of programmed instruction to increase the efficiency in terms of time and energy expenditure of students in achieving stated objectives. They decry attempts to force more and more "content" (another questionable word) upon students and the seemingly ominous pressure to do more things faster.

Rather than bow to such critics, we should be asking the question, "Are we doing all we can to help the student make efficient use of his time and energy?" We should be stripping the nonessentials from our courses, eliminating needless drill and repetition, providing alternate opportunities for fast or slow learners, and constantly challenging all students to set and achieve new objectives. All of these can be accomplished by carefully developed programs but are very difficult to achieve in conventional instructional settings.

Even the casual observer of the typical classroom must agree that many students do not make efficient use of time and energy. While one may argue that this makes school more enjoyable for some, it is also quite likely to be a cause of the obvious disenchantment of many students with their school experiences.

STUDENT REACTION

The most disturbing evidence on the use of programmed instruction concerns student reaction to the technique. The early reports of overwhelmingly enthusiastic reactions to programmed instruction have been contradicted by increasing numbers of neutral and negative reactions. Reports of "dull," "boring," "repetitious," and "uninteresting" have come to be expected. (Of course, we would get the same reactions from many students concerning any instructional technique.) However, the author has studied the reactions of thousands of students and has found a substantial majority who express generally positive reactions. In one study it was obvious that student reaction was not a function of the program used or of the experimental treatment but more likely a reflection of the classroom teacher's attitudes.

It is becoming increasingly clear that the technique itself is no panacea for the pervasive problem of motivating the student to want to learn. Skinner's earlier position that the reinforcement received by making correct responses would be sufficient to sustain motivation must now be discarded in the light of the evidence. The problem is to find a program that is within the subject area interest of the student, has a step-size and programming style that is challenging to the student, and then to use the program in a supportive situation. This suggests the need for a wide variety of programs on any given topic to match the unique characteristics of individual students and the preferences of their teachers.

TEACHER REACTION

There is no question that the large majority of educators are, for real or imagined reasons, less than enthusiastic about programmed instruction. On the other hand, the overwhelming majority of teachers who *try* programmed instruction are generally enthusiastic. The author has worked with hundreds of classroom teachers who have used programmed instruction. In almost every instance, they expressed positive reactions to the *technique*, although not always to the particular program or the way in which it was used.

One of the most often cited reactions is that programmed instruction enables the teacher to have *more* time to work with individuals and small groups. Relieved of the time-consuming tasks of presenting information, monitoring student activity, and checking students' work, the teacher is able to devote his time to the far more challenging—and professional—tasks of clarifying, analyzing, synthesizing and generalizing from the basic content presented by the program. Thus, contrary to the charges of many critics, programmed instruction can actually increase opportunities for interpersonal contacts among teachers and students.

THE FUTURE?

The future directions and use of programmed instruction are inexorably bound to the development of another looming technological colossus—the computer. Programmed instruction as we know it today in the form of programmed texts or simple mechanical type machines will probably continue to be used in school and other educational settings for the next several years.

Even in this primitive form it will continue to demonstrate the feasibility of shaping intellectual behavior in the direction of specified objectives.

In the not too distant future, however, use of the programmed text will be restricted to highly individualized instructional settings. Programmed instruction will have turned to the computer for assistance in overcoming some of its present limitations.

Some advantages of computer-assisted instruction are these:

1. The computer enables the programmer to utilize branching techniques far more effectively than a programmed text.

2. The storage capacity of the computer enables the programmer to provide "feedback" for a virtually unlimited number of responses.

3. The computer can adapt the sequence and rate of presentation of material as a function of student characteristics or performance.

4. The computer can coordinate the use of audio, visual and kinesthetic stimulus and response modes to supplement the verbal mode.

These and other capabilities of computer-assisted instruction (CAI) are being demonstrated and developed in a number of settings throughout the country. The "hardware" will be generally available within 3–5 years. While substantial costs will be a deterrent in the near future, it is likely that CAI will be economically and logistically feasible within the coming decade.

So what is programmed instruction—just another fad—another bandwagon in the educational circus parade? Not at all. Programmed instruction as we know it today represents the earliest phase of a systematic analysis of the teaching-learning process. For one of the first times in educational history, an idea has captured the imagination of psychologists, engineers, technicians, architects, businessmen, publishers—and educators.

The idea can be stated most simply: decide what is to be taught, determine the terminal criteria, and systematically explore the most effective and efficient means of helping the student meet the criteria. The "means" might be a small-step, carefully sequenced series of frames or it might be a film clip, an audio tape, a series of slides, a lecture, a group discussion, or a tutorial session.

The "systems" approach to educational planning requires the precise analysis of the unique characteristics and capabilities of a variety of learning activities which can be used to attain objectives. The approach is based on the deceptively simple but obviously neglected assumption that some learning techniques are more effective for some learning outcomes than others.

In summary, programmed instruction has made a dramatic impact on educational practice in a relatively brief time. There is strong evidence that programmed instruction works although there is considerable disagreement over the most effective techniques.

Perhaps the most significant contribution which programmed instruction will make is dramatizing the necessity of systematic analysis of the teaching-learning process and the determination of the most effective means of instruction for various subject areas as well as various students.

REFERENCES

1. DALE M. BRETHOWER et al. *Programmed Learning: A Practicum.* Ann Arbor, Michigan: Ann Arbor Publishers, 1965.
2. J. P. DECECCO. *Education Technology: Readings in Programmed Instruction.* New York: Holt, Rinehart and Winston, Inc., 1964.
3. J. I. TABER, R. GLASER and H. H. SCHAEFFER. *Learning and Programmed Instruction.* Palo Alto, California: Addison Wesley, 1965.
4. WILBUR SCHRAMM. *The Research on Programmed Instruction.* U.S.O.E. 34034, 1964.
5. B. F. SKINNER. "Teaching Machines." *Science* 128:969–77; October 1958.

THE ART OF TALKING ABOUT SCIENCE

Lawrence Bragg *

As a rule, lectures should be kept short, particularly in junior high schools. Twenty minutes is often considered the maximum for effective lectures in junior-high-school classes. Older pupils can take longer lectures more easily.

The reasons for this recommendation are twofold. One is that after twenty minutes of listening to the average lecture the average pupil becomes restless. The other is that the lecture method does not seem to be a very good way to drive ideas home. Evidently, in order to learn concepts, pupils must do something a bit more active than just sit and listen.

All this does not mean that lectures have no place in the secondary-school classroom. Junior-high-school pupils can listen attentively for a long period to a really interesting lecture, and they can learn much from vivid, well organized lectures—especially if they take good notes and review them. Unfortunately, secondary-school teachers rarely have the time to prepare and deliver lectures well.

Secondary-school teachers, then, should beware of overusing the lecture, but they should not shun it when it seems to be appropriate. When they do lecture, they should attempt to be vivid, interesting, and effective. To this end, teachers should be careful that their lectures do not

* From *Science*, Vol. 154 (Washington, D.C.: American Association for the Advancement of Science, December 30, 1966), pp. 1613–1616. Reprinted by permission of *Science*. Copyright 1966 by the American Association for the Advancement of Science.

cover too much, that they place sufficient stress on the important points, and that the concepts to be learned are re-enforced by illustrations and audio-visual aids. The lecture is one type of lesson that must be planned well.

The following selection consists of the major portion of a speech given by Professor Bragg at a meeting of the American Association for the Advancement of Science, December 28, 1966. The remarks are meant to help lecturers who must address adult audiences. Except for some comments about time, however, they are applicable to lectures in the junior and senior high schools—particularly in large-group instruction. Perhaps Bragg's experience of talking to "many thousands of school pupils every year" has sharpened his awareness of the value of the techniques he recommends. Note that he points out an hour is about as long as one can expect to hold a sophisticated adult audience. Undoubtedly, he would agree that ordinarily the time limit should be somewhat shorter when speaking to secondary-school pupils. Most important of all, though, is his insistence that one must aim at making one's point so that the listeners will understand and remember. It seems such an obvious procedure and yet so few lecturers really do it.

I propose to analyze "Talking about Science." How is it best done? Why is it that a subject presented by A is a thrilling account which leaves a deep impression, whereas the very same material presented by B is dull and boring and produces no impression whatever? How should we present our branch of science to fellow scientists who work in quite another field? How can we present science to those who have little or no scientific background, as is often the case with men of high ability who are important in affairs of state? How can we make the nonscientist understand why its study means so much to us, a passion they sometimes find very difficult to understand? The gap between C. P. Snow's two cultures is not so much due to a lack of understanding as to a lack of desire to understand. There are philistines as regards science as well as regards the arts.

These problems have been brought vividly home to me in a number of ways. I was for many years president of the Physics Solvay Conference. It must be one of the most exclusive of international science gatherings, because only some 20 participants are invited to discuss the subject chosen for the meetings which are held every 3 years. I have listened for 12 years to all the Friday evening discourses at the Royal Institution, where a broad review of some branch of science is given, and the speakers are both well known in their fields and artists in framing their talks. I talk to many thousands of school pupils every year, and find the nature of their response to be a fascinating study. Recently we have been framing courses for men and women who are new entrants to the Civil Service, and who have had no scientific training. I cannot help but be interested in the basic principles which apply to all talks of this kind.

What is the basic character of a "talk"? I think it can be expressed by saying that its primary object is to create a state of mind, or point of view, not to convey information. I can perhaps illustrate what I mean by dwelling on the vast difference between the spoken and written account. Under the heading "talk," I am not including a course of lectures where students take notes and the lectures follow each other as a composite whole. Nor do I include the "get together" of two or three experts in the same line of research, for which no rules are necessary. I am considering the hour's talk to an audience whose attention one has to retain and whose interest one has to arouse. The written account can also aim at creating a viewpoint, but its main function is to be a storehouse of information. The argument can be meaty and condensed. It can be packed with tables, graphs, and mathematical equations. This is possible because the reader can always pause and digest it at his leisure, going back over parts which he finds to be difficult. The written account has a quality also which I find hard to define. It is as if the writer were giving evidence on oath, and had to justify the accuracy of every word. He must be careful to give references and all due acknowledgements. I do not mean to imply that one can be irresponsible in a talk, but one need not cross all the "t's" and dot all the "i's." In fact, the talk would be spoiled by an attempt to do so.

A talk is therefore different altogether from a "paper." To my mind the governing factor which determines its art form is this: The success of the way in which the subject has been presented is measured by the extent to which the average member of the audience remembers it next day.

This may seem an obvious statement, but if we use this principle as a yardstick to assess a lecture we have listened to, or in planning a lecture of our own, it creates a very significant viewpoint. The value of a lecture is not to be measured by how much one manages to cram into an hour, how much important information has been referred to, or how completely it covers the ground. It is to be measured by how much a listener can tell his wife about it at breakfast next morning, or, if she is not interested, a friend in the morning train. If we honestly put this question to ourselves and think how little we can remember of talks we have heard, it gives us a sense of proportion and of values in planning a lecture and makes us realize that what we say will go over the heads of the audience if we set our sights too high. I would like now to list what I believe to be some of the considerations which apply in planning a talk.

For instance, suppose we ask how many main points can we hope to "get over" in an hour? I think the answer should be "one." If the average member of the audience can remember with interest and enthusiasm one main theme, the lecture has been a great success. I like to compare the composition of a lecture to that of a picture. Of course this is dangerous ground on which to venture, because art experts differ so much among themselves. But in simple terms, is it not held that a picture should have one main centre of interest? It may have numerous subsidiary features, but the composition is so cunningly arranged that when the eye falls on these and follows their placing it is subtly led back to the main centre of interest and does not fall out of the picture frame. A lecture should be like that. There should be one main theme, and all the subsidiary interesting points, experiments, or demonstrations should be such that they remind the hearer of the theme. As in a picture, so in a lecture, the force of the impression depends upon a ruthless sacrifice of unnecessary detail. I do not mean that a lecture should be like some modern pictures, consisting of an otherwise blank canvas with one button or other object sewn on it at a place which I suppose has enormous aesthetic significance. It can, on the other hand, be richly endowed with exciting details, but they must be of such a kind that the recollection of them inevitably brings the main theme back to mind. In other words, the lecture must "compose" in the sense of having a pattern because it is this pattern which helps so much to impress it on one's memory.

READING

I feel so strongly about the wrongness of reading a lecture that my language may seem immoderate. I think it is a dreadful thing to do, something quite out of keeping with all that a lecture should mean. The spoken word and the written word are quite different arts. Though the reader can pause and go back to a passage he has found difficult, the listener cannot do so and may lose the thread of the argument. It is boring in a written account to be repetitious; it is right in a spoken account to put a key idea in several ways to make sure the audience has grasped the point. When a man writes out his lecture he inevitably writes it as if it were to be read, not heard. The ideas follow each other too fast. It is, of course, far easier for the lecturer to read than for him to "think on his feet" by constructing his sentences on the spot, because he can frame his sentences at his leisure. I realize that many lecturers read their material from a feeling of modesty, thinking they will give a poor rendering if they have no script. While appreciating their reluctance, I am sure they are wrong. I feel that to collect an audience and then read one's material is like inviting a friend to go for a walk and asking him not to mind if you go alongside him in your car. It is easy for the lecturer to deliver well-considered rounded phrases, but the audience has to follow and to think. If someone says, "I dare not talk. I must write it out," I am tempted to ask, "Then why lecture? Why not send a written account to your friends and let them read it comfortably at home, instead of dragging them all out to a lecture hall to listen to your reading the very same thing?"

We come back, it seems to me, to the essential feature of a lecture which justifies bringing the lecturer and his audience together. It is the emotional contact between lecturer and audience. If a lecturer has to find his words as he speaks, he will be automatically restrained from going too fast because he is thinking along with his audience. Every lecturer knows the trick of watching a few sympathetic faces in the audience and of judging (by noting their response) whether he has been successful in making his points or whether he must put things another way. A lecturer who reads is earthbound to his script, but the lecturer who talks can enjoy a wonderful feeling of being airborne and in complete accord with his audience. It is the greatest reward of lecturing.

Just as the troops used to say "The worst billet is better than the best bivouac," so one is tempted to say in a similarly approximate way "The worst spoken lecture is better than the best read one." But there are exceptions to all rules. Some very fine lecturers read their lectures, and I have tried to analyze the peculiar quality which makes their performance possible. I think they are the people who so refine and weigh every word and sentence that their beautiful prose almost becomes poetry—it is like a poet reading his verse. Eddington read his lectures marvelously, and on the arts side I have heard most moving read lectures delivered with great dramatic effect. But I think one ought not to venture to read a lecture unless one has these considerable poetic gifts.

THE FIRST TEN MINUTES

A lecture is made or marred in the first 10 minutes. This is the time to establish the foundations, to remind the audience of things they half know already, and to define terms that will be used. Again this seems obvious, but I have listened to so much splendid material lost to the audience because the lecturer failed to realize that it did not know what he was talking about, whereas, if the precious first 10 minutes had been spent on preparation, he would have carried his listeners with him for the rest of the talk.

SLIDES

Lecturers love slides, and in a game of associations the word "lecture" would almost always evoke the reply "slide." But I think we ought to apply to slides the same test, "What will the audience remember?" Some information can only be conveyed as slides, photographs, or records of actual events, such as the movement of a recording instrument, for instance, a seismograph. But slides of graphs or tables of figures are in general out of place in a lecture, or, at any rate, should be used most sparingly, just because the audience has not time to absorb them. If the lecturer wishes to illustrate a point with a graph, it is much better to draw it, or perhaps clamp the component parts on a magnetic board or employ some device of that kind. I remember well the first time I was impressed by this latter device, during a lecture on airflow through turbine blades. The lecturer altered the angle of incidence and the air arrows by shifting the parts on the board. It was far better than a series of slides. It is again a question of tempo—the audience can follow at about the rate one can draw; one is forced to be simple, and the slight expertise of the drawing holds attention. One must constantly think of what will be retained in the audience's memory, not of what can be crammed into the lecture.

EXPERIMENTS

Faraday had much to say about experiments that was very wise. The best experiments are simple and on a large scale, and their workings are obvious to the audience. The worst experiment is the one in which something happens inside a box, and the audience is told that if a pointer moves the lecturer has very cleverly produced a marvelous effect. Audiences love simple experiments and, strangely enough, it is often the advanced scientist who is most delighted by them. There are tricks too about demonstration. The wrong way is to do the experiment, ask the audience if they noticed this or that, and then explain what this or that meant. The right way is to start by explaining the significance of the effect you are aiming at producing, tell the audience what to look for, and then, after a pause to make sure you have their attention, to bring it off. These tricks are important because they are all part of fixing your message in the minds of the audience; they have the humble but necessary function of the hypo in fixing a photographic exposure.

THE AROUSING OF INTEREST

Here a most important principle comes in which I think of as the "detective story" principle. It is a matter of order. How dull a detective story would be if the writer told you who did it in the first chapter and then gave you the clues. Yet how many lectures do exactly this. One wishes to give the audience the esthetic pleasure of seeing how puzzling phenomena become crystal clear when one has the clue and thinks about them in the right way. So make sure the audience is first puzzled. A friend of mine, a barrister, told me that, when presenting a case to a judge, if he could appear to be fumbling toward a solution and could entice the judge to say "But, Mr. X, isn't the point you are trying to make this or that?" he had as good as won the case. One wants to get the audience into this frame of mind, when they are coaxed to guess for themselves what the answer is. Again I fear I am saying the trite and obvious, but I can assure you I have often sat and groaned at hearing a lecturer murder the most exciting story just by putting things in the wrong order.

We all know the tendency to go to sleep in lectures; how often have I felt ashamed at doing so myself. Though the best lecturer can never entirely escape from producing this effect, there is much that can be done to minimize it. A continuous even delivery is fatal. There is something hypnotic about it which induces sleep (this is another reason why it is so bad to read). Pauses and changes of tempo are essential. Above all, jokes have a marked and enduring effect. The science lecturer is of course greatly helped by his experiments and demonstrations which make useful breaks.

TIMING

Some try to get the timing of a lecture right by, as they say, "running over it beforehand" and seeing how long it takes. I am doubtful of the usefulness of this exercise when applied to the lecture as a whole. I prefer to divide it into some half dozen portions, and allocate about 10 minutes to each, marking this timing in the margin of my rough notes. One can sometimes fall into a dreadful trap with a subject in which one is a specialist. One thinks "that point will only take a minute or so to explain" and realizes to one's horror in the actual lecture that, having to start from scratch, it takes ten times as long. Of course the way in which each 10-minute section is to be put has to be carefully thought out and its timing roughly estimated. The advantage of dividing the time up in this way is that the pace can be adjusted during the lecture when it is clear that it is going to be too long or (rarely) too short. If time is running short, the part to shorten is the middle where it will be little noticed. The beginning or the end must not be hurried. It is rather like fitting a patterned carpet in a room which is too small for it. If this heroic measure must be adopted, it is much better to cut a strip from the middle of the pattern rather than to cut off an edge. An hour is as much as an audience can stand, and it is most unfortunate when a lecturer has to race through his material at the end and even then runs over the hour. . . .

In conclusion, I hope you will realize that the last thing I want is to seem to lay down the law about lecturing. I have spoken so feelingly about the pitfalls because I have so often fallen into them myself. One has to be constantly watchful if they are to be avoided, and even then one does not escape. It is most dangerous to be complacent about a lecture, to think that it will be all right because one knows the stuff and has given a similar talk elsewhere. Every lecture must be approached as if it were a new problem. No pains are too great in the attempt to make a talk a success, and I believe that, given the right treatment, any subject can be made fascinating to any audience.

TEAM TEACHING—THEME
AND VARIATIONS

Ira J. Singer *

The term team teaching *covers a multitude of practices, none of them especially new or startling, although they have not always received the attention that was their due. The following excerpt discusses several of*

* From Ira J. Singer, "What Team Teaching Really Is," in David W. Beggs, editor, *Team Teaching: Bold New Venture Series* (Indianapolis, Ind.: Indiana University Press, 1964), pp. 16–22. Reprinted by permission of the publisher.

the practices and describes how they operate. Basically, however, all team-teaching plans are methods of school organization that utilize combinations of large classes, small classes, individual study, and/or specialized classes. The strategies and tactics used in the large groups, small groups, individual study, and specialized classes are much the same as those in other classes of the same type with the same goals would be. Therefore, strategies and tactics to be used in team teaching need not be discussed further here.

Most team-teaching schemes currently advocated consist of a group of teachers working together to instruct a combination of large and small groups. Probably this type of team teaching is merely a step to a more sophisticated type of individual instruction. Large-group instruction is not really efficient when other means of presenting lessons are available, because hardly ever are all the pupils in the large group ready for the large-group presentation at the same time. In the future, modern technology can replace the large-group aspect of team teaching. Thus, we see the beginnings of a possible man-machine system developing.

THEME

Despite the many interpretations of the phrase "team teaching," and the numerous acts committed under its name, a basic definition is possible—though it is as flexible as the practice itself.

Team teaching may be defined as *an arrangement whereby two or more teachers, with or without teacher aids, cooperatively plan, instruct and evaluate one or more class groups in an appropriate instructional space and given length of time, so as to take advantage of the special competencies of the team members.*

Though this broad definition does not begin to tell the tale of the many variations of team teaching, it does suggest several major factors basic to any team plan:

cooperative planning, instruction and evaluation

student grouping for special purposes (large group instruction, small group discussion, independent study)

flexible daily schedule

use of teacher aides

recognition and utilization of individual teacher talents

use of space and media appropriate to the purpose and content of instruction.

VARIATIONS

Although few plans are exactly alike, three patterns are emerging from activity across the country. These patterns might be termed the single-discipline team, the interdisciplinary team and the school-within-school team.

Single-discipline team. The single-discipline team usually consists of two or three teachers from the same department, teaming together to instruct a common set of students. Teaching periods may be scheduled side by side or consecutively.

For example, the teachers of two tenth-grade social studies classes may team during the first period of each day so that each teacher can instruct that phase of the course which he can best handle. This arrangement exposes a teacher's specific talents to twice as many students as in the conventional schedule (Tables 1 and 2). Such a team may be organized to permit a new teacher to work with a veteran teacher, providing a built-in service program. With an instructional assistant, a clerical aide and additional planning time, the team members can practice continuous curriculum planning and revision based on the needs of their students as well as their own assets and abilities. To further the activities of this team, community resource specialists, outstanding films, self-instruction programs and other essential technological learning tools can be brought into the pattern.

Although this type of team is most often restricted to a single forty-five or fifty-minute period, alternate possibilities do exist for providing large group—

TABLE 1. *Conventional Schedule*

TIME	MONDAY	TUESDAY	WEDNESDAY	THURSDAY	FRIDAY
8:00- 8:50	Hist. 10A Hist. 10B	Hist. 10A Hist. 10B	Hist. 10A Hist. 10B	Hist. 10A Hist. 10B	Hist. 10A Hist. 10B

TABLE 2. *Single-Discipline Team Schedule*

TIME	MONDAY	TUESDAY	WEDNESDAY	THURSDAY	FRIDAY
8:00- 8:50	History 10AB (LG)	History 10AB1* (SG) History 10AB2 (SG) History 10AB3 (SG)	History 10AB (LG)	History 10AB1* (SG) History 10AB2 (SG) History 10AB3 (SG)	History 10AB (IS) Project work in library, laboratory, music room, art studio, etc.

(60 students, 2 teachers, 1 instruction assistant.)
* One History 10AB-SG can be supervised by an instruction assistant, student teacher or student leader. LG = large group, SG = small group, IS = independent study.

small group—independent study instruction during the fixed period. For example, one team member of a three-teacher team can present large group instruction to sixty students of a ninety-student group. While he lectures to the sixty, the remaining thirty may be broken into two groups of fifteen. Each group is then assigned to another team teacher or instructional assistant. The students may then be rotated through the special size groupings according to a formula set by the team (Table 3). Although this is not the most desirable system, it does afford some flexibility when team activities are restricted to the fixed daily period.

TABLE 3.   *Flexibility for Single-Discipline Within a Daily One-Period Schedule*

TIME	MONDAY	TUESDAY	WEDNESDAY	THURSDAY	FRIDAY
	Group A1, A2, A3 LG-60 students	Group B&C LG-30 students	Group A1, A2 LG-40 students	Group A3, B, C LG-50 students	Group A1 SG-20 students
	Group B SG-15 students	Group A IS-20 students	Group A3 IS-20 students	Group A1 SG-20 students	Group A3 SG-20 students
8:00-8:50	Group C SG-15 students	Group A2 SG-20 students	Group B SG-15 students	Group A2 SG-20 students	Group B IS-15 students
		Group A3 SG-20 students	Group C SG-15 students		Group C IS-15 students
					Group A2 IS-20 students

(90 students, 3 teachers, 1 instructional assistant.)

Occasionally, the single-discipline team may be organized on a block-of-time schedule. However, this arrangement is usually reserved for the interdisciplinary or school-within-school team.

The popularity of the single-discipline team has been due primarily to the ease with which it can be employed within a conventional schedule. Administrators and teachers have not found it too upsetting to combine classes into large groups or break them into smaller groups as long as the master schedule is not radically retooled. In Pittsford, New York, the schedule was revised so that each of the large group classes met twice weekly for double periods of ninety minutes. The large groups were then divided into seminar sections of eight to fourteen students meeting once a week. Seminar sections were ability-grouped with terminal students, excluded from the project, meeting in conventional classes.

In West Irondequoit, New York, a team of five teachers in eleventh-grade English (American literature) share the large group and small group work equally. A teacher conducts two large group lectures (one a repeat), fifteen small group seminar and five conventional classes each week. In addition, he has a double period each day for planning team activities.

Interdisciplinary Block of Time Team. The interdisciplinary block of time team consists of teachers from different disciplines given a common block of time to use as the team sees fit for the instruction of a common set of students in classes of flexible size.

For example, an administrator may assign a two-period block of time to a social studies/English team; a three-period block of time to a social studies/English/science team, etc. Once the block is assigned, the team assumes the major responsibility for scheduling large group, small group and independent study activities within the block (Table 4).

TABLE 4.   *Interdisciplinary Block of Time Team*

TIME	MONDAY	TUESDAY	WEDNESDAY	THURSDAY	FRIDAY
8:00 9:00	Two English teachers team with 2 history teachers to teach 120 students for a 120-minute block of time scheduled as the team desires for LG, SG, IS situations.				
10:00	Team Planning				

(120 students, 4 teachers, 1 aide.)

This type of schedule permits the teacher to reduce such undesirable practices as padding or cutting lessons in order to meet a static bell schedule. In the illustration, the 120-minute block may be treated as a weekly or daily figure. The team may prefer to schedule a weekly 600-minute block (120×5) rather than the daily 120-minute block. They may set certain goals for the week and assign chunks of time for large group, small group and independent study. They may look at the block as a monthly interval and devote entire weeks to one type of activity or another. Whether daily, weekly or monthly, the team can divide the block into modules of fifteen or twenty minutes and fit the various large group, small group and independent study activities into multiples of these modules.

In Racine, Wisconsin, the junior high school established a team teaching system under an English-social studies block organization. Students attended double periods of English and social studies in three sections during the same period in the morning and again in the afternoon. A seventh-grade team of three teachers handled the morning and afternoon blocks of ninety students per block. They then planned the curriculum, schedule, teacher assignment and evaluation procedure cooperatively. The team also utilized a team leader and an instructional secretary serving both morning and afternoon teams.

At Upland High School in Upland, California, the team project operates within the regular school schedule, with all team classes meeting during the first four periods in the morning. However, the team teachers are free to use modules of time in accordance with their instructional needs, shifting from regular academic class sessions to large group instruction. They may team in pairs or assume tutorial roles for independent study. They may group their classes to be tested, group-counseled or for community resource specialist lectures, or they may shift back to small units for individual counseling. All team teachers meet for planning purposes during the fifth period.

School-Within-School Team. The school-within-school team consists of teachers from all disciplines, responsible for the instruction of the same body of students over an extended period of time, usually two to four years. Flexibility in class size and schedule is maintained in this pattern.

The primary purpose of this type of team is to encourage a closer relationship between teacher and student within any and all disciplines. In a large school, the loss of identity suffered by some students might be compensated by placing them in a smaller "division" of the larger school. This "division" may be called a house plan, a form, a school or some similar name. By using the shifting patterns of the team arrangement, teachers observe the behavior and performance of their students in various learning situations during this extended period of time. In the small school, this kind of team attempts to approach the problem of treating individual differences of students in a realistic and continuous manner. Such teams have encouraged members of the various "division" faculties to exchange assignments and have permitted students to take instruction in other "divisions" from time to time in order to introduce greater variety into the pattern.

The Claremont Graduate School in Claremont, California, has sponsored experimentation with the small, integrated school-within-school teaching team. The teams participating in this project usually consist of a group of five to six teachers given a small body of about 150 students for a period of time longer than one or two semesters. Students attend classes of shifting size and schedule (usually block or modular). Teacher strengths are magnified by schedules compiled by the team under the direction of a team leader. Team members are given three to five periods per week to meet for team planning conferences during the school day. The counseling and guidance functions are integral parts of the team operation.

Hierarchical Considerations. Within these three basic types of teaching teams, certain hierarchical differences may be noted. In San Diego, California, groups of 100 met for large group instruction under the experienced teacher in charge; for small group discussions under a certificated teacher (with less experience) and assistant teachers, all of whom were helped by clerk-aides who handled the clerical chores. A number of the assistant teachers were student trainees from the San Diego State Teachers College on a five-year training program.

In Melbourne, Florida, a group of eighty-four students was given algebra instruction by a team consisting of a master teacher, assistant teacher, general aide and student aide. The first two were full-time, qualified mathematics teachers sharing the large group and independent tutoring responsibilities. Small group discussion occurred in groups of seven students conducted by a workshop-trained student leader. The general aide performed the paper grading, recording, mimeographing and other clerical duties. This arrangement worked particularly well in the non-graded, phased education program at Melbourne High School.

In Evanston, Illinois, as part of the English 3 Project, a team of seven teachers divided the work load as follows:

1. Three teachers were responsible for the large group instruction and three of the small class sections.

2. One teacher was responsible for large group instruction and two small class sections.

3. One teacher was responsible for two small class sections.

4. Two teachers were each responsible for one small class section.

Special attention was paid to combining beginning teachers with veterans and to capitalizing on special teacher talents in working with large or small groups. In addition to the teaching staff, one part-time secretary-clerk took attendance in the large group room, mimeographed materials and gave make-up tests. An art consultant prepared visual materials.

TELEVISION TEACHING TEAM RESPONSIBILITIES

Anaheim Public Schools *

Instructional television is an example of a team approach to teaching. The studio teacher prepares and presents the large-group lesson that the classroom teacher follows up. In his presentation, the teacher normally utilizes the large-group techniques of the lecture, bolstered by visual aids.

* From *Instructional T.V. Guide,* James D. Brier, editor (Anaheim, Calif.: Anaheim City School District, 1961), pp. 16–21. Reprinted by permission of James D. Brier for the Anaheim City School District.

The role and duties of the studio and classroom teachers on such a team are well spelled out in the following excerpt from the Anaheim City School District's Instructional T.V. Guide. *Note especially the classroom teacher's responsibility to prepare for the telecast, follow up the telecast, and in other ways help the pupils to use the instructional television well.*

ANALYZING TEAM RESPONSIBILITIES

The studio teacher provides a common learning experience through the telelesson. The responsibility of the classroom teacher is to individualize the telelesson experience and extend the learning opportunities related to the purpose of the lesson.

Joint Responsibilities

Accept the "team approach" concept of teaching.
Plan scope, content, and sequence of curriculum.
Improve instruction through constructive criticism of each other.
Share ideas and materials.
Plan for inter-visitation for the purpose of better understanding of their mutual and individual problems.

Responsibilities of the Classroom Teacher

Physical Climate of the Classroom

Temperature and ventilation
Lighting (best placement of television set)
Tuning of set (check glare on sets from pupils' eye level). The set should be left on until telelessons are completed for the day.
Elimination of distractions
Efficient distribution of materials
Seating arrangements
Orderly movement of groups to and from the classroom, and within the classroom
Definite procedures for such organizational necessities as taking attendance, distribution of papers, leaving the room, sharpening pencils, etc.

Meeting Individual Needs

Provide proper placement of pupils with physical problems.
Be aware of the ability range within the classroom and provide for in the "pre" and "post" lesson experiences.
Clarify and adopt assignments to extend and enrich the learning of each individual within the group.

Before the Telelesson

Evaluate learning activities which pupils are developing.

Thoroughly read and study telelesson guide sheets for each lesson. Know the scope and sequence of each unit and how each telelesson is correlated with scope and sequence guide.

Prepare and have available all materials, texts, etc., for pre-telelesson preparation and related teaching activities in advance.

Create a readiness for learning; discuss lesson and its purpose, what pupils may expect, what they will learn. Introduce new vocabulary.

Organize the classroom so that distribution of materials to be used during telelesson is made before the lesson; television sets are turned on and adjusted, drapes pulled, pupils seated properly, and all materials other than those needed during the lesson are out of the way to avoid distraction.

Watch the time and schedule closely so that the pre-lesson activities are presented thoroughly.

Develop a method in classroom for handling questions asked by the studio teacher.

During the Telelesson

Help pupils who need individual help during a work-type lesson.

Take notes. (Teacher's notes can be used to emphasize main points of the lesson and as a guide for discussion following the lesson.)

List vocabulary for further definition and discussion.

Observe pupil reaction throughout lesson; make notes of any reactions valuable to the studio teacher. Handle behavior problems immediately.

Move about the room to see that pupils understand and are using materials properly.

Give pupils additional directions when necessary during the telelesson.

Become enthusiastic—answer questions asked by the studio teacher during the presentation—if the teacher is enthused and participates, the pupils understand that they are a part of the lesson and should respond to the studio teacher.

Encourage "controlled" overt responses to ideas and questions raised during a lesson. The studio teacher indicates by the way questions and ideas are presented, the type of response that is expected of pupils observing. (He may say, "What famous man, that we have heard about before, died at the Alamo?" He may say, "Can you *think* of other types of plants that adapt to their environment in a different way?" The first question should be answered audibly by pupils in the classroom with the teacher guiding and encouraging the response. The second question requires a covert response from each pupil. which the classroom teacher may wish to bring up after the telecast for further discussion.) Types of response that detract from the intimacy of the studio teacher-pupil relationship should be avoided. (The studio teacher might state, "Let's *think* about why the pioneers went west." The classroom teacher responds, "Mary, what do you think?" Mary may or may not give a correct response. The teacher in the studio cannot anticipate the timing for an oral response to this type of question and the attention and rapport existing between studio teacher and pupil is divided during the discussion in the classroom.) *Participation is an important factor in learning;* it must be developed, encouraged, and controlled by both studio and classroom teacher working together during the telecast.

After the Telelesson

Check pupils' understanding of concepts presented by studio teacher. Stress areas of the telelesson that need re-emphasizing.

Re-teach in area where there is lack of understanding in relation to ability levels.

Check to see that new vocabulary is understood.

Organize class into established groups to summarize lesson and to coordinate and carry out further learning activities.

Use suggested related classroom instruction activities for group work extended over a period of time. Correlate the activities from lesson to lesson so that continuity is established.

Guide discussion according to concepts and understandings which pupils should gain from the telelesson.

Provide experiences to enable the pupil to more fully understand and apply concepts presented.

Provide enrichment activities to meet the special needs and interests of pupils.

Encourage pupil reports of supplementary activities such as experiments, projects, reading reports that grow out of telelessons. Pupil participation is essential to effective education. Participation by using ideas in assignments, projects, discussion and research stimulate active responses so important to good education.

Check pupil's notebooks to assure their maximum value. Folders should be provided for storage of related materials.

Encourage the method of having pupil rise and face the group when speaking.

Guidance, Encouragement, and Assistance to the Studio Teacher

Complete and send to studio teacher telelesson reaction sheets and evaluation reports.

Give constructive criticism at meetings, personal conferences, or by phone —let studio teacher know *what most interests pupils—what teaching techniques "pay-off" in learning.*

Give recommendations for future lessons.

Share materials and projects developed by teacher and pupils.

Professional Support

Give support to the television project in contacts with pupils, parents, teachers and general public.

Give professional support to the efforts of the studio teacher.

RESPONSIBILITIES OF THE STUDIO TEACHER

Teaches Carefully Prepared Telelesson

Well planned
Rich in visuals
Correctly paced
Stimulating and challenging

Prepares Telelesson Guides and Studio Scripts

Professional Support

Be receptive to ideas presented by classroom teachers.
Give support to the efforts of the classroom teacher.
Give support to television project in contacts with parents, teachers, and general public.
Visit classrooms as often as possible.

HELPING PUPILS USE INSTRUCTIONAL TELEVISION

Pupils need to know how to do the following:

Listen attentively and shut out distracting sights and sounds.
Follow sequence of events.
    Outline.
    Take notes and key words (fifth and sixth grade level).
Listen for details.
Interpret motives.
    Note or detect the controversial.
Identify word usage.
    Sounds, pictures, etc.
Maintain emotional control.
See and hear simultaneously.
Follow directions.
Make a conscious effort to select and remember items that will be of special use.
Develop attentive, cooperative and courteous attitudes toward what others say.
Ask relevant questions and avoid repetition.
Form an intelligent opinion from what has been seen and heard.
Interpret dramatization and other creative experiences.
Feel that individual listening, thinking and learning are part of the participation.

Chapter I I

STRATEGIES AND TACTICS
DESIGNED TO PROVIDE FOR
INDIVIDUAL DIFFERENCES

L IKE strategies that help pupils learn skill in thinking, strategies that provide for individual differences in pupils have been sadly neglected in schools. A large number of the strategies are administrative strategies—homogeneous grouping; fast, slow, and medium tracks; acceleration; ungraded classes; and so on. These strategies may ease the problem of individual differences, but they do not solve it. Even in the most homogeneously grouped class there are many, many differences. In order to meet these differences, teachers must individualize their work, differentiate their assignments, and use small-group procedures. Some of these techniques are explained in other chapters—individualized reading techniques in Chapter 9 and the selections on unit teaching in Chapter 7, for instance.

Special consideration has been given to the teaching of gifted, slow, and disadvantaged pupils. In reading these selections, one should remember that there are great differences among such pupils. The generalizations made about slow pupils as a group may not apply to a particular individual. It is especially important to remember this fact when dealing with the disadvantaged—who may vary in intellect and standards all the way from the very highest to the very lowest. These pupils are all too often branded by teachers who do not recognize their potentials. Gifted pupils, too, vary in many ways. In the Douglass selection the author points out several types of gifted pupils. In general, however, gifted pupils respond well to the types of strategies featuring inductive learning, problem solving, research, discussion, and independent study. Teachers seeking ideas for strategies to use with gifted pupils should consult the selections dealing with those techniques (especially Chapter 8) as well as the selections presented here.

GROUPING FOR INSTRUCTION: SOME PERSPECTIVES

O. L. Davis, Jr.*

In this article, Davis describes the pros and cons of ability grouping and tracking in an objective, scholarly fashion that should leave the reader with a relatively clear picture of the problem and the status of the educator's attempts to solve it. The moral of the article seems to be that ability grouping can be an aid or a hindrance. The critical question involves how one uses it in the schools. Administrative devices can make teaching harder or easier; but it is the methods the teachers use (and the way they use them) that make the real differences in how the school affects pupils. In the opinion of the editor of this book, ability grouping and tracking fail, when they fail, because teachers and principals do not seem to be sophisticated enough to make the best use of them. Perhaps, if teachers use other strategies, they can avoid the pitfalls that come with ability-grouping schemes.

I

Grouping is a much discussed topic in present-day American education. Recent clamor to improve the quality of American schooling has increased greatly the attention given to alternative patterns of grouping for instruction. National concern for the academically talented pupil, particularly, has precipitated widespread questioning of accepted grouping practices. Many educators view these questions as ones satisfactorily solved in the 1920's and 1930's. Yet, the issues have been raised again: Why group? Who should learn with whom?

Essentially, grouping is the organization of classes to facilitate learning. It is the process by which boys and girls are organized into manageable classes for instruction. This administrative problem is not to be treated carelessly. As educators have dealt with this problem, a variety of grouping procedures have been developed.

Administratively, when enough pupils are available for only one section of a grade or course, grouping becomes no problem. The teacher simply writes the names of the pupils in his register.

In small schools and in many larger schools, however, when several sections of a course or grade are warranted, two general procedures are used to assign

* From *The Educational Forum*, Vol. 24 (January 1960), pp. 209–216. Used by permission of Kappa Delta Pi, An Honor Society in Education, owners of the copyright.

pupils to classes. The principal or the teachers concerned or some combination of school personnel may take the list of eligible registered pupils, draw names, and assign children to the various sections. This procedure of chance or random assignment might be described as the "lottery" method of grouping. Another widely used procedure, the "cafeteria" method, accepts pupils to sections on a basis of first come, first served.

Generally, in comprising instructional groups in the elementary school, consideration is given the educational achievement of the pupil, but other factors important to successful learning and teaching are reviewed before assigning him to a particular class. Some of the factors considered are the pupil's chronological and mental ages, physical development, special interests, and behavior and emotional problems. Securing satisfactory pupil-teacher relationships is also an important element considered in most grouping plans.

Over the years, such grouping methods have been designated "heterogeneous." Such a term sets them apart from other sets of procedures known as "homogeneous," which uses a single criterion, rather than many by which to group children.

In reality, much grouping is based on a single variable. In the examples described above, the variable was the course offering itself, the pupil's last name, or time of arrival at registration. The most commonly used variable is the grade level of the pupil. His age is another important criterion. Physical education and some music offerings limit participation on the basis of sex. Pupil interest, pupil purpose, career goals of pupils, parental desires, and teacher popularity are other recognized single variables in organizing classes. But these single variables are not adequate as "the best way" to organize classes.

Those who favor homogeneous grouping almost universally favor a criterion of ability or achievement. Scores on intelligence tests and aptitude tests are commonly used to group students by ability. Pupils with IQ 110 and above go in one section, with IQ between 90–110, in another section, and with IQ below 90 in a third group. Students with algebra aptitude scores of 85th percentile or better are assigned to one group, of 70th–85th percentile to another group, below 70th percentile to another.

In recent years, few elementary school children have been grouped according to ability. Some high school students have been grouped by ability, either deliberately or by the nature of the subject offering. Assignment to high school English classes on the basis of ability probably has been practiced more frequently than in other generally required courses. A kind of natural grouping by interest and ability—probably in relation to college requirements and future career plans—has taken place in the election of such courses as advanced high school mathematics, science, and foreign language courses. Similar groupings have occurred in business, agriculture, and industrial courses. Plans for grouping for the education of gifted pupils, as well as other children with exceptional needs, is most frequently done on criteria of intellectual ability or achievement levels in subject fields (11).

Ability grouping on the basis of an IQ has led to the development of several administrative procedures, the most common and most currently publicized of which are designated "tracks" or "rails." Assignment to various "tracks" is made by employing various cut-off points in the IQ range. Schools using tracking arrangements usually employ three or more "rails" but some have only two. Interestingly enough, most "tracks" not only refer to the method of constituting instructional groups, but also to curricular programs. Thus, the high IQ group goes through a college preparatory track or major. The middle-range IQ group enrolls for a "general" course. The below-middle, sometimes designated "S" for "slow" or "significantly below grade level," are assigned to vocational courses. These programs are sometimes organized as honors, general, and remedial, and assignment to a "track" or "major" is generally a horizontal arrangement. That is, the pupil is expected to take all or most of his courses at the level of his track. For example, an honors student takes all honors courses.

Another tracking arrangement calls for grouping by aptitude, or achievement, and sometimes by IQ. Under such plans, a student might be placed in "honors" music and English classes, "general" geometry and history sections, and a "remedial" physical education course. Such plans are premised not on general ability but on aptitude of achievement, or ability in the specific fields. Most tracking programs are found in secondary schools, but some are being introduced into elementary divisions despite bitter opposition by many professional educators.

However simply designed and however precise and "clean" by measurement and administrative standards, grouping by ability, achievement, and aptitude has its problems. Underachievement, aspiring parents, high motivation, sincere interest, ambition, desire to attend college and no desire to attend college are but a few of the problems which daily perplex teachers and frustrate school systems.

When sufficiently impressed with the problems of teaching and learning which ability grouping cannot affect, or affects little, some educators use an eclectic approach to grouping. Some classes are organized on the basis of a student's possibility to succeed (ability), some according to his own desire to succeed (interest), and some according to his role as a person (in such cases, the simple regression to the mean, be it social learning, sex, age, grade or citizenship). One eclectic grouping plan uses an elaborate formula which involves the use of many factors to determine an "organismic" age.

Descriptions of grouping procedures tend to be categorical. Yet, few operational plans exist that are inflexible. Dealing with human beings, most plans provide a tolerance factor for individual variation from the grouping criterion. Pupils may transfer or be transferred from one group, class, or section to another on the basis of established guidelines. Social compatability, schedule conflicts, parental concern, unsatisfactory performance, underachievement, demonstrated ability, and change in vocational objective are a few of the many reasons accepted for altering original groupings in individual cases. While these reasons are sometimes compelling reasons for changing groupings, provision of flexibility in a plan is justified not only on psychological grounds and administrative feasibility, but also on the principle of democracy. Freedom of choice, within limits, is considered by those advocating ability grouping to be a virtue as do those who oppose class grouping by ability.

It is on the issue of "democracy" that much of the controversy about grouping centers. Advocates of differing grouping plans insist that their proposals are consistent with the democratic faith. The point at issue is really the definition and interpretation of our society's philosophy. In an important respect, philosophy determines school practices. Certainly, how one views the role of the school and the goals of instruction is, in essence, a philosophical matter. With respect to grouping, if acquisition of subject matter is the primary goal of the school, then plans to group pupils to achieve this objective probably will be premised on consideration of ability, past achievement, and aptitude. If other goals, such as the development of social, civic, and emotional growth, are held important, other forms of grouping may be practiced. The pattern of a school's organization is intimately related to the goals held for the education of its pupils.

None of these goals for grouping is exclusively "democratic," however; each is developed from different interpretations of our basic philosophic position. Thus, usage of terms like "undemocratic," "education of an elite," "second class citizen," and "intellectual segregation" is an effective procedure to evade thoughtful consideration of educational goals.

Philosophical considerations are seldom the sole determinants of educational objectives. Research in human growth and development has documented some important principles which are useful in formulating goals. Human beings are unique. They develop and learn at different rates, for different purposes, and differently under different conditions. Their uniqueness is expressed in many ways, in ability, development of ability, health, stamina, speed, reaction time, interest, background, emotional stability, anxiety, self-concept, and in many other factors. Development is continuous, but uneven. Growth in one area may be fast, in another, slow. Efforts to devise grouping procedures have been guided by principles of psychological development and philosophical objectives.

II

Some grouping procedure has been used by a teacher every time several children have assembled in a school to learn. By definition, a lad who is being tutored cannot be grouped. But when a teacher desires to teach a number of children on the same occasion, some measure must be taken to make possible instruction appropriate to each individual. The student of 100 years ago— and in some places, a much shorter time ago than that—progressed through a series of books in an ungraded school. In the attempt to manage many students and to systematize instruction in an orderly, sequential fashion, graded schools were established. Not only the school was graded, books were graded, lessons were graded, materials were graded, and teachers were graded. Grade standards were established and the system was put into operation. The Quincy Grammar School in Boston heralded this pattern of organization in 1848. By the beginning of the Civil War, most cities employed it. Since 1870, this school organizational pattern has changed little.

The tradition from great flexibility to a rigidly graded structure had serious problems. Wholesale retardation was the answer of many schools to variability in children. The criterion for grouping for instruction was "grade level," but the massive retardation of learners was shocking. Sensitive schoolmen studied the situation. "Repeating a grade" usually did not help increase a student's mastery of subject matter as much as being promoted would have. "Repeating" did not decrease the variables with which a teacher had to deal; it increased them. Ability grouping through massive retardation was largely discredited by the profession early in the twentieth century. In attempts to break down the lock step of grades, schoolmen turned their attention to individualizing instruction through a modification of the graded structure. As early as 1868, the St. Louis Plan called for reclassifying students every six weeks. The Cambridge Plan, begun in 1893, and the Portland Plan, abandoned in 1915, provided that the brighter pupils could transit the double-mark system in seven years rather than the nine years required for the slower pupils. North Denver, Batavia, and Santa Barbara had well-publicized plans which recognized pupil variation and made some provisions for them within the graded system. Laboratory Plans were introduced later. The Winnetka Plan under Carleton Washburn and the Dalton Plan under Helen Parkhurst were attempts to differentiate "common essentials" and "group and creative" subjects and to encourage pupils to move through the system at their own rate. A recent development in breaking down the rigidity of the graded system is the "nongraded school," "ungraded school," or "continuous progress" plans in elementary schools (6).

The graded system, therefore, made grouping by grade level a primary criterion. The large-scale "individualization plans" having proved inadequate, schoolmen desired other procedures to organize classes for individualized instruction.

Ability grouping was seized as the promise to set the system right. The criterion of ability was the IQ or the M.A. Scientific Education, with its ecoutrement of tests and measurement, held the keys to salvation. The Detroit Plan was begun in 1919 and ABC and XYZ groups appeared soon after across the nation. The solution of the problem of classroom grouping was so simple! Examine the "normal curve," establish cutoff points, and the students were grouped. The rush toward "intellectual ghettos," as some opponents labeled ability-grouping procedures, was itself put to the test of educational research. Eliminating the speculative and emotional chaff from the literature, it is interesting to review the studies to see what the research says.

Most of the research on grouping was conducted before 1936. Much of it was of the comparative type; that is, it contrasted the relative effectiveness of ability grouping generally tabbed as "homogeneous," with "heterogeneous" grouping. Evidence was accumulated, also, to determine the extent variability in achievement is reduced by ability grouping.

Available evidence indicates that group variability is reduced little through ability grouping even when the grouping criterion is general intelligence (3; 15, p. 8–9). Certainly when a number of human characteristics are considered, student variation is great in all groups. Williams wrote recently that ". . . if we have sixty independent measurements, the chance that any individual will be in the median 50 per cent in all is about one in one quintillion" (16, p. 146). When the students are classified into three ability groups, there is a reduction of variability of less than 20 per cent. Pupil variation from subject to subject is great and classification by IQ does not affect perceptibly reduction in achievement variation (1; 2; 8; 9). Segregating the bright and slow learners from the average group on the basis of general intelligence does not reduce materially the "teachable range" (12). Serious questions, too, have been raised about the validity of intelligence tests, on both psychological and sociological bases.

Summarizing the research in 1936, Cornell stated:

The results of ability grouping seem to depend less upon the fact of grouping itself than upon the philosophy behind the grouping, the accuracy with which grouping is made for the purposes intended, the differentiates in content, method, and speed, and the technique of the teacher, as well as upon more general environmental influences. Experimental studies have in general been too piecemeal to afford a true evaluation of results, but when attitudes, methods, and curricula are well adapted to further the adjustment of the school to the child, results, both objective and subjective, seem to be favorable to grouping (4, p. 304).

In a functioning and interacting group, pupils make greater gains in subject-matter mastery under ability grouping than under other grouping plans, provided that there is differentiation of the subject matter to be learned (5). Thus it is that individualization of the curriculum for the variability in any group contributes more significantly to academic progress than the criterion used to comprise the group. Research in the past 20 years has not seriously challenged these conclusions.

Slow-learning children seem to profit most from ability grouping procedures, gifted children least (15). Any advantage to the academically talented children, as with other groups, comes with curricular differentiation, including enrichment and/or acceleration. Sub-grouping within the classroom provides superior results to those obtained by teaching the class without sub-grouping (13).

The research, being inconclusive in some respects, does not demonstrate the superiority of ability grouping. Yet, at the present time, classification by general intelligence is advocated more strongly than at any time in the past quarter century. Pressure of conscience over failing adequately to differentiate instruction in an undifferentiated group seems to be overwhelming many in the teaching profession. Each child must be provided for—and grouping by ability is the straw which is eagerly clasped. The system remains unchallenged and the results of 50 years of research matter little as cumulative records are reshuffled and rapid sleights-of-hand are performed. Altering the marquee in this case may, or may not, mean a new show inside the house.

III

As the problem of grouping is faced critically, schoolmen must come to grips with several very elusive issues. Surely ability must be defined as a multiple characteristic and related to the specific learning situation. The abilities to read, to think in abstract numbers, to write, to participate in a group are not identical abilities.

A group is not a collection of individuals. Recent research in group dynamics offers exciting possibilities for classroom organization. In one sense, a group is an aggregate of persons who interact with one another, assisting and accepting help from one another, and working toward a mutually accepted goal. To group by purpose, by the goal established, seems a rational guide to the utilization of the creativity, intelligence, and other capacities of the individuals involved. In a class organized according to a shared goal, abilities will vary, as with all groups, but the diversities which exist are ones which promise rich learnings to all involved. Increasingly at the high school level, interest and specific ability should play an important role in group compositions (7; 10; 14). The group should be flexible and vary in size and duration according to the purpose for which it was constituted.

Attention to the process of grouping itself is less important than the type of instruction which is given to the group. However constituted, the result of instruction is increased diversity, increased unlikeness, not increased homogeneity. To teach each student in any class, comprised by ability grouping or by any other means, with the same method and with the same instructional materials is gross irresponsibility. The grouping plan can not mask ineffective teaching. Individualization of instruction is not insured simply by the regrouping of pupils.

Our democratic philosophy does not decree educational mediocrity. Equal opportunity is not identical educational environment, educational experience, not educational materials for all. Individual attention to the specific learning tasks, problems, and demands of each pupil who is a member of a group, however constituted, is a covenant kept with the democratic faith. Democracy does not demand that the future physicist, the future musician and the future salesman learn the same things, nor learn all of them together. Our philosophy does call for each person to learn to his capacity. Certainly, it is not educational mediocrity when future citizens of all levels of intelligence and society learn to live and work together for the perpetuation of our democracy.

Careless, indiscriminant assignment to class groups cannot be condoned any more than rigid placement according to general ability. Are there guides to careful organization of effective instructional groups? The teacher should know each pupil well enough to plan for his needs. Class size and pupil-teacher ratio are important considerations in this respect. General class assignments do not obviate the need for within-class groupings for more specific purposes. A good instructional environment, including satisfactory pupil-teacher relationships, should exist in each class. Instructional materials covering a range of difficulty and interest appropriate to the needs and tasks of the instructional group should be available. Groups must be flexible as to size, duration, and purpose. All pupils must not be held to the same requirements. Requirements must vary with the capacity of the pupil and the purpose of the study undertaken. The curriculum should be comprehensive enough to provide for meeting a wide range of aptitudes and interests and combinations of aptitudes and interests. Individual curriculum programs should be planned with and for each pupil, keeping constantly in mind his specific abilities, interests, and needs in relation to available learning opportunities.

Fundamental to coping with the problem of individualization of instruction is the recognition that grouping is not a method of teaching. Grouping, as an administrative device, may facilitate individualization; it cannot guarantee it. Quality teaching which incorporates methods appropriate to each carefully organized group is likely to result in the desired educational achievement for each individual.

BIBLIOGRAPHY

1. Marvin Y. Burr, A *Study of Homogeneous Grouping.* (Contributions to Education No. 457). New York: Teachers College, Columbia University, 1931.
2. Walter W. Cook, *Grouping and Promotion in the Elementary School.* Series on the Individualization of Instruction, Number 2. Minneapolis: University of Minnesota, 1941.
3. —— "The Gifted and the Retarded in Historical Perspective." *Phi Delta Kappan,* Vol. No. 6 (March, 1958), pp. 249–255.
4. Ethel L. Cornell, "Effects of Ability Grouping Determinable from Published Studies," in *The Grouping of Pupils,* 35th Yearbook of the National Society for the Study of Education. Bloomington, Ill.: Public School Publishing Co., 1936, pp. 289–304.
5. Warren W. Coxe, "Summary of Interpretations," in *The Grouping of Pupils,* 35th Yearbook of the National Society for the Study of Education. Bloomington, Ill.: Public School Publishing Co., 1936, pp. 305–315.
6. John I. Goodlad and Robert H. Anderson, *The Nongraded Elementary School,* New York: Harcourt, Brace & World, 1959.
7. May Seagoe Gowan, "Why Homogeneous Grouping," *California Journal of Secondary Education,* vol. 30, no. 1 (January 1955), p. 25.
8. A. D. Hollingshead, *An Evaluation of the Use of Certain Educational Mental Measurements for the Purpose of Classification* (Contributions to

Education No. 302). New York: Teachers College, Columbia University, 1928.

9. C. L. Hull, "Variability in Amount of Different Traits Possessed by the Individual," *Journal of Educational Psychology*, vol. 18 (February 1927), pp. 97–106.

10. Arnold L. Lazarus, "Grouping Based on H. S. Interest vs. General Ability: A Sention High School Teacher's Viewpoint," *California Journal of Secondary Education*, vol. 30, no. 1 (January 1955), pp. 38–41.

11. A. Harry Passow, Jane E. Beasley, and Deton J. Brooks, Jr., "Adapting the Curriculum to the Needs, Capacities, and Talents of Individual Students," *Review of Educational Research*, vol. 27, no. 3 (June 1957), pp. 277–286.

12. Arthur C. Ramey, "A New Look at Ability Grouping in the Junior High School," *California Journal of Secondary Education*, vol. 31, no. 5 (May 1956), pp. 289–291.

13. Eugene S. Spencer, *Intra-Class Grouping of Pupils for Instruction in Arithmetic in the Intermediate Grades of the Elementary School*, Ed.D. dissertation, University of Pittsburgh, 1958. Ann Arbor, Michigan: *Dissertation Abstracts*, vol. XIX, no. 7 (January 1959), p. 1682.

14. Philip E. Vernon, "Education and the Psychology of Individual Differences," *Harvard Educational Review*, vol. 28, no. 2 (Spring 1958), pp. 91–103.

15. J. Wayne Wrightstone, *Class Organization for Instruction*. Washington, D.C.: Department of Classroom Teachers and American Educational Research Association, NEA, 1957, pp. 8–9.

16. Roger J. Williams, "Individuality and Education," *Educational Leadership*, vol. XV, no. 3, (December 1957), pp. 144–148.

CLASSROOM GROUPING FOR EFFECTIVE LEARNING

Louise E. Hock *

The dividing of classes into small groups or committees is an excellent technique often used successfully in the elementary schools, but frequently neglected in secondary schools. Not only is grouping within the classroom an effective means of providing for individual differences, it is also an excellent way to encourage real pupil participation in classes.

* From *Educational Leadership*, Vol. 18 (April 1961), pp. 420–424. Reprinted with permission of the Association for Supervision and Curriculum Development and Louise E. Hock. Copyright © 1961 by the Association for Supervision and Curriculum Development.

Groups can be formed for many purposes. Buzz groups are excellent for getting things started, committees are good for carrying out projects, and so on. In any case, the use of small groups forces the teacher to turn over the carrying out of the learning activities to the pupils and so is a means of encouraging independent learning and thinking.

Would you like to temper Joe's aggressive enthusiasm with a growing sensitivity to others? Do you want to guide Ruth out of her shell? Have you some classroom routines that might well be entrusted to adolescents? Are you eager to meet more effectively the differences found in any class of students, whether grouped at random or by specific criteria? Are you concerned with the scope of information, understandings, attitudes, and appreciations that must somehow be dealt with in a school year of less than 200 days? If your reply to these questions is in the affirmative, then grouping within your classroom can provide one way of accomplishing each of your goals.

The question of grouping is a pervasive, continuing, and insistent one. It covers a multitude of practices and points of view. The issues involved must be explored whenever school people have to make decisions regarding the grouping of students into classes, the grouping of courses into various track-curricula, the grouping of young people into small schools within a large school unit. Throughout educational practice, students are being grouped and regrouped, classified and reclassified, categorized and recategorized.

Similarly, within effective classrooms, students are assembled and reassembled, sometimes as a total group of 30 or 35, sometimes into smaller groups of varying size, sometimes into teams of two or three. The particular focus of this article is on this flexible classroom grouping that makes for sound learning. It will deal with specific questions of the what, why, and how of small-group work.

WHAT ARE GROUPS?

Whether we plan for it or not, we have grouping within our classrooms. There are the social groups—the cliques that develop their own mysterious cement of togetherness; the homework-sharing groups, with profit and benefit to members of the brotherhood; the interest groups that range from the statisticians of the baseball season to the squealing idolaters of the current Fabian, Darin, or Nelson of the popular musical world.

Our adolescents turn to each other for purposes of their own—for social warmth, practical help, identification, assurance, and reassurance in their world of change and growth. Youngsters group naturally and we should use this propensity to group living, no matter how ephemeral and vacillating it may seem at times. When we utilize this need of human beings to be drawn to other human beings, when we channel this need in worthwhile educational directions, we are capitalizing on one more of our reservoir of sound resources in an effort to improve the learning situation.

What are these educational groups we can form and should form? There is the "buzz" group—of short duration and immediate purpose. With these quickly formed groups of five or six, we can provide opportunities for rapid sharing of homework assignments, for exchange of ideas and experiences, for formulation of problems and questions, for discussion of controversy and differences.

Then there are the "job" groups, of short- or long-term duration. Some students can constitute a materials committee, whose function is to locate and arrange for the use of appropriate recordings, films, tapes, filmstrips, and other instructional materials pertinent to a particular unit of study. Or there might be a bulletin-board committee, charged with the responsibility of maintaining attractive and informative displays of pictures, articles, original material relevant to any subject of study or interest to a given class. Current-events committees are another source of study and information for many classes in the social-studies, science, and language-arts fields.

A third type of grouping is represented by "work-study" committees, organized to facilitate deeper and broader exploration of various aspects of a problem or unit. These committees become involved with all the processes of sound research—planning, investigating, organizing, sharing, solving, and summarizing. A science class may have several committees researching the many peacetime uses of nuclear energy. Such a class will have a broader grasp of the role of nuclear energy in our daily lives and deeper insights into issues and implications than will a class that, with one eye and one voice, skims the surface of the brief account found in the standard text.

Buzz groups, job groups, study-work committees—these are only a few of the kinds and varieties of classroom grouping. They can all play an important part in facilitating learning and should be utilized at appropriate times and for appropriate purposes.

WHY SHOULD WE GROUP?

The reasons for small-group work within our classes are obvious and valid, but they cannot be reiterated often enough in this age of conformity.

First of all, we group in order to provide for the vast differences that exist among any aggregation of individuals. The great varieties of interests and purposes, the wide range of talents and skills, the important differences in ability and potential, in speed, depth, and nature of comprehension—all these distinctions necessitate the use of many varied materials and resources as well as classroom procedures that provide opportunities for each student to move as rapidly as possible in reaching his own potential. And these great differences exist, regardless of any effort to implement ability grouping. For while students can be assigned to classes on the basis of similar IQ scores and reading levels, all the other kinds of differences cited here are present and defeat any effort at "homogeneous" teaching, and rightly so.

We can no longer afford the luxury of such homogeneous teaching, wherein 30 students read the same book, answer the same questions, listen to the same words as continuing standard fare during the school year. In fact, the results of such standardized teaching lead us to a second reason for using groups within our classrooms—that of promoting more effective learning. We have much evidence to support the thesis that small-group work, when appropriate, can result in better learning. For example, we know that people tend to learn better that which has meaning and purpose for them; that learning is more effective when the learner is actively involved in the learning process; that the total "power" in a group is often greater than the sum of power found in the individuals involved. Were we to keep only these three guiding principles in mind, we would see how a judicious use of committee and small-group work can improve the quality and quantity of learning.

A third reason for grouping within our classrooms can be stated simply—to vary our teaching-learning procedures. Variety in the learning situation is essential if we are to match method with purpose, procedure with content, approach with maturity level and student needs. The whole concept of method is based upon the appropriateness of any given procedure, technique, approach to the relevant factors involved—nature of the learners, nature of any given content, nature of purposes and goals—to name the major considerations. Therefore, any sound theory of methodology involves the use of varied teaching procedures, which in turn include the use of small-group work.

Another reason for variety in the learning situation lies in the nature of adolescents, who in their early development have a relatively short attention span and need frequent and relevant change of pace. In addition, they need opportunities for productive release of energy, opportunities that can be found in their own involvement in as many aspects of the learning process as possible. The stereotype of the traditional classroom—teacher in front of the room directing a recitation with expected conformity of behavior, response, and attention from class members during the entire period—offers little opportunity for release of pent-up energy and necessary muscular and mental activity so typical of the adolescent age.

Perhaps the most significant reason of all for using small-group work is that by so doing we are helping to achieve one of the most important goals of education—the development of an individual capable of living and working within the society of men. One of the most insistent needs of modern times is the need of men to learn to live together in some semblance of peace and order. Mankind has not yet acquired the know-how for such global existence, although efforts have been made since the dawn of time. It would be fantastic and tragic to believe that individuals are born with the talent to live with others. Rather this is a learned skill, an acquired art; and it is time that the school must recognize its responsibility in teaching the fundamentals of good human relationships.

In many instances we group in the classroom in terms of commonality—of interests, skills, talents, ability. At other times grouping should be based upon differences, involving varied backgrounds, viewpoints, personalities.

These two kinds of grouping play an important role in achieving the aims of the educative process.

HOW CAN WE GROUP?

A usual form of small-group work based on commonality among students is that of small interest groups. Regardless of the nature of the group—work-study, buzz, or job committee—there are many times when students can be grouped on the basis of a common interest. The interest might take the form of decorating for a class party, exploring the relationship of mathematics to architecture, investigating statistics concerning mental illness in urban communities, preparing a bulletin board on Presidential inaugurations. Whatever the problem, topic, or task, it is a common interest in that it ties the students in that particular committee or group together. Together they can plan, investigate, share, solve, accomplish in the pursuit of the specific goals or tasks facing them.

Similarly, a skill or talent brings some students together for working purposes. In an English class study of newspapers and their role in contemporary society, students might decide to prepare a newspaper of their own; or a history class might want to develop a newspaper as it might have appeared in the time of the Revolutionary War. In either case, there will be some students who can type (who will assume the responsibility for that aspect of production); there will be other talented youngsters who will take charge of the artwork; while still others, based upon interest, will work on feature articles, editorials, advertisements, and the like. Not only is this a practical demonstration of essential division of labor but also a working model of the variety of talents and skills and interests needed in producing an essential feature of our everyday life.

In a different way, grouping on the basis of commonality can be utilized in an English class to help with reading skills or in a mathematics class to guide comprehension of various processes. There are many times when teachers of these subjects should meet with small groups of students who have similar problems in increasing their reading rate or understanding a certain grammatical principle or penetrating the mysteries of prime factoring. How wasteful of pupil man-hours is the teacher who "spends" the time of an entire class to drill and review a process, skill, or concept that is understood by a large number, even a majority of the class.

We must not, though, overlook the many occasions when we should be permitting students to group on behalf of differences rather than similarities. For example, where exchange of opinion is desirable, we can provide for buzz-group sessions. During these sessions, adolescents share with each other reactions to books they have been reading or the themes, essays, or compositions that are a part of every writing program. Not only should students have the benefit of the resulting wider acquaintance with literature and their own creative writing, but this procedure also has the merit of saving time. Thirty book reports, given singly, may not only promote boredom but may take precious class time that can otherwise be put to more effective use.

Similarly, when critical and controversial issues are under discussion and study, the therapy involved in letting students exchange ideas, beliefs, opinions, and even prejudices in quick buzz groups may be recommended. Young people must have opportunities to discover how other people—their own classmates—think and feel about many matters, varying from "going steady" to "advantages and disadvantages of foreign-aid proposals." In addition, they are gaining valuable experience in a much-needed art—that of communication for understanding.

GUIDES FOR EFFECTIVE GROUPING

For those who would engage in classroom grouping practices there are some guidelines that are important if maximum values are to be gained. Only a few can be mentioned here.

First of all, it is essential to remember that grouping procedures should be used only when they are appropriate to the task at hand, the goals to be achieved, the nature of the content involved. Also they must be handled in ways appropriate to the maturity level of the students and to their experience with such procedures. Certainly a class that has never experienced small-group work should not be plunged into difficult committee study without careful guidance and realistic expectations.

Related to this caution is another guideline: a constant recognition that group living and group processes are learned skills. As such they are subject to the same helpful guidance and practice and evaluation that are involved in all learning, whether it be ideas, information, attitudes, skills, or appreciations. Patience and imagination on the part of the teacher, along with firm understanding of human behavior, individual and social, are essential for effective teaching of group processes.

In this regard it is wise to bear in mind the maxim, make haste slowly. The teacher must be sure that students understand what it is that they are to do and that they have clear-cut procedures for moving ahead. When false starts are made, teacher and class must reexamine their plans, modify procedures where necessary, try again—and again—and again.

In the final analysis, the role of the teacher is, of course, crucial. The teacher who assumes that, once a class is organized into groups or committees, students should automatically make progress without delays, difficulties, or differences, is unrealistic and naïve, if not incompetent.

On the other hand, the teacher who sees the skills of group living and working as similar to skills in communicating and computing and critical thinking will devote the same patience and understanding and planning normally given to these latter learnings. He will meet with each work committee as often and as long as necessary for its effective functioning. He will see that appropriate and sufficient resource and research materials are available. He will move rapidly from buzz group to buzz group, catching the essence of each in both content and process as he roams. He will develop with his students ways of recording and reporting progress, individual and group. He will note personality clashes and individual problems, and provide suitable guidance. He will expect of his students the best of which they are capable, knowing that few persons ever match grasp with reach.

In short, the teacher who uses groups and committees to further the education of his charges is placing the responsibility for learning where it primarily belongs—in the hands of the students.

JUNIOR HIGH LEARNING LAB

Catherine Dennis Thomason *

The laboratory approach is one of the best ways to provide for individual differences. In schools like Skokie Junior High School, central learning laboratories allow pupils to work independently at their own rates. However, teachers who so desire can arrange their classrooms as learning laboratories and so make them centers of independent study and their courses vehicles for individualized learning.

If the visitor doesn't know that he is in Skokie Junior High School, he might wonder where in the world he is, for the big basement room doesn't look like a regular classroom or laboratory and the youngsters, though obviously of junior high age and obviously busy, don't act as though they are in any class. When period bells ring, some students leave, but others keep working without heeding the bells and still others arrive and start to work.

Lynne and Anne are studying French together. Lynne, more advanced in French than Anne, is brushing up on her own French while she helps the other girl. Although the two are using records, they don't bother anyone else because they are using a record player equipped with earphones.

Next to Lynne and Anne at the long, library-type table with its study carrels is Doris, whose present interest is closer to home than that of her neighbors. Doris is engrossed in a study of the state of Oklahoma and is busy organizing materials she has gleaned from many sources.

* From *NEA Journal*, Vol. 52 (Washington, D.C.: National Education Association, November 1963), pp. 15–16. Reprinted by permission of the *NEA Journal* and the author.

Perhaps it is well that the fascinating story of the Sooner State has such a hold on Doris, for she can't stand rats and mice—even feels squeamish about squirrels—and right behind her Allan is doing research about rodents. Because he has found some published information which conflicts with his own research, he is checking carefully before making his final report.

Tom is making plans for a working model of a water filtration plant which he will build. Tom became interested in the subject of water purification in sixth-grade science, and building the plant was his own idea. Before he started on his plans, he visited the local filtration plant to discuss his project with the director.

Jim has been here since before school, completing a study-guide on cells for those who will use the microslide viewer, but now he and one of the girls have become so fascinated by Bob's study of probability that they have paused to watch him with his cards.

Up in the front part of the comfortably furnished carpeted room, five students are having a lively discussion, planning a panel skit about Greece. Since the group will have a chance to present the skit for the whole class, the youngsters want to give a "professional" performance. They will use visual materials and are recording a commentary to explain them.

This unusual school room is the learning laboratory in the Skokie Junior High School in Winnetka, Illinois. For twenty years Winnetka's small school system has fostered the development of each student at his own rate of speed. The learning laboratory, which enrolled its first students in March of 1962, is the latest expression of this philosophy.

The learning laboratory provides an environment where students can work in a suitable atmosphere on projects of special interest to them. Believing that "self-motivation, self-reliance, curiosity, self-teaching, and the ability to think critically should be characteristic of the educational programs in schools," Winnetka's superintendent brought the laboratory into being after the principal and several consultants from Skokie Junior High, helped by a Ford Foundation grant, had studied similar arrangements in other schools, and after the faculty had indicated its interest in the opportunity for independent study the learning laboratory would provide for students.

In addition to this opportunity, the learning laboratory provides time for creative thinking, and whatever physical equipment a project requires. New media for instruction and expensive equipment from all school departments are pooled in the laboratory, so that youngsters working there have access to a tape-recorder, two overhead projectors, three individual filmstrip previewers with about 150 filmstrips, a record player with some excellent records, programed materials, two teaching machines, and an extensive mathematical library. The main school library is close to the lab.

In the learning laboratory a student works in depth on subjects his class is studying or on a special interest of his own. Guided by the principal, the lab director, and the teacher, a reliable student plans a project that his teacher has approved. He makes time for the laboratory work by doing regular classwork ahead so that he can be excused from class for a period or two or even a week.

Goals for each project are flexible and can be altered as a project progresses and takes unplanned-for directions. Students keep in daily touch with their teachers and are responsible for keeping records of hours spent in the laboratory and of materials used.

The learning laboratory has thrived. Projects came in slowly at first, but as more and more teachers grew interested, the projects became many and varied, sometimes requiring help from teachers in several departments, and sometimes even from talent volunteered by people on the outside.

Soon the learning laboratory will move from its basement quarters to space specifically designed for it in a new addition to the school. It will go into its new surroundings with some problems still to be evaluated: Which children should use the learning laboratory? The gifted only? How long should a pupil remain in the lab? How should experiences in the learning laboratory be evaluated?

As a pilot study, the learning laboratory has been a success. It points out a way in which an educational program can give children the opportunity to progress as fast as their natural ability and inclination urge them.

MODERN FUNCTIONAL ADAPTATION
TO THE ABLER STUDENT

Harl R. Douglass *

There are at least three different types of gifted pupils according to Harl R. Douglass, retired director of the College of Education, University of Colorado. As a result of his vast experience and recent intensive study, Professor Douglass recommends that courses for the gifted be both enriched and streamlined and, in addition, adapted to the many great differences among able students.

It has become obvious that there are at least three somewhat different types of gifted students, for each of which a somewhat different type of planning should be made.

* From *Phi Delta Kappan*, Vol. 47 (Bloomington, Ind.: Phi Delta Kappa, February 1966), pp. 301–304. Reprinted by permission of the publisher.

Most people think of the bright or gifted child as one especially able to learn and retain information appearing in printed materials and recite it in class or reproduce it in written examinations. Many of these students have what is called an "eidetic" or "blotter" memory.

Unfortunately, a rather large minority of blotter-mind students have relatively little ability to organize learned material in ways different from that in which it was learned, in order to apply it to the solution of problems. These students have done exceptionally well on national testing programs. Often their scores mislead admissions officers into believing they are almost certain to be superior college students and will go on for graduate work or make some type of creative contribution.

The facts that the blotter mind and the creative mind are different and that an individual may possess one and not the other have recently become evident to those concerned with national testing programs and the awarding of scholarships. Thus additional types of data concerning the student are being gathered and seriously considered in college admissions and scholarship awards. The National Merit Scholarship Corporation recognizes these facts in its recent *Student Information Bulletin.*

There is also the type of student who has developed the ability to organize what he reads, sees, and hears, or to reorganize his learning around problems in school and in life about him. It is rather obvious that more attention should and is going to be given to this type of able student because of his much greater potential for accomplishment.

The problem-solver and the blotter-mind student tend to behave differently when confronted with the necessity for carrying on a research project for a graduate degree. A student of the blotter type has been capable of making high grades, but he finds it exceedingly difficult to formulate and plan a thesis or other research project sufficiently well to please a committee of the graduate school.

A third type of superior mind which has been receiving much attention lately is the creative type. The creative student is capable of and usually very desirous of using original ideas in planning and executing some unusual achievement. There are creative students in literary production, in composition and arrangement of music, in crafts or shop. There are creative students in planning science experiments. And there are creative students in various aspects of home economics, dress, foods, home planning, and decoration. Indeed, creative students may be found in every subject taught in school.

Furthermore, some students are unusually creative in planning social relations and exercising leadership with other human beings. Most of those individuals who are unusually able to obtain and retain positions of leadership have socially creative minds. They are people "of ideas" who are able to sell or to demonstrate those ideas and to develop a following.

The child who is creative in one field is very frequently uninterested and an underachiever in others. He is independent, curious, skeptical, emotionally committed to his work, energetic, aesthetically sensitive, introverted (usually), non-conformist (frequently), egotistical (occasionally). His interests, whatever his field, often parallel those of artists, psychologists, writers, physicists, and/or musicians.

A considerable majority of students are not of one of these three types only. Some are primarily of the blotter type but are also good at problem solving or creative work in some field, and vice versa. Many are creative and are also excellent problem solvers.

PROCEDURES FOR IDENTIFYING ABLER STUDENTS

Ability grouping has spread so widely that, if it should continue to spread at the same rate, by 1970 the school without any ability grouping will indeed be a rare one. The opponents and critics of grouping usually don't consider that in the very large majority of cases where grouping failed, failure was attributable in part to the fact that the bright and the dull students selected for special sections were not identified at all accurately and heterogeneity was not greatly reduced. Furthermore, such critics rarely mention that it was only in very exceptional cases that the sections of bright students were assigned to teachers who were especially prepared and especially suited for the teaching of the bright, able, and creative children.

It is encouraging to note that today a fairly large and increasing number of schools are doing the following things:

1. Grouping students for particular subjects and not for all subjects.

2. Giving careful consideration to borderline cases. The very brightest and the very dullest students are easily identified. In addition, there are two groups of borderline cases which are given clinical consideration by a committee usually composed of a counselor with special training in psychometry, a representative of the department concerned, and possibly a representative from the principal's office. The fact that there are many more and better-trained counselors today makes this approach more profitable.

3. Employing new criteria in selecting the students, i.e., not only I.Q. or M.A. but previous grades in the subject concerned and the whole file of records likely to contain data on pertinent experiences, character traits, interests, and education of parents.

4. Giving recognition to the cultural and economic level from which the students come, it being recognized that of two students with the same M.A. or I.Q. and somewhat the same grade average, the one who comes from a definitely lower economic and cultural level has more potential than the one who comes from a more privileged environment.

ASSISTING THE ABLER STUDENTS

Few appropriate textbooks are available for abler students, particularly for those with unusual creative ability and interest. Because much time must be spent on developing materials, the alert principal realizes that it is necessary to assign to the teacher of bright students as well as the teacher of the dull students a lighter load, let us say four classes instead of five. (Sections of abler students may well meet only four times a week.) The abler student should be encouraged to carry on "independent" study of two somewhat different types: a) self-planned with little supervision except as a consultant by the teacher; b) study in library, laboratory, shop, or study room as learning activity in connection with units developed in the classroom. Independent study should be stimulated and guided in shop, library, and laboratory.

As indicated in the foregoing discussion, grouping is usually done on three levels, but in some larger schools (e.g., the New Trier Township High School in Illinois and the Melbourne, Florida, High School) there are five levels.[1] In both of these schools the top group is composed of very outstanding students who are given a great deal of freedom and responsibility to carry on their work, which involves much "quest" and discovery. With this type of student, only the specially trained teacher can hope for much success.

Even in schools which prefer to be called "ungraded," grades have not been completely eliminated. What we find is: 1) ability grouping under some euphemistic name; 2) much attention given to individual differences within each group—which of course is as it should be; and 3) encouragement of abler students to take work ordinarily offered to a higher class; e.g., a bright and industrious seventh-grader taking a ninth-grade course.

ACCELERATION OR ENRICHMENT

There naturally arises the question of the soundness of acceleration. Many educators have unequivocally and somewhat arbitrarily opposed all types of acceleration, including of course skipping grades or materials. Unfortunately, their information about the nature and progress of accelerated bright students is limited or faulty. Very careful and reliable studies, including Terman's "Genetic Study of Genius" and dozens of more recent investigations of the bright young student in college, especially those of S. L. Pressey and the author, show that while there are some cases in which bright accelerated students do not do well, the proportion is very low. The bright accelerate was found not only to make better grades but, on the average, to be more prominent in social participation and leadership. An increasing number of educators of all types favor acceleration of bright children—some to a degree not dreamed of a decade or more ago.

In many secondary schools, college-level courses are offered for bright upperclassmen. Newer practice is in the direction of having them complete all or nearly all of their work for graduation at the end of what would ordinarily be their junior year or the first semester of the senior year, and then to re-

[1] See "The Independent Study Program at Melbourne High," by Janet Whitmire, *Phi Delta Kappan*, September, 1965, pp. 44–46.

main on for college-level courses. Many of these youngsters are entering colleges and universities as sophomores, and many others as second-semester freshmen. Universities which at first declined to allow credit for these courses on the basis of traditional beliefs and vested interests typical of college professors were confronted with the choice of providing college credit for those courses or losing many of their brightest prospects. A rapidly increasing number of colleges and universities are recognizing the handwriting on the wall.

High school teachers of college-level courses should be relieved of non-teaching tasks, study hall supervision, and clerical work not directly related to teaching such courses. Moreover, to create the proper climate in their classes, they need special training.[2]

Ideally, regardless of school system size, the gifted child usually 1) would properly be admitted to school prior to the age of six; 2) would become involved in a school program where they can work pretty much at their own rates; 3) would have performance evaluated in terms of their own potential; and 4) probably would, on evidence of reasonably adequate socio-emotional adjustment, graduate with quite a bit of extra learning acquired along the way.[3]

PLANNING FOR THE GIFTED

From the foregoing it should be evident that it is not a simple matter to provide materials and activities for the gifted child. Consequently, as already suggested, teachers of bright sections ought to be given a lighter load, no more than four classes a day to teach, each probably meeting only four times a week. There is need for many individual conferences with advanced students at times other than class periods. It should be clear that planning for gifted students means different kinds of planning for students of different types—the blotter, the problem-solver, the creative student.

It should also be clear that a substantial amount of the material in courses ordinarily taught with average students or heterogeneous groups may be omitted or at least reduced very greatly. Just what is omitted depends upon the individual, his grades in previous years in the subject involved, his interests, his industry, and his performance on a diagnostic test given at the beginning of the course and covering work of the year or semester in that subject.

IMPORTANT VARIATIONS AMONG THE GIFTED

A careful student of the extent of deviations among the more capable students wrote:

[2] Anthony J. Konde, "Selected Practices Used in Administering the Advanced Placement Program in the Secondary Public Schools of the State of New York," *The Journal of Experimental Education*, Spring, 1965, pp. 263–76.

[3] Ernest T. Newland, "The Gifted in the High School," *The High School Journal*, November, 1964, p. 77.

One might conclude . . . that the gifted are a homogeneous group. On the contrary, their individuality is in constant evidence. It has indeed been the most serious problem facing teachers and others who have searched for the best teaching method, curriculum, and management practices for gifted pupils. In attempting to account for the individuality of the gifted it is important to consider their early achievement of independence from adults.[4]

Hollingworth suggests that in general by age twelve the gifted child is more independent than dependent.[5] In her words, he "can use his intelligence independently in gaining control of his own life." A recent study by Lucito [6] confirms Hollingsworth's earlier observations. His results show bright children to be significantly less conforming than below-average children.

It should be constantly borne in mind that students also differ greatly in disposition and reactions to praise, pressure, opinions, and help by their fellows. Isaacs warns that the children themselves must not be made to feel guilty and rejected because of concepts of their potential which originally were not of their personal creation.[7] They need models with which to identify, models which they have themselves discovered and accepted; parents and teachers who are accepting and encouraging; a public climate which not only permits performance at their best possible level of excellence but fully and wholeheartedly encourages originality as well.

From the facts set forth here it seems crystal clear that:

1. Great care must be exercised in identifying and assigning abler students to special sections.

2. Each abler student should be studied very carefully and comprehensively.

3. Sections for abler students should be taught only by teachers with special training and with reduced loads.

4. Both acceleration and enrichment should be employed with abler children.

5. There are great differences among the abler students—differences in temperament, interests, past out-of-school and in-school experiences, in home and family background, in previous school achievement in the subject field being taught, in the degree of ability to study with little supervision, and in creative ability in some one or several fields.

[4] Warren A. Ketchem, "What Do We Know About Gifted Children?," *The High School Journal*, November, 1964, p. 86.

[5] Leta S. Hollingworth, "The Child of Very Superior Intelligence as a Special Problem in Social Adjustment," *Annals of the American Academy of Political and Social Sciences*, Vol. CXLIX, No. 3, 1930, pp. 151–60.

[6] Leonard J. Lucito, "A Comparison of the Independence-Conformity Behavior of Intellectually Bright and Dull Children." (Unpublished doctoral dissertation, University of Illinois, 1959).

[7] Ann F. Isaacs, "Role Expectancy and Its Effect on Performance and Achievement Among Gifted Students," *The High School Journal*, November, 1964, p. 115.

MR. SMITH AND THE SHOP KIDS

David Mallery *

The lessons Mr. Smith taught had little relation to the lives of his pupils. Rather, they were the worst kind of dull workbook exercises. Yet his shop boys, the nonacademic failures, worked hard to do their best in his classes because he treated them with respect and taught them as well as he could, and they appreciated it.

Those C.P. kids get away with anything. The teachers play along with them. If we pulled some of the things they did, we'd get jumped all over.

The boy was in a vocational English class, his school was in an industrial community, and "those C.P. kids" were the college preparatory students in the same school. This vocational section had been colorfully sketched by the principal as he and I stood outside the classroom door. "Now you're going to see how the other half lives! Oh, they won't throw you out or anything. It's just that they're a pretty rough group." Their regular teacher also wanted to brace me for an ordeal before leaving me. "This is the *worst* group. Now tomorrow at 12:30. . . ." But my visit had all been arranged.

"There are twenty-two of them. One is in jail now in New York, a few others have been in and out of trouble with the law here in town. But they're good boys—you know what I mean? And they'll cooperate with you. But they may give it to you in a language you're not used to. They've been around." He had one final whispered word before turning to introduce me to the group and leaving the room: "Remember, these are the lowest IQ group and the toughest of the shop people. Tomorrow at 12:30 you'll get the highest group."

The boys went through courteous, rather formal comments in answer to my opening question about their view of the strongest and the weakest aspects of their school. One by one each boy rose to speak, and the others listened carefully. Then that one boy's comment about "the C.P. kids" swung the discussion into action. Another joined in: "Yeah, you don't have a chance if you're not C.P."

Then with a rush of feeling, they showed eagerness to talk about a real problem:

Somebody roars down the street with no muffler on his car and the teachers'll say, "There go those shop boys!"

In class they tell us we're lazy and dumb.

We have this physics teacher. It turns out you need algebra to do physics. We haven't had it. And he says he knows we haven't had it but we're too dumb to learn it, so we just go ahead with the physics!

I asked them about their mathematics—what they had already had—and one went on: "We've been having the same math now since eighth grade. You don't feel like doing much when you know you've had it before and you know you'll have it again."

When I asked how many would really like to tackle some more advanced work in mathematics, nearly every boy in the room raised his hand. There seemed to be a real respect for and awe of mathematics, and a sense that *here* was something they should at least be given a chance to try.

"We're still doing fractions. I did them in sixth grade. And they wonder why we don't look lively in there!"

They sounded genuinely bitter for a few moments:

We're supposed to be young adults. Teachers should try treating us like young adults and not like kids. It burns you up.

I don't think a teacher ought to swear at you.

They say we come to waste time, us shop kids.

You ask a question and what do you get? "Five points off for you, kid!".

You ask for help and you're stupid. You don't ask for help and you "don't want to learn."

The period was nearly over and I was anxious not to leave these boys in the middle of such a negative, even if heartfelt, discussion. I asked, pointing to the clock, if they would be willing to put in a final word for some experience in their school life which really seemed important and valuable to them. They thought carefully. Then one tall boy in the back rose.

"I had an English teacher last year, and he made you feel like a man as soon as you entered the room."

Others joined in:

"Yeah, he never called you 'hey kid' or yelled at you. When you'd say 'sir' to him, he'd say 'sir' right back to you."

"They talk about respecting teachers. Here was a guy where it went both ways."

Another, seeing the clock's hand approaching bell time tried to bring the ideas together this way:

"I think the best thing here at the school is the really sincere ones—teachers—who go all the way to understand the kids and give them a break."

The bell rang right after his last word. The boys sat still, waiting, it seemed, to be excused. I thanked them, and the whole group converged on the front desk to impress one crucial, suddenly important message on me:

That English teacher's name is Mr. Smith. Be sure to visit his English class.

That Mr. Smith, you go see his class. Come when we meet him tomorrow. We didn't say it very well, but you'll see.

Several boys quickly sketched a diagram of how I could find Mr. Smith's room, and they wrote down the time for his class. The boy who had volunteered to copy my blackboard notes of the discussion's main points handed me his note sheet as he left. The notes were in capital letters, neatly written. In large letters at the end, with three underlinings, he had written: VISIT MR. SMITH'S ENGLISH CLASS. ROOM 321, 7th PERIOD.

A teacher who did not discriminate against "shop boys," one who "made you feel like a man when you walked into the room," seemed more important to these boys, as the final point to be stressed, than their anger about what seemed to be discrimination against vocational students.

MR. SMITH IN ACTION

The next day's visit to Mr. Smith's class showed precisely what the boys meant about this teacher's sincerity and his respect for them. It also showed in action a man skilled in human relations and interested in his students. I could see the things they had appreciated: his light touch, his calling students by name, his way of combining encouragement with dignified expectation that they could do the work. This classroom work in English during time away from the shop, *could* be a strong influence on these boys' powers of thought and expression, even on their own values. Perhaps one of the best ways to destroy any social-outcast stigma attached to non-college preparatory students is to have fine teachers meeting with them in their academic *and* vocational work, supporting them, challenging them, and helping them develop their values, standards, and abilities to the fullest. Here was a man who could do the job.

Mr. Smith's personal achievement with his students seemed even more spectacular to me in view of my impression of the day's lesson. Here was a clear contrast between teacher and curriculum. The boys were using a workbook called something like "English Errors," and dealing mechanically with "*lie* and *lay*," "*raise* and *rise*," as if these were unknown Latin verbs. Words like "*transitive*" and "*intransitive*" were used to explain which forms to use. The sentences in the workbook would have been puzzling to Lord Chesterfield. But the teacher conducted the class with the mastery of a combined artist, football coach, and orchestra director, and the boys enjoyed the process. I could see this by their faces, their way of sitting, their whole response. I myself found the actual *exercises* almost impossible to handle. I am convinced that people do not think this way about language: seeing the setting for a word and then inserting the right form because of a rule on the board. But the boys in this section, presumably limited in what they could do with words and in their hopes for "English," were trying hard to learn the game.

Here was an effective and perceptive teacher, working with responsive, well-motivated students. Their needs in language study and their unusual maturity of understanding could have been met and used in an instructive, valuable way. The actual curricular material got in the way.

What emerged here is a picture of a remarkable relationship between teacher and students, in spite of a serious problem in group reputation ("those shop kids") which these boys felt in the school, and also in spite of course materials of doubtful usefulness for *any* student. I was glad I had seen Mr. Smith. His approach to his students as individual human beings was impressive and valuable. "Didn't we tell you?" one of the boys whispered to me proudly as he gathered his books together to leave the room.

MATHEMATICS FOR THE
LOW ACHIEVER

Irving Adler *

Slow learners get tired of the same old material presented in the same old way. Don't we all? In order to keep up these pupils' interest, teachers need to find new and interesting ways to teach them old material that they have not learned and to introduce new material to them. The pupils should have opportunities to learn the new exciting subject matter. If carefully taught, some of the more advanced material may prove easier for them than the elementary subject matter that has been so frustrating to many of them. Irving Adler, a former teacher who has written much about mathematics, shows some ways to make mathematics sprightly for the slow learner. The basic techniques can, of course, be adapted for other subjects.

A new approach to teaching the low achiever in mathematics is beginning to take hold in the secondary schools of the United States. The old approach, based on the unproved assumption that the low achiever is primarily a person with low innate ability, put a low ceiling over what we expected of him.

* From *NEA Journal*, Vol. 54 (Washington, D.C.: National Education Association, February 1965), pp. 29–30; 44. Reprinted by permission of the *NEA Journal* and the author.

For example, if a ninth grade student with an IQ of 80 performed on the level of the average sixth grade student, we called his work "satisfactory" because he was "working up to the level of his ability." We classified him as "nonacademically minded," implying by this label that he was incapable of dealing with abstractions and was best kept busy doing things with his hands rather than grappling with mathematical ideas. We assigned him to a general mathematics class, where he repeated the same dull routines in "social arithmetic" that had frustrated and repelled him in earlier grades. The net effect of this approach was to perpetuate his retardation in mathematics.

The new approach recognizes that low innate ability may not be the only reason for low achievement in mathematics. It can also result from inadequate motivation, emotional disturbances, cultural deprivation in homes of low socioeconomic status, and even poor teaching in the lower grades.

Inherent in this new approach is the assumption that the low achiever is probably capable of doing better if only the causes of his poor performance can be identified and counteracted. On the basis of this new approach, the school tries to overcome the student's handicaps instead of perpetuating them. It also tries to prepare him and encourage him to enter the regular sequence of mathematics courses at a later time.

Moreover, the new kind of general mathematics curriculum is not dominated by a self-defeating, narrowly utilitarian point of view. It has the same educational goals as the regular curriculum designed for the average and above average student: to develop the kind of mathematical literacy that is needed by a citizen in the era of automation and nuclear energy and to cultivate the intellect and liberate the mind.

To achieve these goals, the new program: (a) presents *significant new mathematical ideas* to the low achiever; (b) helps him *relearn arithmetic* from a new, more meaningful, and more mature point of view; (c) seeks to *arouse and maintain his interest* in mathematics; (d) provides him with opportunities to make genuine *mathematical discoveries* at his level of knowledge and performance; and (e) *crystalizes his learning experience* around ideas that he understands, generalizations that he perceives and verbalizes, and skills that he masters.

Introducing significant new mathematical ideas. A ninth grade course for low achievers can include such significant mathematical ideas as negative numbers, permutations, combinations, probability, and indirect measurements using the tangent ratio and the Pythagorean theorem. The treatment of these topics differs from that used in the ordinary algebra class in at least three ways: There is more reliance on concrete examples, visual aids, and manual activity in developing the underlying concepts; the lessons are paced more slowly; the concepts are applied only to uncomplicated situations in which the underlying principle stands out in sharp relief.

For example, to teach the addition of algebraic numbers, positive and negative numbers are represented first as points on the number line, then as arrows on the number line. Positive numbers are represented by arrows that point to the right; negative numbers, by arrows that point to the left. To add 2 and −5, the student first draws the arrow which represents 2 by starting at 0 and going to the right to 2 on the number line. Then, from the head of the arrow, he draws the arrow to the left that represents −5. The sum is represented by the point on the number line at the head of the second arrow.

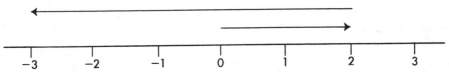

The student can also make a slide rule that performs the addition automatically. The slide rule consists of two strips of cardboard, each bearing the scale shown on the number line. To add 2 and −5, the 0 of the upper scale is placed over the 2 on the lower scale. The student then locates −5 on the upper scale. Directly under it on the lower scale is the sum of 2 and −5.

	−5	−4	−3	−2	−1	0	1	2	
−5	−4	−3	−2	−1	0	1	2		

The student does all additions either on the number line or on the slide rule until he discovers by himself a way of doing the addition mentally.

Relearning arithmetic. The low achiever generally has not mastered the four fundamental operations of arithmetic. Teaching these old concepts in a new way can revive his flagging interest in arithmetic. Addition, subtraction, multipication, and division can be taught as applications of the basic structure properties of the number system which are governed by the commutative laws, the associative laws, the distributive law, the law of zero, and the law of one.

For example, the student develops a better understanding of the usual way of multiplying 3×15 if he first does it in either of the following ways:

Applying the distributive law:
$$3 \times 15 = 3 \times (10 + 5)$$
$$= (3 \times 10) + (3 \times 5)$$
$$= 30 + 15$$
$$= 45$$

or

$$\begin{array}{r} 15 \\ \times\ 3 \\ \hline \end{array}$$

$$3 \times 5 = 15$$
$$3 \times 10 = 30$$

$$= 45$$

He acquires a deeper insight into the meaning of the reduction of fractions to lower terms if he is taught to reduce fractions by using the law of one:

$$\frac{6}{8} = \frac{3\times2}{4\times2} = \frac{3}{4} \qquad \frac{2}{2} = \frac{3}{4} \times 1 = \frac{3}{4}$$

In addition to learning the meaning of the operations in arithmetic, the low achiever must practice using the various operations until he masters them. Practice need not consist of arbitrary and dull drill routines, however; meaningful exercises can be provided that arouse interest and encourage sustained effort.

For example, the following task, which children find intrinsically interesting, gives a student a good deal of practice in addition and multiplication:

Write the base-ten numerals 27 and 13 as base-five numerals. Multiply the base-five numerals. Check your answers by multiplying the base-ten numerals, and comparing the answers.

$$27_{\text{ten}} = 1 \text{ twenty-five} + 0 \text{ fives} + 2 \text{ ones} = 102_{\text{five}}$$
$$13_{\text{ten}} = 0 \text{ twenty-fives} + 2 \text{ fives} + 3 \text{ ones} = 23_{\text{five}}$$

base five multiplication:

$$
\begin{array}{r}
102 \\
\times 23 \\
\hline
311 \\
204 \\
\hline
2401
\end{array}
$$

Note: $3 \times (2 \text{ ones}) = $ six ones
$\qquad = 1 \text{ five} + 1 \text{ one} = 11_{\text{five}}$
$\qquad 1 \text{ five} + 4 \text{ fives} = $ five fives
$\qquad = 1 \text{ twenty-five} = 100_{\text{five}}$

base-ten multiplication:

$$
\begin{array}{r}
27 \\
\times 13 \\
\hline
81 \\
27 \\
\hline
351
\end{array}
$$

Check:

$$2401_{\text{five}} = (2 \times 125 + 4 \times 25 + 0 \times 5 + 1 \times 1)_{\text{ten}}$$
$$= (250 + 100 + 0 + 1)_{\text{ten}}$$
$$= 351_{\text{ten}}$$

Arousing and maintaining interest. Many devices are effective in keeping the student's interest at a high level.

The first is to give him the feeling that he is learning something new even when he is reviewing an old topic. The examples cited above offer some new approaches to the four fundamental operations of arithmetic.

The second is to use problems that are intrinsically interesting whenever possible. For example, in studying the representation of data by a formula, table, or graph, the teacher may use such data as the stopping distance of a car traveling at a given speed.

Third, wherever possible, the teacher should present problems in the form of a challenging game. For example, the problem of writing a number as a base-five numeral can be presented as the *game of five:* A sequence of cafeteria trays has values 1, 5, and 25 as shown in the drawing. A lunch ticket placed in a tray takes on the value of the tray. The game involves using as few tickets as possible to represent any given number. The drawing gives the solution for 63, which is represented by the base-five numeral 223.

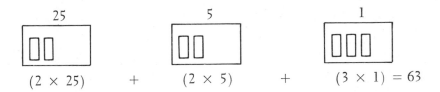

25		5		1
(2 × 25)	+	(2 × 5)	+	(3 × 1) = 63

Providing opportunities for discovery. A student who has done many additions of algebraic numbers on the number line will be able to discover for himself the usual rules for addition. A student who has used many tree diagrams (see example following) in order to find all possible permutations of two out of three objects or three out of four objects will soon be able to formulate in his own words the rule for computing the number of permutations (arrangements) of n things taken r at a time. By allowing the pupil to make these discoveries himself, the teacher gives him the opportunity to experience the thrill of real discovery and to take pride in real accomplishment.

```
        b    (a,b)
a
        c    (a,c)       All  possible  arrange-
        a    (b,a)       ments (permutations)
b
        c    (b,c)       of  two  of  the  three
        a    (c,a)       letters  a,  b,  and  c.
c
        b    (c,b)
```

Crystallizing the learning experience. While using an abundance of concrete illustrative material and providing many opportunities for the student to make his own discoveries, the teacher must be careful not to take for granted the student's ability to use what he understands. The student must not only understand why we proceed as we do in multiplication; he must do enough multiplication to acquire facility with it. It is not enough for him to grasp the meaning of addition on the number line; he should be led to discover the usual rule for addition, to formulate this rule accurately in his own words, and then to apply the rule without reference to the graphic representation of numbers on the number line.

The new approach to teaching the low achiever combines old with new, discovery with application, understanding with mastery, and interest with effort. This combination raises the student to ever higher levels of achievement.

SOME SUGGESTIONS FOR TEACHING
THE CULTURALLY DEPRIVED

Frank Riessman *

Like all other pupils, culturally deprived pupils usually respond well to good teaching. Frank Riessman's suggestions for teaching the culturally deprived are therefore really rules for good teaching. Although these suggestions are useful, teachers of culturally deprived adolescents must realize that teaching them may be difficult because these adolescents have suffered disappointment and disillusionment too long to be easily won over.

Teaching culturally deprived children is not all struggle; it offers an opportunity for personal gratification which few other teaching assignments can match. However, the teacher who hopes to succeed with the culturally deprived must learn to cope with certain problems of discipline and motivation which are not as acute in schools where the great majority of pupils come from middle-class homes.

Handling these and related problems requires no gimmicks or tricks. Nor is there any one right approach, although there are many wrong ones. Perhaps more important than any methods for teaching culturally deprived children are certain basic attitudes on the part of the teacher.

The teacher should be straight-forward and down-to-earth. Some teachers have considerable success with the culturally deprived because they act in a simple, dignified fashion and express a degree of physical warmth without overdoing it. They respect the children, and the children respect them. Superciliousness, toughness, and cynicism are bad, and so are naïveté, softness, and lack of confidence.

Every teacher of culturally deprived children must weather an initiation period which begins on the opening day of school. Sometimes, fear of this initiation sets in before the teacher enters the class. Pupils make a cooperative effort to break the teacher; they try to find out how smart he is, how much he will put up with, and how much they can get away with.

This is the time when the teacher should establish an unvarying routine with simple, clear, enforced rules. The rules need not be imposed on the

* From NEA Journal, Vol. 52 (Washington, D.C.: National Education Association, April 1963), pp. 20–22. Reprinted by permission of the NEA Journal and the author.

pupils as if they were in a prison or be so strict that they arouse pupil resent-ment. The teacher might begin the first class with a discussion of what rules they must all live by if he is to teach and they are to learn.

Establishing rules is not as difficult as it may appear to the teacher on the first day of class. Culturally deprived children welcome limits, but these limits must be clearly defined and consistently adhered to. If the teacher says there will be no gum chewing in class one day, then he cannot allow gum chewing the following day. The teacher, moreover, must abide by the rules himself and he should not introduce changes without advance warning.

Behavior problems which spring up in the class should be handled im-mediately with firmness and fairness. The misbehavior should not be treated as a personal affront to the teacher but rather as an interference with the learning situation of the entire class.

If necessary, parents should be called. Research has shown that most par-ents of culturally deprived children want their children to do well in school and are eager to help the teacher. They depend upon the teacher, however, to establish relationships between the school and the home. The teacher should not confine himself to getting in touch with parents only when a child has misbehaved. If he calls parents whenever the child has done some-thing particularly well, they won't ask themselves, "What has Jimmy been up to now?" every time they get a call from the school.

During the initial testing period, one or two children in the class are likely to accept the teacher much more quickly than the rest. The danger of en-listing their support uncritically lies in the fact that these one or two children are usually not typical representatives of the class and may be rejected by the rest. If the teacher can spot and get the support of the real leaders—the ones who represent the children's own ideal norms—he is more likely to be accepted by the whole class.

The best type of teacher to win these children over to learning is a person of action who communicates in many ways and is not too dependent on words alone as a means of teaching. The leaders in the class and the rest of the children are likely to accept this type of person readily because he is close to the model after which they would like to pattern themselves.

Culturally deprived children are not accustomed to listening to long speeches, and they find it difficult to concentrate very long in a strictly verbal situation. Thus, developing the auditory attention of these children is one of the teacher's most difficult tasks.

This task requires the utmost planning. The teacher must know what question he is going to ask each level of pupil in the class, and he must find a way to involve each child. He cannot leave anything to chance, and yet he cannot plan more than two or three lessons in advance.

One teacher who has had long experience with culturally deprived children uses a simple technique for making sure his pupils are paying attention and understand what is being discussed. He asks a question like "What is twenty-four divided by six?" and has several children respond whether the first one gives the right answer or not. He makes a game out of it by keeping track of and announcing how many give the right answer. Although this technique is too time-consuming to be continued indefinitely, it is a good starting technique for teaching children who find it difficult to listen.

Culturally deprived children also have trouble expressing themselves, and typically do not verbalize well in response to words alone. They are at their best when they talk about things they have actually seen and done. For this reason, extensive use of visual aids and of role playing is effective in improving their verbal expression.

Ask a juvenile delinquent who comes from a disadvantaged background what he doesn't like about school or the teacher and you will get an abbreviated, inarticulate reply. But have a group of these youngsters act out a school scene in which someone plays the teacher, and the result will be a stream of verbal consciousness that is almost impossible to shut off.

Role playing can be utilized in countless ways, such as acting out a history lesson (George Washington signing the Constitution) or teaching arithmetic and economics by playing "store" and "bank." Role playing itself is a marvelous stimulus for discussion, and it appeals to the child's love of action.

The teacher has to develop discussion out of role-playing scenes, however, and not simply capitulate to children's enjoyment of the acting-out process. In other words, role playing should be a trigger for discussion and thinking, not a substitute for it.

In teaching a deprived primary-grade child about a cat, for example, it would be useful to have him draw a cat, "act out" a cat, write the word on the board, and handle pictures of a cat. Similarly, in discussing a musical record, the child should be encouraged to put the record on the phonograph and to take it off. Trivial as this last example may appear, it points up the need to involve the child's motor muscles in every conceivable fashion and to make him an acting participant in the learning situation.

In time, however, the teacher will not have to depend so heavily on these devices, for once the deprived child develops skill through his visual and auditory senses, he is able to deal with the world of conceptual ideas without the need for concrete stimuli at every point.

From what has been said so far, it might appear that the so-called progressive method which emphasizes "learning by doing" is the best approach to teaching the deprived child. However, experience shows this is not true. Permissiveness, accent on the self and creativity as central goals of education—all a part of the progressive approach—are alien to the deprived child's culture.

The most successful teachers in terms of the culturally deprived children seem to combine the traditional concepts of structure, order, discipline, and strong external demands for achievement with the newer methods of down-to-earth learning by doing.

Fear of failure is a big roadblock to learning for the culturally deprived child. Every inch of progress calls for genuine praise. Even making an effort must be fully appreciated for what it is—a sign of maturity, a step forward.

It is difficult for these children to bring themselves to volunteer in class, and the teacher must keep that fact in mind.

But whereas they are slow in getting involved in problems, once their interest is involved, they often seem to be able to work intensely and patiently for longs hours at a stretch. In fact, once they are interested in a task, they want to stay with it and dislike working in short spurts with frequent breaks.

Thus, the teacher of deprived children should aim high—expect more and work for more from these youngsters. There is an exciting challenge awaiting the teacher who realizes that these children need not simply be brought up to grade level, but rather, that they can be encouraged to develop new kinds of creativity.

If this is the teacher's goal, he can help to make the schools far more pluralistic and democratic.

STRATEGIES AND TACTICS USED IN EVALUATION

Evaluation means to place a value on something. In schoolwork we use evaluation for two major purposes: (1) to mark or rate pupils' work; (2) to diagnose the condition of learning as a basis for next steps. Of these types, the first is the more prevalent, and the second, more important.

Most evaluation in schools is based upon some form of measurement. Perhaps the most common measuring device used is the teacher-built test, but there are many other devices available. None of them is very accurate; which one should be used depends upon the situation. As with other strategies, the teacher needs to choose the correct strategy for measuring the quality he wishes to measure. In some instances, objective tests may be best; in other instances, essay tests may be best; in still others, it may be best to depend upon observation of performance, a rating scale, a check list, analysis of written work, or some other device. In the long run, an evaluation is usually best based on a mixture of several measurements of various different kinds. In this way the evaluator can compensate for the weakness of the measuring instruments at his disposal.

So that pupils and parents can have some idea of how well pupils are progressing in their schoolwork, it has become customary to award marks or grades. Usually, these marks are represented by a five-point scale, such as, A B C D F, although they may be represented by percentage points or some other indicator as well. In any case they are subjective and arbitrary. Attempts to make marks seem mathematically exact only disguise this fault; they do not correct it. However, the pupils and parents have a right to know what teachers think of pupil progress. To date no other feasible method of marking that is both accurate and acceptable to parents has been devised. Perhaps the advent of nongraded schools will bring a solution to this problem.

TEACHER-MADE TESTS
AND TECHNIQUES

J. Wayne Wrightstone *

The objectives that one is trying to achieve through one's teaching should determine the types of test items that one should use. Often it is better not to use test items at all, but to use some other device instead. Among the devices available are rating scales and check lists by which to objectify observation, sociometric devices, anecdotal reports, inventories, and the like. The art is to choose the right devices for the right purposes. The result will be a continuous evaluation upon the basis of a reasonable mix of measuring techniques and devices.

When writing or selecting measuring devices, one should check them against the following criteria: Is it valid, that is, does it measure what you want to measure? Is it reliable, that is, can you depend upon it to give an accurate measurement uninfluenced by chance? Is it objective, that is, is the scoring free from chance influences or personal errors? Is it usable, that is, is it feasible to use this instrument under the circumstances?

Evaluation in modern schools should be based upon the concept that multiple learnings develop simultaneously during an educational experience. For example, what is involved if the learner is studying the topic of transportation? We assume that his experience in visting terminals and airports or reading about transportation in a reference book or textbook may at one and the same time influence growth in his information, his attitudes, his interests, his work and study skills, his powers of critical thinking and his personal and social adaptability.

In order to assess the multiple learnings of children, the teacher and supervisor should plan for comprehensive evaluation of major objectives. For this purpose, some of the tests and measures will be standardized and administered periodically. Other methods of appraisal will be informal and will be used daily by the teacher as part and parcel of the instructional process.

* From *Educational Leadership*, Vol. 19 (December 1961), pp. 170–172; 199–200. Reprinted with permission of the Association for Supervision and Curriculum Development and J. Wayne Wrightstone. Copyright © 1961 by the Association for Supervision and Curriculum Development.

COMPREHENSIVE PROGRAM OF EVALUATION

Evaluation involves primarily the gathering of evidence to estimate the degree to which pupils and teachers are achieving educational objectives. Evaluation involves, first, the formulation of major objectives such as: (a) acquiring facts, concepts and generalizations; (b) developing desirable interests, attitudes and appreciations; (c) showing skill in handling facts, concepts and generalizations; (d) increasing powers of critical interpretation of data; and (e) improving personal-social adaptability.

A second step in the evaluative process is to define the major objectives in terms of the behavior of the learner which will indicate that he is achieving the objective. The definitions should outline specifically the types of skills, abilities, understandings, attitudes and interests that the school is seeking to develop in learners. This will serve to clarify the objectives for the purposes of both instruction and evaluation.

Evaluation involves also the limited use of formal tests and measures, as well as the extensive use of informal quizzes, reports, observations and anecdotal records and sociometric methods which reveal pupil growth toward each major objective. The use of teacher-made tests and techniques helps the teacher to guide better the development and growth of each learner from day to day.

Informal Methods and Tests

Informal methods and teacher-made tests are a necessary part of evaluation. This is true, first, because day-by-day classroom appraisal is of equal or greater importance than standardized tests administered usually not more than once per year; and second, because standardized tests and published scales are not available for measuring interests, attitudes and critical thinking at the elementary school level. Many practical suggestions in informal methods of evaluation are given in the Forty-Fifth Yearbook, Part I, National Society for the Study of Education, entitled, *The Measurement of Understanding*, and distributed by the University of Chicago Press.[1]

Information and understanding may be measured informally by teacher-made tests using multiple choice, true-false, or completion types of test items, and exercises. Work-study skills may be assessed informally by observing children systematically as they use reference books, dictionaries, and the index of a book and by examining in oral or written form their ability to interpret maps, graphs, charts and tables in a normal classroom situation.

Powers of thinking may be assessed informally by observing the pupil's ability to draw inferences or to make interpretations or verbal, graphic and statistical data in specially constructed test exercises or in oral and written

[1] National Society for the Study of Education. *The Measurement of Understanding.* Forty-Fifth Yearbook. Chicago: University of Chicago Press, 1946.

reports. In a like manner the ability of pupils to apply concepts and generalizations to specific situations may be observed and examined in special test exercises or as a part of regular instruction.

EVALUATING ATTITUDES AND INTERESTS

Under the general category of attitudes, this discussion will include interests and personal-social adaptability of children. Adequate measurement of achievement of these important, but relatively intangible, objectives is very difficult. There are few formal or standardized measures or techniques which will be valid in many situations. For this reason the informal techniques of evaluation, such as observation, writing of anecdotal records, rating scales and check lists, frequently provide the evidence which teachers use in making judgments about the growth and development of children. In appraising attitudes, values and feelings, the Remmers' multipurpose scales, such as, "A Scale for Measuring Attitude Toward Any School Subject," may be of some value.

In the area of interests there are practically no standard inventories available at the elementary school level. In the area of personal-social adaptability there are some standardized self-descriptive personality tests and rating scales. Both these methods should be used with caution because both self-ratings and ratings by others may contain serious errors of observation and measurement. Even when such measures are used it is wise to supplement the data from them by making systematic observations and anecdotal records of the pupil's behavior. In addition, data may be obtained from sociometric techniques to aid in making more accurate interpretation of the pupil's social behavior and relationships.

TEACHER-MADE INVENTORIES

Interests may perhaps be best defined, for purposes of this article, as those drives which lead the individual to various preferences in personal efforts and conduct. An informal interest inventory of activities may be used to discover pupil preferences. Sample items follow:

	L	I	D
(a) To listen to radio news commentators	( )	( )	( )
(b) To draw pictures	( )	( )	( )
(c) To play the piano	( )	( )	( )
(d) To read about trains and railroads	( )	( )	( )

L means like; *I* means indifferent to; *D* means dislike.

Individual beliefs and attitudes toward ideas, persons and phenomena may be measured by an informal attitude test especially constructed for use with local school children. In such a test the pupil is asked to indicate by + or — whether he agrees or disagrees with such statements as these:

(   ) The farmer is less happy than the city worker.
(   ) The government should help persons who are too old to work.

ANECDOTAL RECORDS

In compiling the anecdotal records, the observer makes notes of sample situations, activities, experiences and expressions of each pupil for the characteristic or characteristics to be evaluated. Thus, for example, an anecdotal record containing descriptions of behavior aids in assessing personal-social adaptability. The following are excerpts about Jane from a teacher's anecdotal record.

9-11-61   Jane cried when she failed to solve an arithmetic problem correctly.
9-18-61   Shoved (without provocation so far as I can determine) Ruth who was standing nearby.
10-3-61   Refused to take part in an arithmetic project because she was not chosen as chairman of the committee to plan and write it.
10-9-61   Used ridicule to belittle Mary, a classmate, who brought in a long report on an arithmetic project. (She has shown jealousy before.)

It is necessary to have an adequate number and sequence of anecdotal entries upon which to base judgments and interpretations of a child's behavior. Some children need more entries than others.

SOCIOMETRIC TECHNIQUES

A common sociometric technique is that involving the choice of classmates as friends. This instrument is a friendship-choice type in which the following sociometric question is asked:

1. Who are your best friends in this class? Name one, two, three or more as you like.

From the children's responses to the sociometric question, it is possible to draw up a table of choices for a class as follows: (a) children chosen by each child as friends; (b) children choosing other children as friends; (c) mutual choices as friends; and (d) children not chosen by any other child.

Another sociometric method involves choosing classmates who are naturally suited for roles in class plays. This device is a variation of the "Guess Who" method used years ago by investigators. This instrument, a pupil questionnaire, is called "Casting Characters for Class Plays." Each pupil in the class is asked to write the name of the classmate who is best suited to play a particular part in a class play because he behaves that way naturally. Sample items are:

1. Someone who is always in good humor; who laughs or smiles a good deal; who makes others happy

2. Someone who is shy about meeting people, who prefers to work alone rather than with others

3. Someone who is snobbish and conceited, who feels superior to others in the class.

Similar items may involve choices of pupils for roles described as co-operative, industrious, dependable, friendly, and outstanding. Other items may ask for choices of roles described as poor loser, bookworm, and show-off.

The following statements provide a summary definition of the qualities by which an effective program of evaluation may be judged:

1. Evaluation is comprehensive. The major objectives of instruction are evaluated by a variety of appraisal methods, including standardized tests and scales, but especially teacher-made tests, observations, questionnaires, anecdotal records, and sociometric techniques.

2. Evaluation is a continuous process. A teacher with a clear concept of instructional objectives evaluates throughout every day the behavior of the children.

3. Evaluation necessitates, on the part of the teacher, alertness and close observation of children in all types of situations in and out of the classroom.

4. Evaluation requires that the teacher interpret appraisal data in terms of the background, the level of maturity, and the personality of each child, for the purpose of guiding his growth and development.

TEACHER-MADE EXAMINATIONS

Isobel Pfeiffer and O. L. Davis, Jr.*

Someone has said that the man who writes the test determines the curriculum. If this statement is a truism, it is a sad one, for evidently the tests used in ordinary classrooms seldom require much use of the higher mental processes, nor do they test any of the affective educational goals. The goals honored by teachers as test makers seem to foster a dry information-glutted curriculum, untainted by pupils' thinking or appreciation. This type of testing cannot be satisfactory. It defeats the central purpose of secondary education.

* From *The Bulletin of the National Association of Secondary-School Principals*, Vol. 49 (September 1965), pp. 1–10. Reprinted by permission of the NASSP and the authors.

Examinations constructed by teachers are a prominent consideration in the overall evaluation of students. They persist in importance from school entry to graduate programs, and their influence is pervasive, particularly upon the manner in which students study but more importantly upon the ways they think and the values they place on intellectual activities.

Tests reflect the objectives held by the teacher devising the examinations. Optimally, objectives for the course, unit, or lesson are stated prior to teaching, thus providing direction for both teacher and students in pursuing commonly understood goals and a reasonable guide to the evaluation of the undertaking. Even when objectives remain unstated, however, tests reflect the real objectives held by the teacher who prepares the examination. Most teachers know that most successful students are "test wise" to some extent. As students review or study for tests, they tend to focus their efforts on the kinds of materials which they expect the questions to require. If, for example, they believe the mathematics test will concentrate on word problems, they probably review typical kinds of problems. If they think that demonstrating relationships among chronological events will be important in a social studies test, they will stress such relationships in their study.

Since tests relate directly to the objectives of a course, a unit, or a topic, an analysis of these tests should indicate the kinds of objectives thought to be most important by the teachers developing them. Do test items require pupils to demonstrate that they have memorized facts? Or do tests require students to think beyond facts, to demonstrate that they can apply their knowledge in a viable situation? Do tests demand that students analyze, synthesize, or evaluate—all "higher" thinking processes? In addition, do tests in different courses, even in different curricular programs of study, emphasize different thinking requirements? This study was designed to gain evidence on such questions and to demonstrate the usefulness of a powerful analytic system. Specifically, its purpose was to determine and note the similarities and differences in the cognitive objectives in examinations used in ninth grade courses in a junior high school.

PROCEDURE

Semester examinations for all ninth grade courses during the 1963–64 school year were secured from a junior high school in Northeastern Ohio. These tests had been prepared by the teachers, as individuals or as members of committees.

Test items were analyzed according to the *Taxonomy of Educational Objectives: Cognitive Domain.*[1] This system has six major categories in a hier-

[1] Benjamin Bloom (Editor) *Taxonomy of Educational Objectives: Cognitive Domain.* New York: David McKay and Co., 1956, p. 207.

archy of increasing complexity: 1.00) Knowledge; 2.00) Comprehension; 3.00) Application; 4.00) Analysis; 5.00) Synthesis; and 6.00) Evaluation. In addition, each of these classes is subdivided into several sections. Examples of the major subclasses used in the study and illustrative test items are presented below:

a) Knowledge of specifics (1.10)—"A list of furnishings and appliances contained in a home is a (an) ——————————————."

b) Knowledge—ways and means of dealing with specifics (1.20) "An atom is to an element as a molecule is to a: (a) colloid; (b) mixture; (c) compound; (d) solution."

c) Knowledge—universals and abstractions in a field (1.30)—"Vital to making a democracy work in a large nation is (1) civil liberties, (2) political parties, (3) rule by an elected assembly, (4) a cabinet system, (5) all of these things."

d) Comprehension—translation (2.10)—"If n + 3 is an odd integer, what is the next larger odd integer? (a) m + 3, (b) n + 4, (c) n + 5, (d) 2m + 1, (e) Zn + 3."

e) Comprehension—interpretation (2.20)—"Read *Pygmalion*. Write a summary being sure to tell what the miracle was."

f) Analysis—Elements (4.10)—"Analyze the following sentence: Mother gave a dollar to the paper boy."

g) Analysis—Organizational Principles (4.30)—"Give two important characteristics of the writing of each of the following: Kipling, Twain, Lindsay, Coleridge."

h) Synthesis—Production of a unique communication (5.10)—"Why is 'Three's A Crowd' considered a romantic play?"

i) Evaluation—Judgment in terms of external criteria (6.20)—"What do you feel is the most important concept you have learned in our study of literature?"

Each item on each test was categorized into the highest appropriate class or subclass. Then, the item frequencies were tabulated and percentages were calculated.

To establish reliability on the classification process, a sampling of items from each test was reanalyzed after a three week period. No change in classification resulted. In addition, another sample of test items was analyzed by another scorer experienced in the use of the *Taxonomy*, and the interscorer agreement was .87.

FINDINGS

COGNITIVE EMPHASES IN NINTH GRADE COURSE EXAMINATIONS

Percentage of test items categorized according to the major classes and their most prominent subdivisions of the *Taxonomy* are presented in Table 1.

In the social studies area, the civics examination emphasized exclusively the knowledge of specific information. The world history examination stressed knowledge of specifics, but also required students to engage in other types

TABLE 1. *Percentage Distribution of Classified Exam Items in Different Level Classes in a Subject Field* [1]

OBJECTIVES	SOCIAL STUDIES		MATHEMATICS		SCIENCE		FRENCH		HOME EC.	BUS. TR.	ENGLISH					
											PR. E		AV. E		AD. E	
	CIVICS	WH	G MATH	ALG.	G. SCI.	BIOL.	FR. I	ADV. FR.			A	B	A	B	A	B
Knowledge																
1.10	100	62	58	34	27	98	21	21	70	95	0	26	21	48	10	22
1.20	0	7	0	0	0	2	0	0	30	0	0	0	15	22	0	22
1.30	0	5	0	18	9	0	0	0	0	0	0	0	0	0	0	0
Comprehension																
2.10	0	0	6	6	0	0	29	7	0	0	0	0	0	0	0	0
2.20	0	4	0	0	0	0	0	0	0	0	0	30	0	0	0	0
Application																
3.00	0	2	36	42	64	0	50	71	0	5	20	10	15	4	22	4
Analysis																
4.10	0	0	0	0	0	0	0	0	0	0	10	30	10	0	15	25
4.30	0	0	0	0	0	0	0	0	0	0	0	0	4	0	0	0
Synthesis																
5.10	0	20	0	0	0	0	0	0	0	0	45	4	25	25	30	25
Evaluation																
6.20	0	0	0	0	0	0	0	0	0	0	25	0	10	0	25	0

[1] *Abbreviations of Subject Fields.*
WH = World History
G Math = General Mathematics
Alg = Algebra I.
G. Sci. = General Science
Biol. = Biology
Fr I = French I

Adv Fr = Advanced French
Home Ec = Home Economics
Bus Tr = Business Training
Pr E = Practical English
Av E = Average English
Ad E = Advanced English

of thinking, including synthesis. Since the world history course was taken by students in the College Preparatory (CP) program perhaps the teacher believed the students could engage in such intellectual operations, whereas the teacher of civics, taken by non-CP students, may have believed his students were not capable of thinking beyond the memory level.

In the mathematics courses, CP students taking algebra again were faced with the demands of using a wide range of mental processes. Students electing general mathematics, on the other hand, had more questions involving memory of specific facts and fewer requiring application than students taking algebra. In science, however, CP students taking biology were asked questions over knowledge only. General science students, most of whom were enrolled in non-CP programs, were required to respond primarily to tasks of application; only about 25 per cent of all their questions were classified in the knowledge category. The examinations in the two French courses were quite similar, although French I demanded more interpretation and less application than did Advanced French.

In the English classes, the differences between the two teachers and their goals was pronounced. Each teacher had sections of the three ability levels. Teacher A, in all her sections, stressed a wide range of thinking processes. Teacher B, however, quite consistently emphasized knowledge (of specifics and ways and means of dealing with specifics) at all levels and gave only slight attention, for the most part, to the other cognitive processes. Whereas Teacher A asked all her students to engage in evaluation, Teacher B asked none of her students to engage in this task, not even those in the advanced course. Both teachers asked their average classes to engage in less complex mental processes than their other groups.

Questions on the home economics examination were entirely in the knowledge classification, 70 per cent calling for knowledge of specific facts. In business training, 95 percent of the test questions required only knowledge of specific facts. The proportion of test items in both these courses calling for knowledge of specific facts seems unusually high, particularly in light of the fact that these courses purport to be "practical."

Cognitive Emphases in Ninth Grade Programs of Study

Findings previously presented indicate that, in general, CP students were required to take examinations encompassing a wider range of cognitive objectives than their non-CP counterparts. This observation is sharpened, however, when the data are grouped according to the three programs of study. Percentages of examination questions categorized according to the major Bloom categories for College Preparatory students (CP) are presented in Table 2, for Business (Bus) students in Table 3, and for Prevocational (PreV) students in Table 4. Because of the differences in objectives evidenced by the two English teachers, data in each program are further subdivided. Thus, these three tables represent the cognitive emphases in the typical course schedules in the three programs.

TABLE 2. *Percentage of Examination Items in College Preparatory Program Courses Classified in Differing Taxonomy Categories*

OBJECTIVES	ALGEBRA, ADVANCED FRENCH, BIOLOGY, ENGLISH		ALGEBRA, ADVANCED FRENCH, WORLD HISTORY, ENGLISH	
	ENGLISH TEACHER A	ENGLISH TEACHER B	ENGLISH TEACHER A	ENGLISH TEACHER B
Knowledge				
1.10	41	44	32	35
1.20	1	6	2	7
1.30	4	4	6	8
Comprehension				
2.10	3	3	3	3
2.20	0	0	1	1
Application				
3.00	34	29	34	30
Analysis				
4.10	4	6	4	6
Synthesis				
5.10	8	6	12	13
Evaluation				
6.20	6	0	6	0

TABLE 3. *Percentage of Examination Items in Business Program Courses Classified in Differing Taxonomy Categories*

OBJECTIVES	GENERAL BUSINESS, GENERAL SCIENCE, GENERAL MATHEMATICS		GENERAL BUSINESS, GENERAL SCIENCE, ALGEBRA	
	ENGLISH TEACHER A	ENGLISH TEACHER B	ENGLISH TEACHER A	ENGLISH TEACHER B
Knowledge				
1.10	50	57	44	51
1.20	4	6	4	6
1.30	2	2	7	7
Comprehension				
2.10	2	2	2	2
Application				
3.00	30	27	32	29
Analysis				
4.10	3	0	2	0
4.30	1	0	1	0
Synthesis				
5.10	6	6	6	6
Evaluation				
6.20	2	0	2	0

TABLE 4. *Percentage of Examination Items in Prevocational Program Courses Classified in Differing Taxonomy Categories*

OBJECTIVES	GENERAL MATH, HOME EC., GENERAL SCIENCE		GENERAL MATH, HOME EC., CIVICS	
	ENGLISH TEACHER A	ENGLISH TEACHER B	ENGLISH TEACHER A	ENGLISH TEACHER B
Knowledge				
1.10	39	45	57	64
1.20	8	8	8	8
1.30	2	2	0	0
Comprehension				
2.10	2	9	2	9
Application				
3.00	30	28	14	12
Analysis				
4.10	2	8	2	8
Synthesis				
5.10	11	1	11	1
Evaluation				
6.20	6	0	6	0

The "recommended" CP program included English, probably the accelerated course, advanced French, algebra, and either biology or world history. Students in the business course, primarily girls, took English (for the most part, the average sections), general business, general science, and either general mathematics or algebra. Prevocational students took either home economics or industrial arts, English (probably in "basic" English sections), general mathematics, and either general science or civics.

Examination of Tables 2–4 reveals that there was great similarity in the cognitive objectives within each of the three programs of study, regardless of choice of major elective course. Table 5 summarizes, according to program

TABLE 5. *Range of Percentage of Examination Items in Courses in the Three Programs of Study Classified in the Major Taxonomy Categories*

OBJECTIVES	PREVOCATIONAL %	BUSINESS %	COLLEGE PREPARATORY %
Knowledge	49–72	55–65	40–54
Comprehension	2–9	2	3–4
Application	12–30	27–30	29–34
Analysis	2–8	0–3	4–6
Synthesis	1–11	6	6–12
Evaluation	0–6	0–2	0–6

of study, the percentages of examination items in each of the major *Taxonomy* categories. The similarity of cognitive objectives within programs persists between programs when one examines Table 5. Overall, the ninth grade examinations show teachers' preoccupation with knowledge of specifics. In all programs, at least half of a student's questions required only memory. For PreV students who took English with Teacher B and civics, almost three-fourths of their examination items called only for knowledge. Emphasis on recall of specific information showed a slight decline along the prestige alignment of programs from PreV to CP. Questions emphasizing comprehension received very little attention in all courses in each of the programs of study. Items requiring application of knowledge constituted quite similar proportions in all three programs, although there was somewhat less attention to application, interestingly enough, in the PreV program. Had it not been for English Teacher A, most students would have had no opportunity to engage in examination tasks requiring analysis, synthesis, and evaluation.

DISCUSSION

The emphasis on memory in the ninth grade examinations analyzed in this study is not particularly surprising. Indeed, that only about half the items, considering tests in all courses, emphasized knowledge alone is interesting in itself. Since its possession is prerequisite to employing it in higher mental operations, teachers must properly be concerned that students acquire knowledge. Nevertheless, to exclude attention to other cognitive areas, as was done in the civics and biology tests, seems excessive. Surely, learning and thinking in these courses can and should involve some attention to operations other than memory. Very interesting, in this regard, is the observation that English Teacher A employed no "knowledge-only" questions with her low ability students.

The overall lack of concern for the objectives in the areas of analysis, synthesis, and evaluation, while not unusual, is surely depressing. In a sense, these junior high school students were intellectually deprived, not having the opportunity, at least on examinations, to deal with much of the basic nature of the courses. Thus, these students, academically able and potential dropouts, were treated to a steady diet of bits-upon-pieces, specific-upon-specific. Only in English and, for a limited group in world history, did students have the intellectual challenge of the higher cognitive processes. Surely, all these courses could have given attention to analysis, synthesis, and evaluation, perhaps in varying degrees, but at least some attention. Only as all courses focus attention on all the intellectual skills and processes will schooling begin to achieve the general goal of fostering thinking. At present, if this junior high school is at all representative of others in the nation, and there is evidence that it is above-average, much concerted attention to this problem is mandatory.

The great similarity within and between the several programs of study in this junior high school reveals inconsistent and perhaps unknown emphases. Are the cognitive objectives in the three programs of study really as similar as they appear to be? If they are, should they be? The apparent similarities certainly indicate that acquisition and application of knowledge are the most important categories of intellectual operations in these junior high school examinations. Even so, the summary similarities conceal the rather striking differences between certain components of the programs, particularly within the social studies, science, and the English areas. Courses in these fields emphasize different cognitive objectives without apparent rationale. Why should civics and world history differ so markedly in their emphasis upon types of thinking? If the reason is that civics is for less-able students, then why does biology, offered to the academically talented students, emphasize memory almost as much as civics? In this junior high school, the civics course was deliberately designed for potential dropouts so that they might have the understandings and skills required for effective community participation. This study would indicate that the aims have little chance of succeeding until the cognitive emphases are re-examined. Is it because general science students are less able that they are required to apply knowledge more than the "better" students in biology? Or might it be that the general science teacher is attempting to make the "meat" of the course more meaningful and more palatable. That the prevocational and business students, because of academic aptitude, cannot handle the higher mental operations is a misconception is clear from the objectives emphasized by English Teacher A. Her "practical English" students were faced with more questions (a total of 80 per cent) in the analysis, synthesis, and evaluation categories than were her "advanced" students who are confronted by 70 per cent of their questions in those areas. It might be argued that she was demanding more than her students could achieve, but hard evidence is unavailable on that point at present. One may conclude, at least, that this teacher was not maintaining her less-able students on a regimen of memorized specific facts, but was encouraging them to go beyond knowledge to using it and thinking with it in different ways.

Probably, each course offered should provide opportunities for students to develop all of the cognitive skills. The extent to which each curricular area emphasizes each of the cognitive objectives surely is not identical. Recognition that knowledge is fundamental to all other cognitive goals is certainly not justification for emphasizing its acquisition to the exclusion of thinking processes.

The teacher-made examinations analyzed in this study clearly emphasized the objective of knowledge acquisition and the mental process of memory. Perhaps the examination items do not adequately represent the scope of intellectual objectives implemented by the teachers as they work in their classrooms. On this hypothesis there can be only doubt at present. Studies should be designed to investigate the nature of teachers' discourse, particularly their substantive remarks, for the cognitive objectives emphasized. In addition, teachers may very well be unaware of the extent to which they emphasize certain types of intellectual objectives and ignore others. Analysis of their own examinations, alone or as members of curriculum study groups, might well lead to better test items and as well, implementation of the general concern for the development of thinking in American schools.

ESSAY AND OBJECTIVE TEST ITEMS COMPARED

Educational Testing Service *

Both essay test items and objective test items have their faults and their virtues. Which one should be used depends entirely upon the situation. Neither should be used exclusively and neither is easy to construct, administer, and score. As far as effectiveness is concerned, it seems to be a case of six of one and a half dozen of the other, but the six of one and the six of the other are not the same half dozen. Their uses and virtues differ considerably.

	ESSAY	OBJECTIVE
Abilities Measured	Requires the student to express himself in his own words, using information from his own background and knowledge.	Requires the student to select correct answers from given options, or to supply an answer limited to one word or phrase.
	Can tap high levels of reasoning such as required in inference, organization of ideas, comparison and contrast.	Can *also* tap high levels of reasoning such as required in inference, organization of ideas, comparison and contrast.
	Does *not* measure purely factual information efficiently.	Measures knowledge of facts efficiently.

* From *Making a Classroom Test: A Guide for Teachers,* Educational Testing Service Series No. 4, by Quentin Stodola and Martin Katz. © First Edition Copyright 1959 by Educational Testing Service, Second Edition 1961. Reprinted by permission.

Scope	Covers only a limited field of knowledge in any one test. Essay questions take so long to answer that relatively few can be answered in a given period of time. Also, the student who is especially fluent can often avoid discussing points of which he is unsure.	Covers a broad field of knowledge in one test. Since objective questions may be answered quickly, one test may contain many questions. A broad coverage helps provide reliable measurement.
Incentive to Pupils	Encourages pupils to learn how to organize their own ideas and express them effectively.	Encourages pupils to build up a broad background of knowledge and abilities.
Ease of Preparation	Requires writing only a few questions for a test. Tasks must be clearly defined, general enough to offer some leeway, specific enough to set limits.	Requires writing many questions for a test. Wording must avoid ambiguities and "giveaways." Distractors should embody most likely misconceptions.
Scoring	Usually very time-consuming to score. Permits teachers to comment directly on the reasoning processes of individual pupils. However, an answer may be scored differently by different teachers or by the same teacher at different times.	Can be scored quickly. Answer generally scored only right or wrong, but scoring is very accurate and consistent.

ABC'S OF TEST CONSTRUCTION

Julian C. Stanley *

Building a test is a simple process that is very difficult to perform well. Basically it consists of three steps:

* From *NEA Journal*, Vol. 47 (Washington, D.C.: National Education Association, April 1958), pp. 224–226. Reprinted by permission of the *NEA Journal* and the author.

1. List the specific objectives of the units or lessons. (This, of course, is done in the initial unit or lesson.) Be sure that the objectives are specific and definite enough so that one can determine whether or not pupils have achieved them.
2. Prepare test items that will measure how well each objective has been reached.
   a. Be sure that the coverage is adequate, that is, all objectives are included.
   b. Be sure you have balance, that is, your test items test the objectives in proportion to their importance.
   c. Be sure that each item is appropriate, that is, it is the type of item that will in fact measure the achievement of the particular objective that it is supposed to measure.
3. Prepare a key.

The following selection by Stanley will give the reader more detailed advice on how to prepare tests; his suggestions fit into the broad outline above and show how to implement them.

Constructing a good test is one of the teacher's most difficult duties. Good tests do not just happen. Actual test construction, therefore, requires much thought and careful planning.

PLANNING THE TEST

A well-planned test will provide the means for evaluating progress toward the expected outcomes of instruction, as expressed in the educational philosophy of the particular school and as defined in the objectives of the particular course.

If the school hopes to produce "good citizens" with "integrated personalities," for example, tests must measure the development of good social attitudes and a widening range of significant interests.

For any given course, instructional objectives must be expressed in terms of the specific changes in pupil behavior or growth which the teacher hopes to bring about.

A teacher, for instance, should be conscious that such an objective as the development of an appreciation of literature may express itself in various forms of student reaction. He sets out then to phrase test questions which will determine whether a particular piece of writing gave individual students a sense of satisfaction and enthusiasm, made them want to read more by the same author, stimulated their own creative expression.

The well-planned test will reflect the relative amount of emphasis each objective has received in the actual teaching of the course. The same test might not be equally valid for two teachers of general science if one has emphasized the memorizing of isolated facts, while the other was more concerned with the interrelation of facts. Each teacher would be helped by drawing up in outline form a kind of table of specifications to indicate not only the objectives of the course, but also the relative amount of time spent on each.

The content of the test should show a similar proportion in regard to the *number* of items to be included but not the *type*, for the type of item depends upon the nature of the objective to be measured.

The well-planned test must be designed to accomplish the purpose it is to serve. If the purpose is to give the basis for school marks or classification, it will attempt to rank the pupils in order of their total achievement. But if the purpose is diagnosis, its value will depend upon its ability to reveal specific weaknesses in the achievement of individual pupils.

Diagnostic tests would cover a limited scope, but in much greater detail than a test of general achievement, and would be arranged to give scores on the separate parts. The range of difficulty of items is relatively less important, also, in diagnostic tests. This is true, too, of mastery tests administered at the end of a teaching unit to see whether minimum essentials have been achieved.

The well-planned test will also fit the conditions under which it is to be administered, such as the time available for testing, facilities for duplicating the test copies, and cost of materials, as well as the age and experience of the pupils being tested.

PREPARING THE TEST

In actual construction of a test, these suggestions have helped:

1. Prepare a rough draft of the test as soon as possible. Many teachers jot down items day by day for possible inclusion to help ensure that no important points will be omitted, particularly those appearing in supplementary material that might be overlooked if the textbook itself is the chief basis of the test.

2. Do not make the test items too easy. Many teacher-constructed tests fail to make the items difficult enough. This, no doubt, is due in part to the influence of the "70% should be the passing grade" tradition. However, the test that is too easy is not an efficient instrument for measuring pupil progress.

3. Include more items in the first draft than will be needed in the final form. This will permit culling out of weak items and those not needed to produce proper balance.

4. Subject the test to critical revision some time after it is drafted by checking items against the table of specifications to see if they show the desired emphasis on various topics. If tests are submitted for criticism to other teachers of the subject, points of doubtful importance can be weeded out and ambiguous wording corrected.

5. Include more than one type of item in the test. A variety of test types

is more interesting to students. The test situation may also require that three or four forms of objective items be used, or that these be combined with discussion or essay-type questions.

6. Place all items of one kind together in the test. Sometimes completion, true-false, and multiple-choice questions are thrown together in random order. This arrangement is rarely, if ever, desirable. When like items are grouped, the pupil can take full advantage of the mind-set imposed by a particular form, and the teacher will find scoring and interpretation of scores easier.

7. Arrange test items in an ascending order of difficulty. The placing of very difficult items at the beginning is likely to produce needless discouragement for the average or below-average student.

8. Avoid a regular sequence in the pattern of responses. If items are arranged alternately true and false, or two true and two false, pupils are likely to catch on and answer correctly without considering the content of the item at all.

9. Make directions to the pupil clear, concise, and complete. Instructions should be so clear that the weakest pupil knows what he is expected to do, though he may be unable to do it.

It is better to tell young children to "draw a line under" than to "underline." In lower grades, teachers find it helpful to read instructions aloud while the class follows silently the written instructions. If the form of the test is unfamiliar or complicated, a generous use of samples correctly marked, or practice tests, is recommended.

Regardless of how carefully a test is planned and edited, it is impossible to know solely by inspection exactly how good it is, or which are the weak items. If possible, therefore, the test should be given some advance tryout which will approximate the conditions under which the real test will be given, show the actual length of time it will require, and indicate what scoring difficulties may result.

Because various studies have shown that a majority of teachers, especially at the high-school level, use a combination of essay and objective questions, the uses and limitations of both will be briefly examined here.

THE ESSAY TEST

The essay test has both unique advantages and serious disadvantages. Some authorities claim that it calls forth less than half the knowledge the average pupil possesses on a subject, compared with results from an objective test, and takes twice the time to do it; that it overrates the importance of knowing how to say a thing and underrates the importance of having something to say; and that the score resulting from an essay test depends more upon *who* reads it and *when* than upon the student who wrote it.

Offsetting the serious scoring difficulties connected with essay tests and their frequently low degrees of validity, reliability, and usability, there is much to indicate that such tests have a legitimate place in the modern school.

Specifically, they are useful for measuring functional information, certain aspects of thinking, study skill and work habits, and an active social philosophy. These are educational objectives which emphasize the *functioning* of knowledge rather than its mere possession.

Such tests are especially valuable in courses in English composition and journalism, where the student's ability to express himself is a major instructional objective, and in advanced courses in other subjects where critical evaluation and the ability to assimilate and organize large amounts of material are important.

Essay tests have at least one other general merit: When pupils expect the test to be of that type, in whole or in part, they seem more likely to employ such desirable study techniques as outlining and summarizing, and to make a greater effort to recognize trends and relationships.

Despite popular opinion to the contrary, a high-quality essay test is more difficult to construct than is a good objective test. These three rules, however, should be helpful in improving the construction and use of essay tests:

1. Restrict such a test to those functions for which it is best adapted.

2. Increase the number of questions asked and decrease the amount of discussion required for each.

3. Make definite provisions for teaching pupils how to take such examinations.

TYPES OF OBJECTIVE TESTS

The simple *recall test* item employs a direct question, a stimulus word or phrase, or a specific direction to elicit from the pupil a response based on his previous experience. The typical response is short—hence its other name, the short-answer question.

The main problem is to phrase these test items so that they will call forth responses from a higher level than mere memory, and so that they can be readily scored.

Example: Eight is what percent of 64?

The *completion test* consists of a series of sentences in which certain important words or phrases have been replaced by blanks to be filled in by the students. This test has wide applicability, but unless very carefully prepared, it is likely to measure rote memory rather than real understanding, or to measure general intelligence or linguistic aptitude rather than school achievement.

Scoring is also more subjective, and complicated by the fact that the missing words are written in blanks scattered all over the page, rather than in a column. This difficulty can be avoided by a form such as this:

1. The man who headed the first expedition to circumnavigate the globe was—————.

2. The Articles of Confederation were in force from 1781 to—————.

An *alternative-response test* is made of items each of which permits only two possible responses. The usual form is the familiar true-false item and its cousins, the right-wrong, yes-no, same-opposite, and multiple-choice questions.

While the true-false type of question is popularly considered easy to prepare, experienced test-makers point out that this type of test requires great skill, and care must be taken in wording so that the *content* rather than the *form* of the statement will determine the response. The following suggestions may be useful in constructing such tests.

1. Avoid specific determiners, that is, strongly worded statements containing words such as "always," "all," or "none," which may indicate to pupils that the statement is likely to be false.

2. Avoid using the exact language of the textbook, with only minor changes to give the true-false pattern, because this puts too great a premium on rote memory.

3. Avoid trick statements which appear to be true but which are really false because of some inconspicuous word or phrase, such as "The Battle of Hastings was fought in 1066 BC."

4. Avoid "double-headed" statements, especially if partly true and partly false, as in this sentence: "Poe wrote *The Gold Bug* and *The Scarlet Letter.*"

5. Avoid double negatives lest pupils versed in grammar conclude that two negatives equal an affirmative, while others think such statements are emphatic negatives.

6. Avoid unfamiliar, figurative, or literary language and long statements with complex sentence structure—for reasons which should be obvious.

7. Avoid words that may have different meanings for different students. "Often" may mean once a week to one child; three times a year to another.

A *multiple choice test* is composed of items which require the student to select a correct or definitely better response from two or more alternatives (at least four whenever possible). This is one of the most useful test forms. It may be used to ascertain the ability to give definitions, identify purposes and causes, similarities and differences, or to ask many other varieties of questions.

In phrasing multiple-choice questions, it is essential to avoid giving irrelevant or superficial clues, and to assure that the question measures more than memory. The diagnostic value of this type of item depends as much on the skilful wording of the incorrect choices presented as upon correct statement of the right choice.

Scoring may be facilitated by arranging the items in groups, putting together all items with the same number of choices, and requiring the simplest possible method of recording the response.

Other useful rules are:

1. Make all responses grammatically consistent. For example, if the verb is singular, avoid plural responses.

2. Use direct questions rather than incomplete statements whenever possible. This helps eliminate irrelevant clues.

3. Arrange the responses so that the correct choice occurs about equally in all positions, and do not consistently make the correct answer longer or shorter than the others.

4. Make all the responses plausible, and when testing at higher levels, increase the similarity in the choices under each item in order to better test the powers of discrimination.

A *matching test* involves the association of two things in the mind of the learner by requiring him to pair the items in two columns: events and dates, events and persons, terms and definitions, laws and illustrations, and the like. Matching exercises are well adapted to testing in *who, what, where,* and *when* areas but not to measuring understanding as distinguished from mere memory.

Since most of the tests used in classrooms are teacher-made, it is highly important that teachers develop proficiency in the building of tests by discriminating use of what is now known, by keeping themselves informed on new studies of testing techniques and methods, and by careful evaluation of their own testing, day by day.

A CATECHISM ON ESSAY TESTS

George H. Cooke *

Essay tests have an important role in secondary education. They should be used as one means of finding out how well pupils have achieved the teaching objectives. These tests should not be used as the only method. They make it difficult to get an adequate sampling of all the objectives. They are difficult to score. Teachers who depend on them, therefore, are tempted not to test as often as they ought to. On the other hand, essay tests can give information that objective tests cannot.

In writing essay tests the following selection may serve as a guideline. Note, however, the difference of opinion implicit in Cooke's question number seven and Norman Cousins' article that follows. The editor of this book feels that the argument expressed by Cooke in his defense of the essay test as a tool by which to measure pupils' ability to organize and write is somewhat specious, and that Cousins' position is sound.

* From *Peabody Journal of Education*, Vol. 37 (Nashville, Tenn.: George Peabody College for Teachers, November 1959), pp. 158–163. Reprinted by permission of the *Peabody Journal of Education*.

Essay tests refer to those questions in which the testee is called upon to plan his answer, to organize his materials, to determine the sequence of presentation; in general, to create his own response. The essay differs in several ways from its forerunner, the oral examination. The essay test requires a written response. In oral examinations the testor may ask leading questions pertinent to the main issue. The oral test is also a measure of the ability to speak. There were so many disadvantages to the oral test that written tests were substituted. There is still a definite place for oral responses in the classroom, and such responses should be an integral part of evaluation, and of teaching.

1. Are all essay tests good?

Many so-called essay tests are really measures of memory. Some questions are outlined to the degree that pupils merely fill in the outlines. Essay tests have many worthwhile advantages but these can only be realized by suitable test exercises, time to respond and through valiant efforts of the grader.

2. Does essay testing have a place in our public schools?

Yes. The emphasis in education today is to make learning functional. If this is true then evaluation must be in similar terms. The essay test has considerable value as a means of general diagnosis. Teachers can learn of a great many characteristics, abilities, weaknesses of pupils by carefully reading their responses to essay questions. The emphasis on Gestalt learning supports one basis for essay testing.

3. Will essay testing provide proper motivation in studying and in learning?

Yes. Most teachers like to believe that certain big ideas, generalizations, principles become a part of the intellectual and emotional background of pupils. These large outcomes are and should be the basis for essay tests. It is assumed that if pupils know they will be called upon to organize, to present an explanation, to show relationships, or to solve a new problem in their field they will study with this in mind.

4. Can essay tests be used in all subjects?

Yes. The subjects taught in our high schools have applications, generalizations, explanations of how, why, effects, causes, etc. Significant ways in which the world judges the degree of understanding possessed by people are clearness of explanation, the degree to which the writer can support a statement, the ease of finding illustrations of a principle or by making application of mastered principles to a novel problem.

5. Must one use considerable time in making up an essay test?

Yes. One of the strong criticisms of essay tests is a lack of sampling of the abilities of the pupils. A test of five questions is not likely to be adequate unless the questions are broad enough to cover the subject and the outcomes. This requires a high degree of subject matter understanding and ingenuity on the part of the testor. Basic to this whole question is: will five questions reveal the truth about the conditions to be measured? In short, the testor has only a limited number of questions. Each question must be good for its intended purpose. One weak or poorly worded essay question may cause disaster, i.e., confusion and failure among pupils.

6. *How much time is necessary to grade an essay test?*

If an essay test is to serve the merits claimed for it, responses must be carefully read. If the test is to serve the purpose of evaluation, written comments by the reader are necessary. Most teachers would want to make note of frequent errors in order to re-teach, or to plan in the future. If pupils spend time and effort to write such papers, they deserve careful, thoughtful reading and analyzing by the teacher.

7. *Are essay tests a measure of the pupil's ability to organize, write, show creativity, etc.?*

Yes. If this were not true there would be little place for this form of testing. Some pupils say they know but are unable to explain. We live in a world where one must verbalize one's ideas and understandings. Hence, skill in communication as an asset is not to be denied.

8. *Can and should pupils be taught to take essay tests?*

Yes. Many pupils lack ability, or fail to use care in reading the questions. Pupils disregard differences among such words as define, distinguish, explain, relate, etc. Students do learn to organize their thoughts, to search for supporting facts, to express themselves clearly. In question seven the thought was expressed that people are often judged in many walks of life on their ability to present their ideas in a clear, logical, and an interesting manner. Hence, this is an ability to be developed and can be taught. Furthermore, this ability to take essay tests with success may be very important in college.

9. *Are there objections to essay tests that demand recalling the authoritative statements of books or teachers?*

These statements may deal with understandings, reasons for or against an issue, or examples of application. There is no answer to this question until the purpose of the question or test has been established. There is no opportunity for personal opinion, nor is there leeway for original thinking. Such a test is calling for knowledge, a repetition of the knowledge and understanding of another. This practice is not to be entirely condemned, but it does not fulfill the usual claims for the essay test.

10. *Do philosophies of education differ in their views toward essay tests?*

Yes. The philosophy of idealism looks for questions to stimulate the mind, questions that will call forth a variety of answers. The idealist pupil would select the most difficult question as a challenge to his powers. The idealist teacher admits subjectivity but relies on his own judgment and insight for grading essay tests. IIe looks for depth, coherence, originality, clearness, vigor, and unity.

The realist is clear with respect to his teaching objectives; namely understanding, knowledge, and ability to use. He seeks methods of testing that are objective, and reliable. Furthermore, he would place his faith in tests made by experts rather than by teachers. He is more interested in using a test to measure than to teach; therefore, he would not favor a choice of questions by pupils.

A pragmatist would agree with the realist in the purpose of tests, i.e., to measure rather than to teach. He does not agree with the realist as to the importance of testing of any kind. This brief statement is to point out that the idealist would certainly favor essay tests of the most general type; other philosophies would differ.

11. *Are there advantages to the essay test not found in objective types?*

Yes. To a question which requires an essay answer, the writer has an opportunity to show what he can do with the question. He can display ingenuity, creativeness, literary ability, originality, and resourcefulness. The degree of validity depends more on the worth of the question than on the form of it.

12. *Are essay tests difficult to grade?*

Yes. It has been pointed out that grading these tests does and should take a long time. Many studies have been made to show the unreliability of grades due to factors of variability of the grader, or even a number of graders. One is faced with many factors such as handwriting, the degree of relevancy of response, misinterpretation of the question, bluffing, and halo effects. Suggestions have been made to make grading more objective but improvements frequently detract from the values claimed for the essay test.

13. *Can essay testing be improved?*

Yes. There are many kinds of essay questions. Some may be suitable for one situation, some for another. The word "discuss" frequently is used and has broad meanings. The exact meaning of this word should be clear to the pupils. The teachers often give such directions as "relate," "devise a new procedure," "explain the meaning, use, operation," "how would you react to such and such a situation," etc. One professor gave as his final examination: "Outline the chapter and fill in the details." It is possible to make the question of such a nature that grading becomes easier and more objective but the test loses its inherent value as a true essay test. It has been already suggested that pupils be given some training in taking essay tests. The use of model answers helps objectivity of grading and reliability but may penalize the student who is original, creative, or who disagrees with the authorities. Essay questions may take almost as many forms as the objective question.

It has been suggested to have more questions calling for shorter responses. But if this is carried to any length, such practice could become almost a recall, or a completion type test. This test may not involve dealing with large ideas and significant generalizations, but would provide better sampling.

14. *How great are the disadvantages of essay testing?*

A brief list should be all that is necessary. It should be realized that these disadvantages are not always present, just as this paper has pointed out that all essay tests are not inevitably satisfactory or defensible. Grading is difficult and time consuming. Bluffing is possible. Sampling is limited. A premium is placed on literary ability, and boldness of expression. A teacher who depends on essay tests is less likely to give tests frequently enough to use them as a teaching tool. Regardless of how good the question may be, subjectivity in grading and inadequate sampling may interfere with validity of measurement.

15. *Are there many kinds of essay questions?*

Yes. Monroe and Carter [1] collected and classified almost a score of essay questions that differed. 1. Interpretation 2. criticism and evaluation 3. statement of purpose 4. how to do 5. cause and effect 6. statement of relationship 7. compare and contrast 8. illustrations 9. application of principle 10. discuss 11. describe 12. summarize 13. list 14. explain 15. devise a plan of research to prove— 16. support your reaction to the following 17. a problem type such as the following: A parent, or your principal asks you how a particular pupil is "getting along" in your class. Discuss the possible meanings and implications of such a query. How do you plan to conduct your classes in order to give a competent, defensible answer to this rather common question?

16. *Should the teacher introduce an essay question calling for a unique approach?*

Yes. This is one advantage to the essay question. To devise a new problem, real or hypothetical, is entirely within the scope of the essay question. The better the question the greater is the challenge for the pupil. The learning of students is improved, and teachers will grow and extend their own thinking.

17. *Should teachers and professors read their own papers?*

Yes. While clerks, graduate assistant may properly read short answer essay papers, or score objective papers, only the class teacher should read essay papers if the usual merits of the essay test are to be achieved.

18. *Will students disagree with the teacher regarding grades given on essay tests?*

[1] Walter S. Monroe and R. E. Carter, "The Use of Different Types of Thought Questions in Secondary Schools and Their Relative Difficulty for Students," Bureau of Educational Research Bulletin, No. 14, University of Illinois, Urbana, 1923.

This can and does happen but not so much as with the objective test. The teacher states he has used his best judgment while grading the answers. How many pupils have the courage to criticize the judgment of their teachers?

19. *Do essay tests minimize the importance of a good knowledge of facts and principles?*

No. In order to write a good essay, students will need a comprehensive knowledge of facts, principles, etc. But what is more, this knowledge and understanding must be selected, organized and applied to the questions in an acceptable form.

A final word on essay tests is intended to encourage the use of this medium. The form of question can and should be improved as the teacher experiments with such tests. It will be an unfortunate time when pupils are not called upon to explain, to meet and solve unique problems, to be challenged by searching questions. Finally, pupils should be given help in order to write better tests. No one should assume from this paper that the essay is the total answer to all the problems of total evaluation of pupils.

HOW TO WRITE WITHOUT THINKING

Norman Cousins *

Sometimes our attempts to teach and evaluate pupil learning get all mixed up. One example of this confusion is the ardent belief of teachers, particularly liberal arts professors, that the only way to test the ability to write or to organize is the essay test. Actually, the writing of an essay or an essay test under the pressure of a test situation is probably more likely to develop poor writing habits than to reveal good writing. Norman Cousins, a master journalist who knows much about writing and teaching, uncovers the fallacy of such testing in the following editorial in which he criticizes the College Entrance Examination Board's attempt to measure youth's writing ability by means of essays written under test conditions.

Our colleague, *The New Yorker* magazine, recently sent one of its men to Princeton, New Jersey, to look in on the Educational Testing Service, an

* From Norman Cousins, "How to Write Without Thinking," *Saturday Review*, Vol. 48 (May 1, 1965), p. 30. Reprinted by permission of the *Saturday Review*.

organization that periodically assembles large numbers of teachers for the grading of College Entrance Examination Board papers. On this particular occasion, 185 English teachers from all over the country were on location, and were reading 68,000 essays by high school students. The assigned subject in the essay was a quotation from George Bernard Shaw's *Man and Superman*:

The reasonable man adapts himself to the world; the unreasonable one persists in trying to adapt the world to himself. Therefore all progress depends on the unreasonable man.

The New Yorker did a straightforward, reportorial account of the event in typical "Talk of the Town" fashion. We confess we read the item with mounting horror, not because there was anything untoward in the way *The New Yorker* reported the story, but because of the basic facts that pertained to the essay question.

We were bothered first of all by the nature of the assignment. Taking an aphoristic, paradoxical syllogism by G.B.S. and attempting to expound or speculate on it can succeed only in spoiling it. Aphorisms, like any form of wit, are not meant to be broken down or hashed over. They derive their beauty from their economy of line and their ability to produce a collision in the mind between two separate trains of thought. There is something highly inartistic and presumptuous about opening up an aphorism, dissecting it, and reassembling the parts into a much larger non-aphoristic whole. You take an aphorism as it is; you don't fool with it or do dissertations on it. An aphorism is like a soufflé; once you start to poke or prod it or take it out of its frame, it falls apart.

This is not all. The notion that the way to test writing ability is to assign a subject gives us the willies. Good writing is something that begins in a man's gizzard. An idea grows inside him until it is ready to pop. The process can be painful or satisfying or both, depending on the idea; but it is a process. We should suppose that the function of the creative teacher is to encourage the student to select his own subject from among the things that are coming to life in his mind. He will never learn to write well unless he develops the ability to dream, to stew, and to be possessed by all sorts of notions that are itching to be expressed.

What is most disquieting of all, however, is the fact of an arbitrary time limit of twenty minutes for writing these essays. What goes on here? A student deserves a high grade if he can think of a good title for an essay in twenty minutes—even before he writes one word. And if it takes two hours or even two days to think through the main points he wants to make in his essay, he will be developing the good habits that go into good writing. What the CEEB does, however, is to separate writing from thinking.

Twenty minutes. Words are not tins of chipped beef to be assembled at so many per minute. The significant thing about a sentence is not how long it took to be written but whether it has its proper place in a sequence of ideas and conveys its message with reasonable clarity and, if possible, style—difficult though it may be to define anything so amorphous as style. The surest way to destroy good writing is to have a clock ticking away in a man's mind. Thomas Mann felt he had done a good day's work if he produced a single typewritten page that said what he wanted to say—not approximately, not passably, but precisely, with the words turning just right, the weight and the accent where he wanted them, and the contour and texture providing the desired effect.

Would we eliminate the essay altogether from English examinations? Certainly not. What might be done is to get the checking questions out of the way on a separate paper, then ask the student to write an essay of an approximate length—on a subject of his own choosing or one he can select from a fairly long list. He would be substantially free of time limitations; that is, he could spend the rest of the day on his paper if he wished. And he would be free to take time out for consulting books or other materials. Even this approach is somewhat squeezed, but it is far better than the twenty-minute straitjacket.

Somewhere in this favored land there must be English teachers who not only do not commit the literary sacrilege of setting a time limit on an essay but who allow and indeed require their students to spend several days thinking about an idea before presuming to commit it to paper. These teachers are as interested in providing the proper environment for creative writing as they are in the writing itself. They encourage the widest possible reflective reading. They recognize the dangers that come from conditioning students to deal in easy, glib answers. These teachers—and we are convinced there must be many of them—ought to go to the mat with the people at CEEB. Perhaps they might even say that if CEEB persists in its twenty-minute essay requirement, they will instruct their students to skip the question—not because they lack respect for the examining body but because they have too much respect for the English language.

Finally, we quarrel about neatness requirements on English examination papers, wherever such requirements exist. The more crossing out, the more reworking and transposing and inserting of second thoughts, the greater the evidence that a student is fully engaged in that painful but also infinitely rewarding exercise of the human intellect, good writing.

MEASURING WRITING ABILITY

Paul B. Diederich *

This short excerpt from a long article by Paul Diederich, of the Educational Testing Service, shows criteria that are used to make the estimates of the readers more reliable. A scale of this type is very helpful in rating performance activities. Although usually they are less complicated and explicit, it is almost a necessity if teachers are to be at all even in their evaluations. Without such a guide, teachers tend to unconsciously give undue weight to extraneous factors that often really should not have any influence in the evaluation at all.

This particular scale, the ETS Composition Scale, was derived from a very detailed study. This study included a factor analysis of the grades of 300 freshmen composition papers given by 53 distinguished readers, a further analysis over a period of one year in three large high schools, and a subsequent workshop in which teachers analyzed a large number of papers that had been rated high, middle, and low on the eight qualities and wrote the descriptions represented here.

Ratings are recorded on 3 by 5 cards by encircling a number representing the scale position of the paper on each quality. In terms of percentages, 5 equals the top 5 per cent, 4 equals the high fifth, 3 equals the middle half, 2 equals the low fifth, and 1 equals the lowest 5 per cent. The midpoints of these intervals are approximately one standard deviation apart. Teachers have recently insisted on emphasizing the importance of ideas and organization by doubling the numbers representing each scale position; hence the numbers after these qualities are now 10, 8, 6, 4, and 2. The scale positions correspond roughly to grades of A, B, C, D, and F.

I. GENERAL MERIT

1. IDEAS

High. The student has given some thought to the topic and has written what he really thinks. He discusses each main point long enough to show clearly what he means. He supports each main point with arguments, ex-

* From Paul B. Diederich, "How to Measure Growth in Writing Ability," *English Journal*, Vol. 55 (Champaign, Ill.: NCTE, April 1966), pp. 444–446. Reprinted with the permission of the National Council of Teachers of English and Paul B. Diederich.

amples, or details; he gives the reader some reason for believing it. His points are clearly related to the topic and to the main idea or impression he is trying to get across. No necessary points are overlooked and there is no padding.

Middle. The paper gives the impression that the student does not really believe what he is writing or does not fully realize what it means. He tries to guess what the teacher wants and writes what he thinks will get by. He does not explain his points very clearly or make them come alive to the reader. He writes what he thinks will sound good, not what he believes or knows.

Low. It is either hard to tell what points the student is trying to make or else they are so silly that he would have realized that they made no sense if he had only stopped to think. He is only trying to get something down on paper. He does not explain his points; he only writes them and then goes on to something else, or he repeats them in slightly different words. He does not bother to check his facts, and much of what he writes is obviously untrue. No one believes this sort of writing—not even the student who wrote it.

2. ORGANIZATION

High. The paper starts at a good point, moves in a straight line, gets somewhere, and stops at a good point. The paper has a plan that the reader can follow; he is never in doubt as to where he is or where he is going. Sometimes there is a little twist near the end that makes the paper come out in a way that the reader does not expect, but it seems quite logical. Main points are treated at greatest length or with greatest emphasis; others in proportion to their importance.

Middle. The organization of this paper is standardized and conventional. There is usually a one-paragraph introduction, three main points each treated in one paragraph, and a conclusion that often seems tacked on or forced. Some trivial points may be treated in greater detail than important points, and there is usually some dead wood that might better be cut out.

Low. This paper starts anywhere and never gets anywhere. The main points are not clearly separated from one another, and they come in a random order—as though the student had not given any thought to what he intended to say before he sat down to write. The paper seems to start in one direction, then another, then another, until the reader is lost.

3. WORDING

High. The writer uses a sprinkling of uncommon words or of familiar words in an uncommon setting. He shows an interest in words and in putting them together in slightly unusual ways. Some of his experiments with words may not quite come off, but this is such a promising trait in a young writer that a few mistakes may be forgiven. For the most part he uses words correctly, but he also uses them with imagination.

Middle. The writer is addicted to tired old phrases and hackneyed expressions. If you left a blank in one of his sentences, almost anyone could guess what word he would use at that point. He does not stop to think how to say something; he just says it in the same way as everyone else. A writer may also get a middle rating on this quality if he overdoes his experiments with uncommon words: if he always uses a big word when a little word would serve his purpose better.

Low. The writer uses words so carelessly or inexactly that he gets far too many wrong. These are not intentional experiments with words in which failure may be forgiven; they represent groping for words and using them without regard to their fitness. A paper written entirely in a childish vocabulary may also get a low rating, even if no word is clearly wrong.

4. FLAVOR

High. The writing sounds like a person, not a committee. The writer seems quite sincere and candid, and he writes about something he knows—often from personal experience. You could never mistake this writing for the writing of anyone else. Although the writer may play different roles in different papers, he does not put on airs. He is brave enough to reveal himself just as he is.

Middle. The writer usually tries to appear better or wiser than he really is. He tends to write lofty sentiments and broad generalities. He does not put in the little homely details that show that he knows what he is talking about. His writing tries to sound impressive. Sometimes it is impersonal and correct but colorless, without personal feeling or imagination.

Low. The writer reveals himself well enough but without meaning to. His thoughts and feelings are those of an uneducated person who does not realize how bad they sound. His way of expressing himself differs from standard English, but it is not his personal style; it is the way uneducated people talk in the neighborhood in which he lives.

II. MECHANICS

5. USAGE, SENTENCE STRUCTURE

High. There are no vulgar or "illiterate" errors in usage by present standards of informal written English, and there are very few errors in points that have been emphasized in class. The sentence structure is usually correct, even in varied and complicated sentence patterns.

Middle. There are a few serious errors in usage and several in points that have been emphasized in class, but not enough to obscure meaning. The sentence structure is usually correct in the more familiar sentence patterns, but there are occasional errors in more complicated patterns, as in parallelism, subordination, consistency of tenses, reference of pronouns, etc.

Low. There are so many serious errors in usage and sentence structure that the paper is hard to understand.

6. PUNCTUATION, CAPITALS, ABBREVIATIONS, NUMBERS

High. There are no serious violations of rules that have been taught—except slips of the pen. Note, however, that modern editors do not require commas after short introductory clauses, around nonrestrictive clauses, or between short coordinate clauses unless their omission leads to ambiguity or makes the sentence hard to read. Contractions are acceptable—often desirable.

Middle. There are several violations of rules that have been taught—as many as usually occur in the average paper.

Low. Basic punctuation is omitted or haphazard, resulting in fragments, run-on sentences, etc.

7. SPELLING

High. Since this rating scale is most often used for test papers written in class when there is insufficient time to use the dictionary, spelling standards should be more lenient than for papers written at home. The high paper usually has not more than five misspellings, and these occur in words that are hard to spell. The spelling is consistent: words are not spelled correctly in one sentence and misspelled in another, unless the misspelling appears to be a slip of the pen. If a poor paper has no misspellings, it gets a 5 in spelling.

Middle. There are several spelling errors in hard words and a few violations of basic spelling rules, but no more than one finds in the average paper.

Low. There are so many spelling errors that they interfere with comprehension.

8. HANDWRITING, NEATNESS

High. The handwriting is clear, attractive, and well spaced, and the rules of manuscript form have been observed.

Middle. The handwriting is average in legibility and attractiveness. There may be a few violations of rules for manuscript form if there is evidence of some care for the appearance of the page.

Low. The paper is sloppy in appearance and difficult to read.

MARKS, NORMS, AND
PROFICIENCY SCORES

William Clark Trow *

Studies of our schools make evident the need for new and better mark-ing systems. Just what those systems should be is yet undetermined. It would seem, however, that the ideal system would indicate in some fashion just how much each pupil had learned of the goals he was sup-posed to attain and that it would be flexible enough to provide the infor-mation when it was needed. Perhaps this is the type of system that will be forced on the secondary schools by the new trend toward ungraded curricula. Meanwhile in the following selection William Clark Trow indicates directions in which one might search to find the ultimate marking system.

I am not a school administrator, but if I were and saw the headline, PRO-FESSOR WOULD ABOLISH SCHOOL MARKS, I would emit the old "ho-hum" and turn on television to the ball game.

Not that marks do not deserve to be abolished. Anyone who has not lived his life in the ivory tower, however, knows that trying to abolish them would be like trying to abolish money. Sometimes a school or college deplores the overemphasis on marks and decides to do without all but the essential "pass" and "fail." But soon such variations appear as "pass plus" and "pass minus," and these are soon followed by "honors," to which plus and minus signs are shortly added, and the same old system is back again.

And in the schools, when a superintendent is daring enough to make the attempt, formerly ill-attended PTA meetings are crowded with protestors, news articles discuss competition as the American way of life, and teachers favoring the status quo explain that "he" is working for a degree at the uni-versity or trying to make a name for himself. Even some of the students, for whose benefit the move was undertaken, want to know where they stand in comparison with others in their classes.

USES FOR SCHOOL MARKS

Of course marks do have their place, such as it is. They represent a teacher's evaluation of a student's performance on a limited academic task or on an

* From *Phi Delta Kappan*, Vol. 48 (Bloomington, Ind.: Phi Delta Kappa, December 1966), pp. 171–173. Reprinted by permission of the publisher.

extended series of such tasks. But they are in reality a multiple-purpose system. Their general utility is revealed by even a partial list of their functions. They serve:

To inform teachers, students, and parents of how well individual students are doing in comparison with the others in their grade or class; and at year's end to designate those destined for promotion and non-promotion.

To provide data for academic and vocational counseling and guidance.

To reward good performance—except for those who cannot do very well. (The rewards are not quite the same as reinforcement, and as a rule not efficiently manipulated.)

To punish poor performance whether or not the student could do better. (If he could not, such action is at least ethically questionable.)

To motivate learning—but students are motivated to compete for marks rather than to attain the more substantial values.

Although marks do serve useful purposes, the good and bad are almost hopelessly mixed in the traditional marking system, and the side effects are mostly on the negative side. The superior are not challenged but are often rewarded for a performance that for them is mediocre; they will "pass" anyway. The retarded are discouraged, as are the disadvantaged, for they are unfairly asked to do things they cannot do, and so get farther and farther behind ("cumulative ignorance"). There is no assurance that anyone, even those in the middle range of ability, are learning as well as they might.

In addition to the functions listed, marks serve as a basis for communicating with the home, for giving special attention to exceptional children, and for such tasks as promotions, award of prizes, and job recommendations. But even for these purposes, taken by themselves marks are dubious criteria for professional judgments.

For the time being, the solution seems to lie not in abolishing marks but in reducing their unwholesome influence by also employing a different form of appraisal.

MARKS THAT DEPEND ON NORMS

Like achievement test scores, marks that depend on norms are based on a comparison of the performance of each student with the others in his grade or class. If the student is in a bright class, he is liable to get a lower mark than he would if he were a member of a slow group.

Even the standardized tests are stacked against him; for they are designed to produce a normal curve, with hard questions included that a large proportion of the students cannot answer—and there may be no good reason why they should. It is uneconomical to spend time and money trying to teach pupils what is known beforehand they will not learn. If they *should* learn such items, they can and should be taught. But if they are taught, the whole class will be able to answer all (or nearly all) of the questions correctly, and "the curve" goes out the window. Or else the teachers would hold to it as an article of faith and conclude either that the test on which every-one gets a good mark is not a good test, or that the students cheated.

As a matter of fact, what has been termed a "mastery test" has been tried out here and there. Is is a test to discover whether pupils have really mastered a given content. If, as in most subjects, there are areas of knowledge about which students should know something but not everything, they might properly receive the top score for answering, say, half the questions correctly, and given no more credit for memorizing further details, which they will soon forget. This would be done on the assumption that their time would be better spent doing something else, e.g., taking a field trip or working on some project.

The current marking system presents an anomalous situation, one up with which we would not put, to paraphrase Winston Churchill's famous declaration, if we had not long assumed that it was the proper procedure. But this is not the end. Raw scores are practically meaningless, so they are transposed into the relative terms of age or grade norms. There is some paper convenience in this arrangement, but it tells us little or nothing of what a student actually *knows* or can *do*, and no one is likely to inquire. Instead, it only tells which students of the same age or in the same grade answered more or fewer questions correctly. To some people "fifth-grade arithmetic ability" may mean something; but what of fifth-grade French ability, or tenth-grade violin, or twelve-year-old typing, or even college algebra?

Marks or scores based on such concepts as those, dependent as they are on the students' relative standing, have been called "norm-referenced." [1] This term is sufficiently awkward to be sure of incorporation into the current technical jargon of education. What we lack and need badly is a content or "criterion-referenced" score based directly on proficiency in subject matter.

MARKS DEPENDING ON PROFICIENCY

The criterion-referenced score is easiest to use when there is some absolute unit of measurement as, for example, in track and field sports. The most accurate mark for ability in running is time in minutes and seconds for a certain distance, and for jumping or throwing it is distance in feet and inches. Similarly, the most accurate mark for typing or shorthand is letters or words per minute. Such measures can be easily converted into a scale, say, of zero to 100, zero being just no ability and 100 that of the top-level professional. Other abilities could be placed along such a scale as this, the ability to play a musical instrument or use a foreign language. In some subjects—social studies, for example—it would be more difficult, but not impossible, to obtain a reasonable consensus on such a sequential arrangement. But almost any planned continuum would result in a more meaningful score than we now have.

[1] Robert Glaser, "Psychology and Educational Technology," *Educational Technology*, May 15, 1966, pp. 1–14.

The criterion-referenced score, then, is a point along a continuum of sub-ject-matter knowledge or skill that indicates the degree of proficiency achieved by an individual without reference to anyone else. Whatever grade he is in, or whoever else is in it, the student's score is the same and indicates *his* level of proficiency. If he is to be instructed, his performance would start at this point and would be expected to move on from there. Sequentially scaled achievement tests to measure his abilities and record his progress remain to be devised.

Some skills might have two or three or more continuums, language skills, for example, having such items as handwriting, spelling, vocabulary, pro-nunciation, and verbal fluency. Similarly for musical skills, such matters as tone quality, technique, reading, and musical feeling might be included. A composite score might be of value under certain circumstances.

OBJECTIVES

It will soon be discovered that to define points on the zero-to-100 con-tinuum the content of instruction in the form of objectives must be clear and definite. And this is the most important reason for moving over to a criterion-referenced marking system. It tends to force attention to the problem of ob-jectives. Just what are students expected to learn?

It is in the formulation of objectives that our educational practice is per-haps weakest. General statements are good enough as far as they go, but they do not go far enough. Specifically, what should young people be taught when the stated objective is "knowledge of history," "understanding of geo-graphical concepts," "appreciation of art," or "realization of the meaning of democracy"?

Actually, every teacher teaches specific concepts and generalizations with-out raising the question of agreement or disagreement with every other teacher. Basic agreements on objectives could be used as a starter. Finer demarcations would be subject to modification based on further research. If instruction is to be effective, the statements of successive objectives should be much more specific than is customary and should indicate just what at different stages the students will be expected to know and be able to do,[2] e.g., to identify, differentiate, solve, construct, list, compare, contrast, etc.

A sequential statement of content objectives has many advantages, among them the following:

It clarifies for a teacher the successive competencies he should expect of a student in progress, and the goal or terminal behavior sought.

[2] See Robert F. Mager, *Preparing Objectives for Programmed Instruction*. San Fran-cisco: Fearon Publishers, Inc., 1962. The excellent suggestions in this little book apply not only to programming but to instruction and testing generally, but they need to be carried further. See also, *Taxonomy of Educational Objectives*, Handbook I, *Cognitive Domain*, by Benjamin S. Bloom *et al*. New York: Longmans, Green, 1956; and Handbook II, *Affective Domain*, by David Krathwohl *et al*. New York: David McKay, 1964. Unfortu-nately, the third handbook on the psychomotor domain has not yet been compiled.

It clarifies for the student what is expected of him and so reduces the strain of uncertainty about "what will be asked on the examination."

It places the emphasis on learning and teaching, where it belongs, and not on school marks.

It provides a succession of check points showing the progress made in the successive attainment of objectives which for the student is rewarding, reinforcing, and motivating, and tends to reduce irrelevant conduct.[3]

In summary, some of the advantages of criterion-referenced marking may be noted:

It gives each student an absolute rather than a relative measure of his achievement or performance that does not depend on what others do.

It provides the opportunity for each student to compete with his own prior record. Over a period of time, a succession of measures reveals the progress that he is making.

It facilitates temporary groupings of students who have actually reached the same level for discussions, TV showings, field trips, etc.

It encourages arrangements by means of which students may proceed at their own rate: They do not have to be held back or pushed ahead.

It makes it easier to adapt instruction to those students who transfer from other schools, since grade standards vary so widely, and to help those who have been absent, since they can go on from the point where they left off.

It furnishes data for obtaining averages and deviations in proficiency for different age groups, and correlations may be found with whatever variables one may be interested in.

It forces attention on content objectives and individual differences in the progress of students. Hence criterion-referenced marks would be useful now and will be even more so in the future when needed for computer-assisted instruction now being developed.

DUAL ASSESSMENT

Should the traditional norm-referenced marking system be continued? For the present, probably yes; partly because it would be more than one's life is worth to try to get rid of it, and partly because it provides a convenient comparison of the performance of pupils with that of others in the same grade or class, though proficiency scores would be more satisfactory for this purpose. It is quite possible that the old norm-referenced system will gradually wither away as the new criterion-referenced individual scores come into common use. The process of development can begin in a small way with the

---

[3] After completing the first draft of this manuscript, I learned that this procedure is being tried out by the Learning Research and Development Center at the University of Pittsburgh. It is briefly reported in the following mimeographed articles: "The Role of Evaluation in Individually Prescribed Instruction," by C. M. Lindvall and Robert Glaser; "The Project for Individually Prescribed Instruction (Oakleaf Project)," by C. M. Lindvall; and "The Development of a Sequentially Scaled Achievement Test," by Richard C. Cox and Glenn T. Graham.

skills that are now measurable in absolute units; gradually we will move out to the other subject-matter areas.

When a number of influential school administrators and teachers become aware of the possibilities and begin to apply pressure, then and only then will the makers of standardized tests evince an interest. As one wrote, "The idea is a good one and practicable. But it took us 20 years to get norms and the curve across to the profession, so why start all over again?" Perhaps this brief paper will suggest reasons for making a fresh start.

REPORTING TO PARENTS:
WHY? WHAT? HOW?

William M. Alexander *

Parents have a right to know how their children are progressing in their schoolwork. In the last few decades there has been much confusion about how this information could best be furnished the parent. Ordinarily, it is furnished them by means of report cards that give the pupils' marks and perhaps some other information. However, the ordinary report card is inadequate. Sometimes it hides more information than it gives. Many other proposals have been made. None of them have provided really satisfactory answers. Perhaps Alexander's suggestions, if taken seriously, might help alleviate the situation. At any rate, educators need to give high priority to this problem of marking and reporting to parents.

For some 25 years now, there has been widespread experimentation with newer types of reports. Reporting to parents has changed in many respects, mostly to the good. More information than percentage marks in the subjects is now commonly given in reports. Much effort is devoted to exchange of information and advice between parents and teachers. Many teachers try very hard to use the whole marking and reporting system as a means of helping their pupils to carry on self-appraisal and improvement.

But have those who are zealous to improve reporting sometimes confused

* From *NEA Journal*, Vol. 48 (Washington, D.C.: National Education Association, December 1959), pp. 15–18. Reprinted by permission of the *NEA Journal* and the author.

parents, pupils, and even some teachers? In trying to communicate better with parents, are teachers sometimes making it more difficult for parents to understand later on when their children encounter other reporting practices? Have some fine efforts to aid pupil progress made it more difficult for pupils to judge their progress?

I would answer yes to these questions, because some teachers and interested parents have frequently overlooked two relevant if unfortunate facts:

1. Differences in reporting practices from level to level and school to school are not easily understood by pupils and their parents.

2. Try as many teachers and parents may to guide learning for learning's sake, there has been far more guidance of learning for the sake of grades and good reports.

Perhaps further improvement in reporting would be aided by more common understanding of the logical answers to three questions: Why report? What to report? How report?

WHY REPORT?

Any boy or girl can tell us why schools send reports home: so that parents may know how their children are getting along in school.

The newer practices have not reduced parents' basic interest in their children's progress. Indeed, informative reports may have whetted the interest of many mothers and fathers. Reporting systems that fail to convey to parents information they understand about their children's progress (or, perhaps more factually, their class standing) invite trouble.

Marks or grades have long been accepted reporting symbols. These marks found their way into school records as well as school reports, and so into college transcripts. From numerical marks or from point equivalents of letter marks, rank in class could be computed for high-school seniors and used by college-admission officials.

Marks could also be reported to prospective employers. Thus, marks and reports became inextricably related, and their purposes were somewhat broadened, especially at the secondary level, to include prediction of college success and even of success in a job.

But the central purpose of informing parents about their children's school progress, and even the related purposes of informing colleges and employers about prospective students and employees, has frequently been subordinated to other purposes: Marks could also be used to decide on promotion and graduation.

Reports become the signposts of passing or failing. Although retardation has been drastically reduced in the past half century, marks still separate pupils by achievement in those schools in which a pupil's previous record determines his assignment to homogeneous groups or tracks.

In recent years, school people, pressed by many needs for better public support of the schools, have awakened to the public-relations aspects of reporting. Here is one place, it was realized, where teachers and parents have a common interest and a reason for getting together. Therefore, reporting systems have been geared in many communities to their potential for interpreting the school and its needs to parents.

However, reports to parents were and are so widely used by both parents and teachers as clubs over the heads of children as to make the report card—and school in general—hateful to many. Are today's parents, whose own parents granted or withheld privileges on the basis of marks on the report card, likely to perceive their child's report as a happy symbol of the parent-teacher partnership?

Undoubtedly, one purpose of reports to parents has been to provide pupils with the incentive to do schoolwork that neither parent nor teacher knew how else to supply. However, indiscriminate clubbing through marks is known to have quite different results from those which well-meaning parents and teachers seek for children.

Of these various and frequently conflicting purposes of reporting systems, two seem clear-cut and justifiable:

1. Parents should have information about their children's progress and standing in school. If this information can be given in a way that promotes understanding of home and school, all the better. But the information needs to be sufficiently factual, even if disappointing, so that the mother and father can use it to understand and help their child. Certainly such information at the high-school level should also be available to college-admission officials and prospective employers.

2. Ultimately, it is even more important that boys and girls have the best information available in understandable form about their own progress. To understand themselves, to capitalize on their strong points, and to remedy, if possible, their weaker ones, they need to know what these strengths and weaknesses are. Many types of evaluative data are needed for this purpose in addition to a six- or twelve-weeks' set of marks, but the accumulation and summary of facts at reporting time may be very useful in the pupil's own plan for continued, improved progress.

WHAT TO REPORT?

Differences of opinion and practice about the purposes of reporting seem almost minor as compared to those which exist about the content of reports. Great variations occur in the items on which information is reported and in the marking symbols. These variations are both vertical, from level to level, and horizontal, from school to school, at the same level.

The educational philosophy in a school or system and especially in the classrooms concerned would be expected to control the nature of the instructional program and the content of the report.

If achievement in subject matter is a central goal, the report card would report pupils' standing in knowledge of subjects of the curriculum. If behavior according to stated criteria of growth and development is a goal, then a description of relevant behavior would be reported. If progress in various work skills and habits is desired, then the report would indicate pupils' status or progress in specific skills and habits.

Since the instructional program typically serves more than one of these goals, the report may give a mark in the subjects and a check on various behavior traits and work habits. Sometimes, however, the philosophy is not clearly stated in the report or understood by either parent or teachers, and what the report is trying to report is not really defined.

The dominant philosophy relates also to the basis on which standing and progress are determined:

Does an A, for example, mean that the pupil is doing top work with respect to his own potential or to the norm determined as an average of the distribution of marks in the class, or by the teacher's expectation of some standard of achievement, or by the norms of some standardized test? And does it describe the pupil's present standing or his progress since some previous time?

An A may mean any of these things in different communities, in different schools in the same community, or perhaps even in different classrooms of the same school.

Confusion arises, at least among some pupils and parents, when the norms and underlying philosophies vary from level to level. The transition from elementary to secondary schools in many communities includes introduction to the use of letter marks for achievement and perhaps elimination of reports on behavior characteristics and work habits.

Even at the same level, teachers may, and sometimes do, disregard the written forms, the check lists or other spaces for reporting on items other than subject achievement. In oral reporting there may be even less uniformity in the items about which teachers and parents converse.

Lack of parent understanding may be increased by varieties in the symbols used in written reports and records. Elementary schools may use S and U, and perhaps also E (excellent) or O (outstanding), or other symbols; and secondary schools, the traditional A's, B's, C's. Or 1, 2, 3, 4 may replace A, B, C, D.

Ability grouping introduces still another problem: Does an A in the low section mean the same as in the high? Indeed, can A's be given in the low section? Actually, these are problems only if the report is used on relative standing rather than individual progress.

I am not alarmed by these variations or even by the confusions they create for parents and pupils. Instead, I see them as encouraging signs of genuine concern by American teachers for finding better ways of reporting to parents in the interest of helping individual pupils.

Although further experimentation with what to report is critically needed, would it not be well, meanwhile, to stick to the two central purposes for reporting mentioned earlier?

Should not the school faculty be certain, first, that parents understand what their children's reports are intended to tell, and second, that the reports summarize data which pupils can use, and indeed have already used, in self-appraisal and improvement? If so, should not the report clearly distinguish between marks and comments related to present standing and those related to recent progress, and also among goals such as subject-matter achievement, work habits, and behavior traits?

HOW REPORT?

Where teachers are certain of the purposes of reporting and of what to report, the form of reporting seems to follow logically. Other articles in this feature show how careful studies of reporting by faculty groups help. Perhaps the great differences in reporting procedures are created by varying degrees of understanding by school faculties on the *why* and *what* of reports. School leaders might reduce confusion as well as the range of practice by providing for more thorough study of the problem.

Certainly our knowledge of communication methods brings into real question the use of written reports alone, especially when these consist of letter symbols and check marks only. Face-to-face communication seems to be as effective in reporting to parents as in other matters. My belief—which has been strengthened by many comments from parents and others—is that the single most effective reporting medium is the teacher-parent conference.

But whatever the method of reporting, there is still the question of how to express that which is to be reported. Marks and checks are simple to write but hard to explain.

The single hardest question to answer—and the one for which most parents would probably settle—is, "How is my child doing?" The complete record, plus samples of work, helps the teacher to explain Johnny's progress but may still fail to answer this question. The teacher, therefore, needs to explain two things to parents: First, how Johnny is doing in relation to his potential, as best it can be estimated (and teachers estimate it very freely among themselves), and second, how he is doing in relation to the class norm.

A satisfactory answer to the basic question in which parents are interested really means a two-way or dual marking system. In the elementary school, this system may be fairly simple. It may be enough, for example, to explain that Johnny is doing as well as he is expected to, although he is below the class average in arithmetic. But in the secondary school, marks are generally needed, and Johnny's status will probably have to be expressed by two sets of letter grades—one for progress or effort, the other for relative standing or achievement.

THE DILEMMA OF REPORTING

This overview of practices and problems in reporting may suggest that the situation has become hopelessly confused. To the contrary, I see it as having been hopefully experimental. However, we do need more widespread understanding of present variations in the *why*, *what*, and *how* of reports.

The perplexity of parents and others caused by varied reporting systems is real and must be recognized. Just as real and to be recognized, however, is the teacher's desire for better ways of helping individual learners.

This is the dilemma we face in reporting systems: A uniform system of reporting throughout the nation might eventually be more easily understood by everyone, but it might also greatly inhibit effective provisions for individual differences among both pupils and communities. In fact, providing for individual differences has already been adversely affected to some degree by greater uniformity of marking and reporting practices in high schools.

I believe that the following items are essential to improve the reporting system throughout the country: agreement among the teachers in each school as to the purposes of reporting and as to what is to be reported; careful explanation to each parent, both on the entrance of his child to school and repeatedly thereafter, of the reporting system used (and of its relationship to any previous systems the parent has known); and careful planning with parent groups as to the method of reporting most useful and convenient for both parents and teachers.

In addition, more systematic publication of relevant research findings, of results of experimentation with different reporting procedures, and of surveys of practices by local, state, and national educational agencies might help to bring about the understanding and spread of good practices.

Chapter 13

MATERIALS AND TOOLS
FOR STRATEGIES AND TACTICS

INSTRUCTIONAL technology includes both methods and techniques of teaching, and the tools and materials one uses in teaching. Obviously teachers must choose their strategies and tactics partially on the basis of the tools and materials available to them. Consequently, the more tools the teacher learns how to use and the more materials he gathers for his classes, the better chance he has of being able to make use of the right strategy or tactic for a particular teaching situation.

It has become customary to speak of hardware and soft ware when referring to technological matters. Hardware refers to machines and gadgets, such as, projectors, television sets, teaching machines. Soft ware refers to materials used. No classroom is complete, nor is a secondary-school teacher a professional, without an ample supply of soft ware. Materials such as books, pamphlets, newspapers, periodicals, mimeographed materials, and so on, are abundantly available. Because so much can be procured gratis, there is seldom any excuse for not having a classroom equipped with materials of this kind. Every month, professional journals run long lists of "free or inexpensive" materials. Even in quite poor communities, there are lots of books, magazines, and other materials ready to be donated to the school. Still, some of this kind of material should be teacher-made to suit the peculiar requirements of particular courses and pupils.

The market is also being glutted with hardware. Machines of all kinds are available and making their way into the schools. Well used, they can be a great aid to the teacher. They can show pupils experiments, dramas, places, and events far more effectively than teachers can. The machines can drill and give pupils information without getting tired. But they cannot take the teacher's place. The human element will always be necessary to guide the machines, pick the programs, to teach the higher learnings, and humanize the schooling. The materials are teaching tools, and teachers should learn to use all of them well so that they can be as effective and efficient as possible. This chapter tells something about a representative few of the teaching tools and suggests some tactics to employ in using them. Imaginative teachers will take steps to incorporate these machines into their teaching strategies. In this way they will make their teaching more effective and efficient.

RESOURCES AT YOUR FINGER TIPS

Roger W. Boop *

As soon as he can, the beginning teacher should start building a class-room resource library. This library should include supplementary reading that can make the subject being studied fuller and more interesting than the single textbook can. The reading matter should include things appealing to both the brightest and the slowest pupils. Sources of materials for such libraries are many and varied. Information about free materials and suggestions for their use may be found in professional journals and books, such as The Educators' Guide to Free and Inexpensive Materials *(Educator's Progress Service, Randolph, Wisconsin);* Patricia Carr's Free Materials of Our 50 States *(Parkman and Associates, Urbana, Illinois, 1962); and the American Association of School Administrators'* Choosing Free Materials for Use in Our Schools *(1201 Sixteenth Street, N.W., Washington, D.C.). To amass a great amount of material quickly is not at all difficult. But no amount of material is useful unless it is readily available for use. Therefore, as soon as he begins his collection, the teacher should set up a plan for organizing and filing its contents so that they will be readily usable. In the following selection, Roger Boop tells how to do it.*

ORGANIZING THE MATERIALS

The materials will be of little use unless properly organized. The students need full and easy access to the library, and once organized it should be kept in an orderly manner with a minimal effort. Most of the materials are of the pamphlet size, well suited to a filing cabinet. A filing cabinet (boxes, if necessary) affords the possibility of organization and separation of the materials into any logical divisions a teacher may desire. Wear and tear are held

* From *The Clearing House*, Vol. 39 (Teaneck, N.J.: The Clearing House, Fairleigh Dickinson University, January 1965), pp. 284–285. Reprinted by permission of the publisher.

down if vertical filing is used. The teacher should also consider the possibilities of lamination or dry mounting protection in the case of fragile items such as newspaper clippings and pictures.

Filing dividers appropriately labeled with topic headings, along with an identification of each drawer and section by numbers and letters, will facilitate checking out and refiling materials. Each teacher can best determine how he or she wishes to organize the materials to bring about a smooth library operation. Small index cards could be used to record the drawer and section from which a pamphlet originated, along with the date and the student's name. These cards are suitable for filing alphabetically by the students' names. When the material is returned the name is crossed off, the card is clipped to the pamphlet, and the pamphlet is refiled using the drawer and section number on the card. This is the system which has worked best for me, but it is by no means the only one.

Each class should play a definite role in determining the criteria for the library's operation. If the students are to be allowed independence in using that facility, they should determine the rules and regulations which appear most meaningful to them. Students, if given the chance, will act with responsibility and abide by their established code of library conduct. Student librarians are also a must. In determining the personal criteria for such a responsibility, each class will usually elect a very capable individual. Participation by the class in these activities is necessary if the students are to feel that this is their library, to be used by them. With the librarians selected and the filing systematic, the operation of the library should not tax the teacher and instead becomes the class's responsibility.

The benefits reaped from these facilities should repay the efforts expended, with profits to both students and teachers. Each should find the regular classroom routine enriched by something resulting from teacher-pupil planning. Personal responsibility in making good use of the available materials for independent study can be developed on the student's part. In addition, pupils and their instructor are given the benefit of a basic research center to which they can refer.

By utilizing materials on subjects ranging from automobiles to Zanzibar, students can begin to develop a total awareness of social studies interrelationships as their interests direct them from topic to topic. They can explore and be exposed to materials of history, geography, current events, social problems, government, and other related areas. Social studies teachers need to encourage their students to search out, discover, and use materials aside from their textbooks. The student classroom library is one way to foster such an outcome. Better informed students of social studies should be the result.

HOW DIFFICULT IS THE TEXT? *

Curriculum Council for Southern New Jersey

To ask pupils to read textbooks that are too difficult for them is somewhat ridiculous—particularly when so much reading material of different reading levels is becoming available. This type of fiasco can be avoided by establishing the reading level of the pupils and matching the reading material to the pupils' reading level. Reading specialists have devised various formulas for this purpose. However, the various formulas for determining reading difficulty are somewhat cumbersome and time-consuming. Most teachers will find that the procedure quoted in the following selection, while not so precise perhaps as other formulas, will be adequate for their purposes in the average classroom.

One of the most important considerations for any teachers is the difficulty of the basic text for his class.

Do students know how to use it to their best advantage?

If the teacher knows the reading grade levels of his students, it is then a simple matter to determine whether a book is too easy or too hard.

There are various readability formulas which have been prepared and have good results.

They have disadvantages, however, which in many cases discourage their use. Most of them take quite a bit of time and require a high level of skill on the part of the user to be sure of the results.

For the teacher who wants to get a rough idea of the difficulty of his book, the following items can be considered:

—Pick several places at random in the book, which appear to be normal in terms of sentence length and vocabulary difficulty.

—Ask each student to read these passages orally, with no time to prepare the material.

—Check the student's reading for errors of: mispronunciation, repetitions, hesitations, omissions, substitutions, insertions, and disregard of punctuation.

—Ask several different types of comprehension questions. Find out if the students can get the main ideas supporting details.

—Evaluate the total performance of the class as well as the performance

* Adapted from "Reading in Grades 7–12," published by the Curriculum Development Council for Southern New Jersey, Glassboro State College. Reprinted from *NJEA Review*, copyright March, 1965, New Jersey Education Association.

of each student. The level of success should be very high for the entire class, or the text is too difficult.

—In the evaluation, the degree of error should not probably exceed three mistakes in each 100 running words of text, and students should not miss more than one out of every five questions asked.

MEASURING STICK FOR NONFICTION

Howard G. Spalding *

Selecting the proper books for pupils will always be difficult. The following two selections recommend yardsticks to be used in the process. None is perfect. Different types of books require different standards. The first list of criteria immediately following would be useful to use in judging the worth of nonfiction books. It can be used by the teachers, but would be most useful if used by the pupils. The second list is designed to be a checklist for use in the selection of textbooks.

1. *Is the author competent to write on this subject?* Is he a person of standing in his own field? Does he have personal acquaintance with public education? Has he previously written on education? Has he had education or experience which would give him superior insight into the subject?

2. *Is the magazine a responsible periodical?* Does it deal in exposés frequently? Is its editorial policy biased in any particular direction?

3. *Is the tone of this article sensational?* Is it presented with "shock" techniques?

4. *Do the titles, subtitles, and illustrations accurately apply to the text?* Is the wording of the titles stronger than statements of the text warrant?

5. *Is the evidence presented factually correct, adequate, and the best available?* Are both the pro and the con of the issue presented? If not, what evidence is lacking that *would* make the presentation balanced and fair to both sides?

6. *Are propaganda techniques in evidence?* Does the author stack the cards in selecting his evidence to prove his point? Is there evidence of name calling? Smears? Innuendos? Loaded words? Appeals to prejudice? Ridicule?

* Reprinted by permission from *Scholastic Teacher,* © 1954 by Scholastic Magazines, Inc.

Personal opinions substituted for facts? Half-truths? Bandwagon techniques? (Commonly used to imply that everyone is up in arms against the schools or some particular practice.) Tricky logic?

7. *Are those whose opinions are quoted identified and qualified to give valid testimony?* If not identified, why not? What evidence is there that the testimony is not fabricated? Does the internal evidence of the person's testimony indicate that he is an objective witness or a crackpot? If a public personage, what is his record? His previously expressed views? What special qualifications does the person have that would make his opinions more valuable than those of others of similar status?

8. *Does the author distort the evidence or omit essential evidence to prove his point?* Is it likely that the testimony of a large number of people would have agreed with that presented? Is there obviously another side?

9. *Are constructive suggestions made for improving conditions complained of?* Are the proposals already in effect in some of our better schools? (If not, they are probably of dubious value.) Have they been tried and abandoned? (Corporal punishment, for example.) Are responsibilities for effecting the improvement properly fixed? (As between school people and the public who supplies the funds, for instance.) Are the obstacles to improvement recognized and means for overcoming them considered?

10. *If the proposals advanced were made effective, would the schools be improved?* For all pupils? For some? For some at the expense of others? Are the changes in harmony with the objectives of a democratic society? Do they rank high on any sensible priority list of changes that would be desirable in the schools? Would they be accepted by the people of your community?

Armed with such a check list, try your hand at the evaluation of several articles.

CRITERIA FOR SELECTING TEXTBOOKS

Leonard H. Clark and Irving S. Starr *

This list of criteria is meant to be used as a checklist to use when selecting a textbook. Not every item applies to all good textbooks. However, any textbook that does not meet most of these criteria should be held suspect.

* From Leonard H. Clark and Irving S. Starr, *Secondary School Teaching Methods*, sec. ed. (New York: The Macmillan Company, 1967), p. 274. Reprinted by permission of the publisher.

1. What is the date of the copyright? Is the information and interpretation presented up to date?

2. Who is the author? Is he competent in the field? Does he write clearly and well?

3. Is the book suitable for the objectives of your course? Does it cover the proper topics with the proper emphases?

4. Are the topics arranged in a desirable sequence? If not, can the sequence be altered or portions omitted without disrupting the usefulness of the book?

5. Is the content accurate and accurately presented? Is the book free from bias?

6. Are the concepts presented clearly? Are they adequately developed with sufficient detail or is there a tendency to attempt to jam in too many ideas too compactly?

7. Is the vocabulary and language appropriate for the pupils of the class?

8. Does it presume background knowledge and experiences that the pupils do not yet have?

9. Does the author make good use of headings, summaries, and similar devices? Does he give opportunity for the readers to visualize, generalize, apply, and evaluate the content?

10. Are the table of contents, preface, index, appendices, and glossary adequate?

11. Does the book provide suggestions for use of supplementary materials?

12. Does it provide a variety of suggestions for stimulating thought-provoking instructional activities?

13. Are these suggestions sufficiently varied both as to level and to kind?

14. Does the author document his sources adequately?

15. Is the book well illustrated? Are the illustrations accurate, purposeful, and properly captioned? Are they placed near the text they are designed to illustrate?

16. Does the book have suitable maps, charts, and tables? Are they clear and carefully done? Does the author refrain from trying to cram too much data onto his maps and charts?

17. Is the book well made? Does it seem to be strong and durable?

18. Does the book look good? Is the type clear and readable? Do the pages make a pleasant appearance with enough white space?

PAPERBOUND BOOKS IN NEW JERSEY
PUBLIC SCHOOLS

Rychard Fink and Max Bogart *

Paperbound books have proved successful in many schools. Their worth was clearly demonstrated in a study conducted in the schools of New Jersey by Fink and Bogart for the New Jersey State Department of Education. Although the project was designed basically as an English language arts study, it was found that the effect of the presence of paperbacks was being felt in science and social science as well. Especially important were the findings that paperbacks seemed to encourage reading in pupils believed to be nonreaders and that they seemed to be encouraging habits of reading in pupils of all ages and intelligence levels. Here are some of the recommendations for the use of paperbacks resulting from the study.

WHAT RECOMMENDATIONS CAN BE SUPPORTED BY THE FINDINGS OF THE PROJECT?

1. *In the elementary school the self-contained classroom should contain an extensive paperbound book collection.*[1] Although there are not enough titles at present to do justice to the reading needs and interests of primary grade students, a modest grouping of such books can be built. In the intermediate and upper grades, there are titles enough available to create rich collections.

2. *In the elementary grades a $2 per year per pupil expenditure for paperbound books would be normal.* Such a sum is not proposed as a substitute or replacement for standard texts and trade books and library books, but as a supplementary cost beyond any existing per pupil book expenditure.

3. *In the junior high school and the high school, each homeroom, study hall, and subject area class should contain an extensive paperbound book collection.*[1] A necessary condition for the creation and support of positive

---

* From *Paperbound Books in New Jersey Public Schools* (Trenton, N.J.: State of New Jersey Department of Education, 1965), pp. 42–45. Reprinted by permission of the State of New Jersey Department of Education.

[1] Neither of these recommendations is designed to frustrate the continued, and very necessary, growth and development of sound central library facilities.

reading habits is an environment in which books are an ever-present feature. The homeroom, where a great deal of conversation and guidance take place, the study hall, where students have a period of free time, and, of course, each classroom should have book centers. Where these are created, each student can live and work for hours a day in the presence of books that challenge and invite responses.

4. *In the junior high school and the high school, a $4 per year per pupil expenditure for paperbound books would be normal.* Such a sum is not proposed as a substitute or replacement for standard texts and trade books and library books, but as a supplementary expenditure beyond any existing per pupil book disbursement.

5. *The creation of such paperbound book collections can be undertaken in a developmental and progressive fashion.* The realities of school finance make it difficult for sudden increases in appropriations to take place; however, any school can begin to build paperbound book collections by making available a portion of the sums recommended above to each grade, level, or subject area in its turn. It must also be noted that the durability factor, as identified in this study, suggests that certain paperbound books can be used for at least three years. This means that the upkeep of a paperbound book collection is less than the initial cost.

6. *Paperbound book purchases should be made by classroom teachers in cooperation with students.* When students choose certain books, their choices involve proposals to read. There is no need to assume that teachers' choices need conflict with students' selections. Both parties should build collections, initially and with respect to replacement and expansion.

7. *Classroom library chores should be managed by students.* The positive involvement of any learner is a principle that needs no lengthy justification. As the Project reports made clear, from the fourth to the twelfth grades, students can manage classroom paperbound book collections. It is even possible for students to build bookcases as industrial arts activities.

8. *Individualized reading programs should be expanded.* Nothing should be done to constrict the expanded desire to read which an immediately available collection of varied paperbound book titles stimulates. One of the basic goals of any school program is an appreciation of, and use of, the literature available in all subject areas. Once the student moves in this direction, nothing should be done to restrict him. A vigorous and exciting reading program will mesh required and collateral reading with a maximum of independent reading.

9. *Reading (literature) should not be isolated from other components of English curriculum.* In certain elementary schools and junior high schools reading (literature) is separated from the other components of English language arts: composition and language. Often literature, a potent motivating force, is isolated and the English class becomes a writing-grammar course.

10. *Where paperbound book collections are used, student opportunities to report on books and exchange experiences should be expanded.* Since en-

thusiasm is contagious, the chance to recommend a successful reading experience must be ever-present. The informal exchange of literary judgments should be planned for as carefully as are the opportunities for formal reports.

11. *Free reading should not be graded.* A large group of teachers in the Project did not grade free reading because they did not want to hinder the enjoyment of reading.

12. *Schools should use every possible device to publicize the books available in the paperbound collection.* Beyond the ever-present bulletin board, there are many ways to call books to the attention of students, such as book reviews in the school newspaper, forum presentations during assemblies, and visits by authors.

13. *Paperbound book fairs and paperbound bookstores should be established where feasible to encourage students to build their own libraries.* Owning books gives students a chance to use them when and as needed. Also, the book that is owned can be underlined and commented in, and thus turned into a peculiarly personal thing. Where students have the chance to buy and keep basic reference books, a level of research and inquiry in all subject areas, for which there is no substitute, can take place. While a school paperbound bookstore can be a complex operation, particularly with respect to finances, there are many ways to solve the problem, including the use of student organization fees. Such a store could be an ideal student council project.

14. *School-community ties can be strengthened by encouraging one or more local merchants to stock recommended paperbound books.* Where school operated book fairs and bookstores are not feasible, such arrangements as this can be most useful to all concerned.

15. *Central libraries should make greater use of quality paperbound books.* Among librarians, attitudes concerning the place of paperbound books in central libraries range from mild acceptance to out-and-out rejection. Such rejection is not completely defensible. Certain valuable titles, long out-of-print in hard-covered editions, are only available in paper, as is true of other original titles on current events written especially for paperbound book publishers. Many scholarly works necessary for research are expensive in bound volumes, but cost less in paper editions. A book club that will show students how to bind books is only one of many ideas that should be explored in order to get paperbound books onto library shelves.

16. *Classroom libraries should display books as any regular library does.* As the world changes, so should the paperbound books in the classroom. Titles and authors can move into and out of the foreground as seasons, sports, world policies, community affairs, and other topics and issues come and go.

17. *School budgets should be flexible enough to allow teachers to order paperbound books for classroom use when and as they are needed.* Routine and rigid budgetary requirements will reduce the spontaneous demands of students to build their classroom libraries. Certainly it is wrong to damage any pleasure and enthusiasm felt by students about reading.

18. *Colleges of education should help teachers-in-training understand the*

consequences of the "*paperback revolution.*" Where the new teacher has an opportunity to help create or enlarge a paperbound classroom library, she must know what to do.

19. *School systems should make provisions for the kind of in-service education that will help teachers learn how to make the most of paperbound books.*

20. *Teachers, supervisors, and administrators should be alert to the opportunities for correlation, integration and broad-fields instruction afforded by the large-scale use of paperbound books.*

LEARNING FROM NEWSPAPERS

Harry Bard, Claire Eckels, Sidney Blum, and Edythe Myers

The newspapers are an ever available source of teaching material—particularly for classes in social studies and English, but for other classes as well, as the fact that one of the collaborators who produced the guide from which the following excerpt is taken was a secondary-school science specialist indicates. Techniques, questions, and exercises similar to the ones suggested in this excerpt could be easily built for classes in mathematics, business, home economics, art, and other subjects.

THE SUNPAPERS IN LANGUAGE ARTS

Students should be taught to skim rapidly to locate information, to read carefully to assimilate facts, and to read critically to develop maturity of thought and judgment. Of the three reading areas, the third can be studied with the newspaper perhaps better than with any other written material. In editorials, letters to the editor, columnists' articles, book and theater reviews, indeed in every story in which a person expresses his thoughts, students may practice the skills of critical thinking.

To become critical readers students must recognize fallacies of thinking and the intentions of the writer. Let pupils discover, identify, and analyze the black-or-white assertion and dire prediction in letters to the editor, the rationalization of Ann Landers' correspondents, the appeal *ad populum* and

* From *Learning Through the Sunpapers*, 2nd Ed. (Baltimore, Md.: The Sun, The A. S. Abell Company), pp. 27–41. Reprinted by permission of the publisher.

the attack *ad hominem* in politicians' speeches, the "figures prove" and band-wagon approaches of advertisements, the over-generalization in the commencement address, the *tu quoque* retort of those apprehended. *Post hoc* reasoning, arguing in circles, "self-evident truths," *ad verecundiam*, and false analogies are other fallacies apparent in the writing of those who, standing on uncertain ground or lacking sufficient evidence, mean to persuade their readers. Obviously, the newspaper becomes the partner of the teacher in presenting material for critical thinking.

The newspaper can also be used to reinforce subjects treated in textbooks, particularly in the field of literature. The following articles, taken from the papers of only one week, are cited to show how classics and old favorites can be brought into the "here and now" for students. An observant teacher will find many such articles and use them constructively in specific classroom situations.

1. Adventure Unit: Eighth grade boys dreaming of space travel may look at *Call of the Wild* in a different light after they read that a Russian cosmonaut took his inspiration from Jack London's book.

2. English Literature Unit: The article dealt with Chaucer's interest in stars. It is good to have seniors see Chaucer out of his usual context—the first section of English anthologies!

3. American Literature Unit: An article on and a photograph of the Old Ichabod Crane Church make a good starting point for a discussion of the real American settings Washington Irving used in contrast to the supernatural elements in his tales.

4. Essay Unit: Theodore Roosevelt's grandson quotes from "The Strenuous Life" to reinforce and carry into the present generation the theory of the active life. For students who feel they have nothing to write after reading an essay, this is a model to show personal application of an idea.

5. Supplementary Reading Units: In an article the modern television sleuth is traced to his prototypes; and the writer speaks of the detectives of Poe, Dumas, Hugo, and others. "Our Yesterdays" noted the growing popularity of Hyman Kaplan twenty-five years ago. Scenes from the films of *Mutiny on the Bounty* and *Gone with the Wind* can send students running to the library for the novels.

Writing practice should develop primarily from work in reading. During a newspaper unit students expect the usual assignments of writing editorials and letters to the editor; yet they can be stimulated to new activity by using the variety of material in the paper. Take, for example, the recent feature story of Bum Rap, the Penitentiary dog. Young students respond to the emotional appeal. They are able to spot the ways in which the dog is given human attributes. Older ones discover that the humor comes from placing the characters out of their proper environment. Such stories will motivate writing creatively about animals or writing with a humorous touch.

Feature articles often illustrate new ways to write the interview type of story. Students must analyze the writing closely to discover the subtle tricks of presenting a personality through responses, gestures, and setting. Many other exercises in writing from reading have been developed by teachers, and some are given below.

READING AND WRITING PRACTICE:

1. Skim to find the late showing of a movie in a downtown theater. Skim to find the Oriole baseball player with the highest batting average. Skim to find which countries are sending freighters to Baltimore.
2. Read carefully to analyze *The Sun's* editorial on "Urban Renewal in Baltimore." What are the main points? Gifted students might be asked to write their own editorials on this subject.
3. Read the lead of a news story. Identify the W's. In subsequent paragraphs skim to find information amplifying each W. Write a news report of a school event, giving particular attention to the lead.
4. Recall the articles read in one day's paper. Which contributed to the acquisition of facts? Which promoted a critical evaluation of events?
5. Compare the treatment of a topic covered in a news story and in an editorial. What is the author's purpose in each? What is the structure of each article? What material is contained in both, in only one?
6. Find examples in a columnist's article of interpretation and background material. What words or phrases does he use to indicate opinion?
7. Find in the advertisements examples of fact and of opinion. What words are used for their connotative value in influencing buyers?
8. Mark paragraphs in book reviews which offer material other than plot development. Discuss the value of the marked paragraphs to determine how they add to a review of the book. Write a report using material other than plot to review a book.
9. Compare headlines and the titles of books. How is the head integrated into the news story? Summarize the main point of a news report by composing a headline for it.
10. Indicate how the viewpoint of an editorial writer is illustrated by a cartoonist. Write a paragraph expressing the artist's attitude toward the subject.
11. Practice reading charts, maps, and diagrams.
12. "Read" a photograph by pointing out significant details. Write a descriptive paragraph of the picture. Remove the caption and write a narrative paragraph based on the photograph.
13. Analyze the review of a current movie. On what factors does the reviewer base his argument? If the movie is based on a book, in what respects does the criticism of the movie hold true for the book?

14. Follow news reports of a topic for one or two weeks. Read an editorial on the same subject. How does the editorial give perspective to the news?
15. Skim the classified advertisements to find a job you could fill. Write a business letter of application.
16. Read a recipe, a clothing pattern, a "how to do it" column. In what order are directions given? Write an expository paragraph to explain how to make something. Give succinct directions for reaching the school library or cafeteria from a particular location in the school.
17. Read critically to determine the purpose of an editorial: Is it to commend, instruct, interpret, or what?
18. Use a background article to write a paragraph of cause and effect. Use a feature story to develop a paragraph by illustration or examples.
19. Study the use of symbolism as it is indicated in book and theater reviews.
20. Analyze the tone of several advertisements. How did the writer adapt his material and appeal to fit a specific group of readers?
21. Discover various types of humor in feature stories, editorials, and advertisements. Classify the types of humor found in the comics.

THE SUNPAPERS FOR VOCABULARY DEVELOPMENT

Words in headlines are used most frequently in beginning vocabulary work. A sequential study, here illustrated by headlines from the papers for one week, may take this form:

1. "Cromwell *Rites* Will Be Held Tomorrow." The opening words are "Funeral services for . . ."
2. "*Probe* Is Asked In Satellite Bill Bribery Case." The lead paragraph reports, "Senators filibustering against the satellite bill demanded today an immediate investigation . . ."
3. "Pressman Blasts 'Real *Renegade*' in Turmoil." Students must read to the fifth paragraph before discovering, ". . . to purge this traitor from its ranks."
4. "Two British Neo-Nazis Jailed For Anti-Jewish *Tirade*." Pupils have to reach a definition by assimilating all the clues in the article, such as the samples of the remarks made by the men.

Short common words used with their less common meanings should not be overlooked. An example of this is "Writ *To Stay* Strike Denied."

News articles bearing directly upon the English language can vitalize the sometimes lifeless chapters on vocabulary and semantics in textbooks. Three such articles appeared in the paper in two days, an indication of the availability of material even in a field of limited news interest. Two, reporting on a new translation of the Old Testament, indicated the change in meaning of *virgin, leprosy,* and *Jehovah.* The third news article, "Latin Locutions and Unwords," cited the additions to the English language through the growth of space jargon.

VOCABULARY EXERCISES

1. List unfamiliar words found often in news reports and in articles in specialized areas such as medicine. Use contextual clues to help discover the meanings.
2. Determine the exact meaning of words frequently used in news reports, such as allegedly, skirmish, pending, contended, and reportedly.
3. Study words frequently used and essential to know in reading the women's page, financial reports, weather reports, and advertisements.
4. Discover words which should be added to the vocabulary in order to understand technological and scientific articles in this space age.
5. Use unfamiliar words in cartoons to stimulate an interest in vocabulary study.
6. Skim sports stories to find words or phrases that add vividness to the writing.
7. Note the connotative power of words (boss vs. leader) in news reports of dissimilar papers. How does the use of words influence a reader?
8. Analyze the use of words in advertisements for influencing the reader.
9. Find synonyms to use in place of underlined words in a story. Find antonyms in the same way. Show how one word can change the entire meaning of a section.

THE SUNPAPERS IN SOCIAL STUDIES

In the teaching of social studies at the secondary level, attention is given to the study of current events, issues and problems. The suggested activities listed below are among many that have been used successfully to develop or strengthen skills; enrich, supplement and bring up to date textbook information; and to motivate and stimulate independent study and research. Current events and contemporary news items make excellent motivation, but they can also be an outgrowing assignment or even inserted to illustrate or supplement the development phase.

SOCIAL STUDIES ACTIVITIES

1. Establish a social studies notebook, and include a section on current events. Set up standards for selection, analysis and organization of the included data in keeping with the grade level and maturity of the group involved. Mere clipping and pasting is prohibited.

2. Follow up a visit to a City Council committee meeting by reading to see what action was taken at the City Council session later in the day.

3. Select a current problem of the city, state or national government and follow efforts made to solve it as reported in the newspapers. Outline two important articles which you have selected and present a brief floor talk using one of these outlines.

4. Select a series of cartoons from the newspaper dealing with the election campaign and use them to show support or opposition to a given issue or platform plank. Select an article and an editorial dealing with the same topic. Compare the effect on the public.

5. Relate the study of early world history to the present day by means of on-going assignments. For example, have students locate in the newspaper the schedules of lectures, museum offerings, and other current activities in the area being studied, which will serve to enrich the regular class study.

6. Secure facts on both sides of current controversial issues to distinguish between fact, opinion and propaganda. In these assignments, require the reading and listing of data on both sides of the issue followed by a judgment or summary statement on the topic by the pupil himself.

7. Select a problem in the political, economic, industrial, cultural or social growth of the United States and study present day aspects of it as revealed in the newspapers.

8. Secure from the newspaper the *text* of the President's "State of The Union" message to Congress and read it. Make an outline of the major domestic and foreign issues discussed by him and list his suggestions concerning them. Use this material as the beginning of an on-going study of action by Congress on these issues and problems during the current legislative session.

9. Make use of the newspaper to follow an election campaign. Keep notes on candidates, issues, platform, convention, and both primary and general election outcomes. Compare differences and similarities of the major political parties as revealed in the press and other mass media of communication.

THE SUNPAPERS IN SCIENCE CLASSES

In a world in which science has not only come to the fore, but has also come to all sides and has completely engulfed us, newspapers play a major role in keeping both the layman and the science-oriented informed about new developments. Teachers capitalize on this immediacy of science and exploit newspapers as a vital resource for classroom instruction.

News stories of local or topical interest help focus attention, stimulate interest, and raise questions. Feature articles are often used to motivate specific lessons, parts of lessons, or even to help establish purposes for studying science. Sunday supplements often feature articles on recreation, commerce, and industry which illustrate concepts in the fields of ecology, genetics, population, conservation, and mechanics. Advertisements and articles on foods, clothing, and housing provide excellent materials for developing concepts and ideas relating to quality, price, worth, and purity of materials and services. Classified advertisements provide information relative to the number and nature of scientific and technical job opportunities. The science of everyday life—involving cosmetics, foods, drugs, machines, weather, and transportation—makes up the essence of every edition of a newspaper.

ACTIVITIES FOR SCIENCE STUDY

1. Write a "news story" describing a possible conference of the American Association for the Advancement of Science in 1984.
2. Write a feature article on a local institution of scientific interest (RIAS, Johns Hopkins, Maryland Academy of Sciences, Chesapeake Biological Laboratory, etc.).
3. Determine the relative space in local papers devoted to science or science-related activities.
4. Using local newspapers as your source of information, prepare a calendar of scientific events or meetings for the next two weeks.
5. Use newspapers to tabulate high and low tides at Fort McHenry for a two-week period. Relate this to the hours at which the moon rises and sets (also found in newspapers).
6. Graph maximum and minimum temperatures as reported in the local newspapers for one week.
7. Identify ambiguities, questionable authorities, or misleading statements in newspaper advertisements.
8. Use newspapers to identify civic problems requiring scientific information for their effective solution.
9. List five topics relating to science that might make good feature stories.
10. Read one science-related news story in a local newspaper very critically. What additional information would you need to understand better or to accept the story? What questions would you ask the writer? What significance do you see in the event or idea described?
11. Make a list of places and/or people of scientific interest mentioned in the newspapers of the last week.
12. Distinguish factual material from opinion in a given newspaper story relating to science. Note any inconsistencies. List any assumptions that the author has made.
13. Use the classified advertisements of a local newspaper to list qualifications that are common for many scientific or technical positions.
14. Examine newspapers for three weeks to prepare a list of 10–15 topics or problems that have been under investigation by scientists.
15. Identify a newspaper item that is more comprehensible to you now than it would have been at the beginning of this course.

TEACHING CURRENT AFFAIRS

Editors of Civic Education Service *

The weekly classroom periodical is a fixture in most social studies courses and many English courses. Unfortunately, teachers have not always known how to make the most of such periodicals. In the chapter of its leaflet Teaching Current Affairs, *the editors of the Civic Education Service describe methods of using these materials. Teachers will probably find the methods that concentrate pupils' attention on one or two articles more effective than merely using a periodical as a basis for a recitation or oral quiz on its contents.*

CLASSROOM PERIODICAL: UPDATED TEXT

Most teachers use basic texts in their current history instruction, just as they do in other subjects. Their current history "text" usually consists of a weekly periodical especially prepared for classroom use. Geared to meet the special needs and problems of this subject, it saves teachers valuable time and effort in gathering material for classroom discussion.

The special school publications sift through the mass of material to be found in all news and opinion media. They present issues clearly and concisely, and summarize the background and development of each news topic. Problems and viewpoints are explained objectively, so that students can more easily form their own conclusions.

The publishers of current history periodicals also offer valuable supplementary services, such as maps and charts, regular tests, study guides, bibliographies on specific topics, and teachers' editions containing a variety of suggestions on current events instruction.

HOW TO USE A CURRENT HISTORY PAPER

There is a great variation in the way teachers use current history periodicals. Allowances must be made for grade level and learning ability of students as well as individual teaching styles. Although the variations are many, here are a few of the most common approaches to using the papers:

Method 1. The weekly assignment covers the entire paper—including the

* Reprinted from "Teaching Current Affairs," published by Civic Education Service, Washington, D.C.

major articles as well as the geographic features on places in the news, stories about people who make headlines, historical backgrounds, career sketches, and other features. The students are given several days to read and study the paper.

The teacher then questions the class for factual information during the first half of the current history session. During this quiz period, use is made of the study guide questions contained in each issue of the paper. In addition, the teacher may ask a number of his own questions to see how much information the students have acquired from their reading.

The second part of the period is devoted to discussion. On controversial issues, students are asked to state the pros and cons which appear in their paper, and also to express their own opinions.

This method does not permit study in depth of the articles appearing in the current events periodicals, but it does enable the students to cover a maximum of issues and topics in the limited time available.

Method 2. Some teachers prefer to select only one of the major topics appearing in each week's paper. They build their study assignments and the subsequent class discussion around this particular subject. They may even have their students read the outside articles on this topic which are referred to in some of the current history papers.

When adopting the single-topic approach, it is a common practice for teachers to assign the leading domestic article in the current history paper one week and the major foreign story the next. This helps to balance class interest between events at home and overseas.

Method 3. An alternate approach to the second method is to assign the major national article to half of the class, and the main foreign article to the other half. Under this plan, the students are participants and observers on a 50–50 basis. During the quiz and discussion on the foreign topic, only those students take part who have studied it; the others merely listen. The same is true with respect to the domestic subject.

Method 4. Some teachers concentrate most of the class period on one or both of the two leading articles in their weekly current history texts, but they hold the students responsible for reading the rest of the publication. During the last 5 or 10 minutes of the period, the students are given a short factual quiz to see whether they have covered the paper generally. Teachers who use this approach feel that the current events periodicals are sufficiently compact so that they can and should be thoroughly read by the students, even though there is not enough time to discuss every article and feature in the classroom.

Method 5. To help get the fullest possible coverage of the current history paper's content in the one classroom period allotted weekly, some teachers appoint groups of from three to six students each to study and report on the various articles and features. Every group is given a certain feature or article to discuss. Student chairmen are appointed for the various committees.

By the end of a given period of time, the various chairmen present summaries on the discussions of their groups. The remainder of the class, under the direction of the teacher, then asks questions and discusses the reports. This committee approach is practiced most frequently in classes of better-than-average students.

Conclusion. Some teachers obtain the best results by using only one or two of these methods. Others feel that it is better to experiment with them all, as well as others, from time to time.

Whatever method or approach is used, every effort should be made to bring as many students into each week's discussion as possible. Since some boys and girls are so much more interested in public affairs than others, there is a temptation to let them monopolize the current history period. The desirable goal, however, is to achieve maximum student participation.

WHAT THE SECONDARY-SCHOOL STUDENT SHOULD KNOW ABOUT THE LIBRARY

John Sherman *

It is often said that the library should be the heart of the school. John Sherman, a college librarian, believes that the young people graduating from our high schools are not well enough prepared to use the libraries properly. They need better schooling in using reference tools, he says, but, more important, they need to learn to respect the library's books and periodicals. Building such skills and such respect is, in Mr. Sherman's opinion, the responsibility of every secondary-school teacher.

What should the secondary-school student know about the library? This question was asked recently at a coffee-break discussion, during which several librarians and teachers were exchanging views regarding college library orientation programs. The question emerged in response to a librarian's statement that freshmen did not bring to college the necessary library skills.

Certainly, there is a core of basic library information which all students should acquire somewhere along the line before they get to college. Not alone in importance is the knowledge of how to use the many kinds of reference

* From *Language Arts Clearing House*, Vol. 1 (Jersey City, N.J.: Jersey City State College, Summer 1965). Reprinted by permission of the publisher and the author. Slightly edited and adapted by the author.

tools generally available in a collegiate library. The student also needs to acquire a cognizance of basic behaviorial attitudes which reflect a social consciousness and a respect for the rights of others. An awareness of the latter values is no less important in today's crowded libraries than the "how to use it" information about reference books.

Despite the wholehearted agreement of educators on what constitutes a working knowledge of the library, they frequently fail to convey very much of that information to their students. This is quite apparent as far as behavior or plain good manners is concerned if perfectly well-meaning youngsters flock into the library with a noisy disregard of their fellows who are trying to study. The lack of knowledge and ethical understanding is not only apparent but also crippling to a library's effectiveness when students thoughtlessly mutilate or steal books and periodicals meant to be shared by all.

No student can succeed in college without at least a minimal use of a library. His failure to understand the nature and use of a library may very clearly doom him to severe academic difficulties. It is just not possible to do a respectable term paper without the intelligent and informed use of *some* of a library's bibliographic tools.

Why then do so many secondary school students go to the college library so ill prepared? In a recent editorial, some information relevant to this point was presented. It may help us with an answer to our question.

Using figures based on a survey in 1962–63 (and the figures haven't improved spectacularly since then), the Office of Education notes that 9,600,000 children and young people (25.7% of 37 million enrolled) go to public schools that do not have centralized school libraries. Of these, 9,000,000 are elementary school children. . . . 41% of all our public schools—that is, more than 34,000 schools—had no school libraries; 55.6% of the elementary schools lacked them; so did 2.6% of the secondary schools and over 10% of the combined elementary-secondary schools.[1]

Supplementing the above is the array of facts presented last year during National Library Week which included the information that for each graduate of a library school in 1964 there were 18 jobs waiting which offered beginning salaries of about $6,000 a year.

Obviously, there is a correlation between the conditions described above and the fact that students who attend schools with no libraries, which of course employ no librarians, are deficient in their knowledge of the use of books and libraries. One can hardly expect a student to develop skills based on an experience he has never had.

*　*　*

Let us return to the teacher's question, "What should a secondary school student know about the library?" If we teachers and librarians are entirely

[1] "School Library Development: a Job for All Bookmen," *Publishers' Weekly*, March 8, 1965 (editorial by G. B. G.), p. 43.

honest we should tell the student quite frankly that he hasn't been given the library instruction he needs. Furthermore, we might add that there is a strong possibility that the student may not find anyone at the college who will have the time to help him learn library research techniques. Perhaps we should tell the student at the outset that it is his own responsibility to learn how to use a library's resources. If we really care about helping him, we can suggest that he read a book like *Guide to the Use of Books and Libraries* by Jean Key Gates.[2]

But let's take a close look at such thinking. Can we honestly feel satisfied in placing the responsibility entirely with the student? If he doesn't know how to behave in a library, which he also doesn't know how to use properly, is it his fault? Should he be expected to have taken the trouble to read a few books on libraries to find out something about them?

This reasoning, pursued far enough, would save a lot of money. It could be applied to many other institutions, and since ignorance is no excuse, people could be held accountable for everything they don't do because of lack of initiative or information.

Surely no person with humanist values can really agree with that. But what do we do, then? We don't have the libraries, the books, and the librarians that are needed now, and with our growing population and increasing costs, it seems unlikely the future will offer any immediate solution to the problem.

One answer would be for other interested professional people to take up the burden of instructing students in the use of books, research techniques, and the proper use of libraries. The grade teacher at the beginning can be most influential in creating a classroom atmosphere in which books are properly used and respected.

The secondary school teacher can augment this by a comprehensive look at the use of special kinds of reference books. Since basic research skills are needed early in the high school curriculum, fundamental library technique is germane to the subject matter and is a natural adjunct to many courses. One has to recognize that such library knowledge as most students have, when they enter college, has probably had its beginning in the work of English and Language Arts teachers.

Finally, it should be pointed out by teachers at all levels that a cooperative social attitude toward one's fellows is a part of any situation in which large numbers of people must share equally. Teachers in the Social Sciences might also talk occasionally about the practical aspects of such cooperation and thereby make a contribution to the order and preservation of libraries.

Returning for a last look at the teacher's question about what a secondary school student should know about the library, one should perhaps answer that, whatever it is he needs to know, he must learn it, if he is to learn it at all, from a teacher who will take the time to instruct him.

2 Jean Key Gates, *Guide to the Use of Books and Libraries.* New York: McGraw-Hill, 1962. 230 p.

USE FLANNEL BOARDS FOR
BETTER TEACHING

E. Milton Grassell *

The flannel board is a versatile tool. In the hands of a skilled operator, it can have a dramatic impact that ordinary chalkboards cannot equal. Furthermore, its exhibits can be prepared well in advance and used again and again. This inexpensive, easily prepared device has been used successfully in advertising, the military, and in sales. Teachers have long used it with success, but it has seldom been exploited to the fullest. It should be used because it, along with the similarly used magnetized metal boards, is one of the few devices that combines dramatic impact, simplicity, and inexpensiveness. It is the sort of device Bragg † meant when he spoke of aids that were more effective than slides.

Do you use a flannel board in your high-school classes? No?

Unfortunately, high-school teachers as a whole do not use this effective, flexible aid. Yet teachers on all other grade levels (including some college professors and many extension specialists) are using it. Now even television has recognized and adapted flannel boards—one of the most inexpensive and easiest of all visual aids to make.

HOW TO MAKE A FLANNEL BOARD

Flannel boards (known by a variety of names, e.g., felt board, story-o-graph, magic board, flannel graph, and so on) can be quickly and easily made from several different materials. The simplest magic board is an ordinary piece of Masonite or Chapco board. Most of the materials that adhere to the more typical flannel boards will stick to either of these common items that are sold in building-supply houses and lumberyards. But usually you will not have to go that far. Your custodian may be able to find a few scrap pieces for you. Flannel is the most popular material for homemade boards. This is

---

* From *The Clearing House*, Vol. 30 (Teaneck, N.J.: The Clearing House, Fairleigh Dickinson University, March 1956), pp. 420–424. Reprinted by permission of the publisher.

† See Chapter 10.

probably due to the low cost of flannel and its availability in local dry-goods stores. One quick construction method is to stretch a piece of flannel over plywood and thumbtack, staple, tape, or nail the cloth to the rear of the panel. The flannel board itself is now ready for use.

You can give this type of board a more finished appearance by nailing four pieces of molding along the front edges, but this is not necessary. Another simple construction method is to sew the flannel together, leaving one end open (like a pillow slip). If you then slip a heavy piece of cardboard or plywood into the open end, a dual-sided aid is ready for use. Some teachers use a different colored background for each side, others put permanent markings (outliner, borders, and so on) on one side, and leave the opposite free.

Flocking materials are becoming more common in most high schools. A flocked piece of plywood or hard board is another type of magic board. Felt boards are made like the flannel-covered boards, but this material is considerably more expensive than any of the others mentioned.

Two other features to be considered in flannel boards are the over-all size and the color. The size depends on the average number of students in your classes and the complexity of the illustrations you intend to use. From my own experiences, I feel the minimum size is about three feet by four feet. Several of my flannel boards are considerably larger. The board should contain enough area so that the illustrations, regardless of their complexity, can be made sufficiently large to be clearly seen by the students in the rear seats. The selection of the background color is important. A brilliant primary color limits the number of colors that can be used in the illustrations. That is why many teachers prefer a less striking background color. A neutral or pastel cover provides more contrast between the background and the display items and allows more contrast among and within display items.

Permanent marks: Permanent outlines, areas, and points are often advantageous on flannel boards. These permanent markings can be made with China marking pencils (grease pencils that are used in stores to write on glassware and dishes); with crayons; with Speedball pen points and various colored India inks; or with commercial felt nib pens. On some pieces of flannel, the inks tend to run. It may be wise to try the India inks out on scrap pieces first.

MATERIALS THAT ADHERE TOGETHER

Some materials that adhere together have been mentioned already. Some, like Masonite, will not adhere to each other but will adhere to other materials. Sandpaper glued to the backs of illustrative material sticks to felt- and flannel-covered boards. Flannel-backed illustrative material sticks to all the types of boards mentioned. Merely glue the flannel on the back of your display material.

FLANNEL BOARDS IN ACTION

Now that we understand the basic construction of flannel boards, let's see how some high-school teachers are using this visual aid.

Audio-visual work: I encourage teachers to use flannel boards to show members of projection clubs the basic operation and care of motion-picture projectors. First, use permanent lines to show the framework of the projector; then cut certain basic interior and exterior parts from felt or flannel. With the actual projector plus the simplified cutouts, the instructor can illustrate, in a general way, interior operation that students would not ordinarily see. As the felt cutout pieces are moved, students see animated step-by-step action of the projector. School audio-visual programs will profit from a basic understanding of the general operation and care of equipment.

Business education: While some typing teachers do not advocate the use of keyboard charts, Mrs. Elizabeth Eckel finds daily use for her flannel-board key chart at Fremont Junior High in Pomona, Calif. This is how she uses it: Blank keys are drawn on her basic flannel board. As each new key is introduced, Mrs. Eckel places a red-lettered disk in position. Before the class meets again, Mrs. Eckel replaces the red-lettered felt disk with white ones to show that they have already been introduced. "This makes the new keys stand out and places emphasis upon them," she says.

"The basic principles of business letter writing are easier to teach with the aid of a flannel board," says Mrs. Elsie Mae Davis, Eugene, Ore., High School. Mrs. Davis uses the board to illustrate various styles of setting up a letter, e.g., block, modified block, indented, and so on. Different lengths of narrow pieces of flannel-backed construction pages are used to represent the major parts of the letter styles. "There is no writing on the opaque strips. This helps to emphasize proper layout," says Mrs. Davis.

Chemistry: Robert D. Van Atta, Stayton, Ore., High School, uses the flannel board in his chemistry classes. Mr. Van Atta has a board three feet square, covered with light blue flannel. Two eight-inch circles represent the nucleuses of the atoms. These were made large enough to accommodate several numerals and symbols.

From a grocery store, Mr. Van Atta obtained some free pieces of show-card material, which he used for spelling chemical symbols—Ca for calcium, O for oxygen, and so on. He backed all of his materials with flocking. "The basic structure of atoms is easily shown with the flannel board," he says. In the teaching of nuclear reaction, the flannel board is more flexible than the chalk board. It eliminates the annoying and disturbing problem of chalk-board erasing while the illustrations are being shifted on the board.

At Corvallis, Ore., High School, Perry Spellbrink uses a flannel board in conjunction with commercial three-dimensional models in his chemistry classes.

Drama: To block out the action of school plays, Johanna Beckham, English and drama teacher at Harrisburg, Ore., finds the inherent flexible characteristic of the flannel board very useful. This simple, easy-to-make device clearly shows the actors just where they should stand and how they should move around the stage.

Driver training: In teacher-education classes, I use a flannel board to demonstrate driver-training techniques. The streets are made on the flannel with India ink and Speedball pen points. Small, lightweight toy plastic cars, trucks, and streetcars purchased from the dime store give the visual aid an unusually realistic appearance. Coarse sandpaper attached to the bottom of the toys with rubber cement holds the three-dimensional aids to the board.

English: Although the parts of speech have been taught in previous grades, it is often necessary to repeat them again and again so that students may become fully acquainted with the name and function of each. Flannel boards provide numerous ways to teach the parts of speech. Some teachers employ matching games, e.g., placing the correct definition beside a certain part of speech.

A sentence can be placed word by word on the flannel board. The unusual flexibility of the flannel board allows for rearrangement to teach techniques by such means as diagraming, placing the parts of speech under each word, and so on. One teacher likes to remove all the words from a sentence except the subject and verb predicate to show that there is still a meaning left. Mrs. Johanna Zeller, English teacher at Beaverton, Ore., says, "There seems to be no end to the things flannel boards can help accomplish."

Health: Willajean Grimes, health-class teacher at Roseburg, Ore., uses a life-sized flannel board. There is a large front-view silhouette outline of the human body on her board. Miss Grimes uses various colored cutouts from sandpaper-backed construction paper to represent certain parts of the human body. She feels that the students gain more from this visual aid because it presents the basic human anatomy in fairly true sizes and proportions.

Home economics: Several teachers in my former classes have used the flannel board for certain phases of home-economics education. One made an effective aid very quickly. She took a commercial graphic aid that illustrated the basic seven foods and glued flannel to the back. After the glue dried, the original chart was cut into the basic seven sections. During class discussions, the teacher and students used these helpful illustrations.

Another teacher decided to try a flannel board for menu planning. She was so gratified, it is still being used in her classes.

Industrial arts: Ivan Burkert, industrial arts instructor and director of audiovisual aids at Corvallis, Ore., High School, occasionally sets the flannel board near a machine in the shop and places on it such words as "THINK," "SAFETY PAYS." On other occasions, he sets the flannel board on a tripod in the halls and uses his three-dimensional letters, cut from Masonite and Chapco board, for pertinent messages.

Because of their unique adaptability, flannel boards are used by some industrial-arts teachers to show the general operation of various machines in their shops. By simple moving of the basic parts, the instructor can easily show movement. Few other inexpensive aids can accomplish this as well.

Journalism: A newspaper is generally regarded as completed when the managing editor O.K.'s the final proofs. "However, the make-up remains to be done in the composing room, and its importance cannot be stressed too strongly," says Alyce Sheetz, journalism instructor at Jefferson High School, Portland, Ore. In her beginning journalism classes Mrs. Sheetz uses illustrations cut from local newspapers and arranges them in various ways to point out good and poor make-up. The ultra adaptability of the flannel board permits this. Also, Mrs. Sheetz and her classes have used the board to plan page layouts for their school yearbook.

Mathematics: Many teachers find various uses for the flannel board in remedial math classes. Fractions can be taught with several identical-sized flannel or felt circles cut into various pieces, e.g., $\frac{1}{2}$, $\frac{1}{4}$, $\frac{1}{3}$, $\frac{1}{6}$. One high-school teacher said, "This is the best way I know for actually showing what $1\frac{1}{6}$ really is." The basic difference among various figures can be shown. I have seen teachers use felt triangles, rectangles, parallelograms, and so on, on the flannel board in advanced math classes.

Music: Mrs. Myrtle Gates, music teacher, Sweet Home, Ore., High School, says, "I have used the flannel board in school music teaching for many years and have found it most valuable. . . . I have found light green flannel to be a useful color because it is easy to see and does not soil quickly. On one side of the flannel I have drawn four music staffs with black crayon. The heat from a medium-hot iron on the opposite side sets the staff lines permanently and stops the crayon lines from smearing." Mrs. Gates uses the flannel board to present scale work. to show the use of sharps and flats, to introduce key signatures, to illustrate triads and chords, to teach the names of the lines and spaces of the treble and the bass staff, and to encourage the writing of original melodies.

Raoul Maddox, music teacher at Mapleton, Ore., High School, uses the flannel board to work out difficult band and choral passages with the students as well as to review the fundamentals of musical notation. "One of the prime assets of this teaching aid," he says, "is that it is something the students can actually handle. Once the students know how the board works, they can be given problems to work out or can help others find the answers to particular questions."

Physical education (boys): When his school played away from home, Ernest Neal, coach at Florence, Ore., High School, found that only one of the high schools had a chalk board in the dressing room for the visiting team. At first, Mr. Neal made chalk diagrams on the cement floors during half time. "But that wasn't satisfactory," says Neal, "because the players had to stand in awkward positions to see the illustrations." He found the flannel board offered unique opportunities. He drew the boundary lines, goals, and so on, on a piece of flannel with India ink. Instead of mounting the flannel on a board, he merely folds and carries it in his pocket. During half time, Mr. Neal fastens the flannel to the wall with masking tape (this doesn't remove paint when the flannel is taken down) and he uses sandpaper-backed symbols to represent players. These, too, are carried in his pocket.

Len Monroe, principal and coach at Maupin, Ore., High School, uses a flannel board for football. Mr. Monroe says, "I have found it to be a valuable teaching aid, especially for new football candidates. Some phases of the game that I have used it for include field layout, kickoff positions, different offensive and defensive formations, the visualizing of certain incidents in the past or anticipated ones in the future."

Coaches in my classes have made flannel boards for nearly all sports. One physical-education teacher summed it this way, ". . . Chalk marks on the chalk board are more limited. Symbolic figures on a flannel board make it possible to show a variable and moving situation. This makes the flannel board a very practical and realistic visual aid."

Physical education (girls): Alice Fish, physical education instructor for girls at Hillsboro, Ore., High School, uses a flannel board to demonstrate zone guarding. "The flannel board," says Miss Fish, "enables me to show the zones as well as the positions of the players and the moves they must make in an easily followed manner. Symbols and figures represent the players."

Marguerite Whitehouse, physical education teacher at Mapleton, uses the flannel board to teach various game skills and to emphasize certain items— posture, clean gym clothes, and so on. To accent posture, Miss Whitehouse sets her flannel board on a tripod near the gymnasium entrance. Then she places on the board such words as "POSTURE," "CLEAN P.E. CLOTHES MONDAY." "The word 'posture' alone," says Miss Whitehouse, "is sufficient. You should see how quickly the students manage to straighten up and walk correctly."

Social studies: Mrs. Kathryn Kumler, Tillamook, Ore., uses a flannel board that resembles a relief map. On large pieces of flannel, she makes outlines of countries. Specific geographical areas are cut out of different colored pieces of felt to show height above sea level. This gives the effect of a general relief map.

At Lebanon, Ore., High School, Dorothy Schulz uses the flannel board to point out our industrial growth since 1800. She uses several circle charts to accomplish this. Since several layers of felt and/or flannel can be built up, her graphic illustrations in sequence have the added touch of animation.

Another teacher who feels that students should have a concrete understanding of our government has been using the chalk board almost entirely until recently. Now she accomplishes most of her objectives with the flannel board. The make-up of Congress, the duties of the President's cabinet, are now more interesting and meaningful because of this easy-to-make visual aid. Some of the students use the aid to help explain certain phases of our government; this in itself helps in another learning process—speech.

CONCLUSION

The flannel board, sometimes roughly compared to bulletin boards and chalk boards, has infinitely greater possibilities because it contains many inherent qualities and characteristics of both. That's why many high-school teachers are beginning to use flannel boards. Ivan Burkert, audio-visual director at Corvallis High School, gives these reasons for the sudden interest: "High-school teachers never realize what opportunities they are missing until they use a flannel board. But when they begin to cut, paste, and use this flexible aid, ideas begin to flow and they soon realize that there is no end to the uses of this device.

"There is one more reason why flannel boards are used. It is very evident that both teachers and students take a genuine interest in their own classroom prepared visual aids. They realize that often their own can be superior to commercial ones." [1]

Space did not permit a detailed list of the numerous uses for flannel boards in high school. However, if you have made some flannel-board teaching devices that were not mentioned, perhaps you will enjoy passing your ideas on to your fellow teachers. This, I am sure, will be appreciated because most high-school teachers never realize what they are missing until they see and use a flannel board.

OVERHEAD PROJECTOR TECHNIQUES

James Klausen and James H. Parsons *

Pictures can make any subject brighter and clearer. Suitable pictures are available everywhere. Libraries have collections; suppliers sell them; but most prevalent of all are the pictures available free in magazines, advertising brochures, and books. These pictures can be cut out and mounted. They can be used to brighten up bulletin boards, or shown on a screen by means of an opaque projector. Seemingly, there is no end to what can be done with pictures.

Filmstrips represent another use of pictures. Projected on a screen by

[1] Milton Grassell, "Flannel Boards in Action," *Educational Screen*, XXXIV (1955), 250–51.

* From *The American Biology Teacher*, Vol. 27 (Bloomington, Ind.: The National Association of Biology Teachers, December 1965), pp. 675–678. Reprinted by permission of *The American Biology Teacher*.

means of a 35mm filmstrip projector, they present a sequence designed to bring out a point. Similar use can be made of 2 by 2 picture slides, which can easily be made into a film sequence with synchronized tape-recorded sound. Such picture sequences, with or without sound, have the advantage of making possible for the teacher of the topic to teach in the way he wants to, rather than in the way some film editor thinks he ought to. Titles and sound effects make the picture sequences more professional, but they are not necessary. Sometimes it is better not to have them so that teacher and pupils can participate in the lesson by answering and asking questions and making comments. Either way, filmstrips and film sequences make admirable aids for use with individual and small groups because the machines are so simple to load and operate.

One of the most effective ways to make use of pictures, diagrams, and so on, is to use overhead projectors. Overhead projection is one of the most useful products of modern educational technology. It is rapidly becoming one of the most commonplace because of its marvellous versatility. In its dramatic impact and simplicity, it is much akin to the flannel board. As with other tools, however, it is only really good when used properly. The following selection suggests several ways to use overhead projection effectively. Most of the suggestions can also be applied to other types of projection.

A visual system that is enjoying increased popularity in the classroom today consists of an overhead projector, screen, and projectuals. The overhead projector transmits light through a system of lenses and mirrors, through an acetate projectual (somewhat like a large slide), and onto a screen. As an "electric blackboard" it has several advantages and has literally replaced the blackboard in many schools.

. . . The screen is located high on the wall, unlike a blackboard. This eliminates the problem of students' vision being blocked by heads and other objects in front of them. The head of the projector is also relatively small to eliminate this problem. The position of the system allows the teacher to constantly face the class while changing materials on the screen and while pointing out objects. The system is used under normal illumination which allows for normal notetaking, drawing, discussion, and control.

Most projectuals are of a permanent nature. Therefore the teacher can afford to spend a little extra time in making the projectual more accurate and colorful than a blackboard diagram done in haste and erased several times during the day. Mounted in frames, they can be filed for use in subsequent years. With the use of suitable solvents, water and alcohol, they can be easily relabeled or revised.

Most biology teachers utilize a large number of diagrams and charts to illustrate concepts under discussion. Every year they are redrawn with some degree of inaccuracy or compromise. What about those teachers with limited artistic ability? The overhead projector system lends itself very nicely to diagrams and charts.

Biology teachers often hold up photographs in books and journals to illustrate a point or pass the illustration around. Certainly the people in the last row cannot see the average photograph held up in the front of the room. Most of these photographs can be made into projectuals. There may be some loss of quality, but this is more than offset by the fact that all students see the photograph at the same time and you can point out things on it or even label it.

The overhead projector system can be used as a testing device. Quizes can be written or typed on a temporary projectual at a moment's notice, administered, and removed completely and easily between periods. Mistakes, additions, or deletions on duplicated tests can be quickly and silently communicated to the students with a temporary projectual. These suggestions can make certain aspects of testing easier.

PROJECTORS

Various types of overhead projectors are available on the market. . . . The Master Vu Graph (A) is a large machine with good illumination. It utilizes a filament bulb, a Fresnel lens, other lenses, and mirrors to project the image onto the screen. The Beseler Porta-Scribe (B) is a smaller machine weighing 17 pounds. This type of projector has the advantages of portability along with a smaller head to decrease screen blockage. It uses a quartz iodine bulb that gives essentially a point source of light. This reduces the number of mirrors and lenses needed in the projector while giving illumination comparable to the larger projectors. The Act-O-Matic Dual Position projector (C) is a special overhead projector designed for chemical and other demonstrations. The lens and mirror system is similar to the Master Vu Graph, but the stage is smaller and can be moved to a vertical position. Clear plastic cells, special meters, and other devices have been developed for use in this projector by Herbert Alyea of Princeton. His ideas are published in each issue of the *Journal of Chemical Education* under the heading *TOPS in General Chemistry*.

SCREENS

The use of a projector implies the existence of a surface on which the image is projected. In a pinch, the wall or even the ceiling can be used for this purpose, but is hardly to be recommended. The most desirable surface is a projection screen, portable or permanently installed.

There are many good screens on the market. The "Flat Mat" type, although the most economical, is very satisfactory. This type permits viewing from a very wide angle. The image does not lose brightness when viewed from the side.

The "Beaded" screen, though having a brighter image, when viewed straight on cannot be viewed from the side.

A recent addition to the field is the "lenticular" screen, boasting the advantages of both the "Mat" and "Beaded" screens. The one major drawback of the lenticular surface is that it must be under tension when in use. When used in a portable screen, this tension is automatically achieved with the supporting stand. In the case of a wall installation, a "tension bar" is required. The additional operation of attaching and operating the tension bar may be sufficient to discourage teachers from using it. Other than this one drawback, the lenticular screen produces an image that is a delight to the eye.

The most practical solution we have found thus far is the use of the "Draper V" wall screen which is not only adequate, but quite economical (approximately $20 for the 60x60 size). It is simply a screen surface rolled on a window screen roller. This unit is attached to an extruded aluminum "V" bar which gives the screen its name.

Ordinarily, the screen is placed above the projectionist. This high placement combined with the short throw (short projection distance) of the overhead projector creates a condition which is termed "keystone effect." The original rectangular shaped image is distorted into a keystone shape, wider at the top than the bottom. This distortion is corrected by tilting the screen until the surface is perpendicular to the projection axis.

This tilt in a wall screen is achieved by using long extension brackets to support the screen at the top. When the screen is pulled open and the bottom attached to the wall, the screen will be properly tilted. Variable extension brackets are available which permit one to vary the angle of the tilt.

The problem of "keystoning" is not as great in portable screens, if the surface is not mounted as high above the projector. Nevertheless, most screen manufacturers provide "keystone eliminators" for use where critical projection is necessary.

If one is confronted with the ever present problem of a very limited budget, it is possible to make a screen from commercial wall board. "Cellotex" which has a white surface, is easily obtained, is quite economical, and light in weight, serves the purpose well. A frame is generally required to stiffen the cellotex which may sag if otherwise unsupported.

PROJECTION SLIDES

There are basically two methods of using the overhead projector, the "quick and easy" and the "prepared projectual." The quick and easy method can be compared to those employed in using a blackboard. This method utilizes a grease pencil and a sheet of clear acetate which is placed on the stage of the projector. With the grease pencil the teacher writes or draws on the acetate and the image is projected onto the screen behind him. When a sheet is full, it can be set aside, available for recall if a student wants a point repeated. When the session is over, if the sheet has no lasting value it can be wiped clean with a cloth and used again. The roll of acetate available for most projectors can also be used in this manner.

The "prepared projectual" method uses projection slides which have been prepared beforehand. These can be purchased from several biological supply houses and publishers of educational materials, or prepared in advance by members of the teaching staff.

In general, it might be said that the major difficulty in obtaining commercially produced slides is finding one that will fit the teacher's immediate needs. Obviously, for a commercial concern to manufacture projection slides in large enough quantities to be profitable, the treatment of the subject must be very general in nature in order to be acceptable to a great number of teachers. The teacher will have to make his own projectuals in order to fill his more specific needs.

There are many benefits to the do-it-yourself approach in addition to the obvious advantage of building up a working library of projectuals. The necessity of rethinking the lesson presentation quite often gives the teacher a new approach to the subject.

The prepared projectual can be as simple as writing or drawing on a clean sheet of acetate with a grease pencil, or as complex as a diagram with several overlays, reproduced from a textbook by one of several reflex transfer processes.

We would suggest that all of these handicraft techniques be tried, if only so you may reject them.

1. Hand letter a text on acetate using a speedball pen and acetate ink (available in any art store). For real economy, reprocessed x-ray film may be obtained from the Johnson Process Co. for 2¢ a sheet.
2. Trace a drawing on acetate using the same equipment as above.
3. Color in the areas of the diagram with a "magic marker." This material will project in color.
4. Cut shapes or symbols out of colored acetate and lay them on the drawing.
5. Attach an extra sheet of clear acetate by a hinge (cellophane tape) to the side of the slide. Additional information (captions, details, etc.) is drawn or lettered on this sheet. Any number of these overlays may be added. The progressive development of an idea is revealed by flopping these overlays in position over the original drawing one at a time.
6. Color photographs from a magazine can be made into a projectual. The technique consists of gluing the ink onto roughened acetate with rubber cement and removing the paper fibers and clay layer by softening in water and peeling or rubbing them off. Seal, Incorporated makes a kit for this purpose.

Obviously, these methods could be rather time consuming if the material produced is anything but very simple.

How extremely useful a technique enabling one to quickly transfer a drawing from a textbook or professional magazine to a sheet of acetate would be! This is possible with a "reflex copier." There are several different brands on the market; Verifax, Thermofax, Contura-Constat, Transofax, etc. Some are "wet" processes (Contura-Constat), others are dry (Verifax and Thermofax) the transfer being effected by heat. If speed is necessary, the dry process is preferable. On the other hand, Contura-Constat produces a more substantial slide using a heavier gauge acetate.

A very popular copier at present is a classroom model of the Thermofax machine, the "Model 70," priced under $150. This device will produce a projectual from any copy in less than 60 seconds. The image can be projected immediately.

In lieu of the above machine, the standard Thermofax copier which more likely is available in the school system, will do a similar job with the exception of copying from books.

The selection of projectual making techniques, projectors, and screens will depend upon the money available and personal experience. Whichever you select, you will find it to be highly adaptable to different subjects and teaching techniques. We have had extensive experience in the use of this system and have found it to be an extremely useful instructional tool.

8MM FILM—AN EDUCATIONAL BREAKTHROUGH?

James Olsen *

Movies are probably the most common type of audio-visual aids in American schools today. They should be used as ordinary teaching tools. The teacher, having properly previewed a film, should introduce it to his class, pointing out what its purpose and salient features are—sometimes with the aid of a study guide—and follow up the presentation with discussion or other suitable activities. Obviously if such procedures are necessary, it is also necessary to show the film at the appropriate time in the course so that it re-enforces or points up the rest of the instruction.

Unfortunately, administration and technical difficulties interfere with

* From *The Educational Forum*, Vol. 31 (November 1966), pp. 103–106. Used by permission of Kappa Delta Pi, An Honor Society in Education, owners of the copyright.

the efficient, effective use of 16mm films. Among these difficulties are the cost of procuring films, the scheduling of films and machines, the need for darkening rooms in which films are being projected, and the economic and practical need for using 16mm films in large-group situations.

Now the advent of the 8mm-film loop projector is overcoming some of these difficulties. It seems probable that film projection of the future can be and should be individualized and fitted into the daily lessons without the undue commotion attendant to 16mm film presentations.

The 16mm films, filmstrips, instructional television—all of these pictorial media have had an established place in the American classroom for more than a half-century now. But at the same time, teachers continue to regard the printed material which is available to them as their prime instructional tool and medium of instruction, education, and communication. The textbook still dominates American education, and film is regarded as supplementary and secondary in importance. 16mm pictures therefore have not had the impact upon education envisioned by the audiovisualists of the 1930's.

There are many reasons for this, not the least of which is that visual learning devices present problems of utilization. In other words, the average teacher in the average school cannot get a motion picture when he wants it. Only a relatively few school systems are adequately funded and equipped to solve this availability problem. Our 16mm educational motion picture prints are stored in central libraries because they are expensive to buy. After the teacher takes the time and trouble to find out what is available and to order it, he then waits for it to arrive so that he can preview it to assess its pertinence to his program.

When the film arrives he must then find a darkened room—often this is not an easy job in an overcrowded school—and project it with a machine that he probably has never been trained to operate. This machine may be complicated for him to operate and, given its age, may break down several times in the course of his preview. After his preview, the teacher may decide that this particular film does not fit his specific needs at this time, and so he must now send it back to the central film library. Film utilization therefore has for many classroom teachers some of the characteristics of preparing for an African safari.

But even assuming that this particular film is appropriate for his class, there are further difficulties, this time of an educational nature. The major difficulty, of course, is that 16mm film, for example, is implicitly designed for large group instruction in which the class is taught as an undifferentiated unit. Suppose a student does not understand a particular instructional sequence. Or suppose another student wants to review some of the concepts presented in the film. What do these students do? The point is that, at least with 16mm film, the individual student has very little choice over what materials are available to him and when he wants to use them. Printed materials, on the other hand, present no such problems. You can read a book when you want, and as often as you want. Books are accessible, available, and in contrast to film cheap.

I suspect that it is precisely because of these reasons—as well as the sacrosanct quality of the printed word in Western civilization—that teachers continue to use printed material as their major learning device even in those situations in which that material is the worst possible choice. It is fairly obvious that given the dramatic immediacy and compelling visual power of film, it can do many jobs more effectively than books. But even so, because of its expense and inaccessibility, I think most of us would agree that film has not generally been used extensively and frequently in the classrooms of the United States, that is, films are not part of our regular instructional pattern.

But 8mm film has inherent characteristics that, unlike 16mm film, make it possible for it to become a prime tool of educational instruction, rather than a supplementary aid.

First, 8mm film can be used in cartridges. The film itself is encased in an inexpensive plastic cartridge that makes it easy to store like a book and that protects it from dirt and damage. Presently, there are more than 1,600 silent film cartridges commercially available and an estimated 50,000 to 60,000 8mm sound and silent projectors are being used in schools and industry. (Sales of 8mm projectors for professional users jumped from under two million in 1962 to five million in 1963.) 16mm films, on the other hand, cannot be used in cartridges except at prohibitive expense both for the cartridge and the projector.

This cartridge format of the 8mm film is crucially important because a film collection can be created in a class or school library. This makes 8mm prints and projectors readily available. Because of cartridge loading, moreover, they can be used effortlessly by anyone at almost any time without breaking the flow of classroom instruction. The projector is loaded by simply inserting the cartridge. Thus 8mm film promotes individualization of instruction in the same way that 16mm film promotes large group instruction. The student, whether he is four or forty, can view the 8mm film again and again *in private*. Students have access to these films on a small-group or individual basis. Therefore, students can learn at their own pace. Skills, for example, can be repeatedly demonstrated *ad infinitum*. (Perhaps some kind of printed material may eventually be correlated with the film presentation.) Some of the 8mm silent cartridges projectors have a control that allows the student to "freeze" the film and study the image as long as he wants. Other styles of projectors permit the learner to advance the film through the projector frame by frame. The possibility of integrating programmed booklets with this presentation is obvious.

Second, the commercial costs of 8mm color prints are, in comparison to the costs of 16mm film, low. Standard 400-ft black and white 16mm films cost about $60 each. Color prints cost approximately twice that. Film rental runs about $4.50 a film, and most teachers have very limited film rental budgets. Four-minute 8mm silent cartridges, on the other hand, cost from $8 to $20. Teachers who make their own four-minute color 8mm films will pay between $5 and $6, including processing and cartridging. As yet, we know little about the cost of 8mm sound cartridged film, but we could probably expect the costs to run about one-third of the costs of comparable 16mm prints.

Third, 8mm films have an educational rhetoric of their own—and this is a vitally important point. To describe 8mm as "single concept" is a mistake, but does indicate that this film form does depart from the conventional format of the standard educational film. 8mm has many possible uses. It can be used to develop single concepts, single skills; and to show demonstrations, illustrations, and stories. In many instances, these films will not have to apply to particular grade levels and can contain a great amount of information that the student will eventually absorb with repeated viewings. There are also no clear beginning and ending points so that the familiar beginning-middle-end pattern is broken.

The advantages of 8mm film over present film media are real and obvious. They are much cheaper to make than 16mm. They can be easily stored and handled and are therefore accessible. And they can be used to serve individualization of instruction and educational innovation. But it would probably be a mistake, I think, to believe that 8mm film will be widely adopted by school systems very rapidly. Rather than expecting an explosive growth in the school instructional materials market, we can look forward to the gradual emergence of a market of moderate dimensions.

The first problem we have, of course, is the traditional lag in the school's acceptance of innovation. The second problem relates to the question of estimating the market for this type of instructional material. Public school systems (K-12) devote about 1.8 per cent of all annual expenditures (including capital outlays) to instructional supplies. Only a fraction of these expenditures can be considered as available for allocation to visual materials. In 1963, for example, $306,000,000 was spent for elementary and secondary textbooks which averages out to $6.11 per pupil, the list price of a single textbook. Or, to put it another way, out of every dollar in the 1963 school budget, 1.25 cents was allocated to textbooks, a startling fact in view of the dominance of the textbook in our curriculum. (Only 0.6 per cent of that 1.8 per cent is spent for the purchase of textbooks.) Thirdly, the diversity in the school curriculum is many times greater than the variety of 8mm programs available. It is likely to be some time, therefore, before much real choice among 8mm films with comparable objectives and quality will be available.

Since we cannot expect a sudden widespread adoption of 8mm loops, we should develop material selectively for those areas of the market that show the greatest potential. Since so much attention is currently being given to the disadvantaged youngster, it would seem there is a special market for deprived youngsters in early childhood programs, preliterate children in the primary grades, and in remedial programs for students who need to catch up or increase their ability in basic academic skills like reading. Since so many of these youngsters are also profoundly disaffected with the printed word anyway, a medium which uses pictures and non-verbal symbols would be especially appropriate.

In keeping with trends in curriculum revision and experimentation, one can also anticipate early applications in science, math, and foreign languages. Additionally, subject matter fields in the secondary school curriculum tend to be more compartmentalized and therefore more amenable to new kinds of treatment.

But as new and better kinds of hardware are developed for 8mm film, it will be important to remember that the device is subsidiary to the program. An early infatuation with the prospects of a "device market" can be financially disastrous to the educational publisher. In other words, we should remember that 8mm loops should be well integrated with other media and techniques so that they can genuinely contribute to the learning situation. What we will need to develop are educationally sound programs that will exploit the potentialities of this medium to their fullest extent.

RECORDINGS AND THE LISTENING EXPERIENCE

John T. Muri *

The record player, like the tape recorder, is another device that has many uses. Modern high fidelity stereophonic instruments are "superlative devices for bringing into the classroom at the moment of our own choosing the spoken word done superlatively well." Good reproduction equipment and a good selection of tapes and records are essential for a well-equipped school. They can be used in all subjects although they fit most readily into the English, social studies, and music classes. With the addition of earphones or sound booths, they are marvelous aids for in-

* From John T. Muri, "Recordings and the Listening Experience," *Using Mass Media in the Schools*, William D. Boutwell, editor (New York: Appleton-Century-Crofts, 1962), pp. 234–239. Reprinted with the permission of the National Council of Teachers of English and John T. Muri.

dividualizing instruction. Although some of the references in the follow-ing article are somewhat old, the article is one of the best succinct presentations of the principles underlying the use of audio aids.

Recordings can help perform at least five important functions:

1. The first function, that of reinforcing learning, may be done by playing a recording after the material in it has been studied and discussed. This is especially effective with selections like Milton's "Lycidas" and Patrick Henry's Speech, which high school students find hard to analyze. Repeated playings are desirable for difficult materials. A record may be heard as a review exercise, days or weeks after a story or poem has been studied.

2. The second function is to supplement reading and learning. To accomplish this, the teacher who has time available for it will introduce new materials by means of recordings, usually short works by authors that have been studied in class (e.g., a short story of Poe, read on [1] Caedmon 1028, Vanguard 9046 and 9007, and Decca 9062, or Edna St. Vincent Millay's "Renascence" on Caedmon 1024). . . . Almost any combination of authors or literary periods, or even of important works of single authors, may be found on recordings.

3. The third function is to teach the student to listen efficiently. This may be done by presenting, on recording, materials that have not been read and asking the student to reproduce what he has heard, and, on the higher levels, to analyze and interpret it. At first, short, easy selections may be used; later, students may be asked to outline and discuss recorded lectures. . . .

4. The fourth function is to stimulate the imagination, the mind's eye. This may best be done through listening to recorded drama, from which the teacher can make many choices. Shakespearean drama is always rewarding; so are *Oedipus Rex* (Caedmon 2021), MacLeish's *J. B.* (Victor LD 6075, a superb recording), *Medea* (Decca 9000), and *Death of a Salesman* (Decca DX-102). Several good courses in drama might be built around a library selected from the dozens of full-length plays that are available.

5. The fifth function is to make comparative studies and evaluations of interpretations of literature. This consists in listening to two or more readings of a literary work and judging which comes nearer to the author's intent, seeing how different interpretations can be valid and enlightening. For this purpose, the teacher may use the numerous recorded performances of Antony in *Julius Caesar*. Students are usually interested in comparing Marlon Brando's performance with those of other actors. Several readings of James

---

[1] In the listings that follow, the names of Caedmon, Spoken Arts, etc., are the trade names of the phonograph record companies, or of what is called their "labels." The number following the name is the one by which the record may be ordered from any record dealer. The abbreviation "SW" represents the company label "Spoken Word"; "SA" represents "Spoken Arts."

Weldon Johnson's "The Creation" are available; they make interesting comparative studies.

The choice of recordings for classroom use is very wide. There is much more material available than any teacher would hope, much less care to use. . . . The teacher who regularly examines the monthly issues of the Schwann Long-Playing Record Catalog (available in most record shops) will be informed about the new recordings, will know what older recordings remain available for purchase, and will be able to make tentative choices of materials. . . .

In selecting records, the teacher may keep in mind four standards:

1. A recorded performance should be chosen for its educational value, rather than for the illustriousness of its performers. Very often readings done by well-known people of the theater leave much to be desired. The differences between exhibitionist theatricality and scholarly excellence should not be confused or ignored. As teachers we should not help perpetuate the myth that so far as poetry is concerned, the performance is more important than the work. There is a time for the study of the performance techniques of art, but it is not usually found in the high school. The most common function of the performer on records for the classroom is to enlighten, to give meaning, to stimulate, and to inspire. If the performer can succeed in only one of these functions, his effort is worthwhile.

2. The recording should add something to the teaching that neither the teacher nor the students could bring to it themselves.

3. The recording should be suitable to the maturity level of the students. Many commercial recordings include passages that could not be defended against the criticisms of disturbed school patrons. In doubtful cases, it would be better for the teacher to omit the passage in his teaching. Other passages may be unsuitable because of their difficulty. A wise teacher will not wish to impose such materials upon minds that are unready.

4. The purpose in using the record should be clearly kept in mind. A distinction should be made between records which are educational (which includes the inspirational and motivational, as well as the informational) and those that are merely entertaining. It is sometimes difficult to distinguish. Some pupils will be motivated by a recording at a time when others are affected little or not at all. The teacher needs to keep in mind the distinction between teaching and entertaining. At times, the latter can be useful in setting the stage for learning, but for its own sake it serves a minor purpose. The teacher needs to keep clearly in mind what he intends the listening experience to accomplish and to buy the records that will best secure those ends.

The tape recorder can be of special value to a teacher, for it can do everything that a record player can, and more. If he wishes, he can prepare a complete lecture-demonstration, putting both his remarks and a tape recording of a phonograph record together. When a recording is no longer available for purchase and the teacher wishes to keep his records from wearing out, he may choose to copy them on tape. Furthermore, when copying on tape, one is able to omit undesirable passages; this is something that cannot be done with a disc recording. It should be remembered that all copying of records should be done with the written permission of the manufacturers of the records.

The tape recorder is a means for making evening radio speech programs available to students during day classtime. Some excellent educational radio may be taken down for permanent use in school. Entire series may be recorded and edited, producing invaluable teaching aids. One device is to record two or three news commentaries in a single evening and ask the students the next day to listen to them, listing the points they hear under the headings of fact, inference, and judgment.

One can make one's own recordings on tape. Spelling drills, dictation exercises, and test instructions, particularly those that are long and which must be repeated several times in one day, may be taped at leisure outside of school. The author has tape recorded the Auditory Comprehension Test of the Diagnostic Reading Test series, which requires the teacher to read almost forty-five minutes; the test results are, in his opinion, just as reliable as if he personally read the material each time the test was given. Much energy is saved, and free time is made available for other tasks.

There are three reasons for putting one's own readings on tape: (1) one's readings on tape, developed through several revisions, can be the best that one can do at the time, (2) recorded readings permit one to listen to himself and to improve, and (3) taped readings can be used on those days when one doesn't feel like reading and doesn't read well, although the material needs to be presented. . . .

THE MASS MEDIA AND
THE SOCIAL STUDIES

Leonard H. Clark *

Obviously, teachers and other educators have not fully met the challenge of the communications revolution and the growth of mass media. As Herbert McLuhan rightly points out,† children of today must come "out of this intricate and complex world of electric information" that they

* From *The Mass Media in Secondary Education*, 1965 Yearbook 130, (Plainfield, N.J.: New Jersey Secondary School Teachers Association), pp. 46–54. Reprinted by permission of the New Jersey Secondary School Teachers Association.

† Herbert Marshall McLuhan, "Address at Vision 65," *The American Scholar*, Vol. 35 (Spring 1966), p. 198.

*live in outside of school "and go into this nineteenth-century world of
classified information that still characterizes the educational institution."
Is it any wonder that pupils are repelled by schools with their dead information and old-fashioned inept methods of communication? As yet,
teachers have not developed the understandings and techniques to take
full advantage of the new media, but there is no doubt that we can use
them in our present context.*

ALL MEDIA

All of the mass media can contribute to the effectiveness of social studies
courses. In the following paragraphs we shall deal with social studies concerns
served by all media and then in later sections turn to specific uses of film,
television, radio, magazines, and newspapers.

LEARNING TO THINK STRAIGHT

In his classic text on the teaching of history Henry Johnson (1940, p. 325)
charges that in their attempts to teach pupils to think discriminatingly, social
studies teachers have emphasized the critical interpretation of information,
but have not taught boys and girls how to determine what the facts are.
Certainly the development of techniques and touchstones for determining
what is fact is necessary. The mass media, especially the news media, provide
excellent means for teaching pupils critical attitudes and skills, such as reserv-
ing judgment and checking the essential facts as bases for straight thinking.

Comparing the coverage of news stories by different newspapers and news-
casters is an excellent way to open pupils' eyes to the uncertainty of many of
the facts we deal with in social studies. Another good activity is to let the
pupils compare something they themselves have witnessed, e.g. a local basketball game, with the account of it in the local or school newspaper. In case
this exercise is not feasible, one can manufacture a reasonable substitute by
having the pupils write and compare their own news reports of a classroom
incident, either contrived or real.

To counteract the failings of the mass media, the social studies teacher,
particularly in the current events class, must help boys and girls create standards by which to check newspaper, magazine, radio, and television reports.
In this process the following questions might be considered:

1. What is the source of the information?
2. Is the information fact or opinion?
3. Are there signs of coloring, policying, or editorializing the news stories?
4. Does the news story check out with information from other sources and
   known facts?
5. Does the particular agency, newspaper, magazine, network or station
   have a reputation for objective, honest reporting?

CURRENT AFFAIRS

Current events are the business of mass media and therefore lend themselves to the teaching of social studies. But they can be misused. Classes in which boys and girls get up to read short clippings from the paper every Friday morning are usually failures no matter how much the teacher tries to develop the news items. Such classes represent inexcusable malpractice. Some exercises which might be more profitable include:

1. Following certain stories over a period of several weeks or months and keeping a file of clippings or a scrapbook with a running commentary and summary of the developments.
2. Designing cartoons representing developments.
3. Collecting cartoons of the issues of the day. These cartoons should be from several papers and magazines and should show different viewpoints. The collectors could explain to the class the implications of the cartoons in a report.
4. Keeping notebooks in which are recorded summaries of the big stories of the day. These can be kept by categories such as: U.S. Foreign Affairs, United Nations, Local Politics, State Government, Business, and so on. Pupils can concentrate on one heading if it seems desirable, or keep an account of all headings.
5. Studying the papers and newscasts to find what the significant stories are in any one week and studying the stories to determine the significant details.
6. Designating certain pupils to become class experts on certain news areas. One person, for instance, could be the stock market specialist and report on the market.

During periods of great news importance it might be wise to assign different pupils to follow the coverage of particular news stories on different television networks and to report to the class.

Several publishing houses specialize in providing weekly news magazines for the pupils in junior and senior high schools. They have several advantages:

1. The reading level is controlled.
2. They supply background material to help pupils understand the stories.
3. They present both information and interpretation.
4. Being weeklies, they are able to tie together, select, and evaluate the news so that events may be seen in perspective.
5. They are usually as objective, authoritative and reliable as their editors can make them.
6. They are supported by teacher editions and study aids which can be very helpful for teachers in preparing and carrying out their teaching.

They attempt to appeal to young people and to write stories in a way that will interest them.

They also have disadvantages:

1. Because they are weeklies, the news may be stale, lacking in immediacy.
2. They tend to write down to the pupils.
3. They tend to take the life out of the stories by over-simplifying, glossing over superficially, and pre-digesting.
4. Consciously or unconsciously the papers tend to present a point of view —the result being a cumulative influence on the readers toward certain biases.

Ideally pupil weeklies should be used only to supplement and complement the live coverage in the mass media. One must recognize, however, that the reading level (12th grade or more) of papers like the New York *Times* is liable to be too high for some readers. Differentiating assignments should take care of this problem satisfactorily. Some pupils can read and report on the *Times*, others the weekly pupil paper.

A STUDY IN THEMSELVES

Because they are sociological phenomena which one must consider in order to have an understanding of the modern world, the study of mass media must be part of our social studies curriculum, particularly in the study of sociology, current events, problems of democracy, current history, and economics. Among the questions which pupils might consider are:

1. Do moving pictures, radio, television, and magazine stories and articles represent American life correctly?
2. What effects do the mass media have on our lives?
3. Are the television and mass media forcing standards of conformity upon people? (See Seldes, 1957, p. 18, for good discussion of this point.)
4. Should the stations and networks give people what they want or what they need?
5. What are the reading, listening and watching habits of parents and pupils?
6. To what extent should T.V. be allowed to enter politics?
7. It is often said that the mass media are responsible for much crime because of their sensationalizing of violence and crime. What evidence is there that this is so? What can be done about it?
8. We are now undergoing a communications revolution. What social and cultural changes are accompanying this? . . .

MOTION PICTURES

Motion pictures have been losing ground to television, but they still remain an important recreational educational medium because the film presents points of view to boys and girls which rub off on them. Any middle-aged American has had much evidence that many of his generation formed ideas of proper behavior, manners, and dress from what they saw at the movies. There is reason to believe that this influence is continuing today. Movies do much of the shaping of young people's ideas concerning other lands, other times, and other people.

Commercial moving pictures provide considerably more for social studies classes than the average social studies teacher can take advantage of. On the day that this paragraph is being written, the New Haven Register—New Haven Journal Courier advertises at least eight feature films based on historical or geographical themes: Mediterranean Holiday, The Longest Day, Zulu, The Unsinkable Molly Brown, Cleopatra, The Long Ships, Becket, and The Island of the Blue Dolphin. Frequently films that one would not expect to be useful have excellent material. An example is The Loss of Innocence, a movie whose theme concerns growing from adolescence to maturity, which has some excellent scenes of the French countryside and French life and customs.

Teachers can hardly be expected to be up on all of these films. There is no reason why they should be. Pupils can do all the scouting necessary by reporting on the movie reviews and on movies they have seen which may be useful. Brief oral reports and bulletins or chalkboard notices will serve to alert other pupils when a movie with social studies impact is in town. In addition, theatre operators will usually be eager to cooperate by providing information about future scheduling and may even attempt to adjust their schedules to fit the school's requirements. Also, many of the best films are now available on 16mm for use in the school itself. (See Mallery, 1964).

THE BRIDGE OVER THE RIVER KWAI

All dramas must take place in time and space even if only "once upon a time" and "the land of make believe." Dramas, also, draw their substance from the behavior of people and their relations with one another. Therefore, movies which can be used to develop social studies attitudes, skills, and concepts are the rule rather than the exception. The Bridge Over the River Kwai is an example of many moving pictures which can contribute to instruction in various social studies disciplines, for example:

1. International affairs: Look up the Geneva Convention. What exactly is the law? Was Colonel Nickerson right or Colonel Saito? What countries had agreed to the Convention prior to World War II? When was it adopted? What is its present status? Do countries of the Soviet Union subscribe to it? How about Red China? To what extent was it honored during World War II?

Prepare a report on Commando operations. Compare the operations of the Task Force with guerilla operations in South Vietnam. Why is it so difficult for any army to successfully combat troop operations such as those of the group sent to blow up the bridge?

2. Sociology: Note the difficulty the Japanese had in controlling the British captives. Why is it that it seems to be so difficult for conquerors to bend captives to their will? Read Steinbeck's *The Moon Is Down,* or see the movie, and compare it to *The Bridge Over the River Kwai.* How do the commanders try to control their captives? Compare their efforts with those of the police in the United States in their attempts to put down riots and stop demonstrations.

3. Geography: Where is the River Kwai (Khwae Noi)? Can you find it on a map? Is there a railroad or highway there now? What type of terrain would you expect to find there? Is the scenery in the picture along the route accurate? Does the picture portray the climate well? Look up the rainfall and temperature statistics for that part of the world and chart them.

4. Anthropology: Find out as much as you can about the people of the area. What level of civilization? What religion? What customs?

5. History: What was the military situation in the early part of World War II in South East Asia? Why would the Japanese need a railroad from Rangoon to Bangkok? What military value would it have? Why would the British wish to destroy it? Report on the principal campaigns and commanders in South East Asia. What was the strategic value of holding this area?

6. Mapwork: Map out a route for the railroad from Bangkok to Rangoon using a large scale map. Draw a series of map overlays showing the position of the various armies in South East Asia during the period from the fall of Burma on. Make a terrain map showing the terrain, vegetation, and principal obstacles.

CINEMATIC HISTORY BOOKS

Old moving pictures such as *Idiot's Delight, The Grapes of Wrath,* or *The Great Dictator,* can give pupils direct experiences in history, for such motion pictures are not movies about history, they are history. Such movies deserve a place in the history curriculum just as much as most of the supplementary readings that we ask our pupils to read.

So do movies like *The Longest Day* and to a lesser degree *Lawrence of Arabia* and *Sunrise at Campobello,* which attempt to portray or recreate historical events. *The Longest Day* is in effect a motion picture history book and *Lawrence of Arabia* is a motion picture biography. They should be treated as such.

History becomes interesting and meaningful when it is studied in depth. Skimming over periods superficially tends to lead to superficial information gathering and not much else. Movies such as *The Longest Day* or *Lawrence of Arabia* make a good base for studying an event in depth. Activities which could be included are:

1. Terrain study.
2. Climate and weather study.
3. Study of strategy and tactics.
4. Study of people of the area—religion, economy, social customs.
5. Map study of campaigns.
6. Study of important individuals.
7. Placing of the event into the context of history. Of what importance was it? What led up to it? What resulted from it? What if it had never happened?

TELEVISION AND RADIO

On the general theory that instruction is much the same in almost any subject or any medium and that introduction, follow up, and so on will be treated well enough in the courses of study, the following paragraphs will be aimed primarily at the enrichment side of television. It will include, however, all types of television programs other than the purely instructional programs, for any type of television program can be used to enrich the curriculum and help cut a window into the world outside its academic ivory tower.

While it is true that much TV programming is fatuous, social studies teachers should try to become familiar with the programs which their pupils watch and especially those programs whose content may pertain to history or one of the social sciences—if for no other reason than to understand where the pupils may be getting some of their misinformation. Information about future television productions may be found in professional journals, e.g. the *NEA Journal* and *NEA Reporter*, as well as in the local press and television guides, or from the TV stations and networks themselves. Usually one will find more programs suitable for his classes than he expects. The February 1964 *NEA Journal* lists an even dozen network programs which have high secondary-school social studies potential. This list could have been greatly expanded. For instance, period drama in addition to being theatre is also a representation of life taking place in historical time and in almost any case can be used by the history teacher.

TV WESTERNS AND HISTORY

Even the formula Western can be used to advantage from time to time. In a unit studying the "Winning of the West", or "Post Civil War", one might assign activities like the following:

1. Read the statement by Gary Cooper (Boutwell, 1962, p. 28) in which he says

"the public has been fed a false concept of the West. . . .
The fact is that the real West was actually populated by
pioneers with guts—many of them with brains, too—and the
gunmen were parasites.

Youngsters growing up today have no real concept of
American history from 1850–1900. . . . What's happened now
is that movies and TV have made a uniform out of the
cowboy's colorful character and put him in a background of
Chicago and New York gangsterism. Only the costumes are
western."

Watch several TV Westerns to see how they falsify history. What elements of the TV story are right? Which wrong?

2. What period of history can be included in the Wild West? What produced this period? What caused it to close? What geographic area is
   represented by the cattle country of the period? What is the mining
   area? What was the purpose of the cattle drives? Where did they take
   the cattle? Do the scenes in the pictures represent properly the type of
   grazing land that was used during this time? Why, or why not? How
   can one find out?
3. Watch *Wagon Train*. What were the vehicles like? What provisions
   were made for water? How many persons banded together? Who was
   the Wagon Master? What was his job? How did he get it? See if you
   can locate the routes of the wagon trains on a map. What sort of terrain
   did they cover? At what speed did they go? How long did it take a
   wagon train to go to California? To Oregon? Read the *Oregon Trail*.
   How does it compare with the representation in *Wagon Train?*
4. Look closely at the land and terrain. What do they show about rainfall,
   fertility of the land, suitability for agriculture?

EDUCATIONAL TELEVISION

Educational or informational programs can be very good sources of enrichment activity. Among the best are such programs as Lowell Thomas' *High
Adventure* and *Bold Journey* which seem to reappear under different names
from time to time. Frequently TV stations schedule publicity or training films
of state, regional, or governmental agencies and sometimes commercial and
industrial enterprises. Many of these are especially useful for social studies
classes in geography, civics, and problems of democracy.

In many communities educational television stations present instructional
programs for adults designed either for self improvement or for college credit.
Often these programs can be used for high school classes. They can sometimes be assigned as the subjects of reports, or as supplementary assignments
for certain individuals. At times these programs require a high level of viewing
or listening skills, but often they do not. Many academically bright pupils can

gain much from them; other boys and girls who are not academically oriented may gain much also. Viewing and reacting to such programs may well be a better activity for them than some of the reading assignments by which we set so much store. For the most part, however, educational and cultural programs on both commercial and educational stations are not popular with pupils. Consequently, in order to get pupils to watch the programs usually they should be assigned. Many teachers have success with bulletin board and chalkboard advertising of "Best TV and Radio Bets" (Anita J. Willens, Boutwell, 1962, p. 254) and class discussion of the programs.

Television and radio programs suitable for classroom use are seldom on the air when the class is in session. This is unfortunate, because the greatest advantage of TV and radio is being able to attend outstanding events. To overcome this difficulty one can rely in part on the use of pupil reports and summaries. Other programs can be taped—both audio and video tape being now available at relatively reasonable cost. Although the video portions of programs such as the *President's News Conference* tend to make the programs more interesting and more meaningful, the audio portions of such programs are sufficient for classroom use.

NEWSPAPERS AND MAGAZINES

Every social studies classroom should be well stocked with newspapers and magazines. Among the newspapers represented should be both local and metropolitan dailies including a newspaper of record, which prints verbatim many of the current documents as well as writing about them. In addition other newspapers, among them one or two reputable foreign newspapers, should be available for classroom use in the social studies or school library. These newspapers, plus news magazines such as *Time*, or *U.S. News and World Report*, should be the bases for lessons on current events.

History, geography, economics, government, sociology, anthropology, all contribute to the news in our papers. In return the newspapers can be used to contribute to their study. In a history class, for instance,

1. Copies of old newspapers might be used to point up the happenings of the time. (Copies of some old papers are occasionally reprinted so that pupils can read the account of the contemporary report.)
2. Contemporary reports may be used to check on the record in our history books or historical novels. Does the *London Times* or *New York Times* report check with the account of Edward VII's funeral printed in *Life Magazine* or *Guns of August?*
3. Pupils might investigate the historical background of a present day social or governmental problem.

Every news story happens in a geography and we should put the story into its geography. For instance:

1. If the story concerns the Aswan Dam: Where is it on the map? What area will the new lake flood? Why do the Egyptians feel the need for a dam? What are the geographical features that make the High Dam desirable? What causes Egypt's great need for water? Where does the Nile get its water? Why does it flood?
2. If the story concerns South Vietnam and the Viet Cong: Where does it take place? What type of land is in the area? What type of climate? What is the strategic value of South Vietnam, etc.

If courses in Problems of Democracy or Modern Problems are to be real problem courses, the use of newspapers is a must. Every week boys and girls should be on the lookout for material on the area they are studying. In their study they can be alerted to particular things that they should look for by means of study guides. Thus in the study of advertising one might look for the following:

1. Study newspaper advertisements to see in what ways the advertisements help business.
2. Set up a set of criteria for advertising in newspapers, e.g. Is it truthful? Is it informative? Is its appeal positive rather than negative, i.e. does it avoid using fear, snob appeal, etc.? Is the advertising logical or deceptive?
3. What would be the advantages of an advertisement free newspaper? What would be the disadvantages?
4. Study the appeal of the newspaper ads in a local paper. To what group or groups do the various ads appeal? Do the emphases change from day to day? Why? How do the advertisers attempt to capitalize on local events, the days of the week, holidays, and so on?
5. Analyze advertisements for propaganda techniques.

Magazines are similar to newspapers, but their authors and editors have more time to prepare their stories carefully and are free to concern themselves less with the news of the moment and more with matters of wider import. Since they are somewhat less transistory than newspapers, radio, and television, they can be used to check the accuracy of news-stories and to follow significant stories into depth. Their semi-permanent format also makes back issues more available for ready use. Thus, if a committee of pupils wished to trace the progress of school integration since the famous Supreme Court decision, it would be much easier for them to do so in the back issue files of *Time* or *Newsweek* than in the newspaper files.

The social studies class should have copies of news weeklies and other magazines readily available. The list of periodicals it would be desirable to have is altogether too long to include here, but if possible it would be proper to furnish pupils with examples of both liberal and conservative viewpoints as well as those that stick to the middle of the road. Among the most useful periodicals are special purpose magazines like *The National Geographic*

Magazine and *Holiday* with their beautifully illustrated articles of places all over the globe. Less well known are the many magazines like *Ford Times, Arizona Highways, Vermont Life, Coming Events in Britain* and other magazines published by Bureaus of Tourism, State Development Agencies, and industrial publicity departments which feature articles, usually with pictures, about the history, geography, and sociology of many parts of the world.

CONCLUSION

Obviously all the mass media are teaching tools of great potential value. But if we social studies teachers use them just to impart social studies information, their potential can never be fully realized. We must use them as means by which to teach pupils to seek out and create knowledge for themselves.

BIBLIOGRAPHY

BOUTWELL, WILLIAM P. *Using Mass Media in the Schools.* New York: Appleton-Century-Crofts, 1962.

JOHNSON, HENRY. *Teaching of History,* Rev. Ed. New York: The Macmillan Company, 1940.

MALLERY, DAVID. *The School and the Art of Motion Pictures.* Boston: National Association of Independent Schools, 1964.

SELDES, GILBERT. *Challenge to a Free Society.* Washington, D.C.: American Association of University Women, 1957.

Part III

THE TEACHER
WE NEED

Teaching is certainly not a sinecure. It calls not only for great skill and knowledge but also for considerable forbearance. Yet, the teacher probably finds more satisfaction in his work than most nonteachers do. Compared to many other professions, teaching is relatively free from drudgery. For good teachers each day is different, full of many and varied challenges. In what other line of endeavor can one find such opportunities for scholarship, service, and enjoyable contact with others?

Beginning teachers straight from college are frequently in love with their subject matter. They picked this subject for their life's work because it meant so much to them. This is the way it should be. Anyone who does not like the subject he teaches is to be pitied. He should not be expected to teach well. Nevertheless, the most important part of the teacher's work is not his subject matter; it is his pupils. His success should not be measured by how well he knows his subject, but rather how well he can teach it to his pupils. This requirement adds a human element to teaching. This human element is the heart of teaching—without it, teaching is nothing. Consequently the teacher we need is one who puts the human element first. His first commitment is to the pupils and their learning; all other considerations, including the academic disciplines, are secondary.

THE TEACHER WE NEED

This short chapter makes up all of Part III. In the eyes of the editor, the selections included in it are especially significant because they point out what the role of the teacher really is and what sort of person a teacher ought to be.

Teachers are paid to teach boys and girls. This is a high responsibility and must be taken seriously. A teacher therefore must choose his strategies and tactics because they seem to be the ones that will be most likely to bring about the learning desired in the pupils—not to build up his own ego or to show off his own abilities. Furthermore the teacher must try to teach all the boys and girls. All boys and girls have worth—and none is worth more than any other. We teachers, then, must try to do the best we can to teach them all well. We can not afford to neglect any of them because they are dull or dirty or poor or "socially undesirable" or "not college material." In our attempt to teach them well, we shall be more successful—with all, rich or poor, sharp or dull, eager or hostile—if we value our pupils as human beings and treat them so in our teaching. When we do, then and then only, we deserve the name teacher, "the friend who makes men free."

THE JUNIOR HIGH SCHOOL
TEACHER WE NEED

Jack E. Blackburn *

In this article, the author pleads for a humanizing of the school. Teachers and pupils are human beings, and, therefore, much should be made

* From *Educational Leadership*, Vol. 23 (December 1965), pp. 205–208. Reprinted with permission of the Association for Supervision and Curriculum Development and Jack E. Blackburn. Copyright © 1965 by the Association for Supervision and Curriculum Development.

of human relationships. This article deals with junior-high-school teaching, but it might just as well have dealt with all teaching, for in every class at every level we need teachers who have respect for the human dignity of everyone and who have faith in the democratic principles. In short, teachers must respect and care for themselves, for their colleagues, and for their pupils as persons. Although it may seem somewhat fatuous to say so, the teacher who tries to live by this prinicple has gone a long way toward becoming the kind of teacher who makes a real impact on his pupils.

One recent Monday morning, a junior high school block-of-time class was having a current events discussion. Albert Schweitzer had passed away during the preceding weekend and much of the pupils' discussion dealt with Mr. Schweitzer. The teacher asked, "What stands out most in your mind when you think of Albert Schweitzer?"

There was a variety of responses from the class. One young adolescent said, "He was all for unfortunate people. I think he was real human. According to a news article I read, Mr. Schweitzer once said, 'You don't live in a world all your own. Your brothers are here, too.'"

The teacher responded, "What does being human mean? How do we distinguish between someone who acts human and someone who acts inhuman? Can you . . . ?"

In one session of a college class in junior high school education, a student asked of the teacher, "Can you help us become more human in our dealings with kids?"

This past session of summer school, the writer attended a one-day conference at New York University. The main focus of the conference was an address centered around humanizing our schools.

The illustrations cited here are only three of many current happenings in which emphasis is on humanness. Concern with this is not limited to educators. We could list numerous projects which are going on in our country and our world which show man's concern for his fellow man.

I, for one, am very pleased with the present emphasis in humanizing education. Never before in the history of American education has the climate been so appropriate for us to declare humanness as an educational goal. Some of us have often been reluctant, for one reason or another, to speak up for qualities which are uniquely human. I get the feeling that today, right now, this is the emphasis we need.

What does all of this talk about "humanizing" have to do with the junior high school teacher we need? To pose an answer to this question, we first need to turn attention to a concept of the purpose of education.

There is nearly unanimous agreement among our citizens that the general aim of education in a democracy is to contribute to the common good through aiding each individual in his process of becoming an intelligent, fully-functioning citizen. Each individual's unique self will determine the degree to which he becomes fully functioning. This is a very human goal.

If we accept this goal as a general aim for education, then what kind of teachers do we need to implement this objective in junior high schools?

TEACHERS WHO CARE

Some attributes of teachers who care have been described by a few people. Other perceptions, insights and skills have not been researched and discussed nearly enough. I would like to describe some qualities which, in my opinion, teachers need in order to aid pupils in their becoming process.

We need teachers who care about democracy.

In a country where citizens subscribe to a democratic way of life, we should not find it necessary to plead the case for democracy in school living. Yet, we are continually doing so. In fact, at least one person I know has raised the question—Is democracy indigenous to this country? When we visit schools and classrooms and see authoritarian practices being used, we might well raise such a question.

Teachers who care about democracy will know it and its opposing ideologies well. They will know that democratic living is learned. Their classroom organization will be such that it allows for pupils to engage in democratic practices.

From where I sit, academic freedom is a hot issue. From many states, teachers and lay citizens, we hear much about the subject of a teacher's freedom in the classroom. We need teachers who not only seek academic freedom for themselves but for pupils also.

Psychologists tell us that the most effective learning and personality development take place in democratic settings. To be democratic, we must have faith in others. Adlai Stevenson said so well:

> . . . I would . . . emphasize first that any discussion of education cannot be cast in terms of national needs . . . For education can serve the ends of democratic society only as it meets those of the individual human being. The essential condition of the system of free choice between conflicting ideas and leaders, which we call democracy, is that it be made up of all different kinds of people—which means that what we demand most of education is the development of informed people who are at the same time unique, different, unpatterned individuals.[1]

We need teachers who care about themselves.

In order for people to fully care about and have faith in others, they must view themselves in positive ways. To appreciate and respect the dignity and worth of another individual, a teacher must have looked within himself to know what is there.

[1] Adlai E. Stevenson, as quoted from Louise Parrish and Yvonne Waskin, *Teacher-Pupil Planning*. New York: Harper & Row, 1958, pp. 155–56.

We need teachers who care about helping pupils develop healthy self-concepts.

Seven years ago this writer participated in research designed to determine the relationship which exists between a nondirective drama technique and the development of reading skills and self-concept. This experience provided me with valuable insight. For example: How a person feels about himself ultimately determines his success or failure whether it be in reading, teaching, basketball, or any other endeavor.

Fortunately, we have available to us today some writings dealing with self-concept development. Teachers must continually strive to understand self and behavior. We need educators who take the time to understand their pupils; who will gather extensive information and use the data in the best interests of pupils.

To care about young adolescents one must understand them in their cultural setting. As Eric Hoffer puts it:

The reasonable approach is to assume that the adolescent's behavior is induced largely by his mode of existence, by the situation in which he finds himself. This would imply that adults, too, when placed in a similar situation, would behave more or less like juveniles.[2]

The young adolescent is essentially a person in search of self in a complex world. He ponders the questions: "Who am I?" "Where am I going?" "What does all of this have to do with me anyway?"

What useful insights teachers can get when they turn directly to the learners themselves! One teacher asked his ninth grade classes the question, "What do you see as being the five biggest problems facing people your age?"

Representative responses were:

We are being rushed along with the world to grow up and act our age.
We need grades for college.
We are worried over problems of the future.
We worry about dropping out of school.
We need to understand ourselves.
We need more recreational activities.
We live with grownups who think all teenagers are reckless.
We are faced with the shortage of jobs because of automation.

The teachers we need for young adolescents realize that *values* and *self-concept* are almost, if not wholly, inseparable. These teachers cherish differences. They help pupils clarify their own values and respect the values of other persons.

We need teachers who care about making content meaningful in the lives of pupils

"What is your class studying now Miss Bridges?"

2 Eric Hoffer, "A Time of Juveniles." *Harper's Magazine*, June 1965, p. 18.

"Oh, we're almost up to the Civil War. You see, it's almost the end of the year and we are supposed to cover American history from exploration to 1865 in the eighth grade."

"Do you mean uncover American history, Miss Bridges?"

"What? Oh, . . . it doesn't really matter. Students must have all of this for citizenship education anyhow."

How often we hear comments similar to these! And we must admit that teachers are not always at fault when they attempt to teach only what is in the book. Yet we know many teachers who use the excuse that a rigid structure is imposed upon them. They do not care whether or not the content has meaning to pupils.

One perceptive pupil, even from a school located in a "culturally deprived" area, said:

My favorite kind of teacher is a scientist. My reason for liking scientists is that they are real intelligent and sensible. They are always discovering things. That's the way I want to be.

This youngster's insight should help some of us to sit up and take notice. In the past few years, teachers have continuously heard that learning by discovery can be most meaningful. Some teachers are so concerned about pouring knowledge into pupils they forget about helping pupils to discover. Teaching procedures might have more promise if we could somehow translate Rachel Carson's ideas into practice. She described experiences she had had with her nephew as they walked on the beach and in the woods of Maine. Mrs. Carson expressed her pleasure in plants and animals which they saw, much as she would share discoveries with an older person. Later, the nephew could easily identify what he and his aunt had seen. "I am sure no amount of drill would have implanted the names so firmly as just going through the woods in the spirit of two friends on an expedition of exciting discovery." [3]

For content to be meaningful to a pupil, he must see its importance to him. In order for pupils to learn skills most effectively, they must need them to get where they are going.

Pupils' opinions of what they need and their teachers' opinions are not always the same. A few educators propose what seems to be a sensible position about content selection. They say that the choice of content is not an either-or proposition; but rather that the learner as well as the world in which he finds himself must be considered in content decisions.

We need teachers who care about teaching in the junior high school.

A safe assumption seems to be that the most effective teachers of young adolescents are those who realize what junior high school education is all about. They are professional educators who understand goals of junior high schools and who work toward implementing these aims.

[3] Rachel Carson, "Help Your Child to Wonder." *Woman's Home Companion*, July 1956.

Because we cherish the dream of providing the best possible educational opportunities for each youth in our contemporary, democratic society, we continually must be involved in experimentation and innovation. The teachers we need have been and continue to be involved in rethinking and reconstructing educational practices for young adolescents.

Teachers who care about being in junior high school are teaching there because they so desire. These teachers are not simply "marking time" until they can be promoted to senior high school teaching. They value the goals of the school. They value the idea of teaching all children whatever their background.

Much needs to be said about changing the junior high school to better meet the educational needs of our young people. We must change the school when it is necessary. To change the school, we must have teachers who are willing to change. To change, we, as teachers, must *care*.

TEMPTATIONS OF TEACHING

Elizabeth Hall Brady *

The teacher's mission is to teach boys and girls something. That is to say, he must help pupils to know something they did not know, or to be able to do something they could not do (at least not as well), or to feel in a way they did not feel. Under pressure of their classes, sometimes teachers lose sight of their main goals. In this article, Elizabeth Hall Brady points out some of the byways that may seduce a teacher from the straight narrow road that leads to really effective teaching.

Many temptations beset the teacher. Who among us has not succumbed? Some pitfalls await college teachers most often, but similar perils confront any teacher. What are some of these temptations?

The temptation to believe that they have heard what we have said
The temptation to believe that we have said what we think we have said
The temptation to believe that because they have enjoyed it, they have learned

* From *Educational Leadership*, Vol. 18 (March 1961), pp. 373–378. Reprinted with permission of the Association for Supervision and Curriculum Development and Elizabeth Hall Brady. Copyright © 1961 by the Association for Supervision and Curriculum Development.

The temptation to believe that if they did not enjoy it, we have taught
The temptation to cover the material at all costs
The temptation to conceal our own biases and beliefs.

Students too often aid and abet us in yielding to the first two errors.

We like to believe that our students will learn and remember all that we say. Despite what we know about the selective ways in which people hear and read and experience, we cling to the myth.

When a student asks a question about a topic which we have just nobly expounded, when the examination answers reveal a failure to grasp our most important message, when students attribute to us conclusions which could never have followed from *our* tightly reasoned remarks, we grow impatient. An accusing "But I told you . . ." or "Just last week I dealt with . . ." rises and escapes. Every such outburst will find some humble learner eager to be culpable, to admit to stupidity or inattention. The fiction is preserved that we can transmit knowledge by telling.

Students consumed with a sense of their own inadequacy encourage us still more toward the second temptation. We choose to believe that we are lucid, organized and succinct. Yet even the most conscientiously prepared instructor at times is vague, diffuse and wordy. Far be it from most students to draw attention to his inadequacies. There are teachers who exploit the tendency. One is the veteran who does not prepare carefully, since he "knows his material so well," and "too much preparation destroys his spontaneity." His disordered words come tumbling out; the students give chase to the ideas in fox and hare fashion.

Another hides the meagerness of his thought or the inadequacy of his preparation behind a barrage of obscure language, vague generalizations, and technical terms. It is for him that certain students reserve the awed comment, "Professor Grandiloquent is so far above us he just can't come down to our level. He knows so much and has such a complicated mind you can't expect him to get through to beginning students." Few statements could be better designed to rouse black anger in the heart of the instructor or graduate assistant whose lot it is to elucidate what Professor G. did not—to do, in fact, the teaching of which the other was incapable out of simple failure to think through what he had to say and to say it in understandable language. The students collaborate in the crime.

THE TEACHER TURNED ACTOR

The next two temptations reflect, not only our confusion about the roles of pleasure and pain, but also our feeling about the virtue of difficulty. The lure to confuse enjoyment with learning is an attractive one. Who does not like to leave a class confident that everyone has enjoyed the hour? For many, the greatest satisfactions of teaching are being liked and approved by students. Each of us has justified wandering into fascinating irrelevancies, anecdotal accounts, and vivid dramatizations by the argument that students will remember what has been pleasurable. It is but one more step to the delusion that where enjoyment occurs, learning necessarily follows. On every campus there is the teacher turned actor. He plays on emotions and uses charm as a substitute for scholarship. His jokes become legend; his personal popularity soars. He entertains; the students appreciate. Who would dare suggest that active effort to learn may yield greater pleasure?

If there are those who are willing to settle for happiness and popularity, there are even more who make a fetish of discomfort. Most often they represent themselves as defenders of standards and believers in hard work. When such a teacher reduces a student to tears or to clenched fists, he is honestly amazed that his superior regard for the integrity of the material to be learned has not been appreciated. The endless work he assigns forces students to neglect other classes; he cites their response as proof that other instructors are soft and have no standards. He confuses making learning difficult with making it worthwhile.

Both errors reflect a failure to distinguish between the task of learning, and the feelings, purposes and problems of the learners. Huston Smith has stated the distinction well:

> It would be good if we could add that education should be permeated with an accepting attitude toward students. Such acceptance has nothing to do with softness—leniency toward work carelessly done, laxity with regard to academic standards, or indulgence toward foolish ideas. Doubtless teachers should be infinitely patient in helping students bring their ideas to birth, but they should stand ever prepared to apply euthanasia to those that turn out to be monsters. Acceptance has nothing to do with indulgence; it is compatible with the most forthright criticism.[1]

There is always more to be taught and learned than can be. The temptation to cover the material at all costs invariably strikes the novice teacher; for some it remains a persistent devil. Queries are cut off; those fascinating excursions through which students discover personal meanings are blocked; the instructor's desire to put the flesh of his own insights on the bones of the text is throttled—all in the interest of "covering the material." Forgotten is Whitehead's terse remnider that knowledge, as bare facts, "does not keep any better than fish." The classroom becomes an arena for a race which must be lost. Even if the last page of the text is completed, the students have not been allowed to acquire the knowledge as their own. The course has been finished, and often so has any real interest on the part of the learners. As one harassed victim of this tendency raced through the final sections of a topic, he would roar as his class, "I know you won't *remember* it, but at least you'll have been *exposed*." But knowledge does not infect as readily as do viruses.

[1] Huston Smith, *The Purposes of Higher Education*. New York: Harper & Row, 1955, p. 97.

Last is the urge for the teacher to suppress his own bias. He withholds, he is detached from the students; he will not reveal his position. Does it seem strange to think of concealing bias as a temptation?

Historically the teacher has been admonished not to impose his prejudices on students. Yet concealment of the teacher's values and beliefs may work an even greater hardship. Joyce Cary describes two of his teachers, Grey in Shakespeare and Irwin in writing. For both he had great regard, but he reports:

> I was perfectly aware that I had gone to school to learn, and Irwin, like Grey, had his preferences, his own formed taste. The only difference between them as teachers was that Grey made no secret of his preferences, and Irwin sought to hide them. He succeeded too well. So, in my essays, I imitated anthology pieces.[2]

Learners must feel that what is being learned *matters*. A teacher's enthusiasm communicates this, but, as Cary points out, "you don't have enthusiasm without bias." [3]

It would be unfair to suggest that the same motivation prompts all who yield to this temptation. Not at all. Some honestly wish not to impose their prejudices on students; they want them to form their own opinions. Such instructions have not distinguished prejudice from bias. As Cary reminds us, immature students may be unable to form opinions without opportunity to know what others value. Others are committed to the virtue of "objectivity," failing to see that it is a will-o'-the-wisp. An occasional instructor keeps secret his most cherished views as a way of setting himself apart. He chooses not to engage in those exchanges with students through which values, ideas and positions are forced into the spotlight of candid reexamination. Whatever the motive, the students lose; in the last case, the instructor loses too.

The catalogue is not complete. Nor, alas, are these temptations to be put down by one strong effort. They hover about us permanently. Which lured you today?

ON STUDENT PARTICIPATION

Richard L. Loughlin *

Richard Loughlin must be a master teacher. At least, he has drawn up a list of ten do's and don'ts for teachers that is hard to beat. The beginning

[2] Joyce Cary, *Art and Reality: Ways of the Creative Process.* New York: Harper & Row, 1958, pp. 44–50.

[3] *Ibid.*

* From *The Bulletin of the National Association of Secondary-School Principals,* Vol. 46 (December 1962), pp. 35–36. Reprinted by permission of the NASSP and the author.

teacher would do well to follow his lead. One secret of good teaching is to involve pupils. The procedures Loughlin recommends will go a long way toward making teaching effective because they will bring about a high level of active pupil participation in the entire class. In this way the teacher can avoid the temptations to self-centered teaching that the two previous selections warn against.

As abilities and desirable attitudes are developed through guided activities, informed instructors seek the fullest possible participation of students in every learning situation. Their rule-of-thumb is: *Do nothing a student is capable of doing.* To increase student participation in a lesson, instructors can adapt the following procedure to the capabilities and needs of each student and class:

1. Encourage student-instructor planning, execution, and evaluation of the lesson.

2. Lead students to suggest possible avenues of approach to and applications of the subject matter.

3. Keep the entire group in the picture, even when working with individuals.

4. Make the group a circle not a triangle. (Do not dominate, judge, or "steal the show," nor permit a student to do so.)

5. Vary activities (dramatizations, panel discussions, audio-visual aids, oral reports, blackboard work, student lectures, committee work, guests).

6. Stimulate socialization, critical listening, and inter-criticism by referring one student's question or reply to another student for comment or additional information. ("What's your reaction to that,   (name)   ?" Then, have the respondent ask another why he agrees or disagrees.)

7. Don't exploit "star" pupils or volunteers; the diffident need encouragement and are often more profound. Involve all in a creative, cooperative, and courteous enterprise to learn.

8. Student errors in fact or in oral or written English should be corrected unobtrusively (merely supplying the correction, without stopping the recitation), unless the mistake is typical enough to require concentrated drill.

9. Cultivate an audience situation by changing your position; *e.g.,* moving to or toward the rear of the room; by insisting on audibility; by using hand signals to get speakers to stand, face the class, and speak up; by discouraging calling out or chorus answers; and by insisting on group courtesy to a student, chairman, or speaker. (At the end of the period, the instructor—not the bell—should dismiss the class.)

10. Students' questions, animated responses, evident enjoyment, rapt attention, and an unwillingness to leave the room at the end of the lesson usually indicate that the instructor has inculcated self-direction—the first step in self-improvement.

THE TEACHER AS A COUNSELOR

Dugald S. Arbuckle *

The teacher-counselor can become the master teacher says Dugald Arbuckle. But what is a teacher-counselor? He is more than just a teacher who counsels, but rather he is a teacher imbued with the guidance point of view, the teacher whose major interest is not subject matter or classes but his pupils as individual persons. The ideal of the teacher-counselor is somewhat new to secondary education. Not everyone feels that this ideal is attainable or even desirable. So let us consider the argument for it by one of its first proponents who, if he did not invent the concept or term, certainly has done much to popularize it. His case for teacher-counselors is very persuasive. In spite of the difficulties, it seems that there really is a place for teacher-counselors in the school, and that teacher-counselors can really become master teachers.

It is only within the last few years that the term teacher-counselor has become recognized as a word, and when the author of this article published a book, *Teacher Counseling*, in 1950, the title was considered to be somewhat revolutionary. This is not the case today, and practically every book that is written in the field of guidance has something to say about the role of the teacher in the total guidance program. In too many schools, however, the change has been somewhat like that which takes place in a college when an academic dean is renamed the Dean of Students. He is still the same person, and he still does the same things. The students are quite unaware that any change has taken place. Elementary-school teachers sometimes brush off guidance in the classroom by saying, "Well, of course we do guidance all the time," while secondary-school teachers are likely to say, "Well, of course, I do have to teach my Latin, you know." Many elementary-school teachers, however, give little evidence of practicing guidance in their classrooms, and many secondary teachers might better be described as *lecturers* rather than *teachers*. In this brief article, then, let us look first at what the teacher-counselor does, and then at those areas where the counseling role may come in conflict with the teaching role.

* From Dugald S. Arbuckle, "The Teacher as a Counselor," *The High School Journal*, Vol. 40 (Chapel Hill, N.C.: The University of North Carolina Press, May 1957), pp. 285–289. Reprinted by permission of the publisher.

WHAT THE TEACHER-COUNSELOR DOES

1. "Working with children" is a term that has a painful sound, since it is dinned into our ears from all corners, and yet the harsh fact in secondary education is that there are still many teachers who do not work with children, who know little or nothing about them, and who, sometimes, care even less about them. The teacher-counselor works earnestly with his children, takes them very seriously, but he does not take the subject or the skill that he teaches too seriously. It is a tool to be manipulated for the benefit of the children. The children are not manipulated for the benefit of the subject. The history teacher is less of a historian than he is a teacher. He must, of course, have a thorough knowledge in the area of history, and he must have an enthusiasm for history, but his primary concern is not history per se, but the extent to which history can really mean something to Mary, and John, and Sally, and Harold. It *must* mean something to each individual child if it is worth being taught to that child, and the "meaning something" may be found in the fact it helps one child to be happier, it helps another to spend his leisure time in a more fruitful manner, it helps another to prepare for an occupation, it helps another to develop a greater interest in the welfare of his country, and so on. But for each child to whom it is taught, it has some deep and personal meaning—it makes sense—and the teacher-counselor spends much time in trying to determine just how it may have some meaning for each of the children in his class. If for John and Mary and Will, history makes no sense whatsoever, then these children should not be in a history class. There is nothing wrong with history, but there is a good deal wrong with the way in which many children are forced to suffer through what is called a "history lesson."

2. "Individual differences" is another term that is done to death, is continually talked about, and in some secondary schools, quite *in*frequently practiced. The teacher's supposed concern about individual differences will have little effect on his teaching unless he knows something about these individual differences. In the better schools, the teacher-counselor will receive a good deal of his information about children from the full-time counselors. Few teacher-counselors, for example, will be able, on their own, to develop an effective testing program, and the teacher can hardly have a real understanding of the child without such a program. With or without the assistance of a formalized guidance program, however, the teacher-counselor does attempt to develop some sort of record system for each child. He must have some indication of the child's intellectual capacity, and while learning is affected by many factors other than intelligence, the teacher is in for trouble if he does not know that Mary, who sits beside John, has an IQ of 83 compared with John's 149! The teacher-counselor can also gather information on the child's interests; his likes and dislikes; his home environment; what he thinks about others, including his parents, his teachers, and his peer group; what he thinks

about himself; what others think about him. The teacher-counselor, then, practices individual differences. He operates on the assumption that thirty children represent thirty individuals, alike in many ways, but also different in many ways. He makes it part of his total job to gather objective and valid information, and thus does not have to depend on his own biased attitudes and subjective reactions to at least some of the children.

3. It may be possible to *teach*, with understanding and sympathy, a group of children, but it is not possible to function as a counselor if one's contacts are always with the group, never with the individual. The teacher-counselor must have time when he is available for individual consultations with some of his children, and the modern school system will provide teachers with this time as part of their full-time load. If the teacher works in a system where this time is not provided, he will have to take some of his own time, usually after class hours, if he is to be able to function as a counselor.

4. The primary function of the counselor, as well as the *real* teacher, is not to dispense knowledge, or to teach an isolated skill, but to develop in the classroom an atmosphere, a relationship, a climate, such that learning of a positive nature must almost certainly occur. The crucial question in the mind of the teacher-counselor is not, "How well did I counsel?" or "How well did I teach?" but rather, "What, if anything, did the child learn?" In such a classroom there may be little in the way of formalized teaching, since teaching frequently gets in the way of learning, but each child does learn.

PROBLEMS OF THE TEACHER-COUNSELOR

1. Some teachers may feel that they can hardly function as counselors since they must, after all, be concerned with teaching a subject. There is little evidence, however, to indicate that concentration on a *subject* has much in the way of positive effect on the learning of that subject. There is much evidence to indicate that learning is directly related to the concentration of the teacher on the learner, rather than on what is being learned. The teacher who fears that his children will get lower grades in history if he becomes more concerned with them and less concerned with history need not worry. If he moves in this direction, he will discover that teaching becomes more of a pleasure and less of a strain, and the children become intrigued and interested in history.

2. The teacher may find that some of the attitudes that might be considered as normal for a teacher are not desirable for a counselor. Most teachers are, at various times, the judge and the evaluator. One must grade papers, one must evaluate an assignment, or in examination, one must periodically make decisions as to the rightness or the wrongness of certain attitudes or actions. Other teachers will say, with justification, that it is difficult to see how they can avoid being, at times, a disciplinarian. They are responsible for the conduct of a group of children, and at times they may have to step into a punitive role. The counselor, on the other hand, is neither a judge nor

a disciplinarian. It would seem that the best the teacher-counselor can do in this regard is to develop the sort of classroom where the children have achieved an inner self-discipline so that the teacher rarely has to function as a disciplinarian. In most classrooms, evaluation can also be drastically minimized by having children work within the range of their interests and their capacities, but it cannot be completely removed.

3. To function effectively, the counselor must have a somewhat ambiguous role. On the whole, it is better that he be a somewhat unknown person to the client. The development of a counseling relationship is probably easier, and the relationship itself is more conducive to client growth, when the client knows nothing about the counselor's religion, his political concepts, his marital status, his nationality, his philosophy of life, and so on. The good teacher, on the other hand, is almost certain to be well known to the children, and it is very likely, since they see him every day, that they have developed a number of questionable or fallacious concepts about him. These concepts may be good or they may be bad, but it does mean that the children already have in their minds a well-developed picture of the teacher. This almost certainly will make the establishment of a counseling relationship more difficult. About the only thing that can be done by the teacher-counselor in this regard is to attempt to develop a warm, but *professional* relationship with the children, rather than a close, friendly, buddy-to-buddy sort of relationship.

4. A final real problem faced by the teacher-counselor in the secondary school is one of time and space and physical facilities. A teacher who teaches six or seven different classes may have contact with several hundred students, and he obviously cannot get to know all of them. Each secondary-school teacher must have the guidance and counseling responsibility for only one classroom. It matters little whether it is called a study group or some other name, but the teacher must be expected to be *personally* responsible for the children in only one room. He should also, of course, have time off to discuss personal problems with his children, and he should, finally, have some private space where he can conduct his counseling sessions. A classroom does not afford much in the way of privacy.

These, then, are problems, but they can be overcome or limited. The teacher-counselor can, in effect, become the real master teacher, with whom children learn, and are so prepared for the days that lie ahead.

WHY TEACH?

John H. Fischer *

Sometimes teachers and writers about teaching seem to emphasize only the bad points about teaching. It is only natural that they should. Everyone's work seems difficult and frustrating at times. And we all tend to complain about the little things that bother us. But really, teaching is a wonderful profession filled with many satisfactions. That is why so many people keep at it when they could have easier, better-paying jobs. As Cicero and John Fischer imply, no other calling is more gratifying.

Let's face it. Teaching *is* frustrating, nerve-wracking, demanding, tiring work. Do what he may, the teacher remains the butt of poor jokes, the object of endless criticism, and the scapegoat for many of society's most widely shared shortcomings.

But it is the teacher to whom parents and politicians, businessmen and clergymen turn, time after time, to set straight whatever is wrong with youth or the world. Are children unmindful of their elders' unrealized ambitions? Are the national goals neglected? Is free enterprise endangered? Do we lack the moral strength we ought to have? See the teacher!

Any teacher can find dozens of reasons, many of them plausible, to feel sorry for himself. But there are more convincing reasons for teachers to feel quite differently about their work and about themselves. For when due allowance has been made for the irresponsible criticism, the foolish expectations, the fuzzy thinking, and the exaggerated claims, the truth comes through, clear and unassailable: The teacher is a most important person.

This new appreciation of the teacher reflects one of the more curious—and welcome—paradoxes of our time. It has taken the enormous increase in the quantity of physical energy within man's reach to remind us that the central element in all our power, in all our plans for using power, is the educated man. We have had to be reminded, for many had forgotten, that technical proficiency, although it is essential, is insufficient, either to build this world nearer to our dreams or to carry us to other regions of the universe.

Fortunately for all of us, the value of education and the urgent need for good teaching are being recognized not only by those who write statements of national policy on education but by growing numbers of able and discerning

* From NEA Journal, Vol. 51 (Washington, D.C.: National Education Association. April 1962), p. 31. Reprinted by permission of the NEA Journal and the author.

young people. Wanting most of all to spend their lives in worthy causes, thousands of our best young men and women are choosing to teach. Improved salaries and working conditions are helping to attract new teachers and to retain experienced people, and continued progress along these tangible lines is highly necessary. But these are at best secondary matters; the more significant change is not in the salaries but in the attention teachers are receiving.

The change is not, however, without its unpleasant side, for while the glare of the spotlight may lend the teacher something of a halo, it also reveals his flaws with a minimum of mercy. No longer can teaching be a sinecure for those who want a job with long vacations or a monthly check to tide them over until something better comes along. Nor is there room in modern schools for teachers who lack the capacity for self-criticism or the willingness to work at a task that is endless and ever-changing.

Why teach? Whether the question is asked by a college student on the threshold of a career or by a forty-year veteran with chalk dust in his blood, the answer can be given many ways. Twenty years ago Lyman Bryson put it gracefully and well when he called the teacher "the friend who makes men free."

Running through all the answers, if they are honest and wise, will be a thread of commitment—a note of faith. To find success or satisfaction in his work, a teacher must begin and end with faith—in the worth of all men and especially in his students; in all learning and particularly in what he teaches. But most of all, the teacher must believe in himself and in the value of what he is attempting to accomplish.

In the days in which we live and teach, it should not be difficult to sustain that faith. Wherever men have believed that the human mind and spirit should be illuminated, the good teacher has been held in esteem and respect. It is so here and now, as it always will be where freedom, opportunity, and excellence are valued. In twenty centuries, no one has been able to answer Cicero's question: "What greater or better gift can we offer the republic than to teach and instruct our youth?"